THE STATE AND ECONOMIC LIFE

EDITORS: Mel Watkins, University of Toronto; Leo Panitch, York University

DAVID LAYCOCK

14 Populism and Democratic Thought in the Canadian Prairies, 1910 to 1945

The first half of the twentieth century saw tremendous political ferment in the Canadian prairies. It was an era of great ideological challenge and political complexity, shaped by cataclysmic events at home and around the world, and expressed in a wide range of political movements. David Laycock offers a close analysis of the publications and speeches of farmers' movements and third parties during that period. He focuses on their conceptions of 'the people,' approaches to the logic and practice of popular democracy, concepts of co-operation, technocratic ideas, concepts of the state, and visions of the good society.

Laycock identifies four populist approaches to the problem of democracy: crypto-Liberal, radical democratic, social democratic, and plebiscitarian. He relates these ideologies to the experience of indigenous political and economic organizations, including the Progressives, provincial farmers' organizations, the Co-operative Commonwealth Federation, and the Social Credit League in Alberta.

He demonstrates the inadequacy of interpreting movement ideologies solely in terms of class without close attention to leaders' and activists' intentions and public appeals. By locating these appeals in coherent structures of democratic thought that transcended agrarian interest, he illuminates the dynamism of prairie politics during this era.

In their brief but intensive experiences with populist democracy, prairie citizens contributed more to Canadian democratic thought than any other regional population. Laycock provides a sympathetic reconstruction of prairie populism's objectives and inconsistencies.

DAVID LAYCOCK is Canada Research Fellow and Assistant Professor, Department of Political Science, Simon Fraser University. He is the author of *Co-operative-Government Relations in Canada: Lobbying, Public Policy Development ~~d the Changing Co-operative System.*

Populism and Democratic Thought in the Canadian Prairies, 1910 to 1945

DAVID LAYCOCK

UNIVERSITY OF TORONTO PRESS

Toronto Buffalo London

© University of Toronto Press 1990
Toronto Buffalo London
Printed in Canada

ISBN 0-8020-2637-0 (cloth)
ISBN 0-8020-6681-X (paper)

Printed on acid-free paper

Canadian Cataloguing in Publication Data

Laycock, David H. (David Howard), 1954–
   Populism and democratic thought in the Canadian
   prairies, 1910 to 1945

(The State and economic life; 14)
Includes bibliographical references.
ISBN 0-8020-2637-0 (bound). – ISBN 0-8020-6681-X (pbk.)

1. Populism – Prairie Provinces – History – 20th
century. 2. Prairie Provinces – Politics and
government – 1905–1945.* 3. Agriculture and politics –
Prairie Provinces – History. I. Title. II. Series.

FC3242.9.P6L39 1990   971.2'02   C90-093151-5
F1060.9.L39 1990

Cover illustration: 'What Makes the Wild West Wild,' political cartoon on the
cover of *The UFA* magazine, Calgary, Alberta, 1 May 1931, courtesy Glenbow
Archives, Calgary (NA-789-89)

This book has been published with the help of a grant from the Social Science
Federation of Canada, using funds provided by the Social Sciences and Humanities
Research Council of Canada.

Contents

Acknowledgments

I have received much assistance preparing this book. Among those who have helped, I wish to mention Professors Meyer Brownstone, Gad Horowitz, C.B. Macpherson, and Kenneth McNaught of the University of Toronto; Reg Whitaker, York University; Ernesto Laclau, University of Essex, England; D.J.C. Carmichael, University of Alberta; John Richards, Simon Fraser University; David E. Smith, University of Saskatchewan; Ian MacPherson, University of Victoria; Deborah Laycock, University of Iowa; and James Carson, Kenyon College, Ohio. James Laycock expertly word-processed my dissertation. Christopher Axworthy, past director of the Centre for the Study of Co-operatives, University of Saskatchewan, provided moral and material support during my four years there. My other colleagues at the Centre offered intellectual life and friendship I will never forget.

For their valuable editorial assistance, I wish to thank R.I.K. Davidson, Virgil D. Duff, and B. Endersby of the University of Toronto Press, and Aina Kagis of the Centre for the Study of Co-operatives.

The Social Sciences and Humanities Research Council of Canada supported me with a generous fellowship during the early years of this maniscript's life. Grants in aid of publication were provided later by the Social Science Federation of Canada, the University of Saskatchewan Publications Fund, and the Centre for the Study of Co-operatives.

Finally, Helia and George Laycock, my late grandparents, inspired me to write about ideas and events that shaped their lives as prairie democrats. I dedicate this book to their memory, and to my son Christopher's future.

Populism and Democratic Thought in the Canadian Prairies, 1910 to 1945

1   Introduction

To many observers, Canadian politics possesses no significant indigenous traditions of practically oriented and critical democratic thought. If we see the current range of political discourse as the culmination of our political experience, we cannot be surprised by this judgment. However, Canadians have not always accepted determination of the legitimate scope and character of democratic politics by governments and élites.

This study addresses one reason why this is so: I argue that, over several decades, Canada's prairie region was the site of concerted and diverse attempts to reconstitute the democratic experience within the Canadian polity. A belief that this task should be paramount in political and social activity was the defining characteristic of prairie populist ideologies. The chapters that follow are an account of the diversity and richness within prairie populist thought associated with this belief. As we shall see, democracy implied substantially different things within prairie populisms; so much so that, as a group, prairie populists contributed more to Canadian thought about the nature and practice of democracy than did any other regional or class discourse.

Studies of prairie political organizations before the Second World War have usually oversimplified by characterizing 'prairie protest' in general terms, or have been so specific as to dislodge the particular populism to which the organization subscribed from its ideological and political contexts. The analytical framework I use in this study is intended to enhance our understanding of prairie populist thought and to deepen our appreciation of the overall dynamics of prairie politics in its crucial formative stages. In demonstrating that prairie populism was anything but monolithic, I show that each variant of prairie populist thought was decisively structured by a distinctive and coherent understanding of democratic goals and practices. My working hypothesis throughout this study is that the relation between populism and democracy best reveals the distinctiveness and complexity of this regional political discourse.

It need not be true that all major variants of prairie populist thought had an equally extensive conception of democracy. It is enough that the elements of each variant cohere around principles concerning redistribution of power among social classes and groups. In this conception, a democratic politics involves extension of the effective right to participate in the determination of political decisions affecting human development. It is, of course, possible that 'participation' can be crudely equated with voting and its results. However, more ambitious democratic projects generally involve attempts to politicize aspects of public life ordered and controlled by privileged sectors of society.

If prairie populist organizations were supported primarily by agrarian producers, should we not attempt to deduce their ideological 'essence' from their class characteristics? After all, this fact loomed large in their perception of issues, objects of criticism, and general social problems. As we will see, however, being independent commodity producers did not circumscribe their political and social visions to the extent that they could entertain only paradigmatic, *petit bourgeois* notions and perspectives. In political life, democratic thought is not parcelled up with the assignment of class copyrights to all of the elements that have constituted it over the years.[1]

I have chosen to examine the prairie populist experience between 1910 and 1945 for several reasons. The 'Siege of Ottawa' and the presentation of the Farmers' Platform by the newly formed Canadian Council of Agriculture took place in 1910. These were the first major demonstrations of prairie farmers' opposition to national economic policy and political colonialism. The defeat of the Liberals and reciprocity less than one year later was, in W.L. Morton's words, 'the first act in the agrarian revolt in Western Canada.'[2]

The 1911 national election was a watershed for many prairie residents who had begun to feel poorly served by the two-party system exported from central Canada. Competing political organizations, strategies, and discourses developed throughout the next three decades to counter central Canada's domination and make a case for western democratic alternatives. This activity was most intense in two periods: 1918 to 1925, and 1930 to 1935. The first period peaked in 1920, when a rapid decline in wheat prices coincided with Prime Minister Meighen's decision to return the grain marketing and price regulation to the private grain trade, after three years of federal intervention in this area on the farmers' behalf.[3] The period from 1930 to 1935 was distinguished by a heightened regional consciousness of class and class conflict, serious hardship in urban and rural areas, tremendous out-migration from the prairies, and the decline of a belief that the West had a special mission in Canada.[4] These developments gave new political forms and social analyses special prominence in the prairies.

By 1945, the dynamism of prairie populist rivalries was largely spent. All of the major populist tendencies had by this time developed an orthodox political practice, or had ceased to be significant players in regional politics. The last really important event in prairie populist politics was the 1944 CCF victory in Saskatchewan.

This victory initiated a long and fascinating administration in which the principles and policy orientations of social democratic populism were put to a revealing test; however, the scope of this study does not allow us to follow the case of the CCF in Saskatchewan into the 1960s.[5] It is also true that, because interest in both class and regional issues was dulled by the Second World War and these issues were denied prominence in the prosperous post-war decade, prairie populisms lost most of their dynamism. Western grievances ceased to be articulated in ways that posed serious threats to the definition and treatment of political issues by the dominant groups in the federal system. Thus, 1945 is an appropriate limit for an investigation of the populism/democracy relation in prairie political thought.

An argument could be made for including an explanation of the influence of similar Canadian events and organizations prior to 1910 here. After all, radical, or at least distinctively agrarian, politics had left their mark on almost a century of Ontario history prior to 1910. Agrarian support for the 1837 'rebellion' in Upper Canada and the activities of the Grange, the Patrons of Industry, and other groups towards the end of the nineteenth century were all noteworthy instances of 'populist' politics.[6]

So were the early agitations in prairie farmers' associations, including those by 'Patrons' in Manitoba and Saskatchewan,[7] the Territorial Grain Growers' Association,[8] and the Grain Growers' Grain Company.[9] All these organizations stood four-square against monopolies in the grain trade ('monopolies and combines which are sapping the life blood of the country'),[10] the tariffs of the National Policy, political corruption, and extravagant government spending. They shared a support for co-operative marketing and trading mechanisms, freer trade with the United States, and a larger measure of local and popular control over the workings of government. These experiences were undeniably important in shaping populist politics on the prairies after 1910.[11]

The reason for the post-1910 focus of this study is simple. This work is not a historical analysis of agrarian populism for the whole of Canada or a history of reform sentiment in the Canadian prairies; it is an account of the distinctive democratic shape and contributions of prairie populisms. Therefore, it is fitting to begin roughly at the point at which the momentum of indigenous populist practice began to have a major impact on national politics and prairie political competitions.

Canadian prairie populism has received much scholarly attention over the last fifty years.[12] Most accounts, however, have focused on the institutional characteristics and political fortunes of prairie social movements and political parties. With the obvious exception of C.B. Macpherson's *Democracy in Alberta*, scholarly studies have not adequately addressed prairie populist thought.

Other academic approaches to prairie politics convey the significance of prairie populist ideas about democracy primarily in terms of challenges to the established party systems, the stresses placed on Canadian federalism, or predictable economic demands and responses by hinterland producers. While valuable for other purposes, these approaches do not allow enough of the depth, diversity, and interest of populist democratic thought to shine through. A new approach is needed to uncover the character of indigenous prairie democratic thought and to supplement accounts of a period of political dynamism and unorthodoxy unrivalled by that in any other Canadian region.

Many prairie populist attempts to address the problems of democracy spoke to issues that are still inherent in North American political conflict. Party discipline and internal democracy, domination of governments and major parties by social and economic élites, and the power of corporate capital to define the limits of acceptable public policy, all remain problems for democrats. In addition, assuring all regions an effective voice in national governments, organizing people into politically efficacious units, and extending democratic decision-making into the economic sphere are all more firmly entrenched problems. Prairie populists rarely offered extensive or erudite solutions to these problems, but their efforts were sincere and often novel. Their prescience with regard to these problems, as well as their oversights, is revealing for those who subscribe to the modern religion of progress.

Finally, I must admit a desire to show the inadequacy of some neo-Marxist writings on prairie populism.[13] Most of these works have characterized prairie populisms as narrowly *petit bourgeois* and chiliastic, or even inherently reactionary. None of them does justice to the historical specificity, cultural milieu, ideological complexity, or considerable achievements of the prairie experience with populist democracy. If current western dissatisfaction with the Canadian political economy used more than a misleading portion of older populist rhetoric, many academics would grant prairie populism more of the uncondescending respect it deserves.

Dimensions of Prairie Populist Democratic Thought

To best appreciate prairie populists' concern with unorthodox notions about democracy, we must order the wealth of data comparatively and thematically. The themes chosen must reveal the underlying structure, strengths, and limitations of the various modes of populist democratic thought.

Explanations of the prairie experience in terms of the West's position as a resource hinterland whose *petit bourgeois* producers toiled for the benefit of central Canadian interests (set out unofficially in the National Policy) form the economic foundation for any analysis of prairie democratic ideologies. However, such explanations only indicate why there would have been opposition to exploitation *per se*, and do not account for the diversity and richness of this opposition. In addition, this analytical framework suggests that democratic thought should have developed in a similar manner in the Maritimes (another hinterland region abused through the National Policy), when in fact this did not occur.[14]

The explanatory model of neo-Marxist political economy is essential to an understanding of why particular aspects of prairie producers' economic subordination were publicly identified and then elevated to symbolize the undemocratic character of social relations. However, we are still left having to account for the diversity in form and ideological substance that bound the objects of economic grievance together in competing populist discourses. This diversity itself indicates that the constitution of political options and ideological perspectives is not an automatic consequence of class locations in the production process. The sum of the economic-experiential parts does not equal or strictly determine the ideological whole. Autonomy must be granted to cultural factors and social actors in explanations of ideologies developing and interacting in particular settings.

In retrospect, we can distinguish among six dimensions that established the dynamism and parameters of prairie populist democratic thought. The first dimension, the concept of 'the people,' identified the movement ideologies' chosen constituencies and became a key element in their social analyses of power and conflict. Second, ideas about 'participatory democracy' outlined the rationale and features of desired democratic practice in political life, for both the political movement in the short run and public life in the long run. Closely related to the first two dimensions of populist democratic thought are conceptions of co-operation, 'the state,' the good society, and approaches to technocratic decision-making. The substance given each of these dimensions did much to distinguish prairie populisms from one another.

The centrality of beliefs concerning desirable political institutions and processes to a body of democratic political thought requires little comment. These beliefs indicate ideological forebears as well as potentially radical implications of group political action. They also demonstrate degrees of cultural and social integration, providing a clearer sense of the limits of intended reform. One may agree that parliamentary or similar systems of representative government place limits upon the socialization of power. However, we must recognize that, to most political actors, such an argument is beside the point, and that consenting to most rules of political conflict does not prevent groups from offering meaningful alternatives to the prevailing distribution of power. In fact, new practices of and proposals for processes of political representation can do a great deal to redefine issues within political competitions.

Since alternative accounts of democratic society identify the conditions of a 'just' distribution of power and material benefits, a popular democratic theory must cope with the problem of co-operation in several senses. Among these are: 1 / whether co-operation implies principles of right relations among persons and groups in public life, and 2 / the implications, if any, for organized political, social, or economic action among those groups agreeing that co-operation does imply these principles. Thus, many ethical and political questions congregate under the rubric of co-operation, which could be a good reason for abandoning so general a concept and dealing with the questions discretely.

For analysis of abstract categories in social and political philosophy, such a procedure is acceptable. However, for an understanding of the dynamics and variations within a regional political discourse, it is not. For many prairie residents, co-operation signified both more and less than an amalgamation of answers to questions of justice, ethical behaviour, proper limits to power, social organization, and so on. Co-operation was more, because it was often seen as an attribute of the prairie community in which some substantial agreement on these issues had been achieved, or as a central characteristic of any democratic society. At the same time, co-operation was less because political competition in the prairies never became so routinized that these issues could be as neatly resolved within this community as they had artificially been in much of central Canada's political party competition. Emphasis on the different aspects of the social problematic posed by co-operation waxed and waned within prairie politics because no political grouping could shape a consensus on the issues related to the idea of co-operation.

Co-operation was so powerfully charged as a symbol in the prairies for two basic reasons. From the moment they settled in the new land, prairie farmers perceived economic co-operation as an obvious alternative to exploitation, especially when it became clear that the federal state could not be relied on for protection from private firms with political connections. Co-operation quickly made sense to those for whom the miracle of the market and the myth of rugged individualism were not ideological blinkers. It was a typical response of people who came to feel themselves part of a community that shared not only occupations but also externally imposed hardships and impediments to self-rule. As such, co-operation might be called a democratic reflex action, or a necessary but not sufficient condition of positive democratic practice.

Co-operation did not imply any specific alternative goals or political strategies, although some co-operative enthusiasts believed otherwise and they were not completely mistaken. Certain benign images of opponents in the conflict could not be sustained, and a rather impressive minimum commitment to redistributive radicalism was assured by experience in prairie co-operative enterprises. But complementary cultural and social supports had to be constructed to guarantee that these economic forms could bear the weight of any 'co-operativist' ideological edifice.

Co-operation was also a key concept in much popular social theory during this period of social change within the Atlantic triangle. By the eve of the First World War, dominant political forces in each country had to address and deflect complaints concerning the power of business interests to shape national policies and social goals. The issue of democracy in economic and political life had been raised to a level of importance unprecedented in each society's experience. America's dominant classes had been more successful than Britain's in deflecting and marginalizing this issue, when by 1896 the populist threat to two-party politics had been squelched through fusion with the Democrats.[15] Nevertheless, residues of American populist and labour radical thought continued to influence thinking about political and social options in Canada, in concert with the impact of British social democracy.

Canada was the last of the three countries to experience a serious challenge to a liberalism dominated by conservative business interests. As Gerald Friesen notes, the war had intensified social and more obviously class conflict in the country and, in the prairies, had led to a 'breakdown of the bi-partisan consensus on political priorities and the regional ideal.'[16] Teachers, social workers, journalists, and Protestant ministers quickly came to play key roles in labour and farmers' movements as the problem of a 'new social order' appeared paramount to rapidly expanding labour and farm organizations.

In the context of a well-educated and democratically optimistic prairie farm population,[17] British and American challenges to the individualistic, competitive ethic helped Canadian agrarian and urban radicals to consider what the co-operative alternative might entail socially and politically. Other

European experiences were relevant in this regard. The large Scandinavian and Ukrainian communities in the prairies were able to draw on co-operative and radical political experiences from their homelands as they attempted to forge social alternatives in the new land.

The point is that even mildly progressive liberals perceived both an imminent challenge to the established order and a vague but widespread support for some 'co-operative' solution in a 'new social order.' It is thus not surprising that everyone from Mackenzie King to Henry Wise Wood, to leaders of the Winnipeg General Strike, attempted to establish political copyright over the conceptual terrain of co-operation. This competition was part of a larger one to define the relevance and practical character of democracy in Canadian society.

The notion that technocratic ideas influenced prairie populist thinking might appear to be misconceived, but such ideas have always presented a subtle yet dangerous challenge to democratic movements. Technocratic thought does not seem threatening when it simply appears to propose elimination of social-organizational constraints on our ability to make efficient use of technology. It takes little reflection, however, to recognize that the social logic of technocratic thought, and consequently its rationality of power, are diametrically opposed to those of popular or participatory democracy. Technocrats locate the problems of social life primarily in technological deficiencies and the unscientific organization of economic activity. They seek narrowly technical solutions to problems that are more fundamentally based on conflicts over the use of social and economic power. This outlook is contrary to that of those committed to participatory democracy, whose primary objective is to redistribute social decision-making power from élites to 'the people.' We shall see that prairie populists were attracted by the apparently scientific, conflict-resolving, and abundance-producing elements of technocratic thought.

In its élitist claims about the necessity of trained intellect monopolizing political decision-making, technocracy has precedents as old as Plato's proposals for philosopher rule. The technocratic perspective received its force in modern thought from the post-Enlightenment assumption that rational techniques can unite intellect and the power of science to resolve all political and social problems. Technocracy in this broad sense is the first principle of social engineering in the tradition of Anglo-American utilitarianism, and has been of great importance in the approaches that western political élites have taken to the problems of policy determination and administration over the last century.[18]

It is in the context of this general bias in favour of technically expert, 'scientific' approaches to social problems that the various notions of democracy have had to grow over this same period. At the most abstract level, we can understand democracy as a demand for and practice of the socialization of power, based on a moral argument for equal human self-determination (as individuals and through communities). From this angle, the idea of technocracy appears to be based on a strikingly different set of assumptions about human needs and the status of people as moral agents, and what these imply about desirable general principles and practices of political life.

However, neither democratic nor technocratic ideas come uncompromised to political and ideological competition. Contradictions between the essences of the two ideas are thus seldom starkly manifest in public life. Because both the democratic and the technocratic ethos had gained legitimacy by the turn of the century, proponents of each perspective have attempted to garner legitimizing force from the commonly accepted features of the other. Technocrats have had to accommodate themselves to a political culture with liberal-democratic values; democrats could not help but be influenced by the entrenchment of the cult of progress through science in most accounts of social change.

Not all 'compromises' made by democrats or technocrats were opportunistically pragmatic. In fact, it is probable that only a small minority of those following both tendencies had thought back to first principles to see contradictions in their positions. Most dedicated technocrats believe they had no moral or social-philosophical objections to democratic practices, but felt rather that current economic and social conditions did not permit democracy to function effectively. Such people would deny that their attitudes were anti-democratic, or that they had accepted a social logic – a logic of power – that was inconsistent with anything except a narrow and institutionally confined democratic practice.

However, many who rejected the abstract idea and social principles of technocracy were not immune to influence from technocratic approaches to economic and social problems. The enormity and urgency of these problems often led participatory democrats to propose variations on scientific management by public officials. Typically, they saw these proposals as alternatives to scientific management by private corporate minions: 'the people's experts' should replace those toiling at the behest of 'organized plutocracy.' When stemming the tide of corporate power and human suffering seemed to be immediately necessary, attention to strategies' implications could easily wane.

Comparative analysis of prairie populisms between 1910 and 1945 shows that the relationship between technocratic and democratic ideas had serious implications for practical political life. Technocratic ideas occupied a prominent, if seldom explicit, place in 'progressive' political thought in North

America during this period.[19] All prairie populisms integrated some of these ideas into their social analyses and proposals for social change. In some cases, the technocratic component reduced democratic theoretical content to a level that seems shocking to us, even with our impoverished sense of democratic possibilities. In other cases, technocracy appeared more to be a benign technique that democrats grasped as a partial solution to problems of social reconstruction. In still other cases, inherited liberal notions about the natural limits on the extension of democracy into social relations made technocratic ideas rarely appear to conflict with formalized democratic routines. On the basis of these variations alone, we can see that prairie populism was not ideologically homogeneous.

There are several reasons why conceptions of 'the state' would feature prominently in populist democratic thought. All social movements view the state from both hostile and positive instrumentalist perspectives.[20] In virtually all populisms, hostility towards the state results from its maintenance of inequitable social relations, and does much to motivate populist political activity. Those populisms that advocate a socialization of power develop a vague conception of the state as the political embodiment of domination *per se*. In this sense, the logical extension of the democratic idea is the elimination of the state itself. Populism here crosses paths with anarchism.

This utopian element in populist thought seldom develops unallayed by a practical recognition that the state must eventually eliminate the power of its current beneficiaries.[21] In fact, the history of populist movements demonstrates that a concern for the positive uses of state power often dominates the political projects of particular movements, and the abstract objection to the state as a coercive force becomes vestigial in populist discourse. Particular state structures and administrations remain the object of populist criticism, but the 'state equals coercion' idea fades. This partly explains the influence of technocratic perspectives: as long as other social forces control state structures, 'the people' have little choice but to attempt a transfer of state power.

Populist ideas about the state are closely related to populists' positions on the desirable procedures of political representation and rule, appropriate principles of justice and relations of power between major social groups, conceptions of human capacity to create and adapt to new social relations, and visions of economic and social systemic order. In the western liberal tradition, a cautious gradualism in the practice of most governments has coincided with a formal optimism about these issues.

Such gradualism is built into the traditions and practices of parliamentary government. All enduringly influential radical political movements and organizations in Britain and Canada have accepted the basic institutional and operational features of the British parliamentary system, as providing an adequate foundation for the development of 'real democracy.' Such acceptance implied agreement with British liberal conceptions of where power was and should be located in state structures. Some prairie social democrats even accepted the liberal idea of the state as a neutral arbiter between contending group interests in a plural society. As is the case for any system that defines the forms and functions of state power, acceptance of the parliamentary system limits, without specifically determining, the options available to democratic thought and practice.

Visions of the 'good society' were key elements of prairie populist democratic thought. From one perspective, normative components of democratic thought can be seen as theoretically condensed abstractions from utopian images of social relationships and individual fulfilment. In the case of prairie populisms, this correspondence is often unclear because of the unsystematic expression of both utopian images and moral first principles. However, we must appreciate the contribution of utopian social visions to democratic goals within popular movements.

The contribution of utopian images to democratic goals is established in two ways. In day-to-day attempts to enhance competitive political strength, populists defined democratic goals primarily in negative terms, proposing to remove certain powers or devices through which dominant social forces maintained inequitable distributions of power and benefits. Identifying specific objects of grievance and their causes in government policy and class power is a crucial step in mobilizing popular support for political alternatives. To sustain large-scale commitment and a growing movement organization, however, activists and leaders must articulate positive goals that suggest the character of the 'new social order.' An essential component of this development is experimentation with approximations of the desired forms of social and economic interaction, within and alongside the political arms of the movement. In this way, the people show themselves the value of their democratic goals.

Where such experimentation and creative utopian thinking are not a part of a movement's activities, its supporters will often fail to see how it constitutes an alternative source of solutions to their problems. The result is generally either passive support for the organization when hard times subside or a drift back towards grudging acceptance of the 'natural' character of established relations of power. Such is often the case with 'single-issue' or moderate reform organizations, which cannot articulate a compelling alternative vision of the good society or suggest why dominated sectors of society should do more than work to maximize individual status and prosperity within the established social order.

Post-war attention to possibilities of a new social order in Canada was especially strong in the prairie provinces. Much of the prairie population was made up of recent immigrants who had come in search of a fresh start. The apparent plenty encouraged settlers to reject the idea that externally imposed economic hardships and political domination were necessary or just.[22] In these circumstances, the quest for individual and community self-determination, and a modicum of prosperity, led quite naturally to organized social action. Campaigns for political and economic reforms were tied to the larger goal of establishing a political community closer to their visions of the good society than to that in the lands left behind. To us this perception and effort may appear quaintly naïve, but prairie populists sincerely believed that they were entering the era of the democratic promise.

Such explicitly utopian tracts such as E.A. Partridge's *A War on Poverty* were rare. To re-create portraits of the utopian visions, we must reconstruct the justificatory logic and assumptions underlying the more mundane proposals for concrete economic and political change, and relate these to other democratic themes under scrutiny.

Populism as a Theoretical Concept

Thus far, I have spoken of 'populism' without explaining its value for this study. In this section, I will demonstrate its explanatory value for the study of popular movements whose appeal transcends class boundaries and challenges prevailing paradigms of democratic political life.

Populism is a notoriously ambiguous concept. It has been applied to everything from Maoism to the political style of Ronald Reagan or John Diefenbaker, to the political activities of a threatened hinterland *petite bourgeoisie*. Unlike liberalism, communism, or conservatism, populism 'is not part of a shared, more inclusive tradition, as far as the subjective orientation of the actors is concerned. Its typological status is solely an analytical one.'[23] The fact that populism is a social-scientific imposition on a disorderly social reality should not relegate it to the conceptual waste heap. The problem is to decide which political phenomena we wish the concept to illuminate. Is it the existence, in analogous socio-economic environments, of similar social and political movements? Or is it an aspect of the political competition into which they enter and which they transform?

The approach focusing on analogous environments usually emphasizes similarities in the class composition and degree of 'modernization' or capitalist industrialization within which populist movements arise. Such a situation imposes marginalization on the social sectors that create populist organizations. Traditional or recently established communities of small agricultural producers are usually the groups identified in this type of analysis, since their livelihoods, status, and overall social survival are threatened by capitalist industrialization. All aspects of their protest are labelled populist. Ideological likenesses among the discourses of protest are seen as direct expressions of these groups' desire to maintain their property holdings and limited independence in the face of unrelenting capitalist modernization.

This approach leaves us with a concept of populism that is little more than shorthand for the predictable political stance of transitional classes in maturing capitalist economies. It offers useful clues to the probable locations of populist experiences, but provides no substantial reasons for searching out and accounting for the diversity within populist thought. The equation of a particular class experience with populism is at the root of this deficiency. Adopting this position denies a priori the very strong possibility that populism is an integral part of other classes' political activity, and requires that wherever we find a marginalized agrarian *petite bourgeoisie*, we will find populism. As this latter proposition is patently false, and because we do not wish to assume what requires proof – that populism is confined to the politics and attitudes of only one class – populism must be conceptualized through other means.[24]

We can rule out the possibility that populism is simply an aspect of political leadership style. This typically journalistic substitute for explanation assumes that any folksy appeal to the 'average guy,' or some allegedly general will, is evidence of populism. Such an approach ignores the mass-organizational requirement of populist experience, thereby going to the opposite extreme of the class-reductionist approach.[25]

What of the possibility that populism constitutes a unique ideological system? Peter Worsley has convincingly rejected this position by noting the absence of definitive populist texts and tenets of social and political philosophy. All manifestations of populism have been ideologically parasitic on what Worsley calls 'neighbouring ideologies' that do not possess 'distinctive boundaries which mark them off clearly from other systems.' Populist movements may share some distinctive ideological characteristics, but it is misleading to speak of an essential populist ideology.

This conclusion does not require us to abandon ideology as one of the factors delineating populism. An attractive alternative is to identify dimensions of ideological expression that reveal commonality among the various political experiences referred to as populist. Worsley contented himself with the hypothesis that populism refers to 'popular participation in general' and a 'constantly recurring style of politics – the eternal attempt of the people to claim politics as something of theirs.'[26] This puts us on the right track, but it offers little as a basis for probing or comparing populisms.

Ernesto Laclau's theoretical writings on populism offer guidance concerning its general nature and ideological dynamics. Laclau's approach gives sufficient recognition to the subjective dimensions of social and political conflict while recognizing the role of class forces in these conflicts. His overall argument focuses on the importance of popularly perceived social antagonisms in political competitions involving anti-establishment groups. To Laclau, populism is an ideological dimension of virtually all political activity. Its significance increases during economic and political crises, when mass organizations' appeals for change are perceived as representative of 'the people's' interests beyond the movements' initial class bases.

According to Laclau, the extension of popular appeals beyond class boundaries is possible because individuals in subordinate classes perceive a kind of overarching socio-cultural antagonism between 'the people' and 'the power bloc' (the interests, the élites, and so on). Appeals made with reference to this antagonism are not detached from class experiences and class politics. Neither, however, are they narrowly restricted by the economic class character of the organizations from which they emerge. Thus while an agrarian *petite bourgeoisie* threatened by industrial capitalism is likely to express a populist ideology, it is not the only class likely to do so. Nor is it likely to appeal for change in terms addressing only its own perceived class interests.

For Laclau, the interpenetration of class interests and political activities with 'popular-democratic' appeals is characterized by disputes over which groups' objectives are consistent with popular values, symbols, and traditions in the community's past experience. These would include demands for popular input into government policy and decision-making, critiques of the institutions of political power and representation, antagonism towards regional inequalities, antagonism towards high-profile wealthy classes, and the yearning for freedom and equality of opportunity. Even established political and economic élites must enter this competition, and represent their objectives as compatible with these values. Laclau calls appeals to such values 'popular-democratic interpellations' and assigns them a central role in 'ideological class struggle.'[27]

The symbols of ideological appeals usually come to have a positive cognitive force with reference to specific historical events, widely read publications, or personalities. In Canada, such things as tariff structures, the 1919 Winnipeg General Strike, the Union Government, Bellamy's 'Parable of the Water Tank,' and William Lyon Mackenzie, all performed this role for a range of social constituencies. They became symbolic of the popular struggle against domination in ways that transcended their contemporary situations and lent themselves to integration into divergent political discourses.

Such popular-democratic interpellations acquire the status of 'popular-democratic traditions.' Their continuity and symbolic strength make them invaluable to any radical discourse, as means of injecting readily grasped meaning into past and present political struggles. For Laclau, populism is the element of ideological discourse that uses these popular-democratic interpellations and traditions to strengthen a case for a substantial redistribution of power among social classes.

Popular-democratic traditions having connotative links with past democratic experiences, and current options for the extension of power to 'the people,' constitute crucial indigenous raw materials for left-wing ideological appeals.[28] The specifically populist aspect of socialism promotes the most radical implications of popular-democratic traditions. The objective is to create a popular perception that these traditions, taken together, possess a historical logic favourable to socialism. Laclau argues that socialists must present the anti-capitalist struggle as 'the culmination of democratic struggles, and socialism as the common denominator in a total offensive against the dominant bloc.'[29] To do this, socialists must champion many of those traditions of democracy and 'rights of the people' that the dominant classes have integrated into their political appeals. Rejecting these traditions and rights as necessarily 'bourgeois' is not only strategically damaging, it also reflects a poor appreciation of established élites' success: their ability to represent concessions to popular-democratic demands as benevolent gifts to 'the people.'[30]

As an element of political strategy and rhetorical style, populism becomes a part of virtually all political organizations and social movements proposing a substantial redistribution of class power. Retrospectively, we can legitimately debate whether an organization is genuinely populist. Has it merely integrated 'popular elements' into an opportunistic political strategy, or has it proposed a seriously 'antagonistic option' to the present power structure?[31] In most cases, the competitive context of political activity provides a firm foundation for assigning populist credentials and gives us a good relative sense of what counts as a meaningful challenge to the power structure.

In their attempts to obtain political copyrights over the most salient popular-democratic traditions, mildly populist organizations and leaders have several common features. They pay little attention to social-structural causes of 'the people's' subordination, often concentrating on a single policy issue without demonstrating what it is symptomatic of. Use of facile moralism also neutralizes the potentially radical implications of popular traditions. More radical populist groups must respond with forceful demonstrations of the diversionary character of such appeals, complemented by culturally appropriate indictments of prevailing political and economic powers. The goal is to have such indictments appeal to all traditionally dominated social sectors in culturally compatible terms. When both status-quo and mildly reformist political groups are forced to address issues presented in this fashion, the complexion of political competition is substantially altered. Competitive articulation of popular-democratic traditions and current feelings of domination becomes the central feature of ideological conflict.

Political and cultural traditions in North America have guaranteed the failure of unambiguously proletarian forms of populism. However, populism can complement a variety of social democratic positions advocating elimination of class inequalities. Populist forms of radical liberal, co-operative–oriented agrarian movements or of reformist liberal movements in conservative political environments have also shown their political viability.

The success of any populist project depends upon the widespread acceptance of a 'system of narration' or distinctive ideological ordering of political and social facts. Political principles and proposals must be integrated into a structure of meanings and connotative associations existing in 'the people's' historical experience. The appeals of populist organizations can vary considerably, as their proponents attempt to alter old and create new elements and relationships within a clearly distinguishable connotative structure.

The point of these efforts is to incline supporters to accept a particular logic of political action and social change. A bridge is thus provided between their constituency's general feelings of exploitation, specific grievances, and the organization's proposals for social change. In a very real sense, this system of narration allows dominated classes to comprehend an otherwise elusive approach to understanding and reforming society. This is the challenge for movement-based democratic thought.

The development of these populist 'systems of narration' owes a great deal to the organizational breadth and depth of particular populist movements.[32] Obviously, large and well–co-ordinated groups of people will present governments with problems of social-conflict resolution and regime legitimation. Beyond this, two aspects of organization are crucial to populist politics. The first is its boost to participants' feelings of political efficacy, ensuring supporters' acceptance of the validity of their alternative political project. Strength and enthusiasm in an organization are reciprocally reinforcing after a certain level of popular participation has been achieved.

Organization also enhances public appreciation of a populist discourse's distinctive features. A sense of 'political community' is difficult to establish in the absence of close contact between supporters and leaders, and is easy to establish with a 'party press,' speakers' network, and widely dispersed propaganda. Open and egalitarian organization of meetings, offices, and activities within populist organizations provide movement participants with an education in democracy. Thus, 'the faith' is sustained and creative thinking concerning the movement's strategies and goals is encouraged. If the organization is authoritarian in these regards, its goals will not escape contamination. In either case, the mode of intragroup organization will affect its system of narration.[33]

Populism never displaces liberalism, socialism, or even conservatism as the ideological backbone of a movement.[34] Instead, it emphasizes a 'people/power bloc' antagonism, by referring to key popular-democratic traditions. When these qualifications to the more basic ideologies become decisive in specific ideological contests, the populist dimension of a regional or national political competition becomes crucial.

Populist contributions to the prairie political competition were characterized by attempts to redefine and reconstitute the processes of democracy. Prairie politics featured contending attempts to establish political copyright over grievances symbolizing the domination of the eastern business élite. Tariffs, freight rates, low grain prices, monopolies in land and finance, and eastern domination of the national party system are only the most obvious examples of elements that shaped indigenous popular-democratic traditions. Their competitive utilization by populist organizations meant that the region's internal political battles were quite distinct from those in the rest of Canada between the wars. Understanding these battles requires us to identify the democratic elements in the populist ideological mix, and to show how they were appropriate to and constitutive of the particular form of liberalism, socialism, or 'hybrid' in question. A concern with popular-democratic traditions and their political uses points us in the right direction in this matter.

Categories of Populist Democratic Thought on the Prairies

From 1910 to 1945, populist political competition on the prairies was expressed in four basic forms: social democratic populism, radical democratic populism, plebiscitarian populism, and crypto-Liberalism. These categories are based on the dominant tendency within each populism and are not meant to suggest that any of the four developed in isolation from the others. Indeed, within any given organization, it was quite common that several populist ideologies found expression.

Within the United Farmers of Alberta (UFA) movement, for example, the radical democratic ideology dominated political discourse. At the same time, the more conventional UFA provincial administration clearly thought and spoke as crypto-Liberals. However, a prominent left-wing faction within the UFA articulated its hybrid radical democratic/social democratic position for many years, most notably after 1930. The Social Credit League and the Saskatchewan Liberal party exhibited much less internal ideological disagreement, and are thus much 'purer' representative cases of plebiscitarian populism and crypto-Liberalism, respectively.

That the UFA provided a home for the discourse of three populisms does not undermine our conceptualization of populism. Instead, it demonstrates the advantage of identifying competitive yet mutually comprehensible means of articulating political and social objectives. Reducing the various tendencies in the UFA to one ideological expression would conceal its dynamism. The UFA experience suggests the value of an approach that encourages sensitivity to different political projects and social visions within one movement.

The four types of prairie populism can be introduced here by noting their principal organizational vehicles and substantive elements. Social democratic populism developed through the early efforts of the Non-Partisan League in Alberta and Saskatchewan, the small urban labour parties across the prairies whose pedigrees and promoters were predominantly British, a small number of socialists working within grain producers co-operatives, and activists in the United Farmers organizations in the three provinces. None of these organizations worked solely through the ideology that its left-wing activists helped to create.

This task was left to the Co-operative Commonwealth Federation on the prairies after 1932, which gave social democratic populism an almost paradigmatic expression. Its most obvious features were rejection of the two major parties as instruments of eastern business, support for state ownership of major industries, advocacy of a farmer-labour alliance against organized business, and support for a full extension of democratic rights and practices within the parliamentary system. It was gradualist without being simply stamped from the Fabian mould, owing more to the traditions and perspectives of the Independent Labour Party of Britain. No rigid orthodoxy defined or limited its adherents; on the contrary, the intellectual eclecticism of many of its leaders encouraged close ties between social democratic and radical democratic populisms.

Radical democratic populism was developed by elements in several of the same organizations that fostered social democratic populism; that is, the Non-Partisan League, United Farmers organizations, and the grain growers' co-operatives. Its intellectual roots were primarily rural western American and entailed a 'co-operativist,' anti-capitalist perspective on questions of economic and political power. A principled rejection of party politics and an insistence on functionally co-ordinated delegate democracy leading into a group government were the most distinctive aspects of this populism. The most complete and certainly most provocative development of the radical democratic themes took place within the United Farmers of Alberta, with Henry Wise Wood and William Irvine as the principal 'theoreticians.' The organizational proximity and reciprocal respect of social democratic and radical democratic populisms were evident in Irvine's importance to social democratic populism, through his work in the Non-Partisan League, the UFA, and the CCF.

Crypto-Liberalism was a western, rurally inclined, more socially progressive and politically experimental version of Ontario Grit Liberalism. It was given form and substance by the National Progressive party, and by prairie provincial Liberal parties preceding, contemporary with, and succeeding this short-lived organization. It provided the dominant mode of thought and discourse for the UFA administration from 1921 to 1935, for the Saskatchewan Grain Growers' Association until 1926, for the long-lived Saskatchewan Liberal government and party, for the Manitoba Grain Growers' Association/United Farmers of Manitoba, for the United Grain Growers, and for the Norris and Bracken administrations in Manitoba. *The Grain Growers' Guide* was the most popular indigenous prairie periodical. It articulated an unmistakably crypto-Liberal perspective. So did J.W. Dafoe's *Free Press*, and most of the urban daily papers in the prairies shortly after the First World War. With these formidable institutional vehicles, one should not be surprised that crypto-Liberalism structured the most influential expressions of prairie protest between 1910 and 1930.

Crypto-Liberalism marshalled and re-presented prairie symbols and traditions of opposition to central Canada's domination, occasionally taking cues from the Clear Grit reformism of mid-nineteenth–century Ontario. Competing populisms were forced to define themselves in relation to crypto-Liberal formulations of prairie people's problems. Crypto-Liberalism generated the lowest common denominator – rurally oriented hinterland regionalism – in prairie populist discourse. Other populisms thus reconstructed this denominator. Their appeals to class, politicians' debasement of democratic politics, and experiences of hardship argued the need for a more forceful rejection of the prevailing structures of power than that proposed by crypto-Liberals.

The least variable and most unorthodox prairie populism was undoubtedly the 'plebiscitarian' populism of the Alberta Social Credit League. The plebiscitarian populism of Social Credit accepted a full extension of the technocratic logic, since its democratic vision was as unchallenging as it was unrealistic. But Social Credit plebiscitarian politics were still populist. Aberhart and the Social Credit League proposed a major revision in parliamentary governmental practice, and considerable redistribution of power between regions and class sectors in Canada. The response of financial and commercial capitalists in central Canada to Aberhart's victory and later proposals indicated that the Social Credit League did indeed present an 'antagonistic option' against the established configuration of class power. Representative government in the British tradition was threatened by Aberhart's conception of a general will, translated into specifics and programs by 'experts,' as the essence of democratic government. There can be no doubt that Aberhart and other Social Credit leaders used popular-democratic grievances against central Canada's domination. Aberhart masterfully presented his crusade as radical, class-transcendent, morally justified, and fully consistent with the basic themes of prairie protest. His success in 1935 seems almost to be an application of a formula for success distilled from Laclau's theory.

Chapters 2 through 5 provide separate constructions of the four major democratic ideologies of prairie populism. In each chapter, I examine one populism's treatment of the six democratic themes that provided the most salient dimensions of common concern and therefore competition in prairie populist thought. In the concluding chapter, I provide a comparative overview of these four patterns of populist democratic thought, address some theoretical questions raised by this analysis, and close with comments on the relevance of prairie populism.

2 Crypto-Liberalism

There are many academic accounts of 'crypto-Liberal' actors during the halcyon days of Canadian prairie populism.[1] However, none of these – not even Morton's classic *Progressive Party in Canada* – has systematically analysed the democratic political thought of crypto-Liberalism. This is the purpose of the present chapter.

W.L. Morton coined the word 'crypto-Liberalism' to refer to the politics of a small group of federal MPs from Saskatchewan and Manitoba from 1921 to 1926. The prefix 'crypto' indicated the questionable dedication of men such as J. Johnston, Robert Forke, and of course T.A. Crerar, to a grain grower politics independent of the Liberal party.[2]

I use crypto-Liberalism to refer to a broader pattern of political discussion and thought about issues central to prairie people. The prefix 'crypto' is warranted because, of all four modes of prairie populism we will examine, crypto-Liberalism broke least with contemporary Liberal party ideology and policy perspectives in Canada. Its populism was thus closest to being a 'disguised' Liberalism. This appellation is most appropriate for the leaders of the National Progressive party from Saskatchewan and Manitoba, and of almost all provincial administrations in the prairie provinces from 1905 to 1944. The term 'crypto-Liberalism' is less appropriate for activist elements within the pre-1926 grain growers' organizations, but is none the less more valid (outside of Alberta) than other categories explored in later chapters.

I begin this chapter by considering major ideological influences upon prairie crypto-Liberalism. Then I discuss the treatment of six basic democratic themes within crypto-Liberalism, paying special attention to the Farmers' Platform of 1910, 1918, and 1921.

A Note on Ideological Heritage

Several tendencies within national Liberal politics were important to the constitution of crypto-Liberalism. The old free-trade Liberalism of Brown, Blake, Cartwright, and the young Laurier had yielded to Laurier's pragmatic, protectionist, and electorally successful Liberalism. Another pragmatic reorientation involved gradual revision of the *laissez-faire* perspective characterizing pre–J.S. Mill British liberalism. The revision was towards a commitment to state intervention, designed to balance the rough justice of the industrial capitalist economy established in the 'empire of the St Lawrence.' Canadian Liberalism gave political credence to a nascent welfare state in response to many 'interest group' representations[3] made to provincial and federal agencies on behalf of the socially disadvantaged. Also influential in this regard were the perceived attraction of socialism to a working class within an unreformed capitalism, the rise of the farmers' movement, and the undeniable intellectual and social interest in a 'new social order.'[4]

The new Liberalism aimed to recruit the growing labour and agrarian sectors of the population, although the latter proved to be most politically troublesome in the decade following the watershed Liberal convention of 1919. Mackenzie King's idealized vision of peace among social classes complemented the convention's qualified support for some demands by contemporary agrarians and 'progressives.'[5] Among the latter were commitments to tariff reductions (to diminish 'the very high cost of living which presses so severely on the masses of the people'), and use of 'the national credit to assist co-operative Agricultural Credit Associations to provide capital for agriculture at the lowest possible prices.' The 1919 platform promised social insurance against unemployment, sickness, and old age; federal incorporation of co-operative associations; and 'the acceptance of the principle of proportional representation.' Also pledged were 'immediate and drastic action by the government with respect to the high cost of living and profit-earning' and 'a grant to the prairie provinces of ownership and control over natural resources.'[6]

Western producers' experiences with the Laurier and Union governments were sufficiently sobering to prevent naïve acceptance of this program. The 1919 program disguised the likely influence of pro-tariff, socially conservative, and unabashedly central Canadian interests on any future Liberal government's policies. Whether King's 'progressive' 1919 platform was opportunist or not, he had not yet conquered the more conservative elements in the Liberal party. These elements were not simply restricted to the 'famous eighteen Toronto Liberals' who had deserted Laurier over reciprocity in 1911.[7] That the party hierarchy and major funders in central Canada were untrustworthy converts to the 'new Liberalism' of 1919 was not lost on the United Farmers of Ontario, who gave up on their erstwhile political cohorts – with some success, for four coalition years – in provincial politics. Prairie producers' organizations developed a realistic sense of the hidden dangers of the 1919 Liberal platform, and moved rapidly to create the National Progressive party.

None the less, Ontario Liberalism continued to influence western political perceptions. Many prairie farmers were immigrants from Ontario, and were thus affected by the legacy of radical, 'Clear Grit' Liberalism. As Frank Underhill states, 'the old agrarian radicalism of the Upper Canada Grits was coming to life again in a fresh incarnation among the wheat farmers of the new West.'[8] This radicalism had been modified by the Grange and the Patrons of Industry in the late nineteenth and early twentieth centuries, with the Patrons doing the most to recommend democratization of political institutions and processes.[9] The Patrons did in fact make a political beginning in Manitoba and Saskatchewan in the 1890s, but were soon displaced by the Territorial Grain Growers' Association.[10]

All agrarian radicalism in southern and western Ontario after 1837 emphasized policies and political procedures that would simultaneously reduce the power of the metropolitan Canadian business community while advancing agrarian interests. These interests should not be construed in narrowly economic terms. Some leadership elements in the Patrons, in particular, were sympathetic to organized labour, to the extent that they attempted to forge an electoral and movement coalition between farmers and industrial workers.[11] This 'populist' alliance was rationalized on moral as well as strategic grounds. Those exploited by 'monopolists' and old-party politicians were adjured to set their differences aside to work towards a more Christian society.[12] This appeal produced successful Patron candidates in 17 of 56 ridings contested in the 1893 Ontario election. A shift of only 3 per cent in 20 ridings would have given the Patrons the largest legislative representation.[13]

While radical Grit traditions reappeared several generations later on the prairies, it was in the form of a 'fresh incarnation' and not simply a duplication. This was especially true in Saskatchewan and Alberta; in Manitoba, similarities with Ontario patterns were more readily apparent.[14] As one moved west, one found a greater tendency to supplement or replace radical Grit and Liberal perspectives with British labourite as well as 'republican' ideas of American Jacksonian democracy, Populism, and eventually, Progressivism. As Morton says: 'the radical democracy of the Old Ontario Grits experienced a new birth on a frontier less constricted and less subject to conservative influence than that of early Ontario.'[15]

By 1919, Ontario Liberalism included three significant strains, which were by no means organizationally separate. There was the compromise Liberalism of Mackenzie King and those whose vision of national Liberal power prescribed reforms to the party's appeal and perhaps even its operative ideology. A second strain gave radical Grit and Patron traditions more of a home. The United Farmers of Ontario entered political competition with no expectation of winning the 1919 provincial election. Thanks to significant rural overrepresentation,[16] luck in the partisan contests in many ridings, and a widespread dissatisfaction with the two old parties, the UFO formed a coalition government with eleven Independent Labour Party representatives.

The UFO platform was not radical by prairie populist standards, partly because the UFO had not intended to become a continuous electoral force.[17] With the exception of support for public ownership of utilities, its program was not noticeably out of step with that passed by the national Liberal party convention earlier that year. None the less, the 'radical democratic' tendencies of two key leaders, W.C. Good and J.J. Morrison, forced a good deal of more radical talk than one found in the election platform, and the physiocratic orientation in the UFO did not sit very comfortably with Mackenzie King's urban reformism.

Most UFO voters saw it as a moderate reform party for rural Ontarians and others interested in 'honest' government. Like its predecessor, the Patrons of Industry, the UFO was not seen by most as a fundamental alternative to either the established party system or the prevailing economic system. Like its federal 'ally,' the Progressives, the United Farmers of Ontario did not manage to pry the majority of its supporters away from their 'old party' (primarily Liberal) home for more than a political moment. None the less, interesting variations on democratic themes were circulating within UFO ranks, and the conflict between the party organization and legislative leadership[18] was instructive for similar conflicts that would occur in prairie politics, especially those in Alberta several years later. This experience did have one significant impact on the Liberalism that followed the UFO electoral collapse (1923) and subsequent withdrawal from direct political action. Ontario's agrarian radicalism ceased to seek expression in direct political competition, or even high-profile criticism of party politics. Agrarian radicals either turned to co-operative organizations or other 'non-political' means of societal change, such as UFO member of parliament and leader W.C. Good,[19] or gradually lost their radicalism.

Also sharing the post-war Liberal party was a Toronto-centred, business-oriented liberalism. It had made its peace with Liberalism via Laurier's acceptance of the core of Macdonald's National Policy. These rural and urban Liberalisms were the Scylla and Charybdis between which King had to steer. The existence and power of Toronto- and Montreal-based business Liberalism[20] led prairie producers to believe that independent political action was on their agenda by 1919 or 1920. Crypto-Liberals believed that King had been seduced by the sirens of central Canada's business liberalism.

Several of the factors leading to the 'freshness' of prairie Liberalism deserve special mention. The idea of 'the frontier,' with connotations of recent settlement, the absence of the range of institutions that reproduce 'received' patterns of thought and activity, a consequent receptiveness to new ideas and practices, and an unequal relation of power between frontier and established centres, captures several of these factors quite nicely. 'Frontier' also usually connotes a regional economy heavily reliant on a few resource industries. The prairie frontier had all of these characteristics, along with rapid settlement, commercial monopolies (the CPR, elevator companies, implement dealers, and land companies), and resentment of central Canadian dominance.[21]

In this context, it is not surprising that prairie inhabitants were suspicious of conservative Liberalism, or even unmodified rural Grit liberalism.[22] Western provincial adoption of parliamentary government did much to maintain continuities with Canadian experience, and to direct political competition within the channels of the 'national' party system. Still, we should not make too much of the homogenizing power of these political institutions. As the whole prairie populist experience shows, adaptive and creative political thought and practice can occur within and alongside parliamentary institutions, including the party system itself.

As a frontier region, the Canadian prairie West was open to the development of a markedly different political culture or ideological climate than existed in English central Canada. Canada's colonial relation and cultural ties with Britain, and its proximity to the United States, meant that these countries would be the main external sources of ideas with which the regional ideological climate could be shaped.

One set of formative ideas came from the British and American co-operative movements, the former more consumer-, and the latter more producer-oriented.[23] To the extent that they engendered a general distrust of big business and a heightened awareness of class conflict, the British and American socialist movements influenced even the most cautious of prairie populists. Finally, the American populisms of the Great Plains from roughly 1880 to 1900 and American Progressivism between 1914 and 1930 had a major impact on grain-grower politics. These influences were felt via imported periodicals and books and through the pronouncements of local political leaders, publicists, and orators.

The main point to be made about the importation of reform ideas into the prairies is that they were highly competitive with and reconstitutive of those coming from 'empire Ontario.' British and American political ideas had cultural credentials similar to Ontario's. Indeed, in some matters, their credentials surpassed those of 'the centre,' largely because Ontario's practices and perspectives were most obviously associated with specific grievances. Hence, for example, prairie residents lauded the tradition of free trade in Britain as a democratic and properly liberal tradition, which had been abandoned by Canadian Liberals.[24] In addition, prairie citizens often viewed the electoral practices of the southern republic – first male and then universal suffrage, experimentation with instruments of direct democracy,[25] the primaries, and open conventions for leadership selection – as superior to those of their own reluctantly democratic polity.[26]

The enhanced competitive power of radical political ideas from Britain and America weakened the established two-party system in the three prairie provinces.[27] In understanding this weakening, one must grant the importance of relative class homogeneity,[28] physical distance, the break with old family and community political 'networks,' the 1911 reciprocity election, and an agrarian region's disenchantment with Union government and non-agrarian representation.[29] One must still see that plausible alternative perspectives did much to give prairie people a sense that the traditional party system imposed from the centre was dispensable.

Finally, mention must be made of the role of the co-operative movement in the prairie redevelopment of central Canadian liberalism(s).[30] Agrarian producer and consumer co-operatives had made an important mark on Ontario's rural political economy by the turn of the century,[31] but never played the central role there that they did in the prairie provinces after 1901. In the absence of organizational and educational contributions of grain growers' associations and their organs (*The Grain Growers' Guide*, *The United Farmers of Alberta*, and *The Western Producer*), it is arguable that alternative political forms would have largely bypassed prairie politics.[32] 'Third party' and 'independent' politics are by no means inevitable in the absence of galvanizing and complementary social institutions, even in a 'quasi-colonial' context.

Lawrence Goodwyn, a historian of American populism, has emphasized the role of co-operative institutions in the agrarian populism of great plains and southern states. 'To describe the origins of populism in one sentence,' he says, 'the co-operative movement recruited American farmers, and their subsequent experiences within the co-operatives radically altered their political consciousness.' These co-operatives were thus the source of the agrarian populist movement and its culture.[33] While too restrictive for the Canadian case, Goodwyn's major point is still valuable for our purposes. Participation in co-operative enterprises gave hard-pressed farmers self-respect and a sense of the democratic possibilities that eventually sustained a (short-lived) crusade directly into politics (the People's Party). This sense was at the centre of 'the culture of the movement,' initiated by attempts to combat the power of eastern American finance capital.

In the Canadian prairies, several factors complemented and facilitated the emergence at an early stage of co-operative institutions and their characteristic 'cultures' as key determinants of the shape of transferred ideological baggage. Among these were the youthfulness of local and regional political institutions and the predominance of grain production in the regional economy. Also crucial was the speed with which grain growers' associations and farmers' co-operatives, such as the United Grain Growers, became the pre-eminent interest groups with which provincial governments had to deal.

One point that cannot be overlooked in the relation of co-operatives to the fate of liberalism on the prairies is the 'anti-political' perspective that traditional co-operatives communicated to the western political environment.[34] This perspective reinforced western producers' tendency to be non-partisan and also reduced their enthusiasm for independent political parties. While the former worked against the success of national Liberalism in the West, the latter, ironically, bolstered provincial Liberalism in Saskatchewan and Manitoba.

The relation of co-operatives to 'established' Liberalism was by no means one-way. Just as Liberalism had to adapt to an ideological environment potentially antagonistic to its *laissez-faire* origins, so co-operatives were often initially rationalized in terms compatible with the liberal rationale of the market: organization and concentration leads to power *vis-à-vis* the sellers and buyers encountered in the exchange of commodities. Prairie co-operative institutions engendered an ethos that often transcended this perspective, and sometimes nurtured support for political alternatives embodying this 'transcendence.'

The development of this ethos speaks well both for the democratic potential inherent in co-operative institutions, and for their leadership on the prairies. As prairie Liberalism came to terms with these developments, it developed more easily beyond the boundaries established in the more restrictive Ontario environment than Grit radicals had successfully managed there. As long as it did not embrace the radical implications of the co-operative experience, however, this liberalism remained *crypto*-Liberalism. This appeared to be the case with the bulk of the United Grain Growers leadership after 1917, partly because T.A. Crerar retained his presidency of UGG during and well after his stint as Progressive leader.

From this brief sketch of the factors conditioning the development of crypto-Liberalism in the prairies, we can look more closely at some of its principal characteristics. Since the fundamental concerns of crypto-Liberalism were rooted in prairie producers' disadvantaged position in the national wheat economy, we shall begin by considering their articulation of economic grievances.

Crypto-Liberalism and the 'New National Policy'

The centrality of the tariff issue in western prairie politics from 1890[35] onwards is well known. This issue provides a good entry into crypto-Liberal discourse, but not for the oft-proffered reason that 'Progressivism' was a one-issue movement and that therefore explication of the prairie producers' class interest in free trade tells us all we need to know about prairie protest. The tariff was a grievance that quickly came to symbolize and connote a revealing range of the social and political shortcomings perceived by prairie producers.

To begin with the obvious: a high ('protective') tariff unavoidably drove up the costs of production, the credit costs incurred as a consequence, and the effective cost of living for all prairie dwellers. As low- to moderate-income earners, the farmers found the effect of the tariff regressive as consumers, as did the working class.[36]

Prairie grain producers relied on many imported goods to keep production costs at a minimum. Because the tariff effectively limited the availability of imports, these producers bore the costs of protective tariffs quite out of proportion to both their relative numbers and their contribution to the national economy. To most farmers, there was bitter irony in the fact that the 'spade work' done in the national wheat economy should be rewarded with disincentives to production.[37] It is not surprising, then, that the age-old agrarian theme of distributive justice *vis-à-vis* other primary social classes should have emerged from the grain growers' experience with the tariff. Noting that these producers were, to date, among the most prosperous in Canadian agrarian history does not render their concern trivial or merely self-serving. As a publicly articulated problem, distributive justice is virtually always couched in terms of relative shares and equity within a given polity.

Whether or not an independent national economy could have been sustained if reciprocity had followed the 1911 election, prairie (and rural Ontario) producers were the biggest short-term losers to sustained high tariffs. Their predominantly Liberal sympathies and their pocket-books drove this home, giving their perception of regional injustice and anti-agrarian bias in the national government a major boost.

The tariff issue had been at the centre of Liberal attacks on Toryism long before western settlers came to place it in their pantheon of political demons.

Edward Blake, Richard Cartwright, George Brown, George Wrigley, and Goldwyn Smith had captured the hearts of Ontario rural folk with their characterization of protection as the bane of social morality and Canada's 'natural' economic progress. Even before 1896, Laurier had castigated 'protection' as the scourge of the people.[38] Edward Porritt had chronicled the history of protection in two books that remained classics in agrarian circles a generation after their publication.[39] And we find a prominent prairie politician and Patron saying in 1895, 'with regard to reform of the tariff much has been promised, little performed, more, perhaps, from want of power than want of will, for the manufacturers seem all powerful at Ottawa – the manufacturers and the CPR.'[40]

With this background, it is not surprising that the central document in the rise of the farmers' movement, and crypto-Liberalism in particular, should place the tariff at the centre of national government and Liberal party failings. The Farmers' Platform, or 'New National Policy' as it was dubbed by its supporters from 1919 to 1926, went through several incarnations between 1910 and 1921. Presented to the Laurier government during the 'Siege of Ottawa,' in 1910, this set of resolutions effectively announced the arrival of an organized interprovincial agrarian group on the national political scene.[41] The Canadian Council of Agriculture (CCA), established in 1909 as a co-ordinating body for its provincial grain grower and agrarian association members,[42] drafted all of these resolutions, as well as the Farmers' Platform of 1916, 1918, and 1921.

In all versions of the Farmers' Platform, the protective tariff of the old National Policy was the main target of economic criticism and reform suggestions, just as it had been for the Patrons a generation earlier.[43] Given the dependence of the established national political economy on the protective tariff, it is not unreasonable to suggest that implementation of the New National Policy 'would have re-shaped the development of the Canadian economy.'[44] For our purposes, it is important to recognize that the campaign against the protective tariff incorporated a plethora of non-economic and reformist objectives at the core of crypto-Liberal democratic thought. The farmers' platforms were far from dogmatic insistence on the extension of British free trade doctrines to Canada, or a poorly disguised 'republican' plot to subvert Canadian nationhood (a point emphasized by the Conservative press of central Canada).

The tariff section took up approximately 40 per cent of the 1921 platform, if one includes preamble and 'demands.' This was considerably more space than was devoted to international relations, treatment of returned soldiers, proposals for settlement, extension of co-operatives, public ownership, or even the twelve-point program for 'other democratic reforms' which ended the document.

The CCA clearly intended to nail its colours to the mast with its tariff position. When the platform was 'ratified' by the provincial grain growers' associations in 1919, they were equally intent on being publicly distinguished by their position on the tariff.

It is significant that the tariff issue maintained prominence after the platform had been used as a litmus test for political candidates and even for political action by grain growers' associations from 1919 through 1921. Because the tariff was widely recognized to be crucial to prairie agriculture, it came to connote a wide range of apparently unrelated social and political issues in current public discussion. The tariff was given pride of place for yet another reason: it was seen by key Progressive leaders and strategists (such as J.W. Dafoe) as the only issue which could force a realignment of national party politics along desirable lines.

The tariff section of the 1921 Farmers' Platform began with a strategic pitch to those interested in fiscal responsibility,[45] which does not seem likely to have appealed to many in disagreement with the rest of the tariff 'package.' It was argued that the 'huge war debt and other greatly increased financial obligations' could most easily and sensibly be met through a national policy that encouraged veterans and 'the large anticipated immigration' to develop agricultural lands. Only a policy that reduced 'to a minimum the cost of living and the cost of production' could draw this surplus population into agriculture. If one accepted the physiocratic premises of the rest of the document, and the drastic consequences of the old National Policy tariff for agriculture, this new part of the tariff section's preamble would ring true.

The rest of the tariff section's preamble replicates the 1916 Farmers' Platform. Under 'Definite Tariff Demands,' only two novel suggestions appear. They suppose a vigorous pro-tariff campaign by 'the interests' (even in the event of a Progressive victory) and the unlikelihood that governments would regulate tariffs fairly:

g) That all corporations engaged in the manufacture of products protected by the customs tariff be obliged to publish annually comprehensive and accurate statements of their earnings.
h) That every claim for tariff protection by any industry should be heard publicly before a special committee of parliament.[46]

Ringing loud and clear in each of these statements are standard prairie producers' assumptions that politicians are manipulated by the 'special interests' protected by the tariff, and that the tariff provides a profit holiday for protected industries.[47]

A more complete sense of the anti-tariff position in relation to non-economic concerns can be gleaned from the 1918 Farmers' Platform. With minor revisions, this version of the New National Policy became the National Progressive party platform in the 1921 election, which clearly marks it as an expression of crypto-Liberalism. This document is reproduced in an appendix to this book.

Democratic Themes in Crypto-Liberalism

The People

Following Laclau, we can say that the way social conflict is represented within a political discourse tells us much about a populism's general social analysis and perspective. This perception is articulated in characterizations of 'the people' and their antagonists, which illuminates the democratic themes with which we are concerned.

The crypto-Liberal conception of 'the people' tended to be the most general among those of the four prairie populisms and had the least radical connotations. For most purposes, 'the people' was a residual category, referring to all those outside of government who were not a part of the scheming 'big interests.'[48] Thus 'the people' were by definition free from the taint of corruption and class privilege that government and big business carried. In characteristic populist style,[49] 'the people' were endowed with common sense and a heightened sense of justice.

The physiocratic and western regionalist tendencies in crypto-Liberalism gave 'the people' a more precise meaning. The physiocratic orientation was evident in many pronouncements of grain growers' association leaders and publicists, and it constituted the lowest common denominator in the politics of prairie protest.[50] By 1916 physiocratic themes were common to agrarian analyses of the effect of the tariff on party politics, the moral tone of public life, the existence of basic exploitation and inequality in Canadian society, and the prospects of the agricultural economy and its human mainstays.

Particularly forceful instances of these physiocratic themes were found in the Farmers' Platform of 1910 and 1916. The Canadian Council of Agriculture pronounced in its 1910 platform that 'the further progress and development of the agricultural industry is of such vital importance to the general welfare of the state that all other Canadian industries are so dependent upon its success, [and] that its constant condition forms the great barometer of trade.'[51] After laying down five propositions for gradual adoption of free trade, the CCA concluded with a concern for the implications of rapid urbanization. 'Believing that the greatest misfortune that can befall any country is to have its people huddled together in great centres of population,' they said, 'and realizing that ... the greatest problem which presents itself to Canadian people today is the problem of retaining our people on the soil, we come doubly assured of the justice of our petition.'[52]

The Farmers' Platform of December 1916 was written in light of the defeat of the Liberal reciprocity option in 1911, and after six years of increasing anti–old party, anti–'big interests' agitation in the grain growers' press and organizations. While the physiocratic orientation is still evident, a more radical critique of the national political economy was now the core of the CCA's anti-tariff position. The CCA focused its preamble to free-trade resolutions on the role played by the 'protective tariff' in fostering 'combines, trusts, and "gentlemen's agreements" by means of which the people of Canada – both urban and rural – have been shamefully exploited,' and on the fact that 'agriculture – the basic industry upon which the success of all other industries primarily depends – is almost stagnant throughout Canada.' It was thus manifest that 'the Protective Tariff has been and is a chief corrupting influence in our national life because the protected interests, in order to maintain their unjust privileges, have contributed lavishly to political parties to look to them for support, thereby lowering the standard of public morality.'

Manitoba Grain Growers' Association (MGGA) presidents also gave voice to the physiocratic tendency in crypto-Liberalism. In 1919 and 1921, they claimed that 'the consciousness of the people has now been awakened,' that 'the Grain Growers have within them the potency and power that will make a democratic state,' and that farmers' proposals are endorsed by 'the people' because their policy 'appeals to their genuine sense of justice – the farmers are not selfishly seeking their own interests merely.'[53] Two years later, after the Winnipeg General Strike, the new MGGA president saw 'the people' in narrower terms: 'those who do not belong to the capitalistic class nor to the other extreme, however you like to designate it, but who belong simply to the great mass of the common, intelligent people of Canada.'

Prior to the 1919 strike and increased labour radicalism, farmers' organizations had generally assumed that labour was a natural and sympathetic ally.[54] After the bitter general strike, condemned by the *Guide* as inspired by 'foreign,' 'Bolsheviki' elements, this assumption was rejected by prairie grain grower leadership and much of the rank and file. Social democratic populists were to work hard to repair this rift among 'the people.'

A less physiocratic and more regionalist conception of 'the people' was found in the Progressives' national leadership, provincial Liberal and Liberal-Progressive administrations, and the writings of the classic western Liberal journalist J.W. Dafoe. In all cases, a desire to retain a large constituency, and to prevent divisions within the farmers' movements, prompted a very general usage of 'the people.' The term thus stood for all westerners – local businessmen included – suffering under artificially high living costs and low incomes resulting from federal tariff, transportation, and grain-marketing policies.

Both Crerar and his confidant, Dafoe, were free-trade liberals. Crerar portrayed the western farmers as the principal victims of the protective tariff, but his hope that the Progressives would found a new, anti-protectionist Liberal party[55] led him to portray 'the people' as all those who suffered under protection. Their antagonists were consequently all those (including the contemporary Liberal and Tory parties) who benefited from it. The tariff was 'morally wrong, inasmuch as it permits a particular group of people to enrich itself at the expense of the rest.'[56] It also prevented the natural development of industry based on Canada's natural wealth – land, lumber, and minerals. Instead, the tariff was 'sustaining a long string of secondary and artificial industries which are often merely of the fabricating type.'[57] Western industry was 'natural' to Canada, and Crerar saw those engaged in these occupations as 'the people.' Special interests opposed to the welfare of the people controlled central Canada's contrived and protected industries. They realized that a corrupt relation with government was their only means of distorting the 'natural economy' to their advantage.

Dafoe was equally a booster of the West, and only slightly less physiocratic in outlook. He too associated the federal commitment to 'protection' with the decline of popular interests, and promoted a party of free trade that could advance 'the people's' interests. His support for the Progressives until 1925 (when the spectre of Tory rule led him back to his true political home in the councils of the Liberal party) was predicated on its supposed potential for re-forming liberalism along its true free-trade lines, while sending crypto-Tories from Quebec and Toronto into the Conservative party.[58] Dafoe continually expressed the worry that a narrow agrarian appeal, especially one based on the doctrines of H.W. Wood, would destroy the Progressives' opportunity to force a political realignment over the tariff question. He thus saw advantage in keeping 'the people' as diverse as possible. Even moderate labour was encouraged to see that their real interests were contained within a liberal position. Finally, for Dafoe, as for Crerar and the United Farmers of Manitoba leadership by 1922, Winnipeg businessmen were also part of 'the people.'[59]

Liberal administrations in Alberta and Saskatchewan did little to alienate local businessmen, except make it clear that the provincial grain growers' associations were their preferred customers. 'The people,' as a result, were portrayed as the whole provincial population, except for hard-core Conservatives. Electoral propaganda of the Saskatchewan Liberal party for 1917 gives us a good idea of how provincial Liberals represented themselves as progressives and the Conservatives as agents of the big interests. On one election handbill, provincial voters were instructed that 'The Liberal Party is the People's Party [which] represents the producers and working classes,' while 'the Conservative Party is the Party of the Big Interests [which] represents the Wealth of Canada.'[60] The remarkable success of the Saskatchewan Liberal 'machine' during even the height of the farmers' revolt testifies to the success of this message.[61]

Characterizing Tories as the 'party of the big interests' was not displaced as the major facet of crypto-Liberal partisan rhetoric until the CCF presented a threat from the other flank. Even then, however, prairie Liberals presented themselves as the 'people's party.' The major difference, of course, was that the threat to 'the people' (in essence, farmers) in the post-1932 period was purported to come from a farm-confiscating, freedom-crushing state socialism. The 1934, 1938, and 1944 provincial elections in Saskatchewan featured an inflammatory attack on the CCF that set Saskatchewan Liberalism on the dogmatic free-enterprise course that led to its victory in 1964 under Ross Thatcher. In Manitoba, an effective coalition between conservative southern farmers and a shrewd Winnipeg business community managed to keep the 'socialists' from the gates of power until 1969. The crypto-Liberal Bracken administrations from 1922 to 1942 laid the solid foundations of this anti-CCF provincial power.[62]

Participatory Democracy and Crypto-Liberalism

Assessing crypto-Liberal thought about participatory democracy is complicated by the wide range of relevant statements coming out of the prairie farmers' organizations between 1911 and 1926, and by the absence of systematic approaches to the issue. We can, none the less, distinguish between positions within crypto-Liberal thought: grain grower rank and file were more enthusiastic about participatory democracy than were crypto-Liberal leaders. This difference is noticeable in the support given to direct legislation, the grain growers' associations' moves into direct political action, their critiques of 'partyism,' the varying emphases on local autonomy, and the intrinsic as opposed to politically instrumental value accorded popular participation generally. For a good indication of how leaders and rank and file agreed on basic 'democratic reforms' to Canadian society, one can examine the 'New National Policy' espoused in the 'Farmers' Platform' of the Canadian Council of Agriculture between 1910 and 1921.

When most fervently promoted, the measures of direct democracy – the initiative, referendum, and recall – have been seen as means of bringing the full force of the popular will into a political arena needlessly complicated by élitist, untrustworthy 'politicians.' In this sense, direct legislation is a quintessential expression of the twin attitudinal pillars of all populisms: distrust of all élites and deep faith in the common sense and ethical wisdom of the common people. From the mid-1890s to 1921, there was widespread support for the initiative, referendum, and recall in most agrarian, labour, and anti–old-party circles.[63] In the decade prior to the Progressives, prairie grain growers offered tremendous support for the devices of direct legislation.[64] Proposals for these devices of popular democracy were natural responses of a population for whom parliamentary institutions had not brought satisfactory federal policy. Direct legislation was desired as the obvious complement to internal democracy within co-operative and other farmer organizations. It was also viewed as a means of forcing unscrupulous politicians to deliver on their promises – on lower tariff rates, most notably.

At one level, direct legislation was favoured by prairie grain growers' associations and those interested in agrarian solidarity as a means of temporarily avoiding internecine, party-defined squabbling, while still availing themselves of the mechanisms of reform. This was the position taken by E.A. Partridge,[65] a later advocate of independent political action for farmers, and by the Manitoba and Saskatchewan Grain Grower associations when they were still informally allied with provincial Liberal parties.

The earliest serious campaign in favour of direct legislation was led by the Direct Legislation League of Manitoba. It soon became a partisan issue, with the premier Tory of the prairies, Sir Rodmond Roblin, excoriating direct legislation as an alien import that ran dead against British traditions of responsible government.[66] The Manitoba Liberal party committed itself to direct legislation in convention in 1910, promptly made it a key campaign plank in elections of 1910 and 1914, and was genuinely dismayed to see its unanimous enactment in 1915 come to naught in a 1916 *ultra vires* ruling by the provincial Appeal Court.[67] This ruling was upheld by the Judicial Committee of the Privy Council in 1919.

The three prairie provinces' grain growers' associations had endorsed provincial direct legislation provisions before the war began. The conviction with which direct legislation was promoted is evident in the following passagefrom an address of R.C. Henders, president of the Manitoba Grain Growers' Association, to the MGGA annual convention in 1911:

The people of Canada have never abrogated their right to rule. If, therefore, custom has introduced a system of legislation by which our legislators can if they desire place themselves at variance with the wishes of the people, for a period of four years irreparable damage may be sustained, and it is up to the people to correct this error and make such reasonable and proper provisions as the case may demand.

First, by providing that when the voice of the majority has been expressed by petition or unanimous resolution this voice should prevail rather than the preconceived predilections of any member or number of members who may be elected as representatives for the time being. Call this if you will direct legislation.

Second, that when any measure has been passed by legislature or parliament which in its working out is likely to affect materially any class of the people, such measure cannot become law until such time as it has been referred to the people and passed on by them, by a majority vote of all who voted thereon.

Third, when any member elected from any constituency shows himself out of harmony with the wishes of his constituency such constituents shall have the power to force him to explain his position and appeal to such constituents for endorsation and re-appointment.

These, gentlemen, are some of the tools with which the people could rule in fact and not merely in theory. These are the planks that will bridge the gulf and keep elected and electors in closer touch; they will reduce to the lowest minimum the possibility of graft and the use of any pre-election pledges.[68]

Henders further adumbrated this radical stance within crypto-Liberalism in his 1912 presidential address:

The people spoken of by the political stump speakers and election campaign literature as the 'sovereign people' have, I might say, no direct efficient control. They are sovereign de jure but not de facto, except at election times. The actual power experienced by the people consists chiefly in the periodic choice of another set of masters who make laws to suit themselves and enforce them until their term of office expires, regardless of the will of the people. We are governed by an elective aristocracy which in its turn is largely controlled by an aristocracy of wealth. Behind the governments and the legislatures are the corporations and the trusts. Behind the machines, the rings and the bosses, are the business monopolists, the

industrial combinations, and the plutocrats; behind the political monopolists are
the industrial monopolists.

This, then, in very brief is the state of affairs. What is the remedy? We answer the
principal remedy is Direct Legislation, because it opens the door to every other
reform. No-one who really believes in self-government can refuse to support the
Initiative and Referendum for they merely enable the people to veto laws they do
not want and to secure laws they do want, that is, they enable the people to govern
themselves.

Did we have Direct Legislation what rapid strides we would make along the lines
of civil service reform, proportional representation, the elective ballot, equal
suffrage, efficient corrupt practices act, and the popular Recall, all of which are
really necessary in order that the people may really own and operate the
government, under conditions most likely to secure wise legislation and honest,
intelligent and economic administration.[69]

The high hopes held for direct legislation here were characteristic of grain
growers' associations and the *Guide*.[70] At a minimum, direct legislation would
restore party activity to its proper functions, by supplementing or checking
policy decisions made by party governments. The New National Policy
platform could not be palatable to its grain grower constituency without
endorsing direct legislation. Many Progressive candidates signed recall
agreements with the constituency organizations that had nominated them.

The records of the three prairie provinces' Liberal administrations in passing
direct-legislation bills are interesting. In all three cases, the governments
responded rapidly to the grain growers' conventions' support for direct
legislation. However, in all cases (Alberta 1912, Saskatchewan 1913,
Manitoba 1916) money bills were exempt from direct legislation, the
percentage of the population required to initiate legislation was quite high (8
per cent in Alberta and Saskatchewan), and recall provisions were left out
entirely. Grain growers were disappointed with the limited scope of these
enabling bills in all three provinces, but particularly so in Saskatchewan and
Manitoba. In Saskatchewan, a referendum on the direct-legislation bill was held
shortly after it had passed through the legislature, with very little positive
publicity and a high required approval rate (30 per cent of eligible voters). The
Saskatchewan Grain Growers' Association contended that the government had
cleverly appeared to sanction direct legislation, while doing little to ensure its
implementation.[71]

In Manitoba, an enthusiastic Liberal government passed the Initiative and
Referendum Act soon after replacing the Tories, then quickly referred the act to
the provincial Appeal Court. The court ruled it *ultra vires* of the province's

power to amend its constitution, and noted crushingly: 'In Canada there is no sovereignty in the people; ... it is in the Parliament at Westminister, and our powers to legislate are such, and only such, as that Parliament has given us.'[72] Morton comments that this decision could not properly have gone the other way: responsible government and direct democracy are hardly to be reconciled with each other without destroying the initiative and responsibility of the former.[73] To this, the three prairie governments would undoubtedly have said 'amen,' but for many rank-and-file grain growers such destruction was not beyond the pale. Their disenchantment with partyism placed them considerably beyond their leading 'establishment' spokesmen and legislators.

Limited support was given to direct legislation by Progressive leaders, the provincial Liberal administrations, and the crypto-Liberal press. The cases of T.A. Crerar and J.W. Dafoe are instructive here, since they were definitive spokesmen of moderate crypto-Liberalism during the Progressives' early period. Crerar had supported the Direct Legislation League before the Manitoba legislation had been struck down, then concluded that it was a lost cause. His 1921 'Confession of Faith'[74] made no mention of direct legislation as a desired political reform or, oddly enough, of the political irrelevance of support for direct legislation in the 1921 Farmers' Platform. His 'Manifesto,' distributed at the height of the 1921 campaign, emphasized the undesirable consequences of the protective tariff, the truly liberal intentions of the farmers' movement, and the need for efficiency in government administration. But direct legislation was not mentioned.[75]

Dafoe supported direct legislation when his partisan support for the Manitoba Liberal party required it (roughly from 1912 to 1916). He backed away when labour and the radical elements in the farmers' movement became its supporters, so as to confound party direction of legislatures' business. His enthusiasm for direct legislation continued only so long as it remained in the provincial Liberal platform and was a clear rejection of the Tory position on the sovereignty of parliament over the will of the electors.[76] By the 1921 election, Dafoe too had come to see tariff, transportation, 'good government,' and party realignment issues as the crux of the Progressive campaign.

Grain grower rank-and-file support for direct legislation was based on a desire to supplement and check the work of representative assemblies. At its most radical, this was to take the form of binding expressions of popular choice, mixed with regulated delegate behaviour in elected assemblies.[77] The logic of direct legislation, if fully extended, could not tolerate crypto-Liberals' ties to the Liberal party. This logic was disguised well by provincial Liberals so long as formal support and, eventually, legislation was provided on this issue.

One might think that prairie Liberal governments would have endured real political travails had the direct legislation statutes remained on the books after 1919. In fact, these governments were on the whole very responsive to demands made at the annual 'farmers' parliaments' of the grain growers' conventions, and tended to anticipate potential policy clashes. The grain growers' real frustrations tended to be with federal matters – fiscal policy, transportation policy, regulation of campaign funding, and so on. Thus, the major object of direct legislation would have been alteration of federal policies, if provision for direct legislation had been made at this level. There is no evidence that such provision was ever seriously considered by a federal administration. Progressive MPs made no sustained attempt to introduce enabling legislation in parliament between 1922 and 1926, probably because economic issues were more pressing, and championing the cause of direct legislation would have been a foregone quixotic affair.

Proportional representation and direct legislation were generally supported as complementary devices in the service of a 'greater measure of democracy in government.' Progressive and labour support for proportional representation was founded on a desire to secure at least minority representation in Canadian legislatures, with seats for farmers and all 'others interested in social reform,' as the *Farmers' Sun* said in 1893.[78] Agitation for this alternative electoral system was neither as intensive nor as symbolically significant as that for direct legislation. Ironically, practical successes in implementing proportional representation were much greater than those for direct legislation, even though enthusiasm for the democratic potential of the latter far outpaced that for the former.

At the provincial level, proportional representation had been promised by the Liberal premier of Alberta on the eve of his 1921 defeat,[79] and had not been provided in either Saskatchewan or rural Manitoba.[80] By 1921, all four western provinces had passed enabling legislation for proportional representation in municipal elections.[81] Seventeen cities had taken up this option by 1922, although twelve had abandoned it by 1929 through plebiscites or provincial ordinances.[82] Proportional representation had not attracted much attention in parliament since its first mention in 1913, despite its inclusion in the 1919 Liberal platform.

Our discussion of the adoption of 'direct' political action by grain growers' associations[83] can focus on what these moves tell us about commitments to participatory democracy within crypto-Liberal organizations. We will examine the Saskatchewan Grain Growers' Association (SGGA) experience with provincial political action, and the 1921 campaign of the National Progressive party.

A large minority of SGGA annual convention delegates had favoured formation of a provincial grain growers' party since 1910. Until 1922, the association's leadership was able to convince the majority that political activity would undermine their economic and educational objectives. The leadership also argued that independent political action was a gratuitous undertaking, in view of the Liberal government's responsiveness to the SGGA The presence of many prominent SGGA members in the legislature and the cabinet (such as C.A. Dunning, W. Motherwell, J.A. Maharg, W.M. Martin) was 'proof' of the identity of objectives. Still, by 1922, after the provincial Progressives had been ambushed by a snap election, a majority favoured independent political action.[84] The 1922 convention instructed its unenthusiastic leadership to prepare for bringing the SGGA into provincial politics. Here is a clear case of the grain grower rank and file forcing an unconventional, that is, anti-Liberal, political project on its leadership.

This grain grower action says a great deal about the passion for 'participatory democracy' in their movement. As at the federal level, grain growers wanted farmer candidates closely connected with an organization of their own.[85] It was not enough to have farmer Liberal candidates committed to responsiveness to the SGGA. There was an irony in this move into political action, however, that suggests a limited appreciation of the difficulties of popular control. After deciding to enter the provincial political arena, the SGGA entrusted preparations to J.B. Musselman, a leader long known as an opponent of this very political project. By leaving the decision regarding political action up to each local, Musselman used the farmers' own commitment to local autonomy to obstruct creation of an effective political organization.

In the full bloom of anti-party sentiment on the prairies, the 1921 National Progressive campaign was characterized by an unprecedented degree of local constituency activity connected to candidate selection. Even before this campaign, local delegates to grain growers' conventions had endorsed the New National Policy of the Canadian Council of Agriculture as the basis for constituency campaigns. Following these endorsements, many Progressive locals designed a method of candidate selection to involve large numbers of local members, as is evident in an excerpt from a guide to candidate selection in the Last Mountain constituency in Saskatchewan:

Any supporter of the New National Policy in the Municipality may hand in the name of a man whom he wishes to have placed in nomination to the chairman or secretary of a polling division, or to the municipal committee man. All these names shall then be sent by the polling division chairman or secretary to the municipal committee man, who shall prepare a ballot or list containing all the names so suggested. The committee man shall then call a public meeting of supporters of the

New National Policy which shall be open from 8 P.M. to 10 P.M. or until any other suitable time of day, for the purpose of giving an opportunity to all supporters to vote on the proposed names. The result of the vote in each polling division should then be sent to the municipal committee man, whose duty it would be to tabulate all the votes in the municipality for each candidate. The man having the largest number of the total votes in all the polling divisions in the municipality would be declared the municipal candidate. His name should be sent to the constituency secretary.[86]

Local control over the candidates, over conduct of internal affairs, and over conduct of campaigns once direct political action had been initiated were also sanctioned by the grain grower's organization.[87] A document produced by the United Farmers of Manitoba at their 1921 convention also emphasizes a commitment to autonomy in these spheres, by guaranteeing binding contributions by local constituencies to provincial platforms and 'full autonomy ... to local constituencies as to the form and conduct of their political organization, the general principle being observed that the constituency recognize itself as one of many working together towards common ends.'[88]

The rank-and-file commitment to local autonomy in organization, campaigning, and candidate selection took away a good deal of the *raison d'être* for a centralized party-like organization. Believing that local autonomy would reduce the Progressives' electoral appeal and increase their public image as a sectionalist party, Crerar struggled to set up such a centralized operation before the 1921 federal campaign began. His attempt was sternly rebuked by the Canadian Council of Agriculture's executive,[89] who recognized that there was little rank-and-file sympathy for such partyish methods. Crerar spoke about the undemocratic character of the Liberal and Tory organizations, but he clearly felt that some of their methods had to be adopted for the Progressives to become a significant political force. Most later commentators have agreed with Crerar on this score.[90]

Academic sympathy for Crerar's position suggests that the more extreme critiques of partyism in the farmers' movement, while understandable, were ill-considered and pre-emptive of feasible yet significant changes in the party system. The Crerar-Dafoe objective of using the National Progressive party to mould national Liberalism into a free-trade, catch-all reform party is thus presented as the only realistic political option open to the Progressives. From this perspective, ridding politics of 'partyism' and party discipline in the context of responsible government is hopelessly naïve and virtually anti-political.

One cannot deny that the Crerar-Dafoe line was more attuned to the exigencies of national campaigning, the potential for lapses in the movement memberships' enthusiasm, and the hazards of a loosely organized party's attempts to play the 'balance of power' game in parliament. However, the Crerarite position on partyism was flawed. At the level of political strategy, one must ask how amenable the federal Liberal party was to Progressive modification. The lesson of 1911 regarding the business community's abhorrence of reciprocity had been well learned by 1921. Potential labour votes would more likely be lost than won on a free-trade platform, at least in Ontario and Quebec. Campaigns were still most easily financed by the 'protected interests.' In addition, being the captive of a volatile and popularly controlled farmers' movement was not an attractive option for any party, as Crerar could himself attest. The Crerar-Dafoe hopes for a 'real' Liberal party were perhaps as naïve as rank-and-file grain growers' hopes for non-partisan politics.

Equally if not more problematic was the effect that soft-pedalling by leadership on political corruption and old-party associations would have had on the rank and file. Given the widespread popular support for local autonomy and non-partisan representation, too many concessions to the old political ways would undermine the Progressive agenda. Among the rank and file, such concessions would engender disillusionment, a willingness to focus primarily on economic organization once again, and eventual grudging acceptance of the inevitability of voting Liberal. As in the case of 'fusion' south of the border a generation earlier, dropping the principled rejection of party politics would rob the movement of its critical edge and its sustaining democratic promise. Neither high prices for grain nor wheat pool campaigns would have damaged the movement in this way; nor, for that matter, would the resignation of Crerar, the creation of the 'Ginger Group,' or the defeat of the UFO government in 1923.

Manitoba Progressives viewed the party system as a machine that, disassembled and relieved of its offensive components, could be put back on the road to deliver good policy mileage with no morally offensive exhaust. For Crerar and his partisans, this new vehicle could be created with the tools of election-financing reform, senate reform, and tariff reductions. These were to reduce the influence of the 'big interests' on the parties. Direct legislation was not seen to be crucial to the outcome. Neither was a democratization within party organization, characterized by local autonomy for constituency associations.

Part of Crerar's 'Manifesto' illustrates this line of thinking. The document presents Progressives as the champions of higher standards of public morality and 'the sweeping away of special privilege in all of its forms.' He then seems to take a radical tack, but retreats immediately into generalities and an exclusive focus on campaign financing:

The new political movement in Canada is ... essentially a movement of liberalism ... that seeks to sweep away abuses in government and to provide policies that will meet the needs of the people. Our appeal is not class, not sectional, not religious. It is to all those ... who desire to see purity in the government of this country restored ... who desire to sweep away the abuse of the function of government for the advancement of the interest of the privileged few.

In nothing is the spirit of the Progressive movement more clearly revealed than in the matter of financing election expenses ... in the past, campaign funds, running often into millions of dollars, have been provided by the managers of the old parties and distributed amongst constituencies ... for use in ways corrupt and altogether indefensible. These campaign funds have been provided by railway promoters, by manufacturers, or by other interests which were actuated ... solely by the sordid hope of getting benefits in the way of legislation. ... The member of parliament elected under this system was not a free agent. ... If he showed signs of independence the whole weight of the party organization was used to crush him ... those manufacturers who desired special favors put up the money to pay election expenses, and then, sheltered behind the tariff they had purchased, exploited the Canadian people in their own environment. Party campaign funds and the sources from which they have come have been the greatest single corrupting agency in the public life of this country ...

I ask you to contrast this sordid spirit, these selfish, corrupting influences, with the spirit followed by those who are taking part in the new political movement in Canada. We are free men and we want a free parliament, and to that end scores of thousands of voters throughout Canada are providing the funds necessary to carry on the election campaign. This is the business of the people ... the supreme issue today is whether our government is to be free or fettered, and whether legislation in the future shall be for the few or the many.[91]

A great deal here rides on the idea that the people will be properly served by parties when they replace 'the interests' as the bankrollers of political organizations. While there is clearly something in this, it is hardly a searing indictment of partyism from the perspective of popular democracy. It should, instead, be seen as the belated venting of anti-tariff spleen in the guise of a rejection of 'old-party methods.' No support is offered to the grass-roots desire for a 'new social order' characterized by meaningful participatory democracy.

Comparison with samples of attacks on party politics in the *Guide* and meetings of the grain growers' movement highlights the mildness of Crerar's critique of partyism. R.C. Henders, the Manitoba Grain Growers' Association president,[92] was one of the earlier outspoken critics of the party system. This excerpt from his 1914 presidential address makes his position clear:

The Curse of Partyism

It has afforded the opportunity for the owners of organized capital to secure positions which gave them undue advantage over their fellow men ... It has converted ... responsible government into irresponsible government by introducing a system of rabid partyism which has succeeded admirably in removing the government so far from the people that, for the most part, they pay little attention to their honest demands. Partyism gone mad, partyism that cannot see any fault in its own party, and cannot see any good in the opposition party; partyism that would use such insane and illogical reasoning as this, 'Oh, well, I know that my party has done wrong, but, then, the other fellows will do just as great wrong if I gave them a chance.' ... My candid opinion, reached after somewhat careful observation and mature study, is that such partyism as I have just described ... is the great curse of present day politics, inasmuch as it opens the way to all manner of political corruption. Nor do I see any way to cure the ills of our political system until the large class of responsible electors, the stalwart, intelligent yeomanry of our country, combine with the robust and independent labour party and cut entirely loose from the influence of such insane partyism, and judge men and measures on their respective merits.[93]

One would expect an address to the troops to emphasize participation by the people. That this was not hollow rhetoric can be seen from two of the watchwords of the grain growers' organizations (and their journal, the *Guide*), 'education' and 'organization.' The more radical crypto-Liberal leaders wished to transfer these into the political sphere from the economic sphere via 'direct' political action. An emphasis on organization in grain growers' associations did not imply the centralized approaches of electoral machines, but rather a multi-layered, open association of mutual advancement. Organization had to be made a boon to democracy. The same held true for education. The *Guide* was conceived as a means of bringing a democratic movement together, by developing a shared understanding of the political, social, and economic obstacles and prospects facing its agrarian elements.[94]

The provincial grain growers' associations were committed to the educational work that could be carried out on a face-to-face basis in the many locals and district councils.[95] In fact, leaders often opposed direct political action because they expected the educational function of the association to suffer.[96] Another excerpt from a 1918 Henders address indicates the link organized grain growers perceived between education and democracy:

Democratic rule requires that the average citizen be an active, instructed, and intelligent ruler of his country, and, therefore, the success of democracy depends upon the education of the people along two principal lines, first political knowledge, and second, what is of far more importance, political morality ... When through the lack of political knowledge, or political morality, citizens fail to realize their responsibilities, when they lose the inspiration which comes through faith in a higher law which neither legislatures nor courts can either justly or safely set aside, then the very foundations of political liberty are swept away, or become a mockery, in which the plutocratic oligarchy grasps the reins of power and the servants of the people become their masters.[97]

In a 1916 speech, Henders combined exhortation to participate in politics with a suggestion that a truly educated farmers' movement would become conscious of itself as a *class* movement:

Our great source of weakness is ... that farmers as a class have not in the past and do not even now readily develop the spirit of class consciousness. We pass many important resolutions all carefully planned and well thought out ... We fail utterly, shamefully fail, when we come to the enforcement of the carrying out of the principles embodied in these resolutions. All other classes, as a result of their combination, and because of the fact that they place class interests above political preferment, are able to wield influence in the halls of our legislature. We pass resolutions, divide our influence along party political lines and so weaken our case politically that in the great game of party politics we play little or no part. The banker, the manufacturer, the railway interests, when they have personal interests to serve, know no politics. With them their business is their politics ... until we go home and practice that lesson, we need not hope or expect to succeed in bringing to rural life that consideration which it merits.[98]

Parts of this argument led in the direction of the 'economic class politics' of the United Farmers of Alberta. Henders and Manitoba Progressives were not willing to follow this path. They none the less felt that an agrarian political analysis that owned up to the class politics shaping party competition was a prerequisite of agrarian political influence at the national level. They rejected the exclusiveness of agrarian political activity proposed by group government theory and replaced it with commitment to a catch-all 'people's party' led by organized farmers. Most Manitoba Progressives were unwilling to see such a party follow the same centralized, élite-dominated route that the old parties had charted. Uncommitted to constituency autonomy or principled non-alignment with the Liberals, Crerar and his followers discovered that, even in their home territory (a United Farmers of Manitoba convention in 1923), proposing a political vehicle too much like the old-party organization would not be acceptable.[99]

The Grain Growers' Guide was a forum for anti-party sentiment from 1910 to 1925. It had led an intermittent campaign for agrarian third-party politics since the 1911 reciprocity 'defeat,' fully nine years in advance of the majority and leaderships of the three prairie grain growers' associations it served. Editorial and feature writers made criticism of the centralized and 'autocratic' character of old-party organizations a central theme in the fight against 'partyism,' with the corollary of support for local autonomy. Prominent Manitoba co-operator and *Guide* writer J.T. Hull put this position succinctly in an article on the three 1921 grain growers' conventions:

One feature in the political organization of the movement deserves special mention, and that is the emphasis that is laid upon the local. The value of this form of organization cannot be overestimated from at least any democratic standpoint. The curse of the old party system was the grip that it laid upon the individual. The party laid down the lines of thought and tolerated no turning to the right hand or the left from those lines. Over his own mind, declared one of the greatest of Liberal thinkers, John Stuart Mill, the individual is sovereign. Canadian political partyism declared otherwise. In making the local the basis of the entire organization, and in stimulating the fullest discussion with the greatest freedom of all questions by the locals, and in bringing the results of that free discussion before the annual conventions, the farmers are doing more to get back to the fundamental basis of real democracy than any other body of men in the country. They are, in fact, the one class that is organizing freedom that the community may gain.[100]

On the eve of the 1921 federal election's announcement, *The Grain Growers' Guide* editorialized on the same theme:

Neither the Liberal nor the Conservative party is democratic in its character nor permanent in its functioning; the organizations of the farmers are democratic in character and they function continuously. They provide channels for individual expression within the movement and the means for keeping the people in touch with the movement in all its phases. These organizations rest on local units; they are built from the bottom up and not from the top down, and it is only by such organization of interest and opinion that partyism of any kind can hope to avoid the evils of an 'odious oligarchy.' And that is not to build on an academic ideal; it is merely recognizing the demand of the time that democracy be more than a pleasant political fiction.[101]

Guide editor George Chipman refused to let the old parties off the hook as easily as Crerar had. The Guide pushed harder on the tariff, campaign financing, business-party ties, and 'class' character of the Meighen government[102] than did Crerar. On the issue of local autonomy and popular control in political organization, the Guide and its principal contributors distinguished themselves in an area that Crerar refused to enter.

It is interesting to note, however, that the Progressives' practical commitment to decentralization of the institutions of representation and administration paled in comparison to that of the Patrons of Industry. The Patrons' 1895 platform included the following:

7. A system of Civil Service Reform that will give each County power to appoint or elect all County officials paid by them, except County Judges; ...
12. Preparation of the Dominion and Provincial Voters' Lists by the municipal officers;
13. Conformity of electoral districts to County boundaries, as constituted for Municipal purposes, as far as the principle of representation by population will allow.[103]

As S.D. Shortt notes, these proposals for reform of electoral machinery and state administration were intended to complement rural political solidarity for the purpose of destroying urban political domination. Farmers, rather than Toronto professionals, would control the functions and administration of most state action bearing upon rural communities.[104] Whether it was the failure of the Patrons to survive the federal Liberal victory in 1896, or the largely federal focus of their policy complaints, prairie Progressives did not see the need to promote so radical a decentralization of state power as did the Patrons. Decentralization of their own representative structures was apparently considered sufficient.

As anti-party sentiment intensified in the West between 1911 and 1921, calls for abolition of 'the patronage system' were central to critiques of partyism. This emphasis meant that the critique was less incisive than the radical democratic critique of party.[105] None the less, it did address a pervasive aspect of party politics, and was an effective means of rallying support within the agricultural community. The attack on patronage was linked to a central Canadian business élite benefiting from the tariff and established patronage network.

A proposal in the 1916 Farmers' Platform for publication of 'political campaign fund contributions and expenditures both before and after elections'[106] followed easily from the preamble's contention that the tariff was responsible for the concentration of industry and inordinate political influence by tariff-sheltered 'trusts.' The suggestion that patronage was the glue for a corrupt political network reflected a widespread prairie belief. There was enough evidence of patronage in federal governmental performance (especially with respect to war-materials contracts and local party 'machines') to make this a very legitimate concern. Patronage was so effectively identified with old-party practices by the early farmers' movement in Ontario and the prairies that all prairie populisms incorporated it into their own accounts of a corrupt political economy.

The patronage issue was seldom treated in isolation from what were seen as closely related practices of party funding by 'big interests' and slick manipulation of public opinion by a pandering party press. Perhaps the most conservative crypto-Liberal account of patronage came from Thomas Crerar. Crerar had left the Union Government in 1919 in response to an unrepentantly protectionist budget, not out of opposition to partyism *per se*.[107] As Progressive leader from 1920 to 1923, he was in fact anxious to organize the Progressives into a centralized political force.[108] Thus, when Crerar attacked partyism, he focused his attack on an uncontroversial target: patronage and bankrolling of old party campaigns by 'big interests.' In his 'Confession of Faith' published in both *Maclean's* and *The Grain Growers' Guide* during the 1921 election campaign, Crerar asserted that 'our criticism is not directed against our federal parliament so much as against the methods by which party managers, fortified by campaign funds derived from the purses of privileged interests, use to manipulate it for their own and their patron's ends.'

The patronage issue figured quite prominently in the *Guide*'s attack on old-party rule, especially in the 1911 to 1918 period. Even after the Civil Service Act of 1920, any hint of the re-emergence of patronage in government personnel appointments was roundly condemned.[109] Unaware of Weber's claim that elevation of the merit principle in government appointments would ultimately subvert democratic control of bureaucracy,[110] the grain growers' organ considered patronage to be the most blatant contradiction of the principles of equity and fairness. Wartime contracts to party-financing businessmen were seen as confirmation of the argument linking government policy to 'the big interests.' Patronage could also be easily linked to the sinister relation between protected industries and high-tariff administrations.

In a dramatic election-eve editorial sheet, *The Grain Growers' Guide* of 30 November 1921 offered two separate seventeen-point scenarios of 'What the People of Canada may expect during the Next Four Years.' 'If the Big Interest Government Wins, ... Big Corporations, financial interests and tariff barons will be permitted to contribute secretly large sums to the government campaign funds, as they are now doing, and will undoubtedly receive government favors in return.' However, 'if the New National Policy Wins, ... Special Legislation will be require full publicity for all campaign fund contributions from all sources both before and after elections.' 'Plutocrats' would have no choice but to terminate their illicit relationships with corrupted politicians. Deprived of this support, governments would surely return to serving the public interest (i.e., following the New National Policy). As unlikely as this scenario seems in retrospect, it was entailed by the democratic reform logic in the New National Policy.

The differences between leadership and grass-roots variants of crypto-Liberalism on the issues of party critique, direct legislation, political action, and local autonomy suggest an important underlying distinction. Whereas many of the rank and file in the grain growers' associations of Saskatchewan and Manitoba accorded virtually intrinsic value to participation in political and economic organizations, crypto-Liberal leadership saw participation in narrowly instrumental terms. Participation was necessary to elect MPs who could remake the Liberal party and national fiscal policy. In this instance they were only one step removed from the position of the Liberal party. For the rank and file, participation was an inevitable component of citizenship. This attitude was fostered in the grain growers' associations' activities. Had the SGGA and MGGA been led by activists who pressed the logic of citizenship in a group government and delegate democracy direction, many of their rank and file would have been 'radical democratic populists' and Crerar would have remained a Liberal.

The State and Technocracy

Celebrations of democracy and critiques of 'old party politics' are prominent themes in crypto-Liberal discourse. Conceptions of 'the state' and the idea of technocracy are less transparently so, but they were, none the less, an important part of the overall democratic theory. The pattern of differences between leadership and rank and file exists in this territory as well.

Technocratic Elements of Crypto-Liberal Thought

The tension between democracy and technocracy within prairie populisms was not often explicitly perceived as a problem or 'contradiction.' This should not be surprising during a period that combined widespread enthusiasm for the new and democratic social order with enthusiasm for scientific and technological solutions to social problems. To most proponents of progress, new horizons of democratic experience were expanded, not obscured, by expert technical direction of public policies. Such direction was generally assumed to be value-free and non-partisan, and thus even more attractive. Few public figures spoke of a trade-off between the technocratic and participatory-democratic outlooks.

Crypto-Liberal leaders' thoughts on the democracy/technocracy trade-off may appear unexceptional to late-twentieth-century eyes, but they reveal a good deal about both crypto-Liberalism's reformism and its commitments to popular democracy.

Crypto-Liberal leadership at both the provincial and federal levels shared with other contemporary liberals the idea that government's proper function was mediation among various interests in the community. National Conservative claims to the contrary, they did not intend government to implement radical policies. Crerar and sympathetic provincial premiers did not come near rejecting traditional parliamentary governmental practices or party competition for office. Incremental changes in fiscal, transportation, and campaign-finance legislation would satisfy them that Canada was becoming democratic. At the provincial level, democratic credentials could be assured by responsiveness to grain growers', other agricultural, and local businessmen's associations.

Because they demanded little from governments and political life that could not have been provided by 'the system,' these crypto-Liberals rarely questioned the relative strengths or virtues of technocratic as compared to popular-democratic determination of public policy. In Crerar's case, inattention to popular-democratic devices for shaping public policy was complemented by an emphasis on 'sound administration' indistinguishable from the two major parties. His 1921 'Manifesto' included the following passage:

The Progressive movement recognizes that while we need a new moral atmosphere in politics, any government has to meet vast problems of practical administration. A new government, then, must bring to its work not only a measure of ideals, but as well sound, practical business judgement and high administrative capacity. Because of the financial condition of this country and the obligations we are facing, *the great need today is sound business administration of this country's affairs.* The best minds available inside and outside the new parliament must be enlisted for the consideration and solution of these problems, and ... the Progressive party ... will apply itself to the discharge of this vast task along the lines indicated. This is a time when patriotism must come before party, when the national well being must be the first concern of every good citizen.[111]

There is nothing wrong with sound business administration or calling on the best minds for policy advice. However, without provision for parallel influence and policy direction from the popular movement Crerar led, this claim concerning 'the great need today' sounds decidedly non–popular democratic. If one substitutes 'Liberal' for 'Progressive' in the passage above, the statement could have been uttered by W.L.M. King in the same campaign. By speaking to a supposed universal public support for 'sound business administration,' Crerar was attempting to 'broaden out' the Progressive party. His grain grower supporters also desired sound business administration, but not divorced from clearly defined popular control of governments.[112]

The same tendency was evident in the three prairie provincial administrations during the 1920s. For example, John Bracken's tenure as premier was characterized by what he understood as non-partisan, administratively efficient, and fiscally responsible direction of provincial affairs. Bracken entered politics with no political experience, a distaste for partisan motivations, and a distinguished career as an academic agricultural scientist.[113] To the victorious but leaderless United Farmers of Manitoba in 1922, his renowned expertise and political detachment made him a desirable premier. Bracken sympathized with the objectives of the UFM, and believed that his premiership might ensure their political success by providing a 'sound, efficient and businesslike administration.'[114]

J.W. Dafoe's support for the United Farmers government was predicated more on its support by the Winnipeg business community and its capacity for accepting 'responsible' leadership than on its enthusiasm for popular democracy. He offered this response to Bracken's acceptance of the premier's chair: 'Professor Bracken is confronted with a business task, calling for powers of organization, foresight, acumen and sagacity – the qualities of the administrator and the businessman. These qualities ... Professor Bracken has ... A highly competent agricultural expert has been placed at the head of affairs in a province which, in its wealth-producing activities, are primarily agricultural.'[115]

Bracken did not disappoint Dafoe. Just before his by-election victory in 1922, Bracken announced that 'our purpose, briefly stated, is to give the province an honest, efficient, and businesslike administration; to eliminate waste and cut down expenses to the lowest possible minimum.' In his first legislative speech, Bracken echoed Crerar: 'We are not here to play politics or represent a single class, but to get down to the serious business of giving this province an efficient government.' When up for re-election in 1927, the Bracken government campaigned on its record, and attributed the province's financial standing to 'what may be accomplished when politics is divorced from the business affairs of the government.'[116] 'Brackenism' was thus a very partial reflection of the democratic aspirations of grain grower rank and file.

The point, once again, is not that this approach was exceptional, or contrary to the traditional Canadian conception of democratic government. It was, rather, entirely unexceptional and consistent with these traditions – albeit taking them more seriously than did most patronage-ridden federal and provincial regimes. The popular-democratic rhetoric of the UFM rank and file would have suggested a greater amount of experimentation and unorthodoxy in democratic government. None the less, the UFM rank and file supported Bracken for over two decades; with little indication that they expected government performance to meet the elevated standards suggested by their rhetoric. The obvious alternative, a return to Tory rule, was one they were loath to accept.

The Saskatchewan Liberal administrations of W.M. Martin and C.A. Dunning frequently made the same public commitment to 'sound administration.' David Smith notes that 'Martin found in Dunning a lieutenant who shared his interest in efficient administration. Sound, or as it was much more frequently described, business-like government was a theme which Martin stressed ... [He was] disposed to value efficient management techniques.'[117]

With our interest in the technocratic tendencies in crypto-Liberalism, we should note the connection between claims about 'non-partisan administration' and the technocratic orientation. The 'non-partisan' spirit [118] was central to early prairie political culture. While non-partisanship was an understandable response to a hinterland wheat economy, it could also offer a beguiling justification for government 'in the public interest' with priorities set by supposedly apolitical administrators. This was especially true at the municipal political level, where the commission-board plan, conceived by American Progressives to prevent corrupt machine politics, was adopted in most prairie cities by 1918.

This form of 'non-partisan' politics was not promoted by principled opponents of partyism, but by local business élites. They felt that by isolating a strong civic administration from party politics, they could ensure that the local 'public interest' could be shaped by business rather than labour priorities. As James Anderson has noted, this kind of municipal reform possessed a corporate and anti-participatory rationale, contending that 'city government ... should be run by administrative experts, particularly successful businessmen, on business-like principles of efficiency and economy; ... the administration of policy should be left entirely to the civic administration or a small executive elected at large, the duties of which [would] correspond to that of the manager of a private business firm.'[119]

These ideas have profoundly shaped public perspectives on municipal politics in Canada. While not accepted so readily in the partisan atmospheres of provincial politics, the underlying logic – that government is essentially an administrative, business-like affair, and that politics should be moulded in this light – was attractive to prairie administrations. Claims of 'non-partisanship' not only suggested unbiased, fair-handed administration, they also tended to isolate senior policy-makers and bureaucrats from the hurly-burly of 'parochial interests' and 'partisan objectives.' Cloaking a government in 'sound, business-like administration' was one covertly partisan means of discouraging popular group pressure on governments between elections. This posture enhanced technocratic attitudes at the expense of popular democracy.

Perhaps the most striking conscious presumption in favour of expert technical policy development occurred in the UFA administrations of H. Greenfield and J.E. Brownlee. By prairie standards, the UFA administration was no more than ordinarily responsive to its grain grower support. Indeed, Carl Betke argues that the UFA administration under Brownlee 'made its decisions on the basis of expert advice, referring regularly to the trust which farmers must necessarily place in such traditionally alien authorities as financiers.'[120] On movement concerns such as monetary and credit reform, the administration arranged a 'replacement of the agrarian wisdom of the UFA by the expertise of special consultants.' This accelerated the decline in UFA participatory enthusiasm and membership.[121]

The UFA administration came to view UFA convention resolutions as unwelcome intrusions into a complicated fiscal and administrative domain. This turned later annual conventions into shadows of their former selves, by undermining rank-and-file belief in the importance of serious policy-shaping contributions by locals and conventions. Their expectations in this regard were undeniably optimistic, but the UFA government did little to accommodate their participatory urge in its policy development processes.

Macpherson, Betke, Morton, and others have explained the relatively low level of direct power that UFA conventions, individual MLAs, and local organizations could exercise over 'their' provincial government. They have pointed to the inherent limits created by responsible government, the federal division of powers, and the party competition in which the farmers' political representatives found themselves.[122] Perhaps these circumstances made the UFA administration's approach to policy development unavoidable. It is significant, though, that the UFA administration developed an early and clear bias against popular interventions, and a presumption that problems raised thereby could only be solved by 'the expertise of special consultants.' While the UFA administration could not have become the direct legislative extension of the UFA movement, it did not have to become such a solid example of 'Brackenism.'

These technocratic tendencies in prairie crypto-Liberal administrations indicate that crypto-Liberalism in office was not the popular-democratic operation that grain grower rhetoric might suggest. Provincial crypto-Liberal leaders never wondered aloud about the technocratic flavour of their style of governing, just as Crerar had avoided or not seriously considered the potential grass-roots opposition to his anti-participatory and 'dirigiste' strategy for policy changes. As we have seen, proper governmental practice was often likened to that of successful corporations. 'Business-like government,' 'sound administration,' and even 'scientific management' characterized the hopes and achievements of crypto-Liberal governments. Like other liberals in the early twentieth century, leading crypto-Liberals had faith that science and technology would progressively eliminate the hardships of social existence. Impartial men of science could be relied on to assess the feasibility of requests made by legitimate interests, and then to determine how requests might be met.

Democracy was thus seen in rather narrowly institutionalized and formal terms, with state functionaries and hired professionals viewed as class-neutral and supra-political. It is not surprising that provincial crypto-Liberal leaders saw little conflict between their popular democratic organizations and their technocratically inclined administrations. Like the national crypto-Liberal leadership, they did not perceive structural or deeply entrenched cultural obstacles in their way. Nor did they carry a passion for collective self-determination rooted in a perception of systematic and sustained exploitation.

The key task of hired experts was not to promote social reconstruction, but to engage in the supposedly post-political administrative business of government. Crypto-Liberal leaders' relatively weak sense of power denied made it difficult for them to see technocrats as another obstacle to greater equalization of power. In these matters, one can see that the crypto-Liberal political leadership was temperamentally and, to a significant extent, philosophically at odds with their grain grower rank and file. This was most obvious in Alberta, but also evident in Saskatchewan and Manitoba. The grain growers' association members and activists supported the use of 'experts' to assist the conduct of sound administration, but they did not accept the priority of 'expert' advice over their conventions' well-considered proposals in matters of basic policy development.

The State

An account of the crypto-Liberal conception of the state follows logically from discussion of its technocratic elements. W.L. Morton puts us on the right track by arguing that 'in the first decade of the century a general reform movement had been growing in the Canadian West ... [which was] at core a demand for positive state action with respect to such matters as the prohibition of the sale of alcoholic liquor, the promotion of social welfare, and the cleansing of political life ... In its demand for action by the state against certain evils, it marked an epoch in the development of Canadian democracy.'[123] The strength of this movement helped shape Mackenzie King's decision to have the Liberal party make a formal commitment to nascent welfare-state liberalism in 1919. He saw that, since the onset of the Great War, there had been increasing public acceptance of an interventionist state, which would soften the blow of inequalities created by the capitalist market economy.

In the moral climate created by anticipation of 'the new social order,' the state also came to be seen as an instrument of moral regeneration. Thus all governments were expected to enact temperance, female suffrage, campaign-financing controls, civil-service reform, and other public morality–enhancing legislation.[124] The same state that had protected individuals benefiting from 'corruption' was now expected to heed the public demand to 'reform itself.' Farmers' groups presented campaigns for public ownership of utilities and railways, and of course tariff reform, as means of cleaning up public life.

For many crypto-Liberals, these demands did not imply a comprehensive state regulation of the market economy. Their liberal-physiocratic view of this 'natural economy' held that monopolies, trusts, and the power of 'plutocracy' in the state resulted from unsound fiscal and economic development policies.[125] They assumed that free-trade liberalism would have prevented the growth of 'interests' holding the state to ransom. From this perspective, the state had a moral duty to implement policies facilitating a re-emergence of the 'natural economy,' thereby ultimately reducing its own role and responsibilities in the economy. Crerar, among others, would have cherished such a reformed state, as he illustrated in 1920 by rejecting a grain grower demand for the re-establishment of the Wheat Board.[126] Crerar did not like being seen to favour free trade while asking for special, market-manipulating state support.

Adherence to a *laissez-faire* doctrine did not prevent Crerar from thinking that the federal state in Canada had been the preserve of one 'class.' He did not idealize the federal government as being equally responsive to all social groups' demands. Trying to defuse the old-party attack on the Progressives as a 'class party,' Crerar commented: 'Liberals of the older school have always had a touching faith that popular self-government would prevent any monopoly of the state by any one class, but our electorate has in the past been too gullible and careless of its real interests to make this cure reliable. The one-class domination, which has hitherto existed, has also managed to poison the system of political democracy which was expected to effect the cure for all our ills.'[127]

Crerar promised that one-class domination of the state would be eliminated if the Progressives came to power.[128] The class in question might be best described as 'Eastern urban professional and protected business interests'; crypto-Liberals seldom referred to it as the capitalist class. The state was at fault, then, because it had dispensed its economic favours to the 'urban class.' When Crerar and others spoke of the 'present economic system ... largely devised for the benefit of a small privileged class,' they were referring to 'financial and manufacturing interests' and their professional hangers-on. 'The system' in question was 'protection,' not capitalism, even though crypto-Liberal discourse contained much anti-capitalist talk.

Most crypto-Liberal rank and file supported an interventionist state well beyond Crerar's wishes. Any number of *Guide* editorial cartoons in the two months before the 1921 federal election demonstrate this optimism regarding the state's potential if the Progressive David could slay the special-interests/Tory Goliath.[129] With their sense of regional mistreatment, they had no ideological problem demanding ameliorative and protective policies for their own industry.

One instance of this was the seventh plank in the 1921 Farmers' Platform. It was clearly designed to benefit the agricultural population, although they argued its implementation would assist all ordinary consumers. This plank proposed 'a land settlement scheme based on a regulating influence in the selling price of land.' To keep land merchants and small speculators honest, and maintain a reasonable price for farm land, 'owners of idle areas should be obliged to file a selling price on their lands, that price also to be regarded as an assessable value for purposes of taxation.' If lands simply gathered speculative value, the unscrupulous owners would pay some price for their greed. With more cheap land brought into production, overall production costs would be lessened and ultimate consumer costs reduced. The prosperity of the farmer would thus benefit society, and validate the platform's physiocratic premise. Where the power of the state (provincial or federal) was required for economic or social advance, farmers were prepared to let it play a major role in their salvation.

Most crypto-Liberals felt an ambivalence towards state interventions in civil society similar to that of contemporary trust-busting Progressives in the United States and reform Liberals in Britain. Grain growers on the prairies were keenly aware of these developments in both countries, partly as a result of coverage provided by the *Guide*. They thus felt more comfortable supporting state action to reform industrial capitalism and the Canadian agricultural economy. R.C. Henders noted in his 1912 address to the Manitoba Grain Growers' convention:

An advance in public industry, or government ownership of industry, is not an unmitigated evil; indeed it may be advanced in aid of the movement towards good government, because in the first place it helps to do away with private corporations which are chiefly the corrupting influence and certainly one of the leading obstacles to good government today. Secondly, it increases the importance of governmental affairs, and intensifies the disasters resulting from corruption, partisanship, and the spoils system and so arouses the interests of the citizens and impels them to demand reforms that will guarantee pure and efficient management. Therefore, except under especially adverse circumstances, sufficiently powerful to overcome the effects just named, government ownership of industrial monopolies tends towards good government and public ownership, both of which tend, of course, to the diffusion of wealth and power and the realization of a more perfect democracy.[130]

Henders had more enthusiasm for public ownership of utilities and industrial monopolies than most grain growers at this time.[131] None the less, all prairie governments were pressured by agrarian organizations to undertake public ownership of utilities, local railways (in Alberta), and even (briefly in Manitoba) grain elevators.[132] Equally notable was the ninth plank in the 1921 Farmers' Platform, which had been ratified by grain grower organizational members of the CCA in 1919. From a strictly class-interested point of view, prairie producers' support for this plank makes sense. It called for public ownership and control 'of railway, water and aerial transportation, telephone, telegraph and express systems, all projects in the development of natural power, and of the coal mining industry.' They saw public ownership of transportation as the only way to regulate the much-detested CPR.

Public ownership of telephone systems was a populist demand accepted early by all three prairie provincial governments. The farming community also viewed cheap and reliable sources of hydroelectric and fuel power as crucial and hence supported public ownership of natural public utilities. State-run monopolies were seen as preferable to private monopolies, which might well influence corruptable politicians (as had the CPR). Support for public ownership of these basic services was thus an expression of distrust in both large private firms and party politicians. Consequently, the campaign for public ownership of utilities and monopolies was widely perceived as an inherently democratic one, transcending petty ideological disputes. Even conservative crypto-Liberals lauded the potential of public ownership to reduce plutocratic power and give agricultural producers the 'square deal' they desired from the state. In this sense, crypto-Liberal support for public ownership may legitimately be taken as evidence of a 'Tory touch' in Canadian political culture.[133]

Unencumbered by a public acceptance of the dogmas of *laissez-faire*, more radical prairie populisms could launch campaigns for more extensive 'social ownership.' By endowing some forms of public ownership with democratic credentials, crypto-Liberalism opened the door to more extensive challenges to the logic of the liberal market on the prairies.

As the rather different case of Ontario Hydro had already demonstrated,[134] public ownership does not necessarily imply socialism. Support for public ownership of 'public utilities' had been a constant of American populism since the 1870s,[135] and has found support in a wide range of agrarian political movements since 1921. The fact that many Canadians now think of public ownership as the legacy of Fabian 'gas-and-water socialism' tells us more about collective political amnesia, the shrunken horizons of contemporary social democracy, and the hegemony of a private-enterprise culture in North America than it does about the nature of the proposal itself.

In view of the mixed results that comprehensive 'free trade' would provide for Canadian grain farmers in the 1980s, it is interesting to review the alternatives to tariffs proposed by prairie farmers' organizations in the era before marketing boards. By 1916, the Canadian Council of Agriculture – dominated by western grain growers – had proposed four forms of direct taxation: 'a direct tax on all unimproved land values, including all natural resources'; 'a sharply graduated personal income tax'; 'a heavily graduated personal income tax'; and 'a graduated income tax on the profits of corporations.'

The first of the revenue proposals shows the influence of Henry George's socio-economic analysis in the prairie West. The direct tax on unimproved land values is presented here as a modified application of George's idea that social inequalities could be largely ameliorated by a 'single tax' on the unearned increment derived by industry and land speculators from land ownership. Under this scheme, taxation of the CPR, the Hudson's Bay Company, and various land companies' holdings would yield major government revenues and maintain manageable land costs to agriculturalists.[136]

The second, third, and fourth tax proposals were relatively radical in 1916. Even the 'progressive' 1919 Liberal platform made no suggestion of income or corporate taxes as devices of wealth redistribution or sources of government revenue. The tax policies broadly proposed by the CCA in 1916 were intended to counterbalance the 'regressive,' hidden tax policy of protection.[137]

It is interesting to note how the redistributionist character of these four complements to 'free trade' contrasts with the corporate power–enhancing logic that pervades the campaign for continental free trade today. Egalitarian sentiments and democratized relations of power between classes have little to do with the current scenario for economic rationalization in a continental market, but they were central to the prairie farm organizations' proposals for alternatives to the tariff.

Co-operation

Complicating crypto-Liberal ambivalence about the state was a strong grass-roots commitment to co-operative enterprise. Co-operatives were the preferred instruments of reform. Even if the state at all levels was responsive to grain growers' requests, co-ops would still have several crucial advantages. They were more sensitive to democratic and local control, and more appropriate as educational forms addressing the specific needs of the agricultural community. Co-operative organizations sprang directly from the experience and needs of the agrarian community.[138]

Additionally, the non-partisan and anti-political tradition in Anglo-American co-operation reduced prairie farmers' willingness to depend on the state's 'favours.' The *Guide*'s coverage of Britain's co-operative movement[139] retained this anti-statist element, and reinforced the grain growers' tendency to seek shelter from the antagonistic National Policy in their own collective institutions. In the minds of many of their supporters, grain growers' associations and wheat pools had almost assumed the status of an 'alternative state'[140] (hence the title 'grain growers' parliaments' for their annual conventions). In the most radical farmers' political organizations, this tendency was amplified into a syndicalist approach to the state.[141] In a different, non-socialist form, this tendency fuelled the 'group government' scheme. In crypto-Liberal circles, however, it was enough to have separate agrarian vehicles of reform, performing the representative function through lobbying rather than farmers' parties. The Saskatchewn Grain Growers' Association's experience provides the best example of this.

Ian MacPherson argues that there were three basic types of co-operators in the co-operative movement in Canada from 1910 to 1945: 'utopian co-operators,' 'pragmatic or liberal co-operators,' and 'occupational co-operators.' The first group was composed primarily of social democrats and 'co-operative idealists' who 'tried to perceive society as an organic whole and thought that co-operative techniques were ideal for establishing a new social and economic order.' The second group saw co-operation as 'primarily a method to protect the legitimate rights of people on the family farm or dependent upon a weekly wage.' Occupational co-operators viewed co-operatives 'as essentially assistants to the farmers who owned them and not as elements of a wider movement.'[142]

There is little doubt that crypto-Liberalism was influenced primarily by 'pragmatic-liberal' thought on co-operatives, although some of the *Guide's* regular contributors presented co-operation in terms approaching the organic, 'utopian' perspective. MacPherson places 'the bulk of farmers in English Canada' and 'such leading figures as C.A. Dunning, T.A. Crerar, and W.R. Motherwell' in the pragmatic-liberal category.[143] Many of these leaders had cut their public teeth in grain growers' organizations or co-operatives, and worked through the Liberal party when pursuing political careers at the provincial level. The Progressives included 'numerous co-operators who were searching for a political home' during its period of prominence in federal politics.[144] This latter attachment was usually made by those like Crerar who hoped to resuscitate 'real' liberalism after being disappointed by the Liberal party.

For these crypto-Liberal leaders, co-operation represented a hard-headed, group-based approach to securing a 'square deal' for grain growers in an economic environment where other economic interests were well organized and holding market and political power as a consequence. Co-operative organizations were also seen as the best vehicles for community education in better farming techniques and flexing political muscle. Co-operation was not thought of as providing a universal paradigm for economic and social relations, except in a very loose sense popularized by moderate expressions of the 'social gospel' at this time.

Crerar spoke in these terms in his 1921 'Confession of Faith,' when he commented briefly on the need for enabling legislation for co-operatives: 'We believe that there is more real happiness to be derived from the creative impulse and the co-operative impulse than from the possessive and acquisitive impulse and the impulse to authority and dominion over others.'[145] This turned out to be a *non sequitur* rather than an introduction to a passage of 'utopian' co-operative thinking, as Crerar went on to extol the virtues of co-operation as a means of reducing the cost of living for the average consumer. Still, with Crerar as president of the United Grain Growers, promotion of co-operative enterprise by crypto-Liberals at the national level was important.

Provincial crypto-Liberal politicians recognized the importance of enacting legislation conducive to the growth of provincial grain growers' associations and co-operatives. This was true especially in Saskatchewan, where the SGGA and the Saskatchewan Co-operative Elevator Company were virtually 'clients' of the Liberal administration from 1910 to 1929. At this level, the crypto-Liberal political response to the growth of dynamic producers' co-operatives involved formal encouragement of a healthy co-operative movement, co-opting its leaders, and assuring the public that established political (and economic) structures could easily accommodate the democratic objectives of the co-operative movement.

Saskatchewan Liberal and SGGA leaders allowed the co-operative movement to feel like a privileged 'pressure group' within the province. For a long time, consequently, the development of a more radically 'co-operativist' or social democratic approach seemed gratuitous to most of their grain grower supporters. Eventually, however, their attempts to neutralize and delegitimize the radical implications of co-operative ideals contributed to the formation of the Farmers' Union of Canada, the United Farmers of Canada (Saskatchewan Section), the Farmers' Educational League, and other populist-socialist alternatives to 'prairie Liberalism.' In retrospect, a clash between the Saskatchewan 'Liberal machine' and the broader democratic vision of the dynamic co-operative movement was probably inevitable.

Within the prairies, co-operation was a veritable religion,[146] and its initiates could thus nod approvingly at the wisdom and progressive implications of the eighth plank of the 1921 Farmers' Platform, which proposed 'extension of co-operative agencies in agriculture to cover the whole field of marketing, including arrangements with consumers' societies for the supplying of foodstuffs at the lowest rates and with the minimum of middleman handling.' For those outside grain growers' associations, it was not evident that producers' and consumers' co-operation, democracy, and a higher moral plane of social intercourse were necessarily connected. Where the spirit of rural co-operation had not left its mark, this seemingly commercial proposal could not inspire. Where it did, rank-and-file crypto-Liberals viewed co-operation as the general philosophical basis on which not just economic security, but also a more complete democracy, could develop. The appeals of the *Guide* and its occasional utopian co-operator columnists – E.A. Partridge in its earlier years, and Salem Bland and J.S. Woodsworth just before the rise of the Progressives – did much to promote this understanding.

A less impressive instance of the crypto-Liberal extension of the principle of co-operation into public life came in the labour plank of the 1921 Farmers' Platform. All levels of government were advised to use 'every means, economically feasible and practicable,' to minimize post-war unemployment. No one was for unemployment, and this proposal committed the Progressives to precisely nothing – as did the Mackenzie King–like recommendation of 'the adoption of the principle of co-operation as the guiding spirit in the future relations ... between capital and labour.'[147] In the context of the bitter labour-capital relations during and after the war, this appeal beyond class conflict trivialized the concept of co-operation, which had proved its importance in agrarian social life. What farm leaders may have seen as support for the just demands of labour and the legitimate claims of employers was likely seen as pablum by each group.

The standards implicit in the accomplishments of the co-operative movement were transposed into grain growers' political activities. These standards related to 'cleaning up' public life, reducing economic inequality, promoting widespread 'civic education' and moral growth, maintaining decentralized popular control of basic activities, and bringing the common people together. When the Progressives failed to make much headway in these areas during their first parliament, such high standards fertilized grain grower disillusionment with political action. The co-operative movement in the United States and Canada had always displayed a deep distrust of competitive organized politics.[148] This distrust had been partly submerged in the period of the National Progressive organization, but it re-emerged quickly following Progressive frustration at the federal level.[149]

Such distrust was displayed in the career of A.J. MacPhail, the SGGA and later Wheat Pool executive whose public life was chronicled in the *Diary* made famous by H.A. Innis. MacPhail was a 'pragmatic liberal' co-operator in MacPherson's terms, but his anti-political sentiments were shared by many more 'utopian' grain growers. He believed that while some politicians could be trusted, grain growers could not hope to obtain their objectives primarily through political action. Political processes could not alter underlying social and economic attitudes – this was the role of popular organizations such as co-operatives. In addition, state action designed to engineer major changes in society implied compulsion, whereas the co-operation encouraged change through voluntary action by an enlightened citizenry. In these senses, he shared a good deal with Henry Wise Wood (as we shall see in chapter 3).

As noted earlier, the farmers' movement developed within a larger environment of reform in the early years of the twentieth century. In the Canadian West, an important part of this was the 'social gospel' of the Methodist and Presbyterian churches, which did much to build bridges between elements in the reform movement. Its most famous spokesmen are best classified under other populist labels: H.W. Wood as radical democratic populist, and E.A. Partridge, William Irvine, Salem Bland, and J.S. Woodsworth as social democratic populists. All of these men, however, were well known and respected in crypto-Liberal rank-and-file circles, not least for their persuasive account of the indissoluble links between the social teachings of Christ, the co-operative ethic, and the achievement of economic and social democracy.[150] The social gospel established or strengthened connections among the various 'democratic reforms' of the day, and then developed connotative links from these to a broad and potentially radical notion of co-operation. It thus played a major role in expanding the democracy/co-operation relationship within the grass-roots version of crypto-Liberalism. The social gospel did not have to convert its audience into social democrats to place the crypto-Liberal rank and file some distance from their leaders.

The last point to note regarding the idea of co-operation in crypto-Liberalism concerns its implications for political action. Crypto-Liberalism was always distinguished from radical democratic populism on this score by its rejection of 'occupational class politics.' Crypto-Liberals consistently proposed some modified form of 'people's party.' Before the Winnipeg General Strike and the Progressives' rise, grain grower association leaders spoke enthusiastically about the potential for political co-operation between agriculturalists and urban labour, as had the Patrons of Industry leaders in Ontario, Manitoba, and Saskatchewan.[151] The crypto-Liberal desire for such co-operation was squelched by the wave of labour radicalism in 1919. From then on, a more general appeal to 'the common people' for political co-operation on the basis of the 'New National Policy' was made. No concerted attempt was made to court urban support, except in Ontario, where the United Farmers administration lived by the grace of support by eleven Labour MPPs, an arrangement that created considerable friction within the UFO organization.

There was, in fact, no substantial effort put into applying crypto-Liberal notions of co-operation to a political strategy. This tells us a good deal about the limits of even the rank-and-file crypto-Liberal understanding of co-operation: for all of its good intentions and high standards, it did not extend beyond agricultural life. As a result, it could not have much of an impact on a national political economy where power necessitated co-operation among disadvantaged classes. As we have seen, there was a strong anti-political (or at least apolitical) bias within the co-operative movement. When translated into the political action of organized farmers, this bias was very likely to discourage systematic attempts to make common political cause with another 'organized interest.' Thus, despite Crerar's claims to the contrary, Arthur Meighen was correct in saying that the Progressives promoted a class notion of democracy – correct for the wrong reasons, but correct none the less.

Crypto-Liberalism and the Good Society

In sketching crypto-Liberal notions of the good society, we must infer a good deal from the aspects of normative democratic theory and social analysis considered earlier in this chapter. It is wise to begin with some of W.L.

Morton's reflections on 'utopian' elements in prairie politics. Morton's comments are meant to apply primarily to the CCF and Social Credit,[152] but they are useful in understanding moderate reform thought as well: 'The reform movement of the first quarter of this century in the Prairie West was ... tinged with millenarianism ... The great majority of farmers wanted only to increase the farmers' returns. But all the farmers' organizations, from the Grange to the United Farmers, had some touch of uplift, and used the methods and even the songs of evangelism. The doctrine of the Wheat Pool was preached with apostolic fervour, and received by the majority of farmers with the abandon of converts.'[153]

The instructive point is that there was a future-oriented idealism even in the most pragmatic of prairie populisms. In noting features common to prairie settlers of different origins and eras, Morton referred twelve years later to 'the hope that the west might be a practical, a really viable, utopia,' a hope rooted in nineteenth-century writings and in 'the democratic dream that men might be free and independent, particularly, as transmitted by young women who taught school in Ontario and the west.' Morton goes on to contrast this utopian inclination with the commercial and utilitarian values predominant in Canadian society. He contends that it was 'the most important fact in the creation of the civilization of the west.'[154]

The predominant characteristic of crypto-Liberal utopias was their physiocratic orientation. As we saw earlier, this decisively informed the various Farmers' Platforms. The rural environment was held to be the only one in which free lives could be pursued, uncontaminated by the moral corruption, inegalitarianism, and class conflict of urban life.[155] The prairie rural setting was seen to possess the additional advantage of being new and thus unconstrained by old modes of thought. It possessed a natural bounty of good land and an impressive array of natural resources, the foundation of a prosperous free-trade economy. Given these advantages, prairie populists generally saw no good reason why political and economic institutions and practices should stand in the way of a 'really viable utopia.' There were several bad reasons why this utopia might be blocked.

For crypto-Liberals, the good society could be unachievable if the corrupting aspects of party politics continued, if the protective tariff were retained, and if agricultural production were not given proper recognition by provincial and national governments. For some prominent crypto-Liberal writers, these obstacles added up to a kind of latter-day 'feudalism.'

In these terms, the force animating this new-world feudalism was the dread 'Toryism.' The conflict enveloping farmers was thus portrayed as involving Toryism, feudalism, and hierarchy, on the one hand, and 'true Liberalism, 'the free market, and democracy, on the other. The promise of the triumph of the latter set of 'forces' was, in effect, the promise of a new Golden Age, where hard-working, God-fearing individuals would have an equal opportunity to lead an honest and rewarding life. The good society would thus prevent a privileged 'plutocracy' from denying a 'square deal' to all those who made an honest effort. Those who worked hard while remaining loyal to the Golden Rule would succeed.[156] The crypto-Liberal conception of justice was thus focused primarily on what an individual merited in return for honest contributions to the social economy. This was qualified by the influence of the 'social gospel,' which bolstered the importance given to charity to the disadvantaged. Still, it is important to see that crypto-Liberal justice was essentially the justice of the 'properly' functioning (and occasionally morally adaptable) free market.

Thus crypto-Liberal justice did not differ significantly from the justice of Anglo-American reform liberalism. If anything, it was less realistic about the prospects for a 'return' to the practices and hence standards of the free market. Paradoxically, this lesser realism gave crypto-Liberalism a more critical perspective on the justice of the modified market society than 'modern' urban Liberalism had, since crypto-Liberalism was less willing to accept the fact and consequences of concentrated corporate power. By itself, this did not push it very far in the direction of generalizing the virtues of collective organization (i.e., of following on the co-operatives' examples). However, one can still claim that 'progressivism should be seen as a step in the development of a Canadian critique of monopoly capitalism,'[157] just as the campaign of the Patrons in Ontario had been a generation earlier. The job of demanding an egalitarian distribution of economic and political power was left to social democratic and radical democratic populisms.

As a consequence, crypto-Liberalism never developed a notion equivalent to that of the 'co-operative commonwealth' of social democratic and radical democratic populisms. Such a notion required that the crypto-Liberal valuation of 'community' be more divorced from the prevailing individualistic liberalism. One occasionally gets a sense of this kind of development from the pages of *The Grain Growers' Guide*, but that is because the *Guide* functioned as a forum for virtually all prairie populism expression.

Clearly, a justice based ideally on a self-regulating market economy and morally self-disciplining population was less in need of a strong state than one that saw neither as 'natural' in human society. Thus, while crypto-Liberals saw a short-term need for strong state action against the organized 'big interests,' their vision of the future good society was decidedly anti-statist and anti-political. Politics had been the most obvious staging ground for corrupt social activity, and had almost always served farmers poorly. Co-operatives had eschewed political involvement, and had seen the state as equally capable of compulsive and voluntary social direction and change.

For all of these reasons, the good society of crypto-Liberalism would have done away with 'politics' as much as possible, while still putting a premium – at least for the grass-roots crypto-Liberals – on participation by common folk in shared public life. The state that became the focus of remaining 'political' activity would be efficient, virtually obsessed with operating economy, and 'non-partisan.' This view suggests a technocratically directed minimum state, if that is not a contradiction. The society it would administer would be characterized by a moral and genuine pluralism, where the interests of the common people would count more than those of traditionally privileged groups. The state would co-ordinate the society that many recent immigrants had believed they were coming to, and would take a modest place in the 'new social order' widely prophesied for Canada.

Finally, to fill out the picture of the normative basis of their democratic thought, it is worth noting that crypto-Liberals were good 'internationalists.' The 1921 Farmers' Platform opens with an endorsement of the League of Nations as an institution capable of guaranteeing national rights of self-determination, fostering international understanding, and 'making the world safe for democracy.' This endorsement complemented nicely their discussion of 'the new social order' for which the Great War was to have been a kind of cathartic prelude. An international organization inspired by recognition of high mutual purposes was welcomed by a variety of agrarian, labour, and political reform groups. This plank was meant as a sign to the public that the farmers' movement's concerns were not 'class-bound,' parochial, or backward-looking, as the Canadian Manufacturers' Association, Meighen's Conservatives, and right-wing Liberals had asserted.

The same could be said of the second plank, proposing 'a further development of the British Empire ... along the lines of partnership between nations free and equal, under the present governmental system of British constitutional authority.' Along with this pledge of allegiance to Anglo-Canadian political structures and traditions came a rejection of any overlording by Britain in such a reformed Commonwealth, as it 'would hamper the growth of responsible and informed democracy in the Dominions.'[158]

3   Radical Democratic Populism

The essence of North American populist thought combines support for popular democracy, agrarian opposition to a polity remade in the image of corporate capitalism, and a fervent desire for supersession of party-dominated political conflict. The most complete Canadian expression of this populist essence was the radical democratic populism of the prairies, ca. 1916-32. All prairie populisms gave voice to some of these concerns, but none presented them as vigourously and consistently as did radical democratic populism. No other populism combined adherence to grass-roots democracy with a vision of a functionally differentiated *demos*, which was co-operatively to set and maintain a public-policy agenda outside the framework of parliamentary government.

Radical democratic populism on the Canadian prairies was distinguished, above all, by a non-British parliamentary, and hence 'radical,' conception of democratic representation. This conception shared with guild socialism, syndicalism, and various forms of corporatism the notion that citizens in modern society are best represented along functional/occupational, rather than territorial, lines. With guild socialism (and with Marx of the *Paris Commune*), radical democratic populism went farther, claiming that such representation must be continuous: that is, maintained between elections through close relations between citizens and their instructed delegates. Such representation would be guaranteed by the common interests of the group, the explicitness of the instruction, delegates' loyalty to their instructors, and the potential sanction of delegate recall. These measures were seen as means of ensuring *de facto* democratic control of the state.

Radical democratic populism would have been inconceivable outside indigenous agrarian political and economic organizations. Locating radical democratic populism in its organizational context is thus the first step in understanding it. We can then examine key dimensions of its democratic discourse.

The United Farmers of Alberta (UFA) provided the most important institutional vehicle for this populism, followed (in order) by the United Farmers of Ontario (UFO) and the United Farmers of Canada (Saskatchewan Section) (UFC[SS]). The UFO experienced an intense and ultimately devastating contest between the principles of radical democratic and crypto-Liberal populism, with the latter dominating through E.C. Drury, UFO premier from 1919 to 1923. The UFC(SS) held fast to the principles of 'industrial action' (farmers as economic lobby group) from 1926 to 1931. Accepting the logical political extension of their position, group government or a kindred anti-parliamentary form, did not become a major issue within the UFC(SS).[1]

Preceding the United Farmer's organizations in Saskatchewan and Alberta was the Non-Partisan League (NPL), a short-lived expression of 'left populism.'[2] NPL support for 'delegated' democratic representation and organization of 'the people' into political units did much promote political action by the UFA. The NPL was also the first significant expression of elements of social democratic populism in Saskatchewan and Alberta. It articulated themes of radical democratic and social democratic populism in response to the perceived weaknesses of crypto-Liberalism.

As one would expect of 'neighbouring ideologies,' radical democratic populism and crypto-Liberalism shared several sources. To take the most obvious case, both were given a *raison d'être* and objects of criticism by the National Policy and the 'quasi-colonial' prairie hinterland condition. 'Alberta Progressives,' as Morton calls them,[3] accepted the crypto-Liberal critique of the tariff, transportation, grain-trade and land monopolies, and federal control over prairie natural resources. However, radical democratic populists located these concerns within a markedly different political analysis and strategy, thereby producing a serious schism in the national 'agrarian revolt' of 1921 to 1926. At the root of this dispute were incompatible conceptions of how democratic movements should engage in political practice.

By 1921, neither of the 'old-line' parties had shown a serious commitment to placing the interests of prairie producers on a par with those of the central Canadian business community. The Liberal party only once possessed the political will to govern consistently with their critique of the 'special interests' and the tariff. The disaster of 1911 convinced the national Liberal party hierarchy that such consistency was a virtue they could ill afford. For crypto-Liberals, this spectacle produced indignation and eventually a desire for an independent, pressure-group politics to force the Liberal party back to its true economic policy home. They did not reject party organization or party parliamentary representation in a principled and decisive way, as did radical democrats.

However, radical democratic populism would have remained a marginal presence in Alberta in the absence of NPL influence. This influence spurred Henry Wise Wood into constructing a socio-political theory that could take farmers into politics without destroying the democratic soul and developmental logic of their young movement.

Wood demonstrated his early reticence about 'politicizing' the UFA in several ways. In 1917, he unsuccessfully contested a Liberal nomination in his own riding. Shortly after, he encouraged the UFA rank and file to seek better representation and reforms within established party structures: 'The machine is all right if it is run right, and it will be easier to run it right than to build another one – another party.'[4]

Wood's early rejection of 'political action' by the UFA organization was premised on his oft-cited concern that the UFA would become misdirected once involved in direct political competition. In his opinion, this had been the mistake of the People's Party in the United States a generation earlier. However, his candidature for the Liberal nomination in 1917 indicates that he was not yet convinced that 'partyism' was the cancer destroying a politics of the people. His rejection of party politics did not occur until the autumn of 1919, after the UFA had enthusiastically authorized 'independent political action' for its locals. To appreciate the genesis of this 1919 convention decision and its significance for the development of radical democratic populism, we must look briefly at the position and strategy of the Non-Partisan League of Alberta.

The NPL spread into Saskatchewan and Alberta from North Dakota in 1916. It had swept the northern state as a 'prairie fire' shortly after its inception, with a 'left-populist' appeal to farmers besieged by credit, transportation, and grain company monopolies.[5] The NPL caught the imagination of Saskatchewan Grain Growers activist S.E. Haight. Within several months UFA activist Henry Johnson met with Saskatchewan NPL organizers, and transmitted the league's dynamic doctrines to William Irvine and several other political activists in Calgary.

Irvine seized on the NPL as a suitable vehicle for building a strong popular alliance between anti-corporate, anti–old party farmers, and wage workers. In his weekly *The Nutcracker* (soon to become *The Alberta Non-Partisan*), Irvine presented the NPL as a champion of agrarian interests capable of forging a popular front against a corporate-party entente. For Irvine, any viable challenge to this hegemony had to carry the battle into political competition; 'the Non-Partisan League believes that nothing permanent in the way of reform can be secured without political action.'[6] Since the UFA was the unchallenged voice of Alberta's agrarian movement, the NPL was left with one practical option: to gain legitimacy as the political expression of UFA objectives.

For many of the politically inclined, left-wing, and non-partisan members of the UFA, this position was more appealing than H.W. Wood's. The strong non-partisan tradition in Alberta helped to set the stage for a movement of farmers into politics. However, NPL popularity among the UFA rank and file would not have mushroomed had the NPL become a labour party *manqué*, emphasizing only the labour-farmer–alliance and state-ownership aspects of its program. The NPL's popularity was primarily the result of its combination of anti-corporate left-populism with a radical democratic populist message. It contended that the interests of 'the people' could only be achieved via a replacement of 'party government' with 'a truly people's government, ... a business administration,' where the business (program of legislation) of the administration and the financing of campaigns was firmly in the hands of constituents.

To some degree, the slogan of 'business government' was superficially similar to those in the rhetoric of 'Progressive' municipal reformers in the United States and Canada. However, for the NPL, business government was not that of a corporate venture. The NPL sought to rein in galloping corruption with a collective effort of scrutiny and control by a politicized citizenry. By contrast, the municipal reform method would rein in the gullible citizenry by replacing a partisan electoral competition with a business-like and depoliticized administration, thereby insulating technocratic decision-making from popular control and partisan manipulation as much as possible.[7]

The NPL platform also endorsed government ownership of natural resources, banks, and other 'fundamental industries feasible to [sic] government control' – including flour mills, packing houses, farm machinery manufacturing, insurance and transportation companies. Irvine and NPL activists[8] recognized that these demands were in advance of the developing agrarian movement, and had to be presented as long-term goals. For any of the goals to be realized, however, the radical democratic component had to be retained. Successful mass participation was required to realize the movement's potential.

The NPL did not become the political extension of the UFA organization. Despite official UFA neutrality in the 1917 provincial election, unofficial support was clearly strong: two of four NPL candidates succeeded. In 1919, the UFA's board of directors and H.W. Wood realized that the question of political action could not be side-stepped any longer. Ten resolutions on political action had been sent from UFA locals. The leadership responded by submitting its own 'moderate' resolution and ensuring that it would be the one debated. The convention supported this resolution, thereby empowering any UFA district association to initiate independent political action, but declined to create a central body to co-ordinate such action. Wood's distaste for political action by the UFA blocked an early start in this direction.

Several months later, a meeting between UFA and NPL representatives sought to prevent a destructive competition based on different political strategies. The NPL executive then circulated a proposal for amalgamation to all NPL members, and advised them to raise the matter as UFA members in upcoming local conventions. The aims were: to maintain a serious opposition to the old parties and the party system; to endorse proportional representation, the initiative, referendum, and recall; to keep the resulting political organization operated exclusively by the rank and file; to set up a central office for political organization; to pass the political program at each constituency convention, clause by clause ('in the interests of education, and also for the prevention of bureaucratic methods'); and to establish *The Alberta Non-Partisan* as the 'official organ of the farmers' political movement.'9

This NPL initiative was followed by several months of regional UFA meetings where these aspects of the NPL amalgamation proposal were debated – in some instances, between Irvine and Wood. The UFA Provincial Political Association was formed in July 1919. The UFA accepted the *Non-Partisan* as its organ, under the new title *The Western Independent*. In due course, all principles insisted on by the NPL as conditions of its assimilation into the UFA were accepted.

The existence of a UFA provincial political association was deceiving, however, because the association related to federal, not provincial, action. In addition, the association had not adopted any program of political action prior to a provincial by-election of 1919, which produced the first UFA MLA in Alberta. Finally, the decision to eschew the 'broadening out' political strategy was not made until the 1920 UFA convention. This decision effected a practical unity among Alberta's radical democratic populists. It assured that UFA political action would be directed by its constituency and convention decisions, and that the logic of functional organization and public activity would not be compromised by systematic political alliances with urban labour.

The UFA's new political principles were first implemented in Medicine Hat during a federal by-election in June 1921. Robert Gardiner, the UFA candidate, demolished the Union Government candidate in a two-way race. Gardiner received an overwhelming majority of support from both farmers and urban labour, despite Wood's frank admission to the latter that a UFA candidate was responsible only to his own group's articulated interests. Gardiner was a transplanted Scot with clear labour sympathies, but once in the house, he quickly became an apostle of farmer/labour unity.

Immediately before this electoral success, the provincial Liberal government called an election for 18 July 1921. Within twelve days, forty-four UFA locals had established provincial constituency associations. Thirty-eight of their candidates were successful, giving the UFA a clear majority in the fifty-eight–seat legislature. Four sympathetic labour MLAs added to this majority, and one became Minister of Labour.

The federal election of 6 December 1921 confirmed the political ascendancy of the UFA, with all eleven UFA candidates winning in Alberta. The remaining seat went to William Irvine in East Calgary. He had run as a Dominion Labour Party (DLP) candidate after the UFA and DLP agreed to split and offer mutual support in the East and West Calgary ridings. Irvine's his victory was savoured by both UFA and DLP organizations. In the House, Irvine caucused with the UFA members in 'the Ginger Group.'

The People

Radical democratic populists shared with crypto-Liberals the idea that farmers were most genuinely of the people. Farmers were the largest single category of productive participants in an economy geared to exploitation of agricultural and exportable staples. Their life-style and moral vantage point contrasted with the urban tendency to distract people from honest pleasures and to sow the seeds of interclass bitterness. In the rural setting, people could more easily recognize common interests and co-operatively work towards common goals. To the extent that the West was agrarian and rural, and the East was industrial and urban, all of these factors favoured Westerners over Easterners for inclusion in the chosen circle of 'the people.'

We can illustrate the distinctiveness of the radical democratic conception of the people by establishing a set of rhetorical antinomies within which this idea constituted one of two poles. Schematically, this connotative structure takes the following form: the people/politicians; the people/partyism; the people/autocracy; the people/plutocracy; and, the people (and God)/Mammonism. The first antinomy implies the whole structure of radical democratic thought. It was usually presented in conjunction with an attack on 'partyism,' but occasionally appeared in a purer form. A 1923 UFA convention endorsement of UFA representation contended that 'it has been fully demonstrated [since 1919] that political activities can be carried on in a systematic and entirely democratic way by *the people* themselves controlling political machinery, instead of this machinery being controlled autocratically by *politicians*, as it has been controlled under the political party system.'[10]

Here politicians' interests are presented as antithetical to those of the people; the example of the party system helps to make the case, but is logically incidental. The same sort of argument is made in H.W. Wood's presidential address to the same convention:

During the past year the conflict between political ideas has been passing through an acute stage. In that conflict, the lining up of the forces of both political and economic autocracy, against democratic citizenship action, has been very marked ... Before the elections of 1921 there was a general opinion among the political party devotees that the organized group system would ... collapse because the people would be incapable of conducting the political activities without the guidance of trained politicians and heelers ... [To] professional and amateur politicians ... a popularly controlled political movement is a monstrosity. The people are not supposed to be competent to become responsible for their own citizenship, but must trust it in the hands of those who are self-appointed and set apart for that purpose. Everything that smacks of political democracy must be crushed, and the supremacy of political autocracy and the rights of the craft left undisputed.[11]

Wood includes other terms to enliven this argument, but its essence is the people/politician antinomy. 'Organized citizenship' is a synonym for 'the people,' with which Wood and Irvine referred to the people in their active, economically and politically self-conscious phase, committing what Wood refers to as the politician's heresy: the collective act of 'taking responsibility for their own citizenship.'[12]

Why were Wood and the UFA so down on politicians? Perhaps the most important reason was their belief that politicians were a breed apart from 'the people,' intent on sustaining socio-political impotence for honest producers. Elimination of these aspects of the people/politicians relationship would eliminate politicians' *raison d'être*. Politicians thus construed were inconceivable outside of a framework of domination and subordination. To the extent that 'the people's' true interests required an end to such domination and subordination, they were ultimately at odds with politicians. A 'true' social order would feature leaders whose activities complemented rather than subverted 'the people's' organized attempts to direct their own lives.

Wood made this point at a UFA nominating convention just prior to the 1926 provincial election: 'I almost feel that I have no business here. You people know what you are here for. It is your work, not mine. I am not a political boss to tell you what to do ... If I were, you would not have me here.

You are fully capable of carrying on this business in your own way ... You have the full responsibility. Nobody as a supreme boss answered for you in the last campaign, and today you have no boss who made rash promises to blame if you have not got satisfactory results.'[13] The upshot of these remarks is that among a democratically mature and self-conscious people, politicians were artificial additions to the political process and a positive barrier to the people's real interests. Politicians prevented (i.e., appeared to remove the need for) organization of people around their interests as functional groups in the industrial system.

Another clue to the logic of the people/politicians antinomy can be found in Wood's brief experience with the ill-fated National Farmers' Alliance and its political vehicle, the People's Party. In Wood's estimation, this promising and dynamic people's movement was ruined by engaging in orthodox political competition and becoming a political party. It thus came to rely on individuals who set themselves up as the saviours of the mass democratic movement. The leaders became politicians when the political became distinct from the economic organization. The average people who had defined the agendas of the Alliance surrendered responsibility when the new organization entered political competition. This surrender culminated in the disastrous 'fusion' campaign of 1896, and the immediate marginalization of the People's Party as a political force. Wood concluded that a people's movement's entry into politics on the terms provided by established political organizations would guarantee the ascendancy of politicians/bosses and the people's arrested development as democratic agents.

A modern cynic might regard Wood's rhetorical opposition of the people and politicians as a manipulative device in the hands of a power-hungry leader. This device is certainly well known to modern political climbers eager to exploit people's alienation from established political leaders by proposing political realignments among 'the people.' As Margaret Canovan has suggested, such politicians adjure the people to 'stand together against the self-serving politicians, instead of dividing along class or sectional lines.'[14] However, this interpretation of Wood's tactics does not stand up. Wood refused to accept the premiership of Alberta, even though it was his for the taking. In addition, his suggestion that 'the people' rise up against the politicians entailed a co-ordinated movement of occupationally self-conscious and well-organized groups, not an unorganized stampede led by one dynamic leader.

The people/partyism antinomy best displays the radical democratic rejection of 'politics as usual.' It appears in a lead article in *The UFA* on the eve of the 1925 federal election. Under the heading 'Why You Should Work and Vote for the Return of the UFA Candidates on October 29th,' readers were told that every representative of the old political parties is responsible to and dominated by a centrally controlled party machine financed and directed by interests inimical to those of the masses of the people, [so that] no pledges and no promises made to the people by party spokesmen in the hope of obtaining votes are likely to be honored; ... the party system involves the dividing of the people into two warring camps, in a sham battle in which the people are left 'holding the sack'; [and] the UFA, Labour and Independent members have introduced a new and virile spirit into the affairs of Parliament, have been free from partizanship [sic], and have fought with vigour and determination for the cause of the people against the centralized financial interests that control both old party machines.[15]

A second instance of this antinomy was provided in a resolution on federal UFA MPs activities, passed 'unanimously without discussion,' to prevent creation of a party-like central committee 'to exercise some kind of autocratic control over the democratic machinery now being operated by the people.' At the 1923 UFA convention, delegates voiced a concern about crypto-Liberal attempts to turn the Progressives into a party, and about UFO Premier Drury's 'broadening out' strategy in Ontario. The convention unanimously condemned any hint of 'partyism' on the part of their own or other farmer representatives.

H.W. Wood and William Irvine had earlier disassociated 'the people' from partyism in equally unmistakable terms. In 1921, Wood argued:

What was wrong with the old [party] system? There was nothing right about it. It was not an organization of the citizens, but of professional politicians ... One party said, 'We are speaking for all the people,' and the other party was doing the same thing. So there you have the people divided in two sections against themselves, farmers divided against each other, labour divided against each other, and all classes that are not so thoroughly organized that they could manipulate the system themselves have been divided.

You can sit down and study out what would be the best way to divide all people against themselves politically ... and you could not think of a better system than the political party system ... The boast of the political party system is that all classes of the masses of the people are divided against themselves, because each rival party claims to represent all elements of the people.[16]

His pitch became more strident pitch in his 1924 presidential address to the UFA annual convention: 'During the past year, political bossism has reared its head from the miasmal swamp-lands of political partyism, and issued a pleading call to the free citizenship of Alberta to return to its infected domain. Little heed was paid to this call. The host of Alberta citizens who in 1921 broke away from the thralldom of party bossism that for generations has herded the masses of citizens into party slave-pens, may not yet fully appreciate the responsibility of their new found freedom, and may have no well-defined ideas as to how they are going to use that freedom, but they have no intention of voluntarily returning to party servitude.'[17]

Irvine defined the basic antagonism between Canadian 'partyism' and the people in two short lines from *The Farmers in Politics*: 'both parties exist to serve privilege, and all their time is taken up doing that. There is no more hope, for the people, in the one than in the other.'[18]

Another closely related antinomy pitted the people against 'autocracy,' a general term embodying all anti-democratic practices by established political and economic élites. From the radical democratic perspective, autocratic power could only be broken when the forces of organized citizenship publicly exposed the forces of autocracy. Wood contended that the political party system 'has always been subservient to autocracy,' and that 'the people are rejecting this system, [having] given it a fair trial.' Wood left no doubt that partyism, autocracy, and professional politicians were necessarily intertwined.

The people/plutocracy antinomy was common in Wood's, Irvine's, and other UFA speakers' public speech. 'Plutocracy' is an old term of popular movement damnation, and had been common in American populist and popular discourse since Jefferson. The term refers to more than 'them': it signifies a general understanding of the prevailing political economy, which features financiers, industrialists, large commercial interests, landowners, and railway companies as the winners, and small farmers, urban-working, and lower classes as the losers.

Wood defined the people/plutocracy contradiction in 'The Significance of Democratic Group Organization,' where he argued that 'plutocracy has gradually built up a competitive strength ... that will eventually reduce the great masses of the people to abject poverty, unless the people can build up a counter-strength equal to or greater than that which has already been built up by the plutocratic classes, among which the Manufacturer's Association is outstanding, and perhaps the most relentless.'[19]

Wood was just as interested in the political nexus inhabited by plutocracy. In speaking of the obstacles to economic harmony among the people ('the primary producer' and 'the ultimate consumer'), Wood told a 1921 Calgary audience that 'the plutocratic classes have ... developed into a dominant political power operating through the political party system, ... a structure ideally adapted to plutocratic control. Through it organized plutocracy holds dominion over both commerce and politics ... Labour can never break into the plutocratic classes. Neither can farmers. We can only serve our interests by developing the true principles of democracy.'[20]

The people/plutocracy antinomy was also featured in Wood's apocalyptic vision of the impending struggle between the forces of 'a false civilization and a new one': 'All through their wanderings of the past, people have been in servitude to the giants of autocracy and plutocracy. This bondage must be ended and the people liberated or else they perish. The conflict is just beginning, and the people will utterly fail unless they mobilize their forces and stand as a solid wall of citizenship in defence of their rights and liberties. It will be the epic of the ages. God will marshall and direct the forces of the people; Mammon, the forces of the beasts. Either Mammon will be overthrown and the beasts destroyed, or the people and the beasts both go down together and God stands alone on the wastes of social desolation.'[21]

Here we see Wood introducing the last of the associated antinomies regarding 'the people': God and the people *versus* Mammon and the forces of the declining 'false civilization.' The success of the people in this epic contest was by no means guaranteed, but God helps those who help themselves by consistently acting in concert with a natural democratic dynamic.

Who were 'the people' within the radical democratic framework? The agents of autocracy and partyism, professional politicians, clearly lacked credentials, as did the plutocratic classes. In their functionalist social theory, the relevant criterion was service to society, viewed from the perspective of the 'new social order.' Wood proposed this criterion in 1917, while defending the UFA approach to 'class organization': 'we are willing to adjust our relationships with all other legitimate classes on the basis of right and service; ... any class that does not give a needed service to society has no rights.'[22]

Who gave a 'needed service to society'? In Wood's eyes, farmers topped the list. Many in the UFA – including its federal MPs, such as Robert Gardiner, E. J. Garland, and Irvine – saw farmers as a species of 'rural worker' within the larger genus of 'working people.' There was a small left-wing minority within the UFA, led by the combative Carl Axelson, that insisted on such a definition of the people. Axelson lobbied for a 'united front of all producers against our common opponents' and regularly addressed his 'fellow farmers and workers' on the need for an effectively syndicalist approach to political action and governmental operation.[23]

A simpler and more widely accepted definition of the people was offered by Irene Parlby, former president of the United Farmers' Women's Association. She noted that 'when I speak of the people, I do not mean a little group at the top of the pyramid, but the great bulk – the manual workers, the clerks and small businessmen, the farmers, the foreign born, the salaried men.'[24]

Radical democratic theory provided a relatively sophisticated account of why the people's natural rationality had not yet been manifested in a rejection of the irrational features of organized political and social life. Both Wood and Irvine continually stressed that effective development of the people's rationality required natural group organization and self-conscious collective identification of group goals and functions ('services'). 'As the individuals make progress in thinking together, they gradually build up their intelligence into the group intelligence, each making his best contribution, and the group ... becomes articulate, and the combined intelligence of all the individuals.'[25]

The anti–*status-quo* feeling generated by the radical democratic usage of 'the people' was considerably greater than in crypto-Liberal discourse. Each of the antinomies with the people was part of a less compromising attack on the established system of power than was ever consistently articulated within crypto-Liberal circles. Given this picture of the people and its foes, we can expect an unorthodox approach to political participation.

Participatory Democracy

The Critique of the Party System

'The UFA, the only branch of the farmers' movement which has survived as an effective political force, has worked out a method of combining constituency autonomy with group solidarity, and local initiative with central direction, which no doubt is not perfect, but does achieve the most complete and real democracy that we have yet seen in Canadian politics.' – Frank Underhill[26]

Suspicion and eventually rejection of partyism by the majority of Alberta farmers was crucial to the development of the political theory of radical democratic populism in Alberta. Early speeches by UFA presidents to annual conventions included support for the measures of direct legislation, with much the same argument that was current across the prairies in crypto-Liberal circles.[27] The anti-party message was not developed beyond this point until William Irvine began publication of *The Nutcracker* in 1916.

Irvine became an avid propagandist for the Non-Partisan League shortly after beginning his journalistic career in Calgary. His colourful attacks on 'partyism' were sprinkled with talk of 'a senseless and pernicious partyism [that is] one of the greatest evils of our public life,'[28] and came down to this basic complaint:

Behind the party system of this and every other country where party rules is economic advantage. Each party is backed, owned and controlled by certain large financial interests, who use these parties to secure their profiteering ends. The first step towards non-partisan politics would therefore naturally be a renunciation of the financial interests that replete the party funds in return for legislation promised or received. A political party which owes its very existence, and the means of attaining power, to private corporations is in a hopeless position when required to render service to the people ... both political parties in Canada are in this position, neither having sufficient faith in the people to break with plutocracy ... there is nothing to choose between them.[29]

The battle against 'partyism' had been joined well before Wood conceded the need for UFA political action. Wood's definitive argument linking partyism, plutocracy, manipulation of the people's business, and administrative corruption and inefficiency had been established before Wood became the UFA's principal political theorist.

Irvine and the NPL did not, however, share several basic premises of Wood's political strategy. The NPL variant of contraparty political action sought to fight cross-class organizational fire with similar fire, rejecting the idea that the plutocracy/party nexus could be challenged effectively with political organizations based in a single class. Divided along political as well as occupational lines, the people would not muster sufficient collective strength to defeat the plutocratic forces in league with partyism. Irvine argued that no democratic organization should exclude like-minded individuals on the basis of their occupation: 'There is no fundamental democratic principle upon which the farmers or any other industrial unit have a monopoly; ... the people in the towns are just as democratic as people on the farms.'[30]

At this point, Irvine still believed that the UFA might participate in an integrated 'people's movement.' When the UFA adopted direct political action, but retained Wood's preferred strategy of 'class-based' political action, Irvine was pleased enough with the former to accept the latter. This acceptance soon blossomed into the most extensive argument on its behalf, in Irvine's *The Farmers in Politics*. As for the Non-Partisan League, its *raison d'être* was largely removed when the UFA Political Association was formed. NPL activists merged with the UFA while continuing to emphasize socialistic proposals for both farmers and labour.

The most complete criticism of the party system in radical democratic prairie populism came from Irvine and Wood after the summer of 1919. Responding to the NPL challenge, Wood articulated his party critique with a rigour not seen before in UFA circles, implying a need for political institutions more unorthodox than any proposed by his predecessors or contemporaries in the prairie farmers' movement.

In singling out Wood as the UFA's principal social and political theoretician, C.B. Macpherson may have slighted William Irvine's achievements.[31] Yet one cannot but admire Macpherson's penetrating account of Wood's critique of partyism. Macpherson begins by noting that the UFA attack on the party system took its point of departure from the perceived use of the party system by 'plutocratic interests.'[32] This orientation was explicit in the radical democratic use of the 'people/partyism' and 'people/plutocracy' antinomies, but did not by itself distinguish radical democratic populism from crypto-Liberalism. The gap between the two began to widen with the second tenet of the UFA party critique: 'the party system was an instrument to divide and rule the people.'[33] As we saw, crypto-Liberal leadership rejected this idea,[34] while some crypto-Liberals were willing to go this far, without propounding a systematic alternative mode of political action.

For Macpherson, the factor most responsible for the UFA rejection of the party system was their idea that 'parties were inherently conglomerate, therefore unstable, therefore incapable of transmitting the democratic force of reform-minded citizens.' Party *qua* party was required to sacrifice everything – especially internal democracy and progressive, unifying principles – to the quest for power. Not surprisingly, a moral conception of democracy as a social order freed from class exploitation was behind the UFA rejection of party as a vehicle for democracy. The critique of partyism was also motivated and sustained by an insistence that popular control of group representatives was central to democratic politics.

The assumptions behind the UFA concern that a party was incapable of transmitting 'the democratic force of reform-minded citizens' fall into two main categories: those informing the radical democratic idea of citizenship and those concerning the necessary context of democratic and progressive political thought. By modern North American standards, the radical democratic idea of citizenship was very demanding. In many ways, it presaged the theory of 'participatory democracy' that has been resurrected and promoted by various radical academics and political activists since the mid-1960s in western capitalist countries. The UFA notion of citizenship also stressed its public character. Isolated citizenship, unconnected to the social and economic institutions moulding citizens' immediate experiences and concerns, was considered a contradiction in terms. It could not foster awareness of the social dimension of individual experience or complementary education in the dynamics of conflict-laden social life. Party activity 'does not raise the citizenship unit' because it obscures the conditions of effective citizenship.

Some of Wood's earliest comments on citizenship were indistinguishable in principle from Chamber of Commerce after-dinner pep-talks, then or since. In describing citizenship as the 'price of democracy' to readers of the *Guide*, he says : 'Citizenship in a democracy is worth something and costs something. Have you been quietly thinking during the last four years whether or not the best man in your party in your district was serving you. If you have not, you have not been doing your duty as a citizen ... Take as much interest in selecting a representative as you would in selecting a horse or a farm ... send delegates to your party convention who will nominate the right candidate. If you fail here you will fail everywhere.'[35]

By September 1917, Wood's increased antipathy towards partyism was still not complete; he was acting as a Canadian Council of Agriculture representative in discussions that led to formation of the Union Government, which he publicly supported. But he had developed a radicalized notion of citizenship. In an Edmonton speech, Wood spoke of the difficulties of maintaining organizational strength among farmers' parties, old parties' efforts to undercut agrarian reforms and parties, and the present inability of the people to rule themselves: 'The lack of intelligent citizenship is the reason why the people cannot govern themselves today. Men are well meaning enough ... but their citizenship is not sufficiently developed to carry on the work of governing the country, with the result that the political forces are in the ascendancy ... We must develop our economic institutions, and then as people become more interested in them they will have their attention drawn away from political institutions and more and more bound up in those institutions which are for the interest of the people themselves ... Instead of building up a political party we ... will be piling up political force and through that force piling up useful legislation.'[36] Accepting the necessity of a socially generated sense of citizenship took Wood closer to the idea of 'the group' as the only sound basis of intelligent and integrated citizenship.

Shortly after the UFA endorsed political action at its 1919 convention, Wood sought to guide such action. He had not rejected party as a vehicle of political action, because he had not yet developed the socio-economic rationale of group organization and government. Wood none the less insisted on a distinctive form of citizenship for UFA political action. He reminded his readers that for years they had been 'meeting together in our local units, in our political conventions, and in our national council, discussing our problems until now we have developed sufficient mobilization to put our ideas in force, [and] to make further progress by taking up the practical duties of citizenship in a sane way.' He went on to contrast locally controlled and vocationally oriented citizen activity with the poorly rooted, ambiguous citizen activity characteristic of party politics. The idea that citizenship and true democratic action could only be nurtured in class-defined and organized activities emerged with the doctrine of group government several months later.

In his 'Significance of Democratic Group Organization,' Wood argues that party division of the people, pursuit of false issues, and distraction of the people from their real interests are possible because 'the unit of citizenship is so low that the masses of the people have no citizenship strength.' This sorry situation could be reversed only if the citizenship 'unit' were raised to a much higher level, on the only basis yet discovered for unified and co-ordinated social citizenship: economic class. When the group is 'stabilized and made permanent, ... [and] individuals make progress in thinking together, they gradually build their intelligence into the group intelligence, each making his best contribution, and the group ... speaks the combined intelligence of all the individuals.'[37]

This pattern of group development would work within agriculture and 'every other legitimate or useful industry or occupation.' It could not work in the power-seeking party organization professing support for a wide range of groups. As Irvine said, 'when the election is over, there is no organization left. The people have only been working together as individuals, they have not been thinking and acting together as a unit, and, consequently, there is no democracy. Voting for a platform, or an "idea" created by some individual, will never develop democratic responsibility ... we have a measure of democracy [when] the people accept responsibility for their thoughts and acts, and as they cannot think nor act until they are organized into democratic units, the units must first exist.'[38]

Creation of these democratic units was assured by 'natural laws' that make economic interest the basis of individual objectives and determine that only group units organized around shared occupational interests will further the expression of legitimate individual objectives. In denying the validity of this approach, parties prevent development of citizen responsibility.

Wood and Irvine saw this responsibility expressed most clearly in two ways. One was citizen control over candidate selection, representative's performances, and campaign financing. The second was really a condition of the first: group education in social, economic, and political affairs. Irvine addresses democracy's dependence on education in the first part of The Farmers in Politics. He insists that 'democracy ... must permeate the whole system of society' and that 'education in a democracy is of supreme importance.' A democratic state 'implies a universal fitness for responsibility which education alone can bring'; consequently, 'we must democratize education, and bring our educational institutions into line with democratic ideals,' since education was designed 'to maintain the status quo, its autocracy and injustice notwithstanding.' Parties had neither promoted nor practised democratic education; by contrast, according to Wood, UFA innovations such as their 1919 provision for district political conventions were 'primarily educational, designed to educate the people in regard to political problems and co-operative methods necessary to [their] solution.'[39]

The UFA rank and file took this educational dimension of citizenship seriously. Discussion of current social, economic, and political problems and theories was central to most locals' activity. At the 1924 annual convention, a constituency resolution captured the concern for informed citizenship.

Whereas, the chief object of the UFA consists of promoting intelligent understanding between all producers, through the means of lectures, press and schools, in order to develop unity of action, as well as general industrial solidarity between the various branches of agriculture and all other industries, in order to thereby secure for ourselves as producers the full social reward to which our labour entitles us; and

Whereas, the only means toward that end is an improved method of education, through the means of lectures, press and schools, by giving unbiased instruction in all natural, economic, political and social laws, and

Whereas, the knowledge of these laws, together with development of co-operative industrial group organizations in all our producing and marketing activities is the only true and scientific method whereby we as producers can develop political power and secure for ourselves socially what is rightfully ours,

Therefore, we respectfully submit as a guide to future political action.
1. That all candidates be chosen on the basis of their ability to expound the principles of economic, political and social laws ...[40]

This resolution passed with a large majority, and indicates the degree to which UFA members believed education, responsibility, and right political action to be interconnected. Like Wood and Irvine's comments, it shows how the radical democratic understanding of citizenship was crucial to their critique of partyism. Partyism was inimical to the interests of democratic citizens and incompatible with the participatory democratic practice of fighting an exploitive social order.

The Positive Image of Participatory Democracy

Democracy is worthless if it does not mean that the people manage their own affairs in such a manner that there can never be any reason for rebellion. Not that management by the people would necessarily result in faultless efficiency, or errorless policy, but rather that, under true democracy, the people would be responsible and, being conscious of responsibility, would not rebel against themselves.[41]

Perhaps no undertaking of the people has ever been harder than adjusting themselves to democratic organization. But nothing has ever promised the people so much, when they have made that adjustment.[42]

These statements by Irvine and Wood provide a fitting introduction to the positive participatory element in radical democratic populism, insofar as they are testimony to the inherent virtues of popular rule. Neither statement stipulates the content of popular rule, but each indicates the animating spirit of the search for such content.

Irvine's statement is reminiscent of Rousseau's logic of participatory democracy. Popular sovereignty allows a community of citizens to be free, ruled by laws that they generate themselves. Citizens freely create laws in recognition of the direct responsibility that they have, *qua* governors and citizens, to identify such laws. While Irvine did not accept Rousseau's idea that 'democratic consciousness' required the group-transcending mechanism of the General Will, he (and the UFA) none the less anchored the notion of citizenship in a context of community. The UFA sense of community was defined in functional economic terms first and supragroup terms only later. The UFA also shared Rousseau's idea that a people would not knowingly govern itself in a way that might provoke rebellion. The faith in developed democratic citizenship provided the foundation for all of the participatory mechanisms and objectives of the UFA movement.

Following the 1921 victories, Wood congratulated UFA supporters on 'adjusting themselves to democratic organization' and reaping promising results:

Three years ago the UFA decided to engage in political activities. We believed that under systematic organization the people themselves could initiate and control political activities ... There was keen realization that the development of democracy was necessarily a slow process ... Consequently we emphasized the necessity of a strict adherence to right foundation principles, rather than those of temporary expediency. The wisdom of our decision has been fully proven by the results of the two political campaigns of the past year; even beyond our clearest foresight or our most sanguine expectations.

It was fortunate that we had two years of preparatory activity before we were put to the test of carrying on an actual campaign. During these two years our membership made unprecedented progress in the study of true democratic principles, and in the mobilization of their forces preparatory to taking democratic action. A wave of democratic zeal, as a prairie fire before a rising wind, swept over our organization and on through the unorganized citizenship of the villages, towns, and cities, until it became irresistible, and in the last election swept the province clean of autocratic political machine representatives ... All this was made possible by systematic organization. Democracy will not, and cannot function except through organization that reaches down to and embraces the people.

Real progress has been made ... in gaining the confidence of the unorganized democratic citizens. These citizens are more than ever impressed with the absolute necessity of some kind of organization that will enable them to initiate democratic political activities. Their problems in doing this will be very difficult, ... but they will eventually solve them. To that end we must give them all possible encouragement and assistance.[43]

Unlike other farmers' organizations across the prairies at this time, the UFA gave little emphasis to the role that public policy proposals played in their electoral victories, as compared to their democratic principles and practice. Democratic political activities ensured democratic and attractive policy and social results, since these goals were identified, developed, and related to necessary institutional action, in the process itself. Only the most general features of the goals themselves – a desire to end exploitation, and a firm foundation for intergroup co-operation and mutual benefit – could precede democratic organization and activity. Potentially democratic citizens would have to organize before achieving a sufficient awareness of their real interests.

What would lead these democrats *in potentia* to organize their own participatory practice? We can get some idea from the UFA's 1919 resolution regarding political action and the 1921 UFA 'Declaration of Principles.' The 1919 resolution's preamble confidently asserts that 'our organization has reached a state of development in freedom from partisanism, in mobilization of thought, and numerical strength that political action not only becomes possible but is now necessary in our continued progress, and ... the nature of this Organization and the very ground-work of its development demands that it should continue to be independent of any class or party and free from any sectional influence, to the end that purely democratic and independent political action shall be promoted.'

The preamble expresses rank-and-file belief that their movement had cleared a major hurdle in establishing a democratic movement: creation of a collective self-understanding within an autonomous social organism. The six resolutions following it detail the control of local associations over UFA political activity.

Lawrence Goodwyn might have said that the 1919 UFA resolution demonstrates an ' "individual self-respect" and "collective self-confidence" [which constitute] ... the cultural building blocks of mass democratic politics, [that] permits people to conceive of the idea of acting in self-generated democratic ways, [and] opens up new vistas of social possibility, vistas that are less clouded by inherited assumptions.'[44]

Another prerequisite of participatory practice was functional group organization, as an antidote to partyism's artificial division and mystification of 'the people.' We can see the importance given to this in the UFA's 1921 'Declaration of Principles,' their definitive pre-election statement.

Believing that the present unsettled conditions in Canada politically are due in large measure to dissatisfaction with the party system of Government, and

Believing that present day political institutions fail to measure up to the requirements of present day conditions in that the present system has failed to develop a sufficiently close connection between the representative and the elector and that the people desire a greater measure of self-government,

Recognizing the rights of all citizens, believing that it is the duty of every citizen to exercise his rights of citizenship in the most efficient manner, and in the best interest of social progress, and believing that individual citizenship can only be made efficient and effective through the vehicle of systematically organized groups;

We, the United Farmers of Alberta, base our hope of developing a social influence and a progressive force, on becoming a stabilized, efficient organization. We therefore place primary emphasis on organization.

Our organization is continuously in authority, and while through it we formulate declarations of principles, or a so-called platform, these are at all times subject to change by the Organization.

We are a group of citizens going into political action as an organization. Our elected representatives are at all times answerable to the organization. Each elected representative is answerable directly to the organization in the constituency that elected him.

We aim to develop through the study of social and economic problems an intelligent responsible citizenship.

Thus organized citizenship becomes the vehicle not only of intelligent voting but also of intelligent guidance of elected representatives.

A full recognition of the supremacy of the organization in all things does not nullify the importance of a platform. Recognizing this importance, we submit the following as a suggested platform to be used by the UFA Provincial Constituencies in the coming Election.[45]

The 1919 resolution and 1921 declaration demonstrate what UFA members expected of a serious commitment to democracy. The crypto-Liberal commitment to participatory democracy was not pushed as far, nor was it as logically dependent on ultimate goals or undergirding faith as was the radical democratic position. The social democratic commitment gave a higher priority to the results from, than to the process of, participatory democracy.

Statements made at the beginning of a political movement are no guarantee that principles will not become empty slogans. However, UFA spokesmen continue to grant their participatory democratic principle pride of place in subsequent years.

One demonstration of this emphasis involved the fundamental dispute over principles of democratic practice between crypto-Liberal and radical democratic populists. This conflict had been evident since the creation of the National Progressive 'party,' but came to a head in November 1922. Thomas Crerar resigned his leadership of the parliamentary Progressive group and lashed out at the sectionalism, 'class orientation,' and political short-sightedness of the Alberta representatives (and Wood as UFA president). Wood replied to Crerar's statement of resignation with an unequivocal rejection of Crerar's politics and approach to movement-building. He denied that any representative can 'represent all interests and still not represent any particular interests,' contended that organized farmers have made more progress developing their own citizenship than any other group, attacked Crerar's approach to political organization as 'political autocracy, as opposed to political democracy,' and counselled farmers to decisively reject it. This critique set the tone for all subsequent clashes between radical democratic and crypto-Liberal populists. In each case, the radical democratic spokesmen championed the functional unity of purpose, institutional autonomy, and self-direction of properly organized agrarian interests.

UFA leaders and activists' rejection of party-oriented approaches to political action was vindicated in provincial and federal UFA electoral victories in 1926 and 1930. In 1926, *The UFA*'s editor, Norman Smith, noted that the novelty and stimulation associated with dethroning partyism (provincially) had subsided. However, Alberta farmers 'have gained a quiet confidence in their own ability to carry on their own affairs in their own way, ... learned much in their own schools of democracy, [and] obtained a deeper insight into the methods and possibilities of democratic political action.'[46] President Wood's assessment of this victory and its aftermath emphasized the novelty of a farmers' political movement emerging from its first election stronger than it was after its first, a result he attributed to 'adherence to true principles' and conscious avoidance of the processes and assumptions of party activity.[47]

For another decade, UFA leaders and publicists explained their organization's success primarily in terms of anti-party methods of group organization, internal democracy, and grass-roots activity. In his controversial *Co-operative Government*, Irvine insisted on the connection between well-informed popular participation along group lines and 'true democracy.' He presented Crerar, Forke, and ex-premier of Ontario Drury as negative cases demonstrating this connection. They would have 'wrecked the whole democratic movement in Canada' if the groups that the Progressive MPs had represented had not been 'properly organized democratic groups of people determined to do their own business.'[48]

The editor of *The UFA* followed the Progressive electoral failure in 1930 with a 'vindication of the Alberta farmers' and their approach to political action. Smith chronicled the rapid reductions in Progressive strength in the 1925, 1926, and 1930 elections, and noted that 'the most ambitious attempt by Canadian farmers to bring into being a new political party had ended in failure,' with only Alberta's agrarian representatives retaining their seats and autonomy from the old parties. Smith left it to the sympathetic *Farmers' Sun* of Ontario (which he had edited in the middle 1920s) to conclude the lesson: farmers' political efforts could be successful only if 'based broadly upon the same independence of spirit and freedom of action that enables the United Farmers of Alberta to ... exercis[e] an influence in the field of politics ... that is as unique as it is salutary.'[49]

While the achievements of radical democratic participatory principles did not match their promise, acceptance of these principles by both leaders and rank and file in the UFA played a crucial role in the life of this movement. Participants developed a strong sense of the superiority of their own democratic commitment and beliefs through their activity in grass-roots formulation of organization policy. In the absence of this activity and belief, UFA members would have been crypto-Liberals with idiosyncratic beliefs in monetary reform and a co-operative future. With participatory beliefs and practice sustaining each other at the centre of the 'movement culture,' the UFA had indeed generated a political experience both 'unique' and 'salutary.'

Local community institutions were crucial to this experience. By considering this link, we can get a clearer sense of its 'participatory practice' and some insight into the reasoning behind the concept of group representation. In 1928, editor W. Norman Smith of *The UFA* wrote an article entitled 'The Contribution of the UFA to Social Progress.' After reviewing some recent criticisms of conventional democratic practice by such an eminent writer as H.G. Wells, Smith describes the basis of the UFA social philosophy. He focuses on the indispensability and natural connection of local institutions of economic co-operation, municipal and school government, and social life to participatory practice in the higher spheres of political life. Smith underscores their importance by describing the political movement as 'merely one of the functions of a farmers' general organization.' Political work at the local, district, and annual convention level were the logical outcome of UFA activities, and of course had the highest profile, but they were never meant to overshadow or, worse, drain necessary energy from these other strictly non-electoral activities. Politics so construed would have been simply unacceptable to all of those for whom 'UFA Sundays,' United Farmer Women's Association, United Farmer Junior Branches, school-boards, and local-level co-operatives constituted the social and cultural foundations of the movement.

Education in the social philosophy and practical arts of progressive rural life took place under the auspices of these institutions, and in turn provided the training in co-operative decision-making necessary for their chosen mode of political activity. Radical democratic political practice is unimaginable outside of such an intensive and extensive institutional and cultural framework of self-directing community affairs. A politics that reduced the democratic potential of community institutions was precisely what led the UFA to counter 'partyism' with their own political intervention.

A 1926 UFA circular refined Smith's account of local UFA activity. It began by noting that H.W. Wood had 'always placed his greatest emphasis on the locals themselves assuming the responsibility of this organization' with the result that 'today the locals feel not only that they are an integral part of the Association, but are, in fact, the Association.' The circular went on to emphasize the unified character of activities at the local level: federal districts of the UFA, as of 1919, 'were authorized not only to carry on political activities, but any other UFA activity.' Consequently, 'there has been no divorcing of the UFA activities from the other citizenship responsibilities represented in political action, but the two things have made a natural weld.' The circular closed by placing the political dimension of UFA activity in perspective, insisting that while 'political action is really a sideline with our organization, ... the striking success in political action is the result of the organization itself, and will be the best assurance the farmers can have that they can succeed in other things they attempt in the future.' Crypto-Liberal and social democratic populist leaders insisted on their close ties to farmers' organizations, but it is unlikely that either would have been willing to devalue the currency of their own political coin as bluntly as the UFA leadership does here.

More evidence of the value given to local community institutions can be found in a 1920 publication of the UFA provincial secretary, *How to Organize and Carry on a Local of the United Farmers of Alberta*. The fifty-page booklet covers a wide range of subjects: procedures involved in establishing new locals and district associations; identification of locals' moral, intellectual, social, and economic objectives; how to make the local organization successful; achievements and long-range objectives of the UFA organization; the importance of UFWA locals and 'junior branches'; and an outline of the Canadian Council of Agriculture's organization and 'New National Policy.' Within this range, the comments on objectives of locals are most instructive.

Included within the category of 'moral objectives' are promotion of group recreation, 'studying of all legislation proposed or passed, both Provincial and Federal,' 'working for the improvement of such legislation which bears unjustly on any class or persons,' and 'making your school house a community centre where the community can regularly meet and discuss all public questions, thereby helping to fulfill and carry out the ideals of democratic government.'[50] Within the category of 'intellectual objectives,' the pamphlet encouraged the development of a community library covering topics of interest to a 'co-operativist' rural population, an organized course of study in various topics for local members, debates and 'paper readings' by members, and whatever the membership felt would 'develop the mentality, public spirit and power of self-expression of every member.' Finally, under the economic/financial category of objectives, co-operative trading was to be aggressively promoted, along with improvements in local marketing, shipping conditions, and member understanding of agricultural and national economies, co-operative methods, and rural credit systems. Previous activities related to these moral, intellectual, and economic objectives had 'helped to create a community consciousness and to establish the spirit of true democracy in many districts.'

In sum, community institutions intimately related to UFA locals were expected to contribute to development of a self-sustaining democratic movement. It could then combine agrarian self-defence and collective socio-economic advancement with an object-lesson in 'true democracy' to other potentially progressive elements of 'the people.'

Fittingly, the last word on the importance of local community institutions to the radical democratic project is reserved for Henry Wise Wood. In an address to the Alberta Institute of Co-operation in September 1929, Wood singled out the UFA locals as the foundation of all UFA achievements in the fields of economic and political co-operation. In fact, 'if one UFA Local could establish a purely co-operative community where all community affairs, both social and business, were dealt with in a practical co-operative way, that pioneer Local would be contributing more to right social construction and human welfare, than any individual that has ever lived.' More praise for the locals can be found in virtually every presidential address to the UFA annual convention between 1923 and 1931, with Wood stressing the threat that declining local activity in the UFA organization posed to realization of its political and social goals. For Wood and UFA activists, membership increases showed that 'the people' were training as responsible and demanding citizens. This was the backbone of the movement culture, without which inspirational leadership, inspired journalism, and electoral organization would have had little significance as adjuncts of the UFA's democratic process.

With this background, the radical democratic populist concept of delegate democracy is easily understood. Following C.B. Macpherson, we can best see delegate democracy as the conceptual and practical centre-piece of democracy as 'a means, a method or type of political organization and responsibility, by which the end ['a non-exploitive, just, co-operative social and political order'] was to be attained.' The logic of radical democratic representation required instruction of elected representatives by electors on particular items of policy. Delegate responsiveness to constituents' wishes was to be guaranteed through a strict form of 'mandated representation.'[51]

The *sine qua non* of such delegate responsiveness was a culturally integrated, constituency-association control over the organization, financing, and conduct of the delegate's bid for elected office. In some cases, this was thought to entail a 'recall' provision. Wood described this latter provision in a 1921 UFA circular, but did not endorse it. 'The idea,' he said, 'is that if after being elected, the [district] committee ... believe he has been false to his trust, they may require him to appear before the district convention and give an account of his stewardship; if the convention decides that his stewardship has been sufficiently unsatisfactory to warrant, it asks him to make his resignation effective [*sic*].'[52]

Well before the UFA 'went into politics,' it instituted delegate democracy as the mode of delegate representation to annual conventions from the locals (one delegate per ten members; changed to one per twenty at the 1921). These delegates in turn elected a president, a secretary, and four committeemen, who, as of 1919, were subject to recall by the convention-at-large. Directors were elected to the UFA board from each of the federal constituencies by those areas' delegates as of 1921. As Macpherson said of the formal structure of the UFA organization-in-convention: 'The delegate relationship existing between the convention and the locals was extended to the governing bodies as far as possible. The officers were regarded as delegates of the convention, and many resolutions passed by the convention were instructions to the board or executive, just as the delegates to the convention had in many cases been instructed by their locals on specific issues.'[53]

This close relation of representation could not help but be a fragile flower in the harsh climate of party competition and pragmatic compromises with the established political economy. Macpherson shows that delegate democracy underwent a radical transformation – in effect, submission – when the UFA found itself trying to extend delegate democracy to cabinet government.

Macpherson notes implementation of delegate democracy principles was limited by the conventions' inability to deal with all local delegate-sponsored resolutions (even after a 1922 ruling that such resolutions should be cleared first through district conventions), and the UFA board's and executive's increased autonomy from local rank-and-file control. However, the primary obstacles to implementing delegate democracy arose after the UFA's electoral successes: cabinet exercised stronger control over UFA MLAs than constituency associations; 'constituency control of the elected member gave way also to provincial convention control';[54] and the annual convention was subordinate to the UFA provincial cabinet over matters of policy.[55]

In discussing the first of these three problems, Macpherson notes the UFA's initial attempts to maintain delegate-directed autonomy for the provincial and federal constituency associations. Internal generation and control of financing of political activities, and regular accounting of elected members regarding their 'stewardship,' were also expected to ensure individual representative autonomy from cabinet or caucus direction. If delegate democracy could not ensure such autonomy from cabinet power, it would be deprived of a good part of its *raison d'être*. To this end, each constituency association 'derived its authority directly from the locals,' and thus possessed a mandate equal in principle to that of the provincial convention.[56]

Macpherson demonstrates that this principle ceased to have practical force shortly after the UFA's accession to power. He shows how successive UFA premiers accepted the conventions of cabinet government on enforcing party solidarity in the legislature with the threat of dissolution. Thus, while the ideological force behind delegate democracy was strong and resulted in a more independent government 'party' caucus than is typical within cabinet government, it was easily overshadowed by a concern for survival. Senior UFA strategists successfully contended that their organization faced a harsh but simple trade-off. The UFA could retain viability as an administration independent of partyism's corruption and subservience to 'the interests' by abandoning insistence upon full-fledged delegate democracy. Or the movement could apply the doctrine to the letter, and forfeit the short- and medium-term opportunity to govern.[57]

UFA leaders at the federal and provincial levels had no public doubts about which nettle to grasp. This was most clearly true of UFA premiers and cabinet, but was also true of H.W. Wood. After 1921, his attacks on the tyranny of party and cabinet control over elected representatives were directed against 'partyism' in the abstract, or the federal parliament. Even William Irvine believed that the provincial organization had no choice but to retreat on the delegate principle. In a 1926 pre-election *UFA* article, Irvine declared: 'Let us not forget that a criticism of the UFA government is a challenge to the intelligence and to the democratic right of every individual member of the movement.' One can partially discount this as campaign rhetoric, but there is still irony in its occurrence in a piece entitled 'Principles That Fortune Has Committed to Our Care Will Save the World; Let Us Be True to Our Own Vision.'

Macpherson describes a second aspect of delegate democracy's decline after 1921. Despite high levels of concern for autonomy from 'central control,' constituency associations' hold on elected representatives declined in relation to the annual convention. This, too, was a consequence of political success in a game whose rules were antithetical to the doctrines of radical democratic populism. The prospect of the movement's respectability declining as a result of perceived inconsistencies among elected representatives made central co-ordination among them essential. Thus, the conventions in the mid-1920s affirmed the responsibility of such representatives to report to and take specific guidance from the 'supreme authority,' the annual convention. President Wood, in fact, sanctioned this practice by emphasizing the folly of constituency independence in view of the ultimate reliance of individual locals/constituencies upon the whole (the common will of which found expression in the annual convention). Constituency associations were thus expected to recognize the higher authority of the convention when instructing their elected representatives.[58]

The third obstacle confronted by radical democratic delegates emerged in circumstances where the annual convention collided with the provincial cabinet on questions of provincial government policy. Theoretically, the convention should have had the upper hand in these disputes. However, the convention never presumed to make demands upon 'their' government, choosing instead to present resolutions on government policy as requests. The government did feel obliged to report on its responses to these requests in convention, through ministers, or through *The UFA*, but it did not justify its behaviour to the degree desired by the rank and file at the convention.

Convention resolutions on provincial credit institutions (in the early 1920s and early 1930s) and debt moratoriums (early 1930s) were notoriously critical of previous or likely government policy, but these did not weaken the cabinet's position in this relationship. As Macpherson argues, nothing that the convention could do could match the threat of dissolution. Few delegates were so committed to delegate democracy that they would regularly force government-endangering votes on particular issues in the legislature. However, on several occasions convention delegates passed resolutions obviously unacceptable to the government, then stepped back from the brink by not insisting that constituency associations instruct their MLAs to vote against the government.

Macpherson denies that this political theatre was simply a disguise for the impotence of delegate democracy in the UFA, even though its power relative to cabinet was greatly reduced. Delegate democracy had left nominating and financing of constituency UFA candidates in local hands, and thus had prevented the emergence of a centralized and electorally opportunistic 'party machine.'[59] It was with this in mind that Wood stated that 'the fundamental principle of political democracy is that the organization of all political machinery must originate with the citizenship.'

It is also true that while no specific reforms to cabinet government practice were achieved, 'the underlying purpose which the particular changes were designed to serve was in some measure realized.' Constituency association and provincial convention activity made the UFA organization a vehicle for the development and expression of popular opinion that has not been rivalled by any political organization in Canada, perhaps not even the Saskatchewan CCF in its halcyon days. Macpherson credits the spirit of delegate democracy ('its reform principles') for the UFA's sustained distance from 'partyism' in other respects; the UFA 'did not become conglomerate, ... unstable or unprincipled in an attempt to hold together a conglomeration of interests, ... did not develop a centrally controlled machine, nor put itself at the disposal of any outside interests.'[60]

This judgment tells us a good deal more about the status of delegate democracy in radical democratic ideology than Macpherson explicitly acknowledges. These achievements were seen as a stage of democratic development, as a means to the goal of a co-operative commonwealth. UFA partisans generally did not believe that delegate democracy could reach its transformative potential in the presence of partyism and unequal market power among economic classes.

The UFA organization did not overcome the euphoria of its initial successes sufficiently to come to terms with this conflict between their goals and the prevailing political economy. Even H.W. Wood, for all his talk about the need for great improvements in efficient citizenship, did not attempt to deflate the unrealistic expectations attached to the doctrine of delegate democracy. The doctrine had, after all, been a powerful inspirational weapon in the fight against partyism at both provincial and federal levels. Admitting shortcomings and contradictions would have been a major tactical error from the perspective of a young political movement. Like the co-operative society, delegate democracy was an ideal whose currency could not be deflated because of poor market conditions. Consumer confidence had to be maintained to enhance the potential for growth in democratic futures.

Lest this sketch of the UFA doctrine's role suggests conscious manipulation of a hopeful public, it should be emphasized that Henry Wise Wood was a true believer in his own movement's doctrine, as were Irvine, Norman Priestly, W. Norman Smith, E.J. Garland, Robert Gardiner, and other UFA leaders. They all sincerely believed, and were able to convince many of the rank and file, that delegate democracy was essential to good provincial and national government. It was the highest expression of 'the people in action,' and hence the logical form of representation. However, its full positive effect could only be achieved when delegate democracy culminated in the structures and processes of group government.

Macpherson convincingly anchors the democratic dimension of the group government proposal in UFA social theory, concerning the dialectic of co-operation and competition in social evolution. 'Occupational grouping [was] the natural and inevitable power grouping, and the only one which, used intelligently by the farmers and other "democratic" forces, could lead to the supercession of the competitive social order.' It is important to highlight several implications and assumptions in the rationale connecting UFA participatory democratic beliefs to the group government theory.

As noted above, radical democratic populists saw the group (variously referred to as 'economic class,' 'industrial unit,' or 'occupational group') as the most natural, complete, and integrated basis for self-directing and collective democratic practice. The group could most effectively retain its links with the local community institutions upon whose health the rationale of delegate democracy ultimately rested.

The group thus provided the only environment productive and supportive of true democratic thought. Individualism, as promoted by the parties and the false laws of competition directing the market economy, could not lead in this direction. No individual could conceive of positive solutions to the conflicts of the social economy without being attached to the combined intelligence of a group determined to recognize and integrate its interests in this social economy. As Irvine says in *The Farmers in Politics*, 'a real democratic thought ... cannot be [developed] by a mob, [but] only ... by groups; and groups must be organized before they can think, and before they can be organized there must be a common interest to bring them together.'[61]

Because the group was the home of integrated democratic practice and the natural source of progressive political thought, it provided the best basis for delegate democracy. Delegates 'went out' into the larger political arena instructed and informed by a coherent, developed, and almost expert sense of their constituents' interests. Delegates 'returned' to the group with a clear sense of what to report and how their constituents would call them to account. The group was thus a much more solid and identifiable point of reference – virtually a political 'super-ego' – for the delegated representative.

Assuming that the example set by early group delegates in such assemblies would encourage other groups to follow the group/delegate model, political parties would gradually lose their predominance in legislative assemblies.[62] Groups' delegates would reconstitute the conduct of legislative and government business, form pluralized group cabinets made up of delegates from the various 'democratic forces,' and lead the fight against the 'forces of plutocracy' inside and outside the legislature. In some fashion, never spelled out in any tactical detail by UFA theorists, the combined forces of organized democracy would defeat the forces of organized plutocracy. They would then substitute a harmonious regime of economic and political co-operation for the existing competitive, divisive, and outmoded one.

This victory achieved, the groups with a legitimate claim to representation (all those providing a genuine service to society) would elect representatives to a true 'group parliament.' Such representatives expect each other to bargain on behalf of well-informed group interests, and still have a clear sense of the interdependence of all 'functional units' in the whole co-operative framework. Delegates would become expert functional representatives, balancing responsibility to their specific group with that to the collective, finely tuned co-operative enterprise that politicized society had become.[63]

While group representatives would not abandon their responsibility to plan and resolve issues in accordance with their groups' interests, such planning and resolution would be facilitated by the 'higher intelligence' of co-operation that the changed circumstances of representation and group interaction in the economy would foster. Both delegate democracy (which assures high-quality and popularly controlled representation) and group government (which removes artificial and destructive adversarial relations between groups of representatives within the legislature) are required for this 'higher intelligence' of co-operation to take hold – just as regard for the benefits of organized co-operation is necessary to get economic group units started.

The 'enlightened self-interest' facilitating co-operation between groups in policy making and executive matters cannot, however, exist in an antagonistic social climate. Undergirding a successful group government is, at one level, the public triumph of the co-operative perspective over the competitive perspective; at a more fundamental level, it is bolstered by settling 'economic questions ... on a co-operative basis, [in which] the industrial exploitation of one class by another is done away and economic freedom realized.'[64]

Group government, delegate democracy, and the 'higher intelligence' of co-operation are all dependent upon one another, but the maximally positive results of their reciprocal dependence do not emerge until some time after the decisive battle between democracy and autocracy has been waged. In the same sense that the young Marx spoke of the period before the supersession of capitalism as the 'pre-history' of humanity, we can say that radical democratic populists saw the period before the epochal confrontation as one of 'pre-democracy.' Only some aspects of a full democratic social and political practice (the 'co-operative commonwealth') could be realized before the transition, just as, for Marx, only some could develop their potential humanity before the transition to socialism.

The State and Technocratic Thought

Radical democratic populism has been best known for its theory of group government. No one has seriously entertained the possibility of group government at the national level since the UFA was politically obliterated in 1935. None the less, the theory has fascinated students of Canadian political thought. This is as it should be. It is the only theory of government that rejected the British parliamentary model and still commanded more than marginal support in a mass democratic movement in Canada. Central to this rejection was a conception of democratic practice that was fundamentally at odds with the only system of political organization – the party system – to become inextricably intertwined with the prevailing state system.

Before discussing the institutional framework and logic of the group government idea, it is best to examine the negative and positive images of the state in radical democratic populism. As we have seen, radical democrats believed that politicians worked with the support of plutocracy and party organizations to subordinate the common people through the various agencies of the state.

Within the UFA leadership and rank and file, this aspect of the state's negative image was taken in two distinct directions. The most widely accepted direction was defined by Henry Wise Wood, in which the state was a necessary evil (except under very special circumstances) because the use of state power – i.e., adoption of the roles of politicians – was inherently at odds with the interests of the people as self-directing agents. Even common people's past efforts to exercise or obtain state power demonstrated the pernicious effects of this 'iron law of statism.' When the state came to be regarded as that institution which could, above all others, determine the public interest, it would undermine democratic citizenship. Only a state form that took its logic from the self-determining organization of legitimate economic interests could avoid this trap.

It would be wrong to see only a *petit bourgeois* perspective and deluded individualism in this dimension of radical democratic populism. As in the crypto-Liberal case, the anti-statist impulse involved co-operatives. For radical democratic populists, however, co-operatives were virtually a metaphor for the type of democratic public institutions that could shoulder the major burden of social and economic organization.

Wood and his UFA constituency expected the practical experience and social philosophy of co-operatives to show the way for democratic organization of other producers' and consumers' groups. The framework for relations between these groups would be a group government deriving its authority from the groups' legitimacy and success. In a much stronger sense than has been asserted by traditional pluralist theories,[65] the anti-statist element in radical democratic populism would be countered with a systematically pluralist state. Only such a pluralism could remove the possibility that the state would subvert or misrepresent the pluralism and interdependence of group interests that structured a co-operative social order.

The other perception of the state as a negative force focused more on the historical experience of 'class government' and less on the idea that the state *per se* was antagonistic to organized citizenship. This nascent social democratic framework was established by the Non-Partisan League and sustained by William Irvine and others who led the UFA into the Co-operative Commonwealth Federation in 1932. The Non-Partisan League's antipathy towards politicians delegitimized the connection between state, politicians, partyism, and plutocracy, without delegitimizing the state as such.

A 'sound business administration,' free from partisan or plutocratic manipulation, would be composed of citizens delegated to decide issues in the interests of the people. This response was the appropriate one to the negative image and practice of the state. Such an administration was necessary because the economic transformations desired by the NPL[66] could be implemented only through positive state action. The non-partisan government was expected to be responsive to its non-plutocratic constituency's demands and interests, but there was no logic of group representation that mapped a pluralized society onto a pluralized legislature, as in Wood's plan. Worries about subordination of democratically organized group interests to those of the state, while present, did not develop into serious anti-statism.

When Irvine and other left-leaning leaders promoted a non-partisan yet interventionist state in the UFA movement, they emphasized Canada's history of 'class government.' Irvine devotes a lengthy section in *The Farmers in Politics* to an overview of class governments in Canada from confederation to 1920. He characterizes the National Policy as the quintessential production of a class-biased state. While contending that the New National Policy was democratic and in the interests of all, he boldly submits that if any class should reap the benefits of state power, it should be the farmers. They were, after all, the most numerous and had suffered most grievously at the hands of Canada's established 'ruling class.'[67] Hence, for this more collectivist element within the UFA, the negative image of the state was shaped primarily by a perception of class legislation and favouritism, not by opposition to the state as a 'false divinity.' This negative image was informed by different assumptions as to what such a state form could or should achieve.

Much of the positive image of the state underpinning the group government theory has been implied above. The positive value of the state would be clearly revealed only in the future. In the short run, organized groups could publicize and support desirable legislation, while demonstrating the regressive nature of political parties. In the long run, group representation would include enough of the legitimate economic classes in the country for the government to operate democratically and efficiently. Wood believed that group government could not function before the forces of democracy triumphed over the forces of plutocracy. The positive image of the state would then reflect successful co-operation between non-exploitively related classes.

The basic lines of the group government proposal were only sketched in by Henry Wise Wood. After 1920, he referred to the proposal in ways that seemed to assume his audience intuitively comprehended its more problematic features. His defence of the proposal usually involved a rapid move to the social-evolutionary and moral basis of the idea of co-operation between groups, or to an attack on the impossibility of democracy and co-operative social relationships in a context of partisan and plutocratic manoeuvring. Even with his quasi-religious social theory and reading of history, Wood had no trouble asserting that economic interest was the motor that turned the social-systemic wheel and powered the vehicle of progress. In 1922, Wood contended that 'economic interests are at the very base of our social structure ... if the relationships between the economic classes can be adjusted in accordance with true social laws of life, other social problems will almost automatically adjust themselves.' He continued:

The immediate problem before us is that of economic class adjustments. These adjustments must be made on the basis of equity and justice ... The value of each industry or occupation must be measured by the value of its service and remunerated accordingly. In making these adjustments each and every *legitimate industry* or occupation must be represented by the highest possible intelligence. There is just one logical hope of getting such a *representation in conference* where these adjustments will be dealt with. Those who control each industry must, through organization, develop capacity to speak with the highest intelligence concerning their own interests or industry. This will be done by the economic class groups.[68]

Powerful economic class groups would not do this, because they were driven by the 'false social law' of competition. They could not provide good service to society or work within the co-operative framework of 'representation in conference.' Wood rules out participation by plutocratic groups in the 'representative conference' in this same article, claiming that 'plutocracy ... will exist and dominate all other social elements so long as our social system is based primarily on competition, [but] could no more exist under a scientifically operated co-operative social system than a fish could live out of water.' Only economic class groups with neither the power to dominate others nor the intention of doing so could participate in this 'representation in conference.' Farmers had progressed farthest in organizing themselves for such representation, and labour was showing signs that it would soon do so.

What did Wood say beyond this? Were group candidates to be elected in non-territorial 'constituencies,' with some form of preferential ballot, by members of that group only? How would cabinet be structured? How would government business be prosecuted, without a government party responsible for the introduction and staged processing of legislation? Was legislation still to be passed on the basis of majority vote within the 'conference'-style government, or was a broader, more demanding consensus among all groups' representatives required? Wood did not offer public answers to any of these questions. Some answers were essayed by Irvine, or other UFA leaders or supporters, but we cannot be sure that Wood would have sanctioned them. None the less, such answers as were provided – most elaborately by Irvine – were consistent with the logic underpinning Wood's exposition of group government principles. Irvine's critique of party and party/plutocracy linkages was more effective, concrete, and less self-righteous than Wood's. His activities in the labour movement, as a muck-raking journalist and as a crusading political activist, gave him the feeling that a strong case had to be made for the group theory outside the farmers' movement. *The Farmers in Politics* was intended to bolster the existing forces of organized farmers, and to recommend delegate democracy, group organization, and group government to labour, progressive intellectuals, and farmers outside of Alberta.

Irvine sets the problem encountered by progressive political forces in these terms: 'The mission of the United Farmers and of all organized workers is simply to construct a repository for the new spirit of justice. To pour the new wine of co-operation into the old, dried-skin bottles of cut-throat competition, or, if you prefer, to pour the new wine of political democracy into the old bottles of party politics, is, in either case, to lose the new wine.'[69]

The 'new spirit of justice' had already found two conduits in the organized farmers' and organized labour movements, but no socially representative state 'repository' had yet been created. For Irvine, Canadian government could not continue indefinitely to be mismatched with the dynamic of the social economy. According to Irvine, 'Governments take their forms from the economic basis upon which they rest, and for which they function ... the plutocratic oligarchies of the United States and Canada are the natural outgrowth of an era based on industrial individualism, and as these earlier forms of the state have been the reflex of the societies of the time, so also must the governments of tomorrow be re-shaped to correspond to the industrial democracy which is now in the process of being established.'[70]

Irvine's optimism shows here, but his sense of the necessary socio-economic basis of group government is clearer than Wood's. Irvine presented group government as a logical political outgrowth of the social stratification engendered by industrial capitalism. Because 'industrial classes know less of each other's requirements than they did in the less complicated society,'[71] the state could treat them democratically only through guaranteed, functionally defined representation.

Irvine realized that the case for group government had to be made along less 'deterministic' lines to be attractive to liberal-democratic pluralists, the *sine qua non* of any viable North American political thought. The group 'system' might seem to impose too rigid a set of guide-lines on free exchange of ideas within each group organization, because it required committed representation of common interests. Irvine argued that the group system would entail such representation, but that intragroup pluralism would ensure greater freedom of expression and variety of perspective with an interest-based focus. As he put it, 'if our nation is to be veritable factory of ideas, people of many different thoughts must be able to unite; ... by the interplay of different minds, a creative social thought becomes possible, and every individual becomes a part creator.'[72]

Irvine was confident that a heightened awareness would assist all organized groups in their fight for economic justice. Each group would benefit from its own and others' appreciation of their economic interdependence. While such advances by industrial classes would yield positive results even in the absence of a 'representation in conference,' the full benefits of group organization could emerge only with a correspondence between socio-economic organization and state forms.

In *The Farmers in Politics*, Irvine briefly indicates what this proposal might be profitably compared with. He mentions two revolutionary 'group proposals,' syndicalism and that of the 'Bolsheviki,' only to pronounce them severely flawed. Syndicalism has the virtue of being based on 'group formation,' but leads to anarchy by preaching 'the abolition of the State,' and neglects to make provision for 'the unification of the syndicates so as to regulate the interlocking and common interests of all.' The Bolshevik plan grants too little rather than too much autonomy to the 'industries and professions,' because 'rigid state control,' culminating in dictatorship, centralizes the industrial system to the point that it 'becomes a bureaucracy which may in time become as intolerable as private ownership under Czarism.' Each 'group system' has debilitating inadequacies because neither 'has followed the natural co-operation which underlies the group organization.'[73]

By contrast, the guild socialist system was a 'group system which is, perhaps, the sanest and most practical of all European theories of social improvement,' by attempting a 'synthesis between the anarchy of Bakunin and the bureaucracy of Marx.'[74] 'The guild is to have democratic control of the industry, but according to guild socialism there must also be a central control or state for the supervision of all industries for the common good, and to prevent strife arising between one industry and another. But this central body, or parliament, is to be elected in a manner similar to that in vogue at the present time. This is the weak spot in guild socialism. The parliament should be the elected representatives of the various guilds, and thus preserve he opinions, and represent the interests, of each democratic unit in the state.'

Irvine argues that the UFA's scheme was superior to these three group proposals: 'The industrial group system as taught by the United Farmers of Canada implies all the good points of the systems reviewed, and none of their weaknesses or errors ... As an industrial organization the farmers' movement will direct and control its own affairs as an industry, allowing the same privilege to all other groups, but it insists that representatives of organized industries shall compose the parliament. The key to the political philosophy of the United Farmers is co-operation. The co-operation which brought individuals together in a group must be applied between the groups, until the highest form of co-operation is reached, namely, a fully organized co-operative State.[75]

This account of guild socialism on the matter of parliamentary composition is significantly but understandably mistaken. However, by endorsing the guild plan with only one qualification, Irvine implicitly tells us a good deal about his preferred group government option. Most important, he implies that the most crucial pre-condition of the 'fully organized co-operative state' is the supersession of the capitalist economy. For Irvine, as for G.D.H. Cole, this would involve 'self-government in industry,' via state-sponsored socialized control and co-operative enterprises.

Irvine also marshalled a pragmatic argument in favour of group government. Since all reasonable people could see that economic interests are the basis of all serious divisions, why not make the most of this, by granting full political legitimacy to the organizations working on this basis? This would mean arranging their political interaction through the medium of the state in a way that recognizes the overwhelming fact of economic interest. Once recognized and accommodated in the structures of state representation, such interests could be honestly portrayed. They would rely on the glare of public scrutiny, and the push of enlightened self-interest, to supplement the higher rationality of co-operation in their search for legislative solutions to intergroup problems.

This understanding of the group-based state receives little elaboration in Irvine's writings. But he does offer a suggestive analogy between the logic of the interdependence of labour and expertise in the modern industrial economy and the logic of functionally divided yet interdependent representation of economic group interests in government.

While one group cannot get along without the others, yet they know little of each other's immediate needs. Miners do not understand the needs of store clerks, farmers do not understand those of wage workers, wage workers those of professional people, and so on. But the laws that govern the lives of all these people are made without consulting a single group apart – no member of which is in contact with any other group.

[Parties and their candidates] to be successful, must find an issue that is on the surface of things, that everybody knows about ... [as a consequence] party majorities ... make no provision for expressing, and have not themselves the means of expressing the specialized intelligence developed through specialization in industry ... party governments invariably represent the lowest intelligence of the nation. The intelligence of an industrial unit is infinitely higher than that which any individual may have respecting all the groups.

He then proposes a solution to this state of affairs:

Science, applied to industry, has led to the division of labour, and specialization; this in turn has led to industrial group organization based on particular group interests; these groups are seeking representation in parliaments; and once they get to parliament the two party system becomes inoperative, and some form of group government is necessary. In this way the party system will pass away, and a new form more suitable to modern conditions inevitably replace it.

Every industrial group to-day knows that it cannot live by itself. If one group were to secure political power and use that power to the detriment of any other group, it would ultimately kill itself. Farmers cannot live without coal miners, city dwellers without railroad workers, nor industrial workers without farmers. Each depends on all, and all depend on each. This social unity is not overlooked by group politics. And surely when the various groups are necessary to the lives of all, all ought to be represented in that parliament which deals with their common life, so that *in bringing to the service of the nation the best knowledge from every group*, they may be able, co-operatively, to arrive at the highest justice.[76]

Interdependence within the modern 'social organism' is sufficiently finely tuned that no one group could benefit (over the long run) by trying to rearrange the interdependent relations to its advantage. It is hard to reconcile this contention with Irvine's belief that Canada had a 'ruling class' using government to do precisely this. One can say only that Irvine wished to demonstrate the ultimate necessity of 'fitting' modern political forms with modern economic forms. If people believed that the new society/state relationships were required by 'social laws' and guaranteed to yield 'the highest justice,' a large part of the debate would be won. Irvine supplements this rather formalistic argument later in *The Farmers in Politics* by suggesting how group selfishness assists the resolution of intergroup conflicts, and rules out class rule and class legislation:

that group representation will lead to co-operation instead of class rule is obvious. Suppose that there are three classes represented in parliament, the Farmers, the industrial workers, and the commercial interests. There will be other classes ultimately, but these three classes already are factors to be reckoned with. Well, we will suppose each class to be selfish and to want more than its share. When one of them attempts out of all reason to legislate for itself, ... the other two classes will combine to prevent the legislation of the first class from becoming operative. The only check on the selfishness of the one class is the selfishness of the other class. Thus the competition that had hitherto taken place between individuals will take place between groups, and will lead to a higher order of co-operation ... the experience already common on the lower planes of [intragroup] co-operation will be sufficient to warrant the adoption of a higher co-operation among the groups.[77]

The positive case for group government could not rest on these foundations. Because such a heavy burden was borne by the functional dimension in the case for group government, the policy-making and conflict-resolving virtues of functional representation had to be addressed. It is at this point that a tension between participatory-democratic practices and technocratic assumptions emerges in the group government 'system.'

Irvine's *The Farmers in Politics* presents functional specialization and interdependence of the economy as the basis of a scientific political organization. Modern economic activity and problems resulted from the natural operation of 'economic laws.' Resolution of these problems, then, would involve working with rather than against such laws. 'Things would be very different if in Canada,' he says, 'if people understood the economic laws that are at work, and if the nation were organized in conscious co-operation with these laws, instead of blindly running in the very face of them.'[78]

These references to 'natural laws' of economic and social development were not just rhetorical devices designed to ensure audience approval. Like Wood, Irvine felt that representation based on functionally defined group organization was the sole scientific basis of good relations between an interdependent civil society and a welfare-maximizing state. In *Co-operative Government*, Irvine sets the problem from the state's perspective: 'It is the business of government to see that all the essential functions of society are performed and that due regard is given to their interdependence.' Party politicians and governments either misunderstood or ignored these distinctive functional interests, thus producing serious conflicts. Group politics would 'admit the existence of economic differences, but while admitting them would, at the same time, face and solve them.'[79]

Organized farmers who had taken the step into political competition had recognized this need to resolve differences by affirming that 'economic and political questions are inseparable, [and that] politics ... is but the direction of economic affairs.' By 1929, Irvine believed 'functional group interdependence' had begun to manifest itself politically, even in parliamentary representation, to the point that 'a new form of government cannot be infinitely delayed.' Economic groups, he claimed, 'are contending for a co-operative system of government which will correspond to the interdependence of our economic life today as the bi-party system did to the competitive system brought about by the industrial revolution.'[80]

What can be said about the operation of such a government? We have seen that group representatives were to be instructed and responsive delegates. Their experience in co-operatively establishing group policies would enhance their ability to forge mutually acceptable policies with other group representatives. As products of mature functional organizations that understood group needs, interests, and activities in an interdependent industrial system, delegates to the group parliament would express the 'highest intelligence of the groups.' In this sense, they would have successfully solved what Irvine calls 'the democratic problem,' namely, organization that facilitates 'a knowledge of the responsibilities of citizenship.'[81] The democratic problem is thus defined to reconcile popular democratic control of political and economic activity with the need for expert direction of the state by group representatives and technical support staff. In the absence of efficient,[82] scientifically ordained, and popular-democratic organization, the democratic problem would be unresolvable. Functional organization permits its solution.

Irvine attempts to clarify the political implications of this functional logic in *Co-operative Government*. He says:

Governments have no business to govern people. People, on the other hand, must learn to govern governments. It is the highest function of a government to apply intelligence to the 'things' which affect the life and happiness of the people, to the end that human beings may be less and less hampered by governments ... The various functions of social and economic life are all interrelated and interdependent. A government ... must be in possession of all the facts in relation to each function. The best and easiest way to obtain the required information is to obtain it from those engaged in the performance of the function. A Parliament composed of representatives on a functional basis would be in possession of all the expert economic knowledge available with respect to the various functions. If it is agreed that representation of each functional group is a just and sound basis for government, then some way must be found by which each group may obtain adequate representation.[83]

Here, Irvine addresses a problem that Wood identifies only vaguely: how can the need for popularly controlled representation of distinctive 'class' needs and concerns be reconciled with an efficient and co-operative resolution of policy questions? The latter part of the 'formula' should be understood for what radical democratic populists saw it as: a scientific method for government policy planning and implementation. We can pose the problem simply: how can pluralistic, popular democracy be reconciled with a scientific state?

The answer was to make popular democracy and the scientific state necessary conditions of each other. Only popular democracy within the economic groups could satisfy democracy's moral requirement of political self-determination, while facilitating emergence of the 'highest intelligence' of groups in the social economy. Only popular democracy extended through delegated group representation could guarantee a state structure fully responsive to the needs and interests of all significant groups. At the same time, only a 'scientific' state structure could produce policies that fulfilled the potential of popular democracy.

The rationality and legitimacy of both state and organized political activity would thus be complete. Organized group politics would not make sense unless it 'produced' representatives articulating the most well-informed contributions to policy-making. The co-operative, plural-group state would not make sense unless it provided democratic group organizations with clear practical incentives to make expert contributions to state policy-making. The logic of linkage between democratic group politics and the co-operative group government was functional-democratic. Group representation was democratic because the process was highly participatory and responsive. Group representatives were, in a sense, also technocrats, because they articulated expert positions on matters of public policy in a legislative environment where crudely political considerations had no place.

The idea that political considerations would play a much smaller role in group government than in party government is perhaps the most striking element in the group government rationale. Of its presuppositions,[84] perhaps the most crucial is that politics has heretofore entailed domination of unorganized classes by powerful, organized classes. With a state structure premised on a rejection of class domination, the links between organized group activities and group government will be solid. Politics would then involve open and informed representation, instead of closed and manipulative representation for the purpose of achieving domination. The processes of policy formulation and group conflict resolution could become much less political, in the older sense of the term.

The group government scheme may seem to have been designed to produce the same results as policy development by a 'representative bureaucracy.' Group delegates' intimate knowledge of economic activities and needs, combined with a spirit of co-operation, would produce a higher rationality that elevates policy contributions above the sectional environments from which they came. But the difference between models of representative bureaucracy and the group government model is crucial. Expert group representatives' contributions to the policy process would necessarily be accurate reflections of their groups' 'highest intelligence' and vital interests. This would be guaranteed by the inherent safeguards of delegated representation.

Representative bureaucracy, as commonly conceived, provides no guarantee that representatives would not be co-opted by the logic of state-bureaucratic policy formation, which easily becomes manipulative of specific group interests. Representative bureaucracy could easily lead to a corporate state where group representatives came to identify more with the state (as rational planner) than with their respective groups (as equal participants in a responsive and rational planning process). At least in theory, delegate democracy would prevent the elevation of the state to the status of a distinct 'class' or social force with interests detached from, and eventually opposed to, those of the groups in co-operation.

The group government scenario placed a very heavy burden on delegate democracy and the almost mystical spirit of co-operation. Would members of group organizations continue to direct, advise, and scrutinize their representatives if the group government were accorded decisive powers of policy formulation? Popular faith in the rationality of the new state had been a *sine qua non* of optimal group organization. Could it not become an obstacle to active and informed delegate democracy, once group government got on its feet? The logic of the 'popular technocratic' group government theory is tight and very dependent on assumptions about a transformed politics and group behaviour. A tension between democratic and technocratic direction of public policy was bound to emerge. Which orientation would begin to overshadow the other, and why?

Irvine indicates the likely source of the tension without realizing he has demonstrated the problematic assumptions on which the democracy/technocracy relation is based. A chapter in *Co-operative Government* entitled 'The Need for Science in Government' includes an argument for a 'greatly extended' and much more influential Bureau of Statistics, which would obtain all facts relating to every phase of national life, as well as all facts in relation to the important economic, political and social experiences of other countries; assist in forming a national policy based on those facts; and conduct proper experiments with new proposals and policies.'[85]

He goes on to suggest that, ideally, 'the Bureau might be expected not only to aid but to give the final word on national policy,' and that 'a much greater degree of accuracy than is now possible [in the "science of politics"] could be reached were government policy determined by a national bureau of expert sociologists.' For Irvine in 1929, there was no question that 'when all available facts have thus been impartially collected, the facts should be allowed to tell their own story as regards their application to future policy.' Their import and implications would be clear to all rational individuals with a capacity to transcend the confines and categories of partisan politics.

This argument does not even hint at the problems that its logic would raise for delegate democracy. What would become of the group representatives and their role as providers of 'all the expert economic knowledge available with respect to the various functions'? Irvine proposes to reduce them to 'a dozen or two of the best informed men and women from the various functional groups of the country,' to achieve a more efficiently operating government. And what of these representatives? When proposing permanent heads for government departments, Irvine argues that 'representatives of democratically-organized functional groups, co-operating with each other and directly responsible to the people electing them, would constitute a Parliament supreme over all administrators. Such a Parliament would be forced to engage the best administrators to be found in the country, and to hold them responsible for their several departments ... the country would gain by the experience which years of service would bring to its administrative staff, and would be saved from the possibility of the perpetual incompetence which the party system makes inevitable '[86]

This proposal's attractiveness comes from the added expertise and administrative efficiency of the state. The population of group constituencies might benefit from better and more consistent policies, but not because delegate responsiveness to group demands and claims had increased. Irvine's assurance of a 'Parliament Supreme over all administrators' here is merely a formal promise. Standards for judging the performance of administrators have been detached from specific group perspectives, which may conflict, and defined instead in terms of objective 'facts' that are collected by government social scientists. In telling 'their own story,' these facts are beyond politics – not even easily disputed by 'alternative experts.' Their correct policy implications are not arguable.

Regardless of what the highest intelligence of group organizations has to say on policy matters, their representatives must defer when group proposals are inconsistent with the facts. In placing the standards of assessment for policy and administration beyond politics, Irvine undermines many potential contributions of popular democracy in group politics. It takes no great insight to see that popular democracy is subordinated in the policy process when the standards of policy choice are derived from a socially detached realm of facts.

Facts (and compilers of facts) that are ascribed this power are the trademarks of the technocratic perspective in modern politics.

Irvine did not develop the technocratic logic of the group government theory with a conscious desire to subvert popular democracy. Nor should his relatively undeveloped thoughts on the role of social scientists and officials be taken as representative of rank-and-file radical democratic populists. Their distaste for a politics detached from their needs and experiences, and their support for co-operatives and other locally controlled institutions, would have prevented acceptance of Irvine's technocratic proposals. However, the direction Irvine takes the group government theory does suggest that it contained several questionable assumptions about rational resolution of intergroup conflicts and social problems. Delegitimation of politics and elevation of social scientific rationality in the group system exacts a price from the participatory democracy that offers its *raison d'être*.

Betke's study of the UFA government and organization indicates the effect that even a partial presumption of the priority of government expertise can have on its electoral supporters. He argues that UFA organization locals began to defer to their governments' policy decisions only several years after they took office, and continued to avoid making potentially controversial demands until economic catastrophe struck in the early 1930s. There were many first-term attempts by UFA activists to persuade their government to adopt radical credit, banking, and group government policies. Failures to elicit favourable government responses to many of these took their toll. Betke claims that the organization, in effect, 'conceded to the government superior wisdom and therefore the right to make decisions for the agricultural future of Alberta.'[87]

One could counter this bleak picture by arguing that the annual convention continued through these years to keep the UFA government relatively responsive to its electoral base, or that the basis for a proper group government did not exist in Alberta during the UFA regime. The rapidly developed preference for government expertise over popular organizational proposals should, consequently, not be taken as a repudiation of the functionalist democratic logic posited by Irvine. However, it is significant that in the one area where activists' proposals might be expected to be considered authoritative – agriculture – the government denied their merits. The UFA government brought its members to grudgingly accept the superior status of supra-organizational 'expert' advice. This should have been a sobering lesson for Irvine and others who sought a reconciliation of functionally co-ordinated participatory democracy with technocratic policy direction.

Political and State Reform before the Triumph of Democracy

Our emphasis on radical democratic populists' rejection of the prevailing political process may have created the mistaken impression that they had no political objectives short of apocalyptic change. However, several of their objectives did not necessarily involve the processes of delegate democracy. They included eliminating party patronage in government administration, passing direct-legislation statutes in federal and provincial legislatures, freeing elected representatives from various constraints of party solidarity and cabinet government, and promoting true citizenship through enhanced public education.

An important common denominator of anti-party sentiment in the West was opposition to party patronage. Crypto-Liberals focused on this to the point of obsession, and targeted federal much more than provincial governments. Radical democratic populists saw partyism, plutocracy, and patronage as indivisible, and their elimination almost an all-or-nothing matter. The UFA administration quickly eliminated most serious cases of patronage in their provincial administration while, in Saskatchewan, Liberal patronage became the stuff of legend.

The state was also expected to ensure honest and responsive administration by accommodating the various measures of direct legislation. The second item in the UFA's 1921 'Reconstructive Legislative Program' endorsed 'the principle of the initiative, referendum, and recall.' However, the UFA government attached a low priority to this endorsement, leaving the 1920 provincial Liberal legislation in this area intact. UFA locals placed little pressure on the UFA government to strengthen this legislation. The achievement of group representation by Alberta farmers made such reform seem less pressing, and the courts would have stopped them after the Manitoba ruling. In any case, the theory of delegate democracy and group government virtually eliminated the rationale behind direct-legislation proposals.[88]

The expectations created by the UFA's anti-party, pro-delegate democracy crusade were significant for the movement's short- and long-term objectives for state action. To take the provincial case, the first legislature involved pitched and even public battles between a traditional cabinet and back-benchers enthusiastic about their new delegate-representative functions. Their organization had promised during the campaign 'that no government be considered defeated except by a direct vote of want of confidence.' Many freshmen MLAs believed that this promise could be at least partially implemented. This expectation led to some rather unusual legislative scenes, when Cabinet introduced legislation without any assurance of support by all thirty-eight UFA MLAs. After one year, the cabinet convinced back-bench

MLAs that their veto power over any cabinet-favoured legislation eliminated the need to embarrass the government and the movement. This was as close as the UFA government came to implementing the non-confidence promise.

One of the many reasons for William Irvine's reputation as an unorthodox parliamentarian was his stubborn advocacy of the non-confidence voting principle in the House of Commons. Irvine spoke in support of such a change in parliamentary procedure in *The Farmers in Politics*, in his first parliamentary speech,[89] and sporadically until 1935. He presented it as a major step towards unshackling representatives of 'the people' from the manacles of 'partyism.' Irvine recognized more clearly than did early UFA MLAs that the reform could only partly assist the rise of independent, occupationally representative groups in legislative assemblies. In this campaign, Irvine had the support of most Progressive, Labour, and UFA MPs during the 1920s.[90]

We have already seen that radical democratic populists emphasized citizenship education in their reform campaign. On the left of the UFA, Irvine spoke regularly of education and the new social order. H.W. Wood's convention speeches presented a more conservative approach, which accorded greater educational responsibility to co-operatives. Both preached the necessity of making education and community cultural forms into instruments of democracy. Only in this way would citizenship meet the demanding participatory criteria of delegate democracy and group politics.

The UFA organization did much more to facilitate this political education than the UFA government. While university extension courses and a stronger public secondary school system emerged during the UFA tenure in office, the government's educational achievements were not exceptional by the standards of prairie provincial governments. UFA convention resolutions in the 1930s urged teaching of co-operation rather than competition in public schools. These met with some sympathy but no substantial response in financially and politically precarious years.

By contrast, the UFA's official organ took its educational duties quite seriously. *The UFA* kept the scattered locals informed of one another's activities, and presented editorial comment, special articles, and columns that were generally ahead of rank-and-file opinion. This was especially true of early 1920s and 1930s coverage of Social Credit monetary and credit theory, and of sympathetic coverage of the CCF from 1932 to 1935. *The UFA* was crucial to development of a 'movement culture' and political discourse within radical democratic populism, thereby promoting the radical democratic ideal of citizenship.

In Saskatchewan, *The Western Producer* went some distance in performing this movement-building function between 1923 and 1931. It injected sympathetic accounts of delegate democracy and group government into an environment where the populist competition was rapidly polarizing into crypto-Liberal and social democratic camps. Lacking an institutional vehicle, radical democratic populism could not develop an independent base in this province. As we shall see, however, something akin to the radical democratic conception of citizenship was fostered in Saskatchewan through co-operatives' and social democratic organizations' emphasis on political participation.

Superficially, radical democratic populist demands for minor reforms of state process and practice resembled those of crypto-Liberals. However, crypto-Liberal attacks on patronage and calls for honesty in public life were not connected logically to a root-and-branch critique of partyism, or to an account of the dynamic within which patronage was embedded. For all of its pseudo-scientific baggage and unrealistic expectations concerning a non-partisan state, the radical democratic position on this matter was at least part of a more systematic whole. The same can be said for their belief that the state was obliged to promote a more complete citizenship via enhanced educational opportunities. This fits nicely into the logic of participation and representation developed within radical democratic populism. By contrast, improvement of education and citizenship in crypto-Liberal circles lacked distinctive criteria for assessment. No alternative proposal for political representation and decision-making depended on systematic changes in this area. Thus despite financial support for 'educational grants' to provincial organizations within the United Grain Growers, and similar expenditures within the grain growers' organizations of Saskatchewan and Alberta, the task of popular education on matters of political reform seemed less compelling to crypto-Liberal leaders.

Of the political reforms mentioned, measures for direct legislation were promoted more aggressively by crypto-Liberals. Yet this also demonstrates the weak co-ordinating political logic in crypto-Liberalism. The crypto-Liberal demand for initiative, referendum, and recall statutes proposed supplements to existing mechanisms of policy choice and electoral direction. It offered no alternative representative structure to alter the relationships between organized civil society and state structures. Direct legislation, once facilitated, says nothing about the process of bargaining or relations of power among contending social forces, and says nothing substantive (rather than simply procedural) about balancing social forces' interests. Radical democratic theory speaks to both of these key issues, since it is based on a social theory rejecting existing class relations and calls for alternative political forms to alter them. We may not see a logical connection between the critique of plutocracy and the group government proposal, but there is no doubt that Wood, Irvine, and other UFA activists did.

Radical democratic populists' short-term economic demands were not substantially different from those of more mainstream prairie populists. Most radical democratic populists whole-heartedly endorsed the crypto-Liberal critique of the National Policy, and promoted the CCA's New National Policy. William Irvine insisted on the democratic character of each reform advocated in the farmers' platform[91] in an attempt to refute the Liberal and Conservative arguments concerning the farmers' organizations' desire for 'class legislation.' Characteristically, Irvine linked the farmers' demands to a critique of the existing configuration of political and class power. Radical democrats also joined crypto-Liberals in calling for state support for co-operatives. The UFA had originated as a typical prairie grain growers' association, concerned with farmer control over grain marketing and related commercial activities. These were to redress the imbalance created by financial, transportation, commercial, and grain-trade monopolies. Eventually the UFA saw the Wheat Pool as a further advantage for grain growers.

Enthusiasm for the pooling crusade has been widely recognized as contributing to the decline in support for direct 'political action' in all three prairie provinces. Where group-oriented and self-directed development of economic power was not distinguished from the larger area of group politics, such economic activity was not seen as detrimental to direct political activity. The group's interests, political and other, were seen to be enhanced by the successes of the pooling movement. When grain grower pressure on the federal government to establish a prairie-wide pool was unsuccessful, Alberta farmers turned to a receptive provincial administration to clear the path for a provincial pool. The Alberta Wheat Pool was created in 1923, and in 1928 the UFA government did much to promote co-operative ventures and agencies of co-ordination for agricultural marketing and consumer co-operatives.[92] Radical democrats thus did not hesitate to request support for co-operative institutions from sympathetic governments; their distrust of the state did not render them politically naïve or economically self-defeating.

Non-Partisan Leaguers showed considerably less antipathy towards and distrust of the state *per se* than did Wood. Irvine and other NPL leaders advocated provincial ownership of banks, grain elevators, major transportation and communication companies, agricultural-product processing industries, power utilities, and key natural-resource industries. They argued that accountable public monopolies were required for farmers to prosper through their co-operative and individual agricultural enterprises. Social ownership would minimize disadvantages farmers faced from private monopolies' influence over terms of trade. The NPL did much to increase UFA rank-and-file support for an interventionist state.[93]

Support for the Douglas Social Credit doctrine and panaceas was widespread among UFA members. However, President Wood and the UFA cabinet were unalterably opposed to credit-reform proposals long before it was clear that they could not be implemented provincially. These leaders were all fiscal conservatives who could not sanction stimulative budget deficits. Nor did the cabinet's wish to maintain good relations with outside financial institutions incline them to attack the banks as the central villain in the farmers' plight. It is also true that Wood's past experiences in the American Midwest made him suspicious of 'Greenback' or 'Free Silver' surrogates that might distract farmers' attention away from class organization, co-operative development, and education.

Wood's economic philosophy was a combination of free-trade liberalism and moral injunctions against destructive competition. This contradictory combination left little room for an economic doctrine appearing to require substantial state control over the conditions and relations of trade. Social credit doctrines were attractive to radical democratic populists less taken with the prevailing liberal economic philosophy, or less worried about the state as a democratically pre-emptive force. In Alberta, Norman Priestly, Norman Smith, George Bevington, and federal MPs George Coote, Henry Spencer, and E.J. Garland were outspoken advocates of social credit doctrine. William Irvine led the UFA left wing's social credit proselytizing as early as 1921,[94] and continued until 1937.

Social credit policies were attractive to this group for a variety of reasons. Belief in the necessity of state action to establish 'right relations of trade' between economic groups opened the door to the appeal of the underconsumptionist, inflationary social credit doctrines. This was especially true in the absence of any well-developed left-wing plans for assisting debtor grain growers. Widespread support for social credit (and other underconsumptionist) doctrines in Independent Labour Party and Labour circles in Britain during the 1920s and early 1930s[95] gave social credit doctrine an aura of legitimacy for the UFA's left wing, with its influential group of displaced British socialists.

For Irvine and his associates, public control of banking, money, and credit was seen as the *sine qua non* of a democratic economic life. One did not have to be a nascent social democrat to find the social credit doctrine attractive. It promised 'just prices,' a fair return to labour, an end to financiers' extortions, transition to an era of abundance, and community control of credit. All of these linked quite naturally with the radical democratic vision of a social economy where no classes exploited 'the people,' thus allowing local control over economic life.

Enthusiasm for social credit policies within the UFA peaked in the early 1920s and once again in the early to mid-1930s. Social credit advocacy was showcased in 1922 and 1923 UFA annual conventions, with calls for a provincial bank and easy agricultural credit, and in the 1923 House of Commons Banking and Finance Committee review of the Bank Act. The latter featured Irvine, Spencer, and other UFA MPs grilling Canadian banking magnates, and asking leading questions of 'Major' C.H. Douglas and several other unorthodox credit theorists imported for the occasion. The enthusiasm displayed for social credit analysis and remedies in Irvine's initial parliamentary speech was still evident in *Co-operative Government*, where he presented social credit as a transitional instrument in development of the 'co-operative commonwealth.' 'The New Economics' (chapter 7) is presented as the logical complement of groups' democratic and policy-creating abilities. The whole book is much more technocratic than *The Farmers in Politics*. We can assume that a decade beginning with real promise and ending with set-backs for organized 'progressive' politics, coupled with an increasing obsession with social credit solutions, largely accounts for this change.[96]

Alberta farmers' interest in social credit nostrums grew rapidly with the onset of the Depression. By 1933 UFA locals and the annual convention pressed their government to translate social credit theory into practice. Earlier than this, however, *UFA* editorials and feature articles presented social credit policies as integral to the UFA's agenda. After 1931, increasingly strong attacks on capitalism and promotion of 'the co-operative commonwealth' were combined with support for vaguely defined social credit policies. They were presented as weapons to be deployed against a decaying but none the less destructive capitalism. Their value for the UFA membership was proclaimed in the same selective and cautious way that socialist ideas were integrated into 'the people's' battle. *The UFA* finally could not convince Alberta voters that social credit policies made sense only as part of a larger transformative policy package. However, articulation of social credit ideas in conjunction with those of group government, 'radical democracy,' co-operation, and CCF-style socialism indicates that radical democratic populism could be quite accommodating on questions of state economic policy.

Co-operation and the Good Society

Co-operation is the true social law, and a true social system must be founded primarily on that law. – H.W. Wood, 1922

The key to the political philosophy of the United Farmers is co-operation ... It is in the expectation of bringing about a truly co-operative commonwealth that the farmers are entering politics as a group. – William Irvine, 1920

Three ideas of co-operation informed radical democratic visions of the good society. Most simply and generally, co-operation was portrayed as the 'true social law,' a historically inevitable but none the less moral principle of human intercourse. Co-operation was also seen as a key dimension of economic relations preventing interclass exploitation while allowing for individual ownership of agricultural land. Finally, co-operation was presented as a means of establishing first a countervailing, then a victorious, political power in relation to the foes of 'the people.'

Logically, the radical democratic good society was not merely the sum of these three dimensions of co-operation. It presupposed much about human nature, and about desirable relationships between and within civil society and the state. These relationships cannot be implied directly from ideas about co-operation. The notion of co-operation as the true social law bound together ideas of economic and political class action, by enjoining political co-ordination of 'the people,' justifying delegate democracy as the expression of co-operating group intelligence, and providing the moral basis for group government. UFA speakers all made co-operation the centre-piece of UFA activity and inspirational power.

Henry Wise Wood located co-operation in the UFA social philosophy with a simplistic but compelling dialectic in a theory of social evolution. He presented this theory concisely in an article that ran in the first four issues of *The UFA*:

True and False Social Laws
It is interesting to study the effect of the operation of the laws of competition and co-operation upon each other in social development. Competition is the false social law, and no social system based primarily on this law can ever reach perfection. Co-operation is the true social law, and a true social system must be founded primarily on that law.

All past social progress has been founded primarily on the law of competition, but the law of co-operation has been operating secondarily. These laws are ever acting and reacting upon each other, the destructiveness of competition forcing co-operation to higher development, and this in turn increasing the destructiveness of competition. Competition is the law of destruction, and all the destruction that has ever been wrought by man against his fellow man has been wrought by competition. All construction of social strength has been done by co-operation. By co-operation men have built nations, by competition these nations have destroyed each other ...

Practically all the strength that has been developed in the past through co-operation has been used for competitive purposes. This will continue to be so as long as our social system is based primarily on the law of competition instead of co-operation. As soon as we begin to develop co-operation for co-operation's sake, realizing that it is the true law, we will begin to force our social system from the basis of competition to that of co-operation. Then will begin the real test of the ability of the human race to become truly civilized.[97]

Wood portrays a general social antagonism between competition, Mammon, organized plutocracy, and partyism on the one hand, and co-operation, God, organized democracy ('the people' organized into groups), and group government on the other. Co-operation will guide organized democracy in its quest for justice and human fulfilment.

Wood returned to this theme repeatedly during the next nine years. In 1929, he stated that 'co-operation is the true law of life and only hope of humanity, and it must be developed to perfection.' Speaking to the Alberta Institute of Co-operation, he argued that 'when we accept co-operation as the true guiding principle of life's activities, it follows logically that it should be applied to all of those activities.' On a slightly different note, Wood spoke in 1922 of co-operation as 'a method, embracing order, system, law and spirit ... that must be systematically and scientifically developed.' As the UFA moved from local to provincial group levels of co-operation, the 'larger unit will be much stronger and have much more capacity for co-operating with other like groups.'[98]

Wood portrayed co-operation as a 'natural law' that had guided some human action to date, and would eventually come to prevail, with the appropriate 'scientific' assistance from good democrats. Co-operation was not simply one of several social philosophies to be applied to social relations: it was ordained to be, and scientifically predictable as, the organizing principle of civilized life. A democratic theory that was scientific and in concert with a higher spiritual design would implant the principle of co-operation at its very core.

Reference to natural law as justification for political reform had deep roots in both British and American radicalism,[99] and appears to be directly related to what Ramsay Cook has identified as the tendency to replace theology with Christian social science in the reform movements in late–nineteenth-century North America. This strategy associated such reform with divine purposes and the scientifically discoverable 'nature of things.'

One cannot avoid noting the connections between co-operation as described thus far, and the various social-gospel currents influencing prairie Canada at this time. Wood traded heavily on a set of virtually apocalyptic themes in his presentation of the UFA message on co-operation. His association with the Cambellite sect in Missouri, and the millenarian touch that this gave his social theory, put him outside of the Protestant mainstream of Canadian social gospel. This by no means rendered his message suspect in Alberta, with its many non-mainstream Protestant sect members.[100]

Closer to the social-gospel mainstream were two other UFA spokespersons, William Irvine and Irene Parlby. Irvine was well known as a student of Salem Bland, perhaps the most influential voice in Canadian social-gospel circles at this time. In his political journal from 1916 to 1920, Irvine spoke continuously about 'the new social order' that would follow the Great War, and regularly ran columns on related themes by both Bland and J.S. Woodsworth. All three men championed the spirit and practice of co-operation among prairie grain growers. Salem Bland contributed a preface to *The Farmers in Politics*, offering fulsome praise: 'I question if any more constructive and distinctively Canadian contribution has yet been thrown into the discussion of our national problems.'[101]

Irvine's text begins with a section on 'the New Social Ethics,' in which he argues that many Canadians, 'in the midst of economic oppression,' finally recognize the connection between obsessive money-making and immorality. They could thus see the need for a new ethics of 'brotherhood extended to all practical affairs. Co-operation is but another aspect of the same thing.'[102] The section identifies those social forces that are carrying the new message and struggle to the public realm: 'to the agrarian worker in his environment of honest toil, and to the awakened worker of the industrial system in our cities, we look for the new measures and the new men which our times demand.' Irvine argues that the 'new social order' required wholesale changes in political leadership: 'Those who were most efficient in individualism will be, for that very reason, the most inefficient under co-operation. Most of our leaders in industry, religion, education, and government, are not qualified for leadership in a new social order ... Objectionable as it may seem to some, the new leaders are coming from the ranks of those who have been up till now "the despised and rejected of men." The agrarian and industrial organizations are the Nazareth from which are coming the prophets of a new day.'[103]

Irvine spells out the particular role that Canada's organized farmers would play in post-war reconstruction:

The farmers are in a position to do great national service, not only because they awoke to consciousness in the midst of a changing world, but also because their aims are synthetic. Although fathered by oppression, the farmers' movement has escaped that bitterness of feeling against capital, and that extreme rashness both of expression and action, so characteristic of labour. The farmer ... is both capitalist and labourer. He knows that production is not furthered when war is going on between the two. He sees, also the hopeless deadlock between organized capital and organized labour in the world of industry and commerce, and is thus led to the discovery of co-operation as the synthesis without which progress cannot be made. In this way the United Farmers have become the apostles of co-operation; they have captured the imagination of the nation by combining true radicalism with scientific moderation, and it is safe to say that they are the most hopeful factor in Canadian national life to-day.[104]

While other groups exist by co-operation, they do not see that co-operation must be applied between competing groups. Capital, highly organized, is engaged in a fight to the death with organized labour. The farmers come ... with a new discovery, namely, that farmers, labourers, manufacturers, and all other groups must co-operate to make a commonwealth of human happiness ... Natural law is on their side, and co-operation will win. Competition cannot go much further without endangering the lives of the competing classes. Co-operation will ultimately be forced into existence between the competing groups, but if its mission could be realized and consciously striven after by all groups, as well as by the farmers, Canada might be saved a great deal of unnecessary suffering.[105]

Irvine's demonstration of the relevance of co-operation broke new ground with the suggestion that farmers are in the vanguard of social and political change because their vocation comprehends the positions of both labour and capital. His close ties with social democratic labour likely account for his desire to show where farmers fit into the struggle between capital and labour.[106]

Co-operation's status as guiding moral principle and 'true social law' for radical democrats found a more practical expression in a 1927 article by Irene Parlby, then minister without portfolio in the UFA government. Parlby became the first female cabinet minister in the British Empire in 1921. She was highly regarded in agrarian circles, and her comments on co-operation can be seen as a folksy and popular articulation of the moral conscience of radical democratic populism. 'If the seed of co-operation has been sown on the stony ground of economics alone, it will wither up and die ... Co-operation is not fundamentally an economic movement. It has its roots in the things of the spirit; the soil in which it flourishes and grows into a mighty tree, is composed of love, service, loyalty, honor. These are all spiritual qualities and without them the co-operative movement can never reach its full development, can perhaps hardly hope to survive over any great period of time. With these qualities as a foundation it can in time transform a world made hideous by the competitive system, into a democracy of hope, justice, and happiness for all.'[107]

This is not the stuff of compelling political philosophy. It was, however, typical of the social philosophy regularly consumed in UFA locals. Parlby neatly suggests how co-operation was the religion of radical democratic political thought. Even shorn of related claims concerning the scientific, natural law, or evolutionary basis of co-operation as social philosophy, a principle so easily connoting democracy, justice, honour, service, and hope had a great deal going for it in the prairie political community between 1920 and 1935.

While co-operation as principle transcended co-operation as economic practice, radical democratic populism would have been unthinkable without the institutions and successes of the latter. It was on this foundation that their 'movement culture' was erected. Tangible accomplishments in the line of co-operative marketing, pooling, and even retailing were central to rank-and-file enthusiasm for unorthodox political and economic structures and practices. H.W. Wood knew this well. All of Wood's addresses to UFA conventions from 1919 to 1931 insisted on the inseparability of organized economic and political activity. Wood brought the UFA membership to appreciate the necessity of learning practical lessons for social and political experimentation in the local activities of co-operative agricultural enterprise.

For Wood,[108] as for Irvine[109] and most other UFA leaders, the heart of political questions and conflict was economic. Effective organization and activity along economic lines would necessarily lead to victories for associated political organizations. Economic justice among the various occupational groups would comprehend political justice. Intragroup and intergroup co-operation in production and trade would only occur in concert with true political co-operation among these groups' representatives. Very generally, economic co-operation was to prevent intergroup exploitation while allowing individual farmers to own agricultural land. It involved creating agricultural producers' marketing mechanisms so farmers could influence the final selling price of grain by 'eliminating the middle man.' Those on the left felt that wage labourers should maximize their relative economic power through union activities in socially owned productive facilities. Such productive activity was seen as compatible with co-operative trading relations. Those on the left also felt that most of the retail trade could be carried on under co-operative direction.

Radical democrats with a more liberal economic philosophy saw definite limits to co-operative enterprise. It was appropriate for marketing agricultural products, when the alternative was to allow private monopolies to control prices for agricultural products. Co-operatives were not seen to be appropriate to many other forms of commodity production by those on the right, as these co-operatives could hold farmers to ransom for products whose final selling prices were not influenced by world markets, or could threaten state control over industrial production.

Nor were those on the right enthusiastic about co-operative enterprises coming to dominate the retail trade. The retail trade might become too much of a distraction from the business of agricultural production, and too far removed from the areas of essential concern and expertise for farmers. While President Wood was not likely to denounce small-scale co-operative retail ventures that related closely to farm production and farm life, he was far more supportive of grain-marketing activities. Half-way through his thirteen-year presidency of the Alberta Wheat Pool, Wood told an Alberta Institute of Co-operation convention that 'as farmers, the supreme problem before us is to learn to sell our products on the same level of prices that others are sold; ... it will [then] be possible for industry to function efficiently in the interests of all.'[110]

This is more or less a practical extension of his 1922 claim that 'commerce, systematically used in accordance with the true social laws of life, would be the greatest binding tie in the social system ... it would destroy competition and establish co-operation.' Wood extended this thought to indicate how crucial co-operation in economic life was to social life generally: 'If the relationships between the economic classes can be adjusted in accordance with the true social laws of life, other social problems will almost automatically adjust themselves.'[111]

Wood believed economic co-operation and group government must be indissolubly linked for the former to confer its potential benefits. When the group government idea did not catch on outside of Alberta or inside the Alberta legislature by the late 1920s, Wood increasingly devoted his time to leadership of the Alberta Wheat Pool and other attempts to establish orderly and equitable grain-marketing practices. His addresses to UFA annual conventions charted progress on this front, and emphasized progress in local and regional co-operatives for the overall objectives of 'the movement.' However, Wood realized that members might revert to a belief that the political aims and accomplishments of the UFA were separable from economic ones. He was thus careful to claim that 'the UFA political movement and the Alberta Wheat Pool are the two greatest products of the UFA, and ... are both founded on the same general basic principles.'[112]

In the 1935 provincial campaign, an insecure UFA stressed its achievements in fostering co-operative agricultural enterprises. Vice-President Norman Priestly produced a pamphlet entitled *Has the Organized Farmers' Movement in Alberta Justified Its Existence?* It portrayed the Wheat Pool, Dairy Pool, local selling agencies, and a fledgling consumer co-operative network as achievements 'providing farmers effective weapons in the competitive struggle and giving them experience in commercial organization.' This more pragmatic demonstration of the virtues of economic co-operation returned to the 'bottom line' established by crypto-Liberalism. Co-operation was a weapon in a market biased in favour of other interests. As we shall see, however, the 1930-5 period was also characterized by reference to the 'co-operative commonwealth.'

The third radical democratic notion of co-operation involved a political strategy for achieving first defensive, then systematic political power by the forces of 'organized democracy.' We saw earlier that radical democratic populism was forged in Alberta under circumstances of profound disagreement over political co-operation. Irvine and the Non-Partisan League, and some prominent figures in the UFA, had favoured the 'open door' in the UFA's political organization and activities. This would allow sympathetic social democrats from the labour movement to work closely with radical agrarians against partyism and plutocracy. When Wood recognized that the UFA would 'enter politics' with or without his direction, he yielded – but his condition was 'the closed door.' Wood successfully insisted on the necessity of the 'group' and its internal, self-directed development, for generating true democratic principles and socio-economic objectives.[113]

In 'Political Action in Alberta' (May 1919), Wood attempted to provide direction to the organization that had endorsed political action several months earlier. He emphasized local-level democratic control, the development of 'democratic citizenship,' and the 'closed door,' which was especially crucial in 'political activities of the group, for there is where the most vital principles of the group are involved, and the group itself must, at all times, be in position to govern its own utterances and guide its own actions.' He insisted that 'the first stage of democratic organization is to bring the individuals of an organization together, ... and the second stage is to gradually bring the several organized groups together through co-operation.'[114]

This admittedly vague proposal was directed against the Non-Partisan League. Wood says nothing here about the identity of other 'democratic groups.' But by the fall of 1921, following the inclusion of a sympathetic Labour MLA from Calgary in the UFA cabinet, Wood was under pressure to speak to the question of co-operation with Labour candidates in the upcoming federal election. He did so at a joint meeting of the East and West Calgary UFA district association, fully aware of the joint campaign that East Calgary Dominion Labour candidate William Irvine had been conducting. Wood contended that neither group should adopt the other's platform, but each could offer its 'voting strength' to the other group, without expecting to have any control over the other group's successful candidate.

This control would occur only when labour and farmers were integrated in the same democratic organization, sharing the same economic interests, following a profound transformation of the economic environment. Since 'we are all creatures of environment and the viewpoint of Labour is the product of the environment of Labour, and the viewpoint of farmers is the product of the environment of farmers, ... you cannot organize labour and farmers into one organization.' That would be tantamount to a political party that had proved its inability to foster or transmit democratic thought and relations. So the only option for the present was 'co-operation in votes.' This was to remain the official UFA position until Wood stepped down as president in 1931. What Wood left unspoken here was his fear that labour would come to dominate farmers ideologically if a federation developed.

Acceptance of Wood's strategy by the 1920 UFA Annual Convention ushered in a divided approach to political co-operation within the UFA organization over the next fifteen years. Wood's approach predominated. The class-based organization would accept 'co-operation in voting' in the short term, partial co-operation in policy development in existing legislatures, and eventually full co-operation of this kind in reconstituted group governments. On the opposite end was the position stoically adhered to by Carl Axelson, whose interpretation of group government and delegate democracy made him an 'agrarian syndicalist.' Axelson's advocacy of One Big Union–style economic and political action received thin support from the UFA rank and file.

The principal challenger on the question of political co-operation was thus William Irvine. He managed to argue for practical common-frontism in all but name, while formally remaining an effective advocate of the closed door. The UFA rank and file wavered between Wood's and Irvine's positions until the early 1930s. A change in leadership led the UFA into common-frontism informally, then formally, in 1932, following affiliation with the CCF. Political co-operation with organized labour was never achieved, because of a variety of perceived antagonisms and organizational blunders.[115]

Interestingly enough, Labour candidate Irvine professed adherence to Wood's line during the 1921 campaign. He told a reporter for *The Alberta Labour News:* 'I have never advocated group government in this campaign. I have written a book on it and I believe in it but I am, if elected, going to do what the labour people wish.' Labour supporters might have been concerned that Irvine would turn out to be a propagandist for UFA nostrums; ironically, Irvine used UFA-sanctioned political strategy on 'co-operation with votes' to defuse labour doubts about his likely preoccupation. Following his election, Irvine represented what he perceived as the common interests of farmers and labour in Canada, often in ways that only Alberta farmers had acknowledged conformed to their stated concerns. This was displayed in his advocacy of social credit policies, group government principles, and elimination of 'confidence' votes on government bills. At the same time, he was a determined and eloquent defender of labour.[116]

When Irvine publicly retracted his opposition to separate political activities for farmers and labour, he did so in the belief that common cause was required to achieve the larger goal of UFA political action. Irvine and his associates believed that when farmers came into politics as a 'class-conscious' grouping, co-operation with labour would soon follow, even if initially over organizational boundaries. The catalyst to more extensive and effective farmer/labour co-operation was to be ideological. Irvine's *The Farmers in Politics* demonstrates great optimism in this regard, with favourable references to labour, suggestive associations of labour with the organized farmers, and a long analysis of how both labour and farmers' organizations grew in response to exploitation by the same capitalist interests. Labour comes off in a much better light in this classic of the farmers' movement than in any of Wood's public pronouncements.

Irvine continued to insist on this community of interests and perspectives in terms that required political co-operation. In his 1925 nomination convention speech, he argued that the labour and farmer movements had three crucial things in common: 'both looked to the day when political issues should not be divorced from economic need, as had been done through the evil genius of partyism; ... both desired that co-operation, not only in industry, but also in politics, should be substituted for the "old tooth and claw method" of competition for political power; [and] both had a belief in common in democratic political organization.'[117]

Irvine's desire to arrange more than an alliance of voting convenience was supported by a majority of UFA members in resolutions at UFA annual conventions in the 1920s and 1930s. 'Fraternal delegates' from the Alberta Federation of Labour and the Canadian Labour Party commonly addressed the convention. Following an address by AFL President (and Irvine's close friend) Elmer Roper in 1924, UFA delegates resolved 'that steps be taken to co-operate with Labour, in view of the coming elections, in order to counteract the influence of the combining of the two old parties, whose purpose is to defeat the UFA.' *The UFA*'s coverage of the 1925 annual convention reported enthusiastic adoption of 'a resolution calling for close co-operation with the Labour forces ... and the very cordial reception given on the following day to [labour representatives], reveal[ing] the general desire of the Convention for co-operation with an organized group which is, second only to the farmers, the largest group of citizens of progressive outlook in this country.'[118] UFA delegates had been eager to explore new strategies for political co-operation well before 1932. Irvine, Robert Gardiner, E.J. Garland,[119] and other UFA MPs were more sure of the value of an integrated political vehicle than were average radical democrats, but they were not voices in the wilderness.

UFA editor Smith was thus on safe ground when commenting on the 1933 UFA convention's decision to affiliate with the Co-operative Commonwealth Federation:

the Convention [has] carried to its logical outcome a quarter of a century of unremitting struggle towards the attainment of an equitable social order ... Alberta farm people have been laying the foundations ... for the day when, with effective allies of the same mind as themselves, they might aspire to stride forward towards the realization of their larger aims ... In the Federation has been found the means by which all classes possessed of a common social philosophy can operate on a national scale ... to win power to translate their ideals into reality.

The UFA has at all times been ready to co-operate with other groups of citizens ... in a form which, leaving the autonomy of the Association unimpaired, and the UFA unit free to carry on unhindered all of the work in various fields in which it is engaged, yet makes coordinated action with other social units possible. The Federation is in fact a concrete expression of the spirit of the UFA movement, a means whereby co-operation between groups may become not merely a name, but a workable plan.[120]

With the Depression as catalyst, UFA leaders had convinced convention delegates to reject Wood's strategy of slowly evolving political co-operation. As Smith intimates, achieving group government would be inconceivable without integrated political co-operation among 'progressive social units.' While Alberta farmers were attracted to Aberhart's more sensational social credit option after two more years of grinding suffering, their district representatives had not been hypnotized into supporting CCF affiliation in 1933. The 1924-34 record of UFA resolutions and electors' support for advocates of something beyond 'co-operation in voting strength' demonstrates that radical democratic populists could quite easily sanction an approach to political co-operation that was consistent with social democratic populism. H.W. Wood's doctrinaire position on this issue had done much to separate the two tendencies for a decade. When he voluntarily stepped down, the UFA movement's (not government's) distance from a social democratic political strategy lessened. Even though many UFA members who supported the new political strategy went on to vote Social Credit in 1935, few did so in conscious rejection of the modified common-front approach. As we will see in chapter 5, Aberhart did much to generate the impression that Social Credit was the proper political vehicle of such a common front.

Radical Democracy and the Good Society

The distinctiveness of utopian visions in radical democratic populism can be summarized in comments on several elements of the radical democratic good society: 1 / its conception of human nature; 2 / its valuation of community; 3 / the centrality of co-operation to the vision; 4 / the preferred relationship between state and civil society in the 'co-operative commonwealth'; 5 / the ambivalent perspective on politics as a dimension of public life; and 6 / the expectation of a coming era of abundance.

Henry Wise Wood's dialectic of social progress, featuring the true social law of co-operation doing battle with the false social law of competition, can easily be seen as an extended metaphor for the nature of man. Men were both good and evil, and the preponderance of either depended on social circumstances. Wood argued that time was running out for the false social law, if only because men were finally realizing that it atrophied their individual and group-related potentials, and even threatened survival when expressed in international conflict. Circumstances increasingly required organized groups of men and women to give expression to the higher dimension in their character, by adopting co-operation as their guide in social relations. An increasingly democratic society required environmentally induced development of the positive side of human nature.

Irvine was less cautious than Wood in predicting the arrival of a society peopled by such individuals. In the few years following the end of the war, Irvine predicted the rapid victory of 'the new social ethics.' They would help initiate a 'new social order,' not merely follow in its wake. Irvine was also less inclined than Wood to explain regressive social attitudes in terms of the dialectical social-evolutionary model, and more likely to attribute them to the human agency of Canada's 'ruling class.' He presented human nature as something structured by environment and opportunity far more than by 'natural laws,' without rejecting the analogy from social-evolutionary dialectic to human nature. The church-going prairie community was impressed enough with the precepts of a dualistic human nature that speaking of personal capacities for both good and evil had political value. Situating one focus of the moral challenge for democratic change within independent prairie farmers' personalities made common sense in prairie politics.

Both Wood's and Irvine's perspectives on human nature enhanced the radical democratic sense of community. Crypto-Liberalism had already provided prairie residents with a certain base-line perception of community, in physiocratic, western-regional terms. Radical democratic populism heightened the Alberta agrarian community's sense of economic and political distinctiveness. While not developed to the satisfaction of orthodox Marxists, their class-consciousness still contributed to a more communitarian vision of the good society. The good society would be a community of self-governing groups in co-operation. Group government could only make sense if a structured state pluralism encouraged the development of a democratic plurality of communities.

Working towards group government through integrated 'industrial' and political action[121] created a strong sense of community-in-development. The radical democratic emphasis on grass-roots delegate democracy and development of 'group thought' did much to give their movement a sense of distinctiveness in community. But distinctiveness did not imply exclusivity. Wood's strategy of political and economic co-operation stopped short of this, and Irvine's common-frontist strategy was intended to nip group 'separatist' tendencies in the bud.[122]

Even Wood believed that only a community of 'democratic forces' could vanquish the 'plutocratic forces,' and then build a co-operative, socially pluralistic community. A participatory public life would originate in but not be exclusively channelled through industrial group organizations. This group basis of public life would ensure that meaningful community attachments would go beyond the rural regionalism of crypto-Liberalism.

Many left-of-centre Anglo-American social and political movements had made the 'co-operative commonwealth' the ultimate object of political action before the rise of radical democratic populism in the West. By 1931, it was closely aligned with the social democratic vision of the future. Prior to this, radical democrats' occasional use of the phrase implied co-operation facilitated by group government. In *The Farmers in Politics*, Irvine suggested that all economic groups come together 'and, in the spirit of co-operation, find a solution that will give most satisfaction to all.' The hope that such co-operation will succeed was, Irvine claimed, the animating principle of United Farmers activity: 'It is in the expectation of bringing about a truly co-operative commonwealth that the farmers are entering politics as a group.'[123] He was thus able to address moderate and left-wing radical democrats simultaneously.

Henry Wise Wood had only the former audience in mind in a 1929 speech, which assumed a general understanding of the goal, then immediately pulled back into the world of short-term objectives: 'I assume that the ideal of a co-operative commonwealth involves inclination at the present time to extend the scope of these activities. This is manifest among Canadian Farmers as it should be; but we must not forget the fact that co-operation ... must have a practical, systematical manner ... readjustments cannot be made quickly or violently.'[124]

How did these two leaders conceive of the co-operative commonwealth? It could not abide the exercise of exploitive power by any group. The commonwealth could thus not include Canada's plutocracy; as Wood said in 1922, 'plutocracy could no more exist under a scientifically operated co-operative social system than a fish could live out of water.' Who would build the co-operative commonwealth? It was 'the great masses of the people,' who had 'failed in the competitive struggle,' but were now 'marshalling their forces into stable groups.' These groups would be 'gradually federated into one great co-operative force, mobilized on the common ground of all-embracing democracy.'[125]

For Wood, this was a long-term prospect, about which little detail could be revealed. He was none the less confident that the good society would be envisioned and built by economic organizations controlled by their members. The primary force in the creation of the co-operative commonwealth was not to be political. Political action could help to mobilize and consolidate economic strength, but it could not perform the leading role. Wood alluded to this relative priority for economic action carefully in his last presidential address, asserting that 'while governmental legislation is only secondary and supplemental in scientific social construction, it nevertheless wields a tremendous influence for good or evil on social progress.'[126] 'Co-operation in practically all industrial activities' would be expressed in and partially co-ordinated by the state (group government), but the state had to continue to be recognized as a 'false divinity,' with a tendency to threaten democracy by enforcing compliance.[127]

As we saw earlier, the state was not nearly so suspect for Irvine and others on the left of the UFA, providing it became the instrument of both delegated democratic groups' representatives and 'the people's experts.' Elimination of class exploitation required the state to deprive plutocratic forces of their superior political and economic power. From *The Farmers in Politics*, through his long advocacy of state-directed monetary and credit policies, to his advocacy of affiliation with the CCF, Irvine gave the state a much more prominent role in the transition to the co-operative commonwealth. For eleven years, UFA leadership rejected this, as is evident even in the 1931 UFA Board's 'Manifesto to the Farm People of Alberta.' According to the manifesto's authors, the crisis they were facing demonstrated the need for a co-operative commonwealth, but its creation was still to be the result of 'orderly organization and united movement and a developed capacity for collective responsibility.'[128]

This manifesto was quite consistent with Wood's anti-statism, despite its recommendation of nationalization of credit and immediate provincial action in providing relief for farmers. A year of left-wing executive leadership, radicalized *UFA* messages, and worsening economic conditions led the 1932 UFA convention to pass a much more 'Irvinesque' manifesto. The 'Definition of the Co-operative Commonwealth' was discussed clause by clause on the floor, and all clauses were either carried unanimously or with radicalizing amendments. (This resolution, and the next year's 'Declaration of Ultimate Objectives,' are discussed in the next chapter.) The UFA leadership by this time were radical democratic/social democratic hybrids, and their analysis and proposals fall more easily into the latter category.

However, we should note here that through its transition from radical democratic to social democratic status within UFA discourse, the co-operative commonwealth retained several key elements. One was the idea that it would be 'a community freed from the domination of irresponsible financial and economic power,' with 'all social means of production and distribution ... socially owned and controlled either by voluntarily organized groups of producers and consumers, or – in the case of the major public services and utilities ... by public corporations responsible to the people's elected representatives.' Another crucial belief was in 'rapid development of social units, and the aquirement [*sic*] by individual members of such units of an intelligent understanding of the nature and evolution of social forces.' Finally, this conception of the co-operative commonwealth contained the belief that 'because community of industrial interest is the basis upon which any group of the people can most easily organize, it is on this basis, primarily, that organization needs to be undertaken.' This would 'not involve the narrowing of social sympathies,' but 'a training in the habits of co-operation within each industrial unit, and at the same time the preparation of the industrial unit for co-operation with other social units in the effort to realize broad social purposes.' The result would be 'common action by all such units to bring the Co-operative Commonwealth into being.'[129]

By 1932, radical democratic populists had assigned the state a much greater role in the creation and operation of the co-operative commonwealth. The emphasis remained on ending exploitive relations between classes, the value of group organization, and the almost mystical role of co-operation. Political activity continued to possess a confusing status. Politics often connoted unsavoury, manipulative activity, since the outcomes of 'politics' had always been disadvantageous to the people. However, politics by the people's own design – as an informed and democratic extension of their social and economic lives – was the natural activity of responsible citizenship. The co-operative commonwealth would thus be highly political in this positive sense.

A problem arose when Irvine tried to reconcile policy determination by both delegated representatives and government experts (social scientists). In trying to detail the specifics of group governmental activity, Irvine ended up giving the key role to technocrats. Granted, their actions were to be at the service of 'the people,' since any correct reading of 'the facts' of economic and social life would necessarily be to the people's advantage.

However, where benign science and popular democracy meet, there is no guarantee that the former will not remove the dynamism of the latter. The reverse is more likely to be true, at least when the rationale for popular-democratic activity is centred on creation of a functionally defined 'highest intelligence' of group actors. Radical democratic theoreticians failed to develop an explicit rationale for popular democracy in self-developmental terms, except when the powers of organized individuals were seen to be diminished by state power. When this potential diminution was not seen as a problematic possibility, popular democracy's role in the good society was not as safe as its initial proponents required.

This problem had roots in the radical democratic tendency to insist that politics was almost exclusively about economic interests. The notion that 'when we have learned to trade right, we will have learned to live right' contains the seeds of eventual trouble for participatory politics. To sustain a dynamic conception of participatory politics at all levels of the public realm, politics has to be seen as more than the work required for some version of economic justice. The irony for radical democratic populism is that this did not occur, even though the institutional life generating its movement culture was strong enough to demonstrate the supra-economic benefits of co-operative political activity.

Closely related to this confusion concerning the role of politics in the good society was the idea of a coming era of abundance. Prairie social and political thought had been suffused with this expectation since the turn of the century. Immigrants to the agrarian frontier were exposed to the wishful thinking of Ontario imperialists[130] and the propaganda of Clifford Sifton's Ministry of the Interior on the virtual paradise of plenty that sturdy yeomen could create in the prairie environment.

Even such critics as William Irvine pursued the age-old radical theme of 'poverty in the midst of plenty.' His enthusiasm about this had three sources, all of which influenced many prairie radicals. The first source was his British socialist background, in which Robert Blatchford and Keir Hardie had promised the coming plenty of the co-operative commonwealth. The second source was Irvine's sense of Canada's vast undeveloped resources, particularly in the prairies. The third source was C.H. Douglas, who argued that the underconsumption and stunted technological development imposed by a faulty financial system had created 'poverty in the midst of plenty.'[131]

From a different perspective, H.W. Wood also contended that the problems of production and consumption had been solved. The force preventing 'the people' from taking full advantage of the potential for abundance was 'efficient middlemen' who exploited both producers and consumers.[132]

By the early 1930s, social credit doctrines and the faddish nostrums of Technocracy, Inc., combined to influence UFA leaders and rank and file. Prominent UFA spokesmen such as E.J. Garland and W.N. Smith contended that the economy producing misery could actually produce abundance for all. The first two 1932 issues of The UFA featured Garland on 'The Age of Plenty and Social Credit.' Smith, the editor, introduced it as a crucial topic, concerned with policies designed to dislodge 'the tyranny of financial capital upon an international scale through the unofficial league of bankers.'[133]

Garland observed that 'the potential productivity of the machine is staggering.' He marshalled figures to demonstrate the productive potential of the United States and Canada, and announced achievement of the eternal human goal –'that it might be able to produce all that it needs for keep and comfort for the least possible labour.' The limiting factor had become the inability of many to buy what was produced. The age of leisure was thus artificially postponed by those controlling financial institutions. Garland used Major Douglas's 'A plus B' theorem to explain why underconsumption and underutilization of 'machine power' continued. To conclude, he exhorted his audience to agitate for change in the monetary and credit system. If successful, they could 'look forward to the appreciation of the dividends that come to all the people from the result of the generations and generations of cultural and scientific advancement of the human race.' Social Credit would pave the way to abundance for all.

Later that year, Norman Smith wrote a feature article in The UFA on 'the disclosures of Technocracy.' He began by referring to 'the Age of Plenty – when the means of production in the hands of man are capable of providing for all a standard of living incomparably higher than that of any other age in human history.' Smith endorsed Technocracy's predictions of massive technological unemployment, and rapid increases in industrial efficiency and productivity. 'The information which has been given publicity by Technocracy,' Smith asserted, was 'sufficient to show the immense power of modern industry to supply mankind ... with all its needs with a small expenditure of human labour.' Smith then integrated Technocracy's claims with Social Credit writers' musings on 'the leisured state,' in which the bulk of human activity would be freed from compulsion. Men 'must realize the Leisured Social Order or perish.' Hope was to be found in the activities of the

CCF and the Canadian Monetary Reform League, whose efforts could guarantee that 'this superabundance of good things which the engineers can give us can be distributed to the community in the form of commodities and leisure.'[134]

This combination of socialism, Technocracy, and social credit was not commonplace in the mind of the average UFA member. None the less, its articulation by one of the key proponents of radical democratic populism is significant. The same can be said for Garland's disquisition on Social Credit. The point is that if the reason for political activity is achievement of economic interests in a class-harmonious social environment, a large part of the rationale for participatory democracy would seem to vanish in the future. Politics in the short term would clearly require mass political organization, so that existing obstacles to abundance could be removed. However, the achievement of abundance would seem to make participatory politics almost redundant. The technocratically successful state-as-provider renders 'politics' unnecessary, except as a means of organizing efficient economic activity by groups of producers.

This seems an odd utopia for a political theory based on the centrality of participatory politics, but given the assumptions adumbrated here, it is also a logical one, despite its contradiction of much of what they said about the co-operative commonwealth. The anti-political tendency dormant within radical democratic populism shows its full colours in plebiscitarian populism. But radical democratic populism had a more powerful and positive legacy, stemming from its achievements in the theory and practice of popular democracy.

This interpretation of the radical democratic populist vision of the future presents an unfortunately misleading picture of the overall ideology. It is appropriate, therefore to close this chapter by reaffirming that by the standards of modern democratic theory, radical democratic populism in the prairies dealt with shortcomings of a partially democratic society as impressively as any North American social or political movement.

4   Social Democratic Populism

Social democracy signifies an extension of popular power, opportunity, and welfare beyond liberal democracy. It assumes that formal rights to participate in voting, political and social-organizational activity, and public office do not in themselves lead to an equitable distribution of power, opportunity, and welfare. At its best, social democracy recognizes the power relations inherent in the institutions citizens encounter daily.

Social democrats differ as to the depth and character of this democratization of power, but agree on what might be called a 'social democratic minimum': a redistribution of economic goods and societal resources (such as education and access to culture) among classes and communities to make equality of opportunity reality. Social democrats may argue that meaningful equality requires popular participation in the institutions of social and economic power. This demand, which takes many forms, usually arises from a perception that systematic class power in major societal institutions prevents the realization of meaningful equality.

Democracy thus requires a more egalitarian, state-enforced, and co-ordinated distribution of goods and opportunities, flowing from extensive citizen participation in social institutions. In its most radical form, social democracy insists on 'workers' control' of all economic, as well as social and political, institutions, while rejecting the Leninist claim that social democratic governments' accommodation with prevailing political cultures and institutions reflects the acceptance of 'bourgeois' political norms.

Social democratic populists on the prairies[1] articulated these concerns in different ways. For example, the welfare 'distributionist' concern was sometimes emphasized at the expense of concern for equalization of social power. Some prairie social democrats had more penetrating or consistent critiques of capitalism and class power than others. Many tended to see the 'new social order' in more agrarian than labourist terms, while a minority viewed farmers as another species of exploited industrial worker. A few stressed the need for wholesale reorganization of political institutions to enhance 'economic democracy,' while the great majority were satisfied with British parliamentary institutions as amenable to social democracy. Some gave state ownership tremendous responsibilities in the new economic order, while others leaned more heavily on agrarian-style co-operative ownership. Finally, some social democratic populists foresaw a technocratic administration that would have made H.G. Wells blush, while others were suspicious of the state while profoundly committed to public control of economic resources.

All social democratic populists believed, however, that reversing the injustices of the Canadian capitalist order required producers to unite in a political struggle for social control over the economy. This belief animated a set of ideas expressed in a populist discourse – populist, because, as Laclau argues, the essence of populism is a perception of opposition between 'the people' and 'the power bloc,' articulated with reference to popular-democratic traditions. Of all the prairie populisms, social democratic populism did the most to identify the character of this opposition, and to present an alternative to it.

We have already seen that the Non-Partisan League and the United Farmers of Alberta provided a home for the expression of social democratic populism. This populism ceased to be the prevalent discourse in the League in 1919, when political strategy seemed to require a greater emphasis on achieving popular agrarian representation through non-partisan, delegate democracy than on achieving particular economic reforms. The Non-Partisan League did, however, manage to popularize an Independent Labour Party–style socialist analysis among radical farmers in Saskatchewan and Alberta.

The UFA's openness to NPL, credit reform, single tax, and transplanted Labourite ideas made it the 'omnibus' radical party in rural Alberta. Even the syndicalist Carl Axelson found a place in the movement. From 1921 to 1935, UFA MPs and their supporters in *The UFA* provided a contact point for socialist and labour organizations in the prairies. Their collaboration with J.S. Woodsworth in supporting the struggles of urban labour across Canada provided a fitting background to the UFA's entry into the CCF in 1932; in fact, many have argued that UFA activists' and MPs' efforts were crucial to the creation of the CCF. UFA legislators' desertion for the Social Credit mirage was a blow from which social democratic populism in Alberta never recovered.

Of the two other 'United Farmers' organizations in the prairies, the United Farmers of Canada (Saskatchewan Section) (UFC[SS]) was both more predominantly social democratic and more inclined to seek common cause with labour than was the United Farmers of Manitoba. The UFC(SS) was formed in 1926 when the Saskatchewan Grain Growers' Association merged with the Farmers' Union of Canada (FUC). The FUC was formed in 1921 to express dissatisfaction with the Liberal ties and the conservative tactics of SGGA leadership. The FUC had advocated a kind of agrarian industrial unionism[2] and proposed a socialistic analysis of the farmers' position in society, but like the SGGA, had consistently eschewed direct political action. The UFC(SS) extended this strategy until 1931.

From 1926 to 1934, the UFC(SS) was dominated by the left wing of the agrarian movement in the province, most notably by CCF leader-to-be George Williams. The UFC(SS) supported the UFA line on occupational organization and representation, but never made a commitment to electoral competition. Like the UFA, the UFC(SS) included many for whom social credit economic analysis blended readily with a commitment to widespread state and social ownership. The UFC(SS) linked up with the tiny but influential Independent Labor Party (ILP) of urban Saskatchewan in 1932 to form the Saskatchewan Farmer-Labor Group, which became a federated member of the CCF later in the year. There was more ideological common ground between agrarians and urban labour in Saskatchewan than in Alberta from 1932 to 1945, which was partly attributable to the British labour background of many in the Saskatchewan leadership.

In Manitoba, the Independent Labour Party's connections with organized farmers were formal but strained and seldom electorally valuable to an integrated social democratic movement. Closer agrarian ideological ties to Ontario liberalism, conservatism, and eventually 'Brackenism' were obstacles here, as was the divisive Winnipeg General Strike, for which agrarian Manitoba had little sympathy.

However, Manitoba made the greatest urban labour-oriented contribution to prairie social democratic populism. Winnipeg's working class was the largest, most politically and socially complex, and most ideologically interesting on the prairies.[3] The Independent Labour Party's socialism was clearly British, gradualist, and ethical. They were committed to extensive public ownership, and to many reforms that prairie farmers supported – such as direct legislation, steeply graduated income tax, tariff reductions, and the single tax.[4]

The same set of commitments could be found in ILP organizations in Saskatchewan in the 1920s and early 1930s, and in the Dominion Labour Party and then Canadian Labour Party organizations in Alberta from 1918 to 1935.[5] In the sympathetic and strategic connections that developed between labour party and united farmers, rural organizations' preoccupations always had a stronger influence on labour's than vice versa. In practice, the presence of many agrarian activists with previous experience in British labour/socialist organizations prevented a suffocation of urban labour in these relationships. Only in more conservative Manitoba were the organized farmers likely to perceive a greater community of interests with the local urban bourgeoisie than with the local urban workers. Manitoba's crypto-Liberalism (especially as expressed by the *Free Press*'s J.W. Dafoe) promoted this orientation. The same effort was made by the crypto-Liberal daily press in Saskatchewan and Alberta, but less strenuously in view of their smaller urban working classes.

The CCF requires only two points of introductory clarification. First, the CCF's origins in farmers' and workers' organizations, as well as its national and loosely federated character, virtually guaranteed that its analysis, appeal, and programmes would reveal a clearly populist stamp. Second, it is misleading to draw a hard distinction between populism and socialism when populism as ideology, rather than as a sociological category, is the subject of inquiry. Populism as ideology incorporates socialism as a subspecies if, as Laclau suggests, it is the mode of ideological appeal, as opposed to its content, that identifies populist ideology. In one sense or another, capitalism was 'the system' to which twentieth-century North American populists objected. Insofar as socialism attempts the most comprehensive critique and alternative to this system, socialism can be understood as 'the highest form of populism.' Socialism gives a particular shape to a populist appeal, providing a 'unifying principle of the ideological discourse.' The same is true of social democracy, situated somewhere between reform liberalism and Marxist socialism. The concept of social democratic populism removes the need to make 'either/or' judgments; it in fact denies that a precise boundary between populism and socialism exists.

The People

In a capitalist society, that populism whose identification of social conflict is most clearly anti-capitalist is, by definition, the most radical form of populism. By this measure, social democratic populism was the most radical of all four prairie populisms. One way of gauging this radicalism is to look at the rhetorical use of 'the people.'

We can begin with a comparison of the social democratic to the radical democratic populist perception of the 'people/power bloc' relation. In a sense, the latter was more complex: the radical democratic concept of the people connoted a set of political structural antagonists of the people that was of greater importance to its discourse, while maintaining a sense of antagonistic opposition between the people and an exploitive economic structure.

H.W. Wood and like-minded radical democratic populists articulated an elemental opposition between the people and politicians, the people and partyism, and the people and autocracy. By contrast, social democratic populism did not talk of irreconcilable differences between the people and 'politicians' or 'partyism' *per se*. Generally speaking, social democratic populists objected to those politicians and parties directing the state in the interests of the wrong classes, rather than to politicians and party activity in all conceivable forms. Given democratic connections with their supporters and socially progressive objectives, politicians could perform useful – indeed necessary – works of social reconstruction. Democratic party structures would ensure that politicians would implement the will of the people.

This account has to be qualified immediately to register the influence of the radical democratic critique of partyism on prairie social democrats. Many 'hybrid' social democratic/radical democratic populists in the UFA took their critique of party very seriously indeed – to the point that UFA MPs and leaders emphasized the CCF's federated, non-compulsory, highly democratic structure. They insisted that the UFA would retain complete autonomy and its delegate democracy as an element of the larger people's movement that the CCF was to become. The CCF was portrayed as the social movement equivalent of a group government.

In Saskatchewan, FUC(SS) and UFC(SS) suspicion of politicians and partyism contributed to their reluctance to engage in direct political action from 1921 to 1931. They maintained that the people could easily be diverted from their most important goals (such as control over the marketing of wheat), as demonstrated by the experience of the SGGA with the Liberals.

We can also note E.A. Partridge's idiosyncratic yet revealing position. Partridge established the short-lived[6] No-Party League of Western Canada in 1913. He denounced politicians and partyism until at least 1926, when the remarkable *A War on Poverty* adumbrated a politician and party-free[7] co-operative utopia in western Canada. Partridge argued that local and regional communal producers' organizations would represent citizens in his projected classless society.

Finally, the Non-Partisan League contended that partisan organization and competition disguised the control of the people's business by a self-selected corporate élite. Corporations used the mock battle between old-line parties as a cover for their control of the state. The NPL alternative, 'business administration,' would deal with issues on their own merits and in the people's interests. Politicians from party machines merely 'played politics,' which is to say they provided state-sanctioned favours for their plutocratic benefactors, or did what they could to prevent the people understanding this unofficial tenet of public policy. The Non-Partisan League's analytical coupling of party politics with corporate control was a pioneering effort in prairie social democracy, and left a significant legacy in the public perception of the people/party politics relation.

The 'people/plutocracy' opposition in social democratic discourse was more complex than in that of radical democrats because so much more of the social democratic populist case turned on a public understanding of capitalism. They expected that successful articulation of this antagonism would demonstrate the undesirability of Canadian capitalism.

Like radical democratic populists, social democratic populists frequently referred to the fundamental economic antagonism between 'the people' and 'plutocrats.' However, social democratic populists turned to various socialist analyses to explain this antagonism. To link up with 'anti-plutocratic' popular-democratic traditions of Anglo-American popular movements, social democrats used a variety of synonyms for 'capitalism' and 'classes' in their public appeals. For example, a 1917 Saskatchewan Non-Partisan League pamphlet claimed that 'these two classes, *viz.* the "down-east" nabob on the one hand and the common people on the other, are the only two recognized "classes" of society in Canada.'[8] Ten years later, the Farmers' Educational League Manifesto claimed that 'the poverty of the masses of the people is due to the fact that modern society is divided into two classes – those who produce and do not possess, and those who possess and do not produce.' The authors go on to argue, however, that 'the existence of poverty side by side with superabundant wealth is caused by the exploitation of the masses of the people,' agricultural and industrial alike, by 'the capitalistic class.'[9]

E.A. Partridge made similar claims in *A War on Poverty*, contending that 'society is divided into those who produce and do not possess, and those who possess and do not produce: of those who live without working and those who work without living.'[10] A 1938 Calgary CCF pamphlet provided another variation on this theme, arguing that 'effective power is in the hands of a powerful and wealthy oligarchy, whose money finances elections and ... line[s] the pockets of legislators.'[11]

This account of the people/plutocracy antinomy also appeared in the federal CCF organization's official publications in the late 1930s and mid-1940s. *Make This Your Canada* offered a national political sociology that spoke frankly about antagonistic relations between capitalists and workers in farms and factories. Authors David Lewis and Frank Scott claim that 'the basic struggle today is between the 99% who are reaching out for the economic and political power which the 1% now effectively control.'[12] And in *Left Turn, Canada*, M.J. Coldwell says that 'the issue of our time is that of public power, responsible to the whole of the people, against private power exercised by a self-interested financial and economic autocracy.' He further states that 'the people ... will not be supreme until our government has asserted its supremacy over business interests.'[13]

These excerpts are all taken from analyses designating capitalism – not merely 'the big interests' or 'the forces of Mammon' or 'organized plutocracy' – as the source of 'the people's' exploitation. Capitalism was often portrayed in ways that modern socialists would deem idiosyncratic or misleading. For example, prairie socialists often spoke of capitalist conspiracies between 'the 50 big shots,'[14] or capitalism as co-ordinated by super-powerful financiers,[15] or as a system producing misery by enforcing underconsumption,[16] or of the threat posed to capitalism by ethical co-operativist critiques. None the less, all of these drew on established British and American socialist traditions, and helped to distinguish the social democratic from the radical democratic conception of the people.

Construction of a politically effective popular discourse requires a clear delineation of its audience. Social democratic populism included many definitions of 'the people' in its political appeals and popular educational efforts. It provided a variety of distinct yet generally compatible answers to the question 'who are "the people"?'

For all social democratic prairie populists, 'the people' included at least farmers and wage labourers. Including wage labour was necessary because, whatever their socialist education, social democratic populists stressed the historical importance and contemporary plight of those selling their labour for a living. A belief that the working class was to be the principal force behind economic and political change was a possible but not necessary corollary to this identification of the people. Even the mildest forms of labourite socialism would have suggested that capitalism was inconceivable without the wage labour responsible for industrial production. And if capitalism were identified as the major obstacle to social progress, 'the people' would have to include the group on whose efforts the material success of capitalism was primarily built.

Stemming from the organization of Canadian society were factors guaranteeing that a concept of the people must incorporate farmers as well. In national terms, farmers and those employed on farms made up just over 34 per cent of those considered gainfully employed in 1911, and just over 25 per cent in 1941.[17] Thus any viable opposition to the existing power system had to postulate the compatibility of farmer and worker interests. On the prairies, the need to interest agrarians in a program of anti-capitalist political and economic change was even greater. Any prairie political project that did not modify its proletarian orientation was doomed to failure.

Prairie social democrats took several approaches to political incorporation of farmers and workers into the 'class' of the people. Most popular was an assertion that the differences between farmers and workers were insignificant when seen from the perspective of the need for change and the forces working to obstruct such change. This assertion could take two forms: to treat farmers as a subspecies of the working class or to acknowledge differences in perspectives and some specific interests, while stressing their complementarity.

The more militant farmers' organizations and activists[18] took the first approach. They contended that farmers' independence was completely illusory, and that they were wage workers for the various financial, commercial, and industrial monopolies with which they dealt.[19] If it could be demonstrated that the relation of agrarian producers to capitalists was similar to that of industrial workers, the political objectives and class perspective of farmers should coincide.

The more common approach to encouraging farmer-worker solidarity was to admit the differences in the two classes' situations and particular interests, but to insist these were secondary to their common status, grievances, and needs as subordinate producers. In the absence of farmer-worker co-operation, the common enemy – capitalists and their political agents – would continue to exploit both farmers and workers.

This approach was expressed most simply in the Saskatchewan Non-Partisan League's claim that 'the League only endorses one class. That is the farming and working class,' and further, that 'the main issue is the political supremacy of the common people.'[20] Here a difference is implied, but rejected as irrelevant for practical political action. In the same year, William Irvine wrote in *The Nutcracker*: 'How does it come about that the farmers and all the industrial workers of western Canada combined have less power in Edmonton and Ottawa than twenty-three Money Kings?'[21] This question set up a brief analysis of 'plutocratic' power over both farmers and workers, and a suggestion of political remedies. NPL promoters, including J.S. Woodsworth, often spoke of the need for a 'united democracy of farmers and workers,'[22] so that democracy could be 'a full and free expression of the spirit of the people as a whole.'[23] Defining the people as a combination of workers and farmers continued when the CCF became the vehicle of prairie social democracy. In 1943, T.C. Douglas referred to 'the common people, the workers and farmers [who] should have an opportunity of owning, controlling and operating the facilities by which they live.'[24]

CCF speakers more commonly used an expanded conception of 'the people' to attract the politically crucial 'middle classes.' They argued that the middle class would also benefit if the existing system were replaced. The CCF alternative could guarantee economic security for all, true democratic political activity, intelligent economic and social planning, and a standard of social justice superior to that of capitalism. It was presented as the intelligent choice of both the middle class and the more obvious victims of capitalism. Thus, 'the people' became all those who suffered in some way under the old order, and who could now participate in creating the co-operative commonwealth. New political realities had to be accommodated if a regional social democratic populism were to become a national 'people's movement.'

Social democratic populists had occasionally defined the people broadly before the CCF emerged. E.A. Partridge, in the preface to his 1913 'Manifesto of the No-Party League of Western Canada,' spoke of 'the complete community of interest of all who live, and desire to live, by useful labour, whether of hand or brain.'[25] The commonly expressed antinomy between producers and non-producers also encouraged a broad range of participants in 'the people's movement.' However, explicit incorporation of groups outside the farming and wage labour communities occurred much more after 1931. Agnes Macphail's House of Commons speech in support of Woodsworth's famous 1932 resolution for the creation of a co-operative commonwealth is a good example. Referring to the CCF, Macphail argues that 'this orderly mobilizing of the people's forces does not consist of farmers and labourers only, but is augmented by these new, insecure groups, namely the business, professional and smaller industrial peoples.'[26]

At the 1933 Regina CCF convention, Woodsworth described the new party as 'essentially a drawing together of the common people.' He identified the people as labourers, farmers, small businessmen, clerics, and professionals.[27] This quickly came to be the official understanding of 'the people' in the CCF In *Democracy Needs Socialism*, League for Social Reconstruction (LSR) authors note that 'it is difficult to draw rigid class lines in Canada, but it is not difficult to recognize the common interests and sympathies which unite all wage and salary workers as against the small group who wield the predominant industrial and financial power.'[28] Several middle class groups, including farmers and small businessmen, had interests in siding against capital in the Canadian 'class struggle.'[29]

A long section in *Make This Your Canada* is devoted to describing the participation of various classes and regional groupings in 'the people's movement' responding to the increasingly monopolistic character of Canadian capitalism.[30] Lewis and Scott also argue that the powerful had consciously manipulated the powerless: 'To retain its power, finance capital must and does exaggerate and distort differences between sections of the people through its control of the major organs of education and propaganda.'[31] This had been a popular theme for many years in the prairie farmers' press. On this and the other themes noted above, LSR publications merely extended and provided updated evidence for the arguments that had long been staples of prairie populist rhetoric.

While the importance of attracting middle-class participants and electoral support was clear to movement leaders, farmer rank and file needed a more satisfying rationale for seeing urban non-labourers as part of 'the people.' This was most often provided with the notion of 'service' or 'useful labour.' Farmers had long believed that they worked harder than any other group in society, and that justice required they should be fairly rewarded for their labours. By extension, only those who provided some other essential service to the national community should participate in a just distribution of its benefits. Anyone who deserved a share of the social product was, by definition, a part of 'the people.'

In attempting to explain the idea that 'workers' should control and benefit from productive facilities in society, a Saskatchewan CCF pamphlet stated that 'when we say workers we mean anybody who renders a service to society – teachers, farmers, doctors, railwaymen – all are workers, all render a service, and all deserve to be rewarded for their labours.'[32] CCF criticism of the national governments' war effort from 1940 to 1945 also took up this theme. It suggested that 'dollar-a-year men' and others recruited from the business élite were serving their own interests, while the government was denying many of 'the people' making selfless and patriotic contributions to the national welfare – farmers, labour, and many professionals and technicians – their role in 'democratic planning.'[33]

Treating 'service' as the criterion for membership in the people was an old idea in British socialist thought. It was a recurrent theme in Robert Blatchford's *Clarion*, perhaps the most widely read British socialist periodical in the nineteenth and early twentieth centuries.[34] Strikingly similar to the *Clarion* in format and style, William Irvine's Calgary periodicals often followed this theme by excoriating the 'idle rich' and exalting the honest working man. Keir Hardie's influential ethical socialism also advocated the service criterion. As he said in 1920, 'the term "working class" is not used in any restricted sense, but includes all who by head or hand are rendering useful service to the community, and are dependent upon wages for a livelihood.'[35] Hardie used 'working class' and 'the people' as synonyms ('the ILP aims ... at the conquest of political power by the people').[36] In Canada, Hardie's considerable audience learned to appeal to farmers with anti-capitalist grievances of their own in their attempts to build a mass-based socialist movement.

Even academic British socialists used the 'service' criterion to draw effective lines in political struggles. In *The Sickness of an Acquisitive Society* (1921) and other writings, R.H. Tawney argued that the standard of function or service should direct distributive justice. G.D.H. Cole applied this idea to structures of political representation. He insisted that the only sensible approach to democratic decision-making in social institutions was to opt for representation by functional economic activity (or 'guild socialism'). Not only would service be the prerequisite of reward, thus favouring all of those not parasitic or exploitive, but service would also furnish the appropriate organizing principle for co-determination of industrial activity.

Service as a criterion for 'the people' was never systematically extended by socialists along guild socialist lines in Canada. It did help rationalize less worker-centred policies by the CCF, even though the notion of service was not inherently deradicalizing as long as the CCF portrayed capitalist society as inherently exploitive and unjust. However, prosperous middle classes experiencing temporary hardship are fickle allies of radical movements, even when they are presented with the parallels between working class, agrarian, and salaried employment in ways stressing common foes. In appealing to middle-class values of security and stability, a radical movement will almost certainly lose some of its critical and reformist zeal. If the middle-class–oriented political discourse claims that all but the 'big interests' serve the community usefully, workers and farmers will become less and less able to distinguish their interests and expectations from those of the middle classes. When the community in question is one of secure middle-class aspirations, the notion of service as a key to the people/power bloc antagonism loses much of its critical value.

None the less, these various notions of 'the people' are, as a group, the most radical of any in prairie populist discourse. The underlying social theory and philosophy was the most consistently and perceptively critical of the 'going system' available on the prairies.

Participatory Democracy

In its most complete yet simple sense, social democracy stands for the democratization of social relations. Historically, social democrats have identified 'democratic deficits' primarily as the effects of capitalism on the distribution of power and resources in social relations. Where capitalist or landed interests have restricted the franchise to their own class and its allies, the social democratic project focuses on achieving universal suffrage and other political rights. Where formal political rights have been extended to small property holders and propertyless labour, the focus shifts to achieving safeguards for these groups in their struggle to reduce their material disadvantages and to increase their power in relation to dominant economic groups.

Depending on such factors as political and cultural traditions, political stability, and the condition of the national economy, the social democratic political project will also focus on transforming the socio-economic system to remove the dominant capitalist class from its position of hegemony. A great emphasis on this objective is generally rationalized in terms of democratic reform. However, if it does not reject the right of capital to determine the social agenda, social democracy cannot mount a coherent campaign to democratize social relations, and transfers onto the omnibus of reform liberalism.

A participatory democratic element in social democratic thought is not guaranteed by the social democrat's commitment to eliminating the exploitive power of capital. This must be accompanied by a belief that power in social relations is equalized only when 'the people' become the subjects rather than simply the objects of power, exercising power at many levels of social life. It is not enough to believe that power will be sufficiently equalized if the people's representatives and government can provide them with a higher standard of living and better working conditions. Participatory democracy assigns a high priority to the widespread expression of rational human agency in the use of social power. In this section we will examine the social democratic populist commitment to such participation.

What was the nature of this discourse's indictment of the 'state of democracy' in Canada? We shall look briefly at two indexes of this: the expression of dissatisfaction with the 'depth' of democracy in Canadian public and social life, and the more specific criticism of existing political parties.

The Critique of Existing Democratic Practice

In the inter-war discussion of 'a new social order' on the prairies, William Irvine's contribution was typical in emphazing an extension of democracy. As editor of *The Alberta Non-Partisan*, Irvine expressed his belief in the necessity of this extension, by arguing that: when the common people, through education and organization, secure power, the whole social structure will gradually be moulded according to democratic principles. Industry, commerce, and education alike will readily conform to the new spirit ... [but] without political power the democratization of institutions is impossible ... When autocracy is overthrown, and democracy comes to power, these [public] institutions will serve the people, but not before.[37]

The UFA, *The Western Producer*, and the western labour press regularly portrayed Canadian economic and social institutions as inconsistent with democratic principles. By 1932, the CCF continued with the contention that a democratic 'gap' existed in Canada. Saskatchewan CCF notable Carlyle King provided one of the more sophisticated examples in a pamphlet entitled *What Is Democratic Socialism?* King covers a good number of the points made by other CCF spokespersons:

In the democratic countries of the Western world most of us have been taught to believe in responsible government, that is, that the people entrusted with positions of political governorship are answerable to those whom they, for the time being, govern ... But what about those who rule us in the economic sphere, [who] determine far more fatefully than political governors the ways in which we live out our lives? ... What control do we the (supposedly) sovereign people exercise over them? To whom are they responsible? In our capitalist democracies we choose our political rulers (or think we do); but who chooses our economic rulers?

All adults in a democracy have a political voice through the vote at election times, but very few have any voice in determining the conditions under which they must work, ... [and] little or no control over or check upon the economic decisions which may make or mar their lives.

This, says the socialist, is surely the denial of a democratic responsible government ... What it comes to is this: we have the principle of democracy in one area of citizenship, the political, and the principle of dictatorship or tyranny in another area, the economic, which at the very least is equally important ... we must extend the principle of democracy, of responsible government, from the purely legislative or parliamentary sphere to the economic sphere ... unless we have democracy in economic affairs we have only a limited democracy, at the worst a sham, at the best a shadow of the real thing.

In fact we cannot even have effective political democracy until we have democratic control in the economic sphere as well ... those who control the bulk of the economic resources of a nation have large sums to spend upon the election to government bodies of persons sympathetic to capitalism, while their opponents are comparatively handicapped. Furthermore, many citizens are so poor that they cannot afford to buy the books and papers they need to read if they are to make sensible political judgements. Capitalism, that is, keeps people in ignorance and thereby limits their exercise of full political citizenship. And on top of all that, capitalists through their ownership of the means of wealth production are also able to own the means of production of ideas; through their control of the nation's wealth, they also control what people read in the newspapers, hear over the radio, see in the newsreels, and learn in school, college, and church.

Observe, too, how the undemocratic control of economic wealth adversely affects the practice of the traditional democratic rights and liberties: freedom of speech, freedom of religion, freedom of association, freedom of the press, and equality before the law ...

For these two reasons, then, i) that men may be free to enjoy the rights and perform the duties of citizenship, and ii) that they may be free from the dominion of irresponsible power in the places where they work, socialists advocate the democratic government of commerce and industry.[38]

This argument for economic democracy is much more comprehensive than the typical piece of social democratic populist oratory or writing. However, it is typical in arguing that the logic of political democracy should extend beyond parliament, especially to the economic realm. Even prairie folk of less radical stripe were prepared to admit that economic power often distorted political competition to the advantage of 'the big interests.' King's argument thus encapsulates a key part of the social democratic populist strategy in attacking the existing order: the appeal to 'popular-democratic traditions' of support for popular choice of those who rule, and opposition to the illegitimate power of monopolies and other 'big interests.' National CCF publications such as *Democracy Needs Socialism* (1938)[39] and *Make This Your Canada* (1943)[40] also used this approach.

As one would expect, a significant element in social democratic criticism of Canadian democracy was an attack on 'the old-line parties.' Much of this came from Alberta, where the NPL and UFA organizations resolutely criticized partyism *per se*. The non-partisan spirit was also in evidence in Saskatchewan social democratic circles.

An early expression of the anti-party element in prairie social democracy appears in E.A. Partridge's No-Party League Manifesto (1913). Partridge argued that creating another party was a futile endeavour. Partisan attachments were still strong among farmers but, more seriously, parties would ignore the educational and propaganda purposes to which a radical movement must commit itself.[41] Additionally, any democratic organization must 'avoid that centralization of power in a group of general officers which characterizes party organizations and makes them easy of control [sic] by influences that render them useless as instruments of popular government.'[42] Partridge did not reject political action; instead, his league endorsed only that which followed extensive education by branch locals and majority support for the league's candidate prior to an election campaign. Unqualified constituency control over the candidate's program and campaign was also to be mandatory, thus ruling out centralized direction of local political life.

A rejection of centralized party control was also part of Alberta Non-Partisan League and United Farmers' objections to partyism. Neither, however, ruled out guidance from the organizational centre of the movement. Their attacks on partyism had more to do with party ties with organized business interests ('plutocracy') and party's inability to produce representative democratic thought than with party's purportedly inherent tendency to centralize power. Hybrid radical democratic/social democratic populists were also concerned that the strength of movement commitments would weaken if their political organization became the focus of member activity. As Walter Young has demonstrated,[43] this latter concern was influential throughout the national CCF organization until at least 1945.

Both the Farmers' Union of Canada (Saskatchewan Section), and its successor, the UFC(SS), demonstrated considerable anti-party and social democratic sentiment during the 1920s. When combined with its members' support for the provincial Liberal party, this stance prevented either organization from establishing an independent political wing during the decade. Ironically, non- and anti-partisan feelings were less widely held in Saskatchewan, which had no party strictly for farmers, than in Alberta, which did. The FUC (SS) saw itself as the rural equivalent of an industrial union, rejecting direct political action in favour of industrial action. The latter was thought to develop agrarian class consciousness more effectively and, consequently, to be a more effective weapon against the economic ruling class.[44] The FUC's main concern was establishing a 100 per cent compulsory wheat pool, the agricultural equivalent of 'One Big Union.' Many FUC members appreciated the quasi-syndicalist nature of UFA doctrine, but did not extend their support for group organization and internal democracy to support for direct political action.

The UFC(SS)'s more moderate political line also eschewed provincially co-ordinated political action from 1926 to 1931, even though its left wing was convinced of the eventual necessity of partisan activity by the organized farmers. George Williams had founded the Saskatchewan Farmers' Political Association (SFPA) in 1925, and presented it as an organization for all producers working against capitalist interests.[45] Williams and others devoted little attention to the SFPA after the 1926 merger, supplementing it with the Farmers' Educational League (FEL), a kind of Waffle group within the UFC(SS). Party-focused political action was not a major concern of the FEL; however, criticism of existing parties definitely was, when it could be linked to a criticism of capitalism and 'capitalist governments.'[46] When Williams and his FEL colleagues captured executive positions in the UFC(SS) in 1929, this criticism became a central part of the United Farmers' propaganda and program.

At the 1929 convention, several UFC district associations expressed support for the 'Industrial Organized group system of representation,' or 'co-operative

Government,' to 'replace the present party system.'[47] A majority opposed entry into politics on 'the UFA plan,' on the grounds that 'up to the present more has been accomplished for the benefit of the farming community by the organization working as an educational and economic body than by direct representation in parliament.'[48] In 1930, the non-partisan forces carried the day again, but faced stiff opposition from those who agreed with the District No.16 convention resolution contending that because 'the freeing of the wealth producers from economic slavery hinges upon the conquest of [political] power,' the convention should support 'political action by farmers as a class, preferably in conjuction with other bodies of wealth producers such as organized labour.'[49]

At the 1932 convention, both the president of the UFC(SS) and Louise Lucas, Women's Section president, condemned the party system's links with vested interests. This convention overwhelmingly endorsed joint political action with the small Independent Labor Party.[50] The ILP's leader, M.J. Coldwell, had cut his Canadian political teeth as a provincial candidate for the Progressives, and had condemned undemocratic 'partyism' as late as 1929.[51] ILP criticism of 'orthodox partyism' clearly made it a more attractive ally to the UFC(SS).

The non-partisan tendency in radical prairie farm organizations from 1920 to 1930 is widely recognized, though the early position taken by J.S. Woodsworth is less so. His activities as an organizer for the Non-Partisan League in 1917 (primarily in Alberta) were not just undertaken out of friendship for Irvine or a desire to hasten the political alliance of farmers and urban labour. Woodsworth did in fact subscribe to a critique of party almost as rejectionist as Irvine's for several years before 1920.[52]

Even after Irvine became a key spokesman for group government, and Woodsworth became the leader of the ILP in Manitoba, the latter spoke in favour of occupational representation and a form of group government.[53] Woodsworth contended in a 1926 Edmonton speech that while partyism was corrupt and unnatural, occupational representation and group government were both natural and desirable.[54] An echo of his contempt for Canadian party activities is even evident in his presidential address to the 1933 Regina CCF convention: 'the democracy we have known in this country has been government of the people by the party machines for the profiteers.'[55] Contrary to Walter Young's suggestion, Woodsworth's early revulsion with the practices of party politics was based on more than his quasi-religious orientation to the CCF as movement.[56] He had absorbed a radical agrarian critique of party despite his support for British parliamentary institutions.

With influential figures in the early CCF carrying their animus against partyism into the new federation, the CCF was a party that 'dared not speak its name' in its early years on the prairies. Its leaders insisted that if it were a party in some sense, it was in no way comparable to the 'old-line parties.' This was especially true in Alberta, where the UFA's passion for organizational independence seriously hampered the creation of a viable political organization until it was too late – i.e., after the Social Credit victories of 1935.[57] Even in Saskatchewan, where the alliance between the UFC and ILP was more effectively co-ordinated, 'CCF' did not replace 'Saskatchewan Farmer-Labor Group' as the alliance's official name until 1937.

The prairie affiliates' reluctance to display 'party-like' characteristics to their intended constituency affected national CCF publications. In the 1932 *The CCF (Farmer, Labour, Socialist): Outline of its Origins, Organization and Objectives*, the national CCF office emphasized the new movement's federated character, portrayed it as a logical extension of previous farmer and labour organizations, and insisted that the CCF was 'not a political party such as the two traditional parties ... but a close alliance of social units which have fundamental aims in common.'[58] The notion of the CCF as a 'united front' of progressives found a clear expression in the Farmer-Labor Group's offers of electoral co-operation with Social Credit, Communist, and even Conservative organizations from 1935 to 1938. No self-respecting party would have engaged in such political follies, temporary as they were.

When CCF affiliates and provincial associations acted more self-consciously as parties, they criticized other parties primarily in terms of their relations with capitalistic interests, and their hopelessly undemocratic character.[59] National CCF publications took this line for many years. *Democracy Needs Socialism* singled out the Liberal party to demonstrate how undemocratic party organization and policy-making lead to undemocratic government policy, and to warn 'those who think that progressive young men can revitalize old parties.'[60] Five years later, in *Make This Your Canada*, Frank Scott and David Lewis contended that because 'democracy is frustrated by political machines and huge corporate funds,' the people had become 'politically cynical in a disturbing way.' By contrast, 'the CCF was not formed from above by bosses.' It was controlled by a range of co-operating interests and opinions, and hence capable of forging a 'dynamic unity' on questions of policy and the people's needs.[61]

For all of the residual critique of partyism in the new social democratic organization, there remained a recognition of the need for a party as a political instrument of social change. It was not just based on the widespread belief that farmers' interests had to be represented by their own in legislatures.[62] As David Smith noted of Saskatchewan, the Depression had a critical effect. 'Previous inhibitions about partisan activity were swept away in the economic collapse, and the farmers approached partisan politics with the same desperation as they had supported the abortive campaign for the compulsory pooling of wheat.'[63] S.M. Lipset makes a similar point, arguing that Saskatchewan farmers emphasized producer co-operation schemes in good economic times, but saw the need for co-ordinated political action when times were bad.[64]

The anti-capitalist, anti–old-party position taken by prairie labour parties made them more politically attractive to most prairie farmers by the early 1930s.[65] Effective political alliances with labour had to be forged and sustained with more than declarations of mutual support. The 'democratic class struggle' of electoral competition virtually assured the importance of party-like discipline, co-ordination, and leadership for the alliance's prospects. This was recognized early in Saskatchewan,[66] and belatedly in Alberta. Retaining separate political extensions of rural and urban workers' economic organizations was no way to challenge the prevailing order.

Reaching unradicalized sections of 'the people' required a strong social democratic voice inside and outside the legislatures. Pooling organizational, financial, and ideological resources was crucial if popular dissatisfaction with a failed economic system was to be translated into a popular program for change. Federally and provincially, the CCF thus had to act as more than a loose federation of groups with broadly similar concerns.

There was, however, a major and unavoidable complication for this strategy. As social democrats, CCFers believed that democratic results could not flow from undemocratic processes. More precisely, prairie CCF supporters and leaders insisted that democratic structures and practices within the movement's organization were prerequisites of social and economic objectives. Thus, conflicts and disagreements within the movement often reduced the competitive political strength of the organization. Thus the CCF's decision to aim for the political power that only party could achieve was frustrated by its incomplete devotion to party-style electoral promotion and centralized direction of the movement's political work.

These complications did not have a completely negative impact on the CCF. Two examples are germane. In the first place, where the orientation of the groups in the political 'federation' is ideologically close and stable over a significant period, emphasis on democratic process within the party is an advantage. This was true in Saskatchewan, where the numerically dominant agrarian contingent in the Farmer-Labor Group/CCF had the most socialistic perspective of any agrarian community in Canada. In addition, and partly as a consequence, it managed to cultivate a sensitive appreciation of agrarian problems among labour groups in the province's small urban centres.

It is also true that however much the CCF's internal democratic practices hobbled its competitive strength after the early years, the CCF would not have emerged as a significant national force had those practices not been guaranteed at the outset. Provincial CCF organizations' and affiliates' insistence on autonomy was not simply a function of provincial jealousies or member-organization stubbornness. It was rooted in the long-standing agrarian political principle that organizational autonomy was a guarantee of democratic responsiveness. If the invitation to federate with other 'people's organizations' had hinted at the need for centralized decision-making and leadership domination in the federation, prairie farmers' organizations would have declined.[67] As it was, only eastern intellectuals and west-coast Marxists would have preferred such a structure for the new party, and they were not instrumental in initiating the Calgary conference. (Both groups were highly suspicious of prairie farm organizations' commitment to serious socialist measures and objectives.)

It may well be that a socialist labour party would have laid more solidly radical foundations without agrarian allies, but it is not likely that this political creation would have matched the political impact of the CCF – at least for a generation after 1932. The viability of a national social democratic organization in Canada was predicated on integration of both labour and farmer organizations within a democratic structure. This is true even though that structure contributed to problems for the efforts of the organization as a competitive party.[68]

Positive Alternatives in Democratic Practice

Social democratic populists were anxious to demonstrate their distance from 'old-line parties' in matters of internal democracy. They recognized that their constituency would find any political alternative wanting if the infamous old party practices found a home there. None the less, no social democratic populist appeal matched the radical democratic emphasis on internal democracy.

The Non-Partisan League of Alberta stressed its anti-monopoly, public-ownership, and 'business government' appeals more than its status as the people's instrument, but the latter was increasingly prominent as the campaign to involve the UFA in political competition intensified. In 1918, Irvine wished to clarify the socialist tendencies of the NPL program while portraying the league as an open and popularly controlled organization. In a characteristic appeal, he argued: 'The Non-Partisan Movement is the first logical step for the socialist but is is only the first step. We are not a socialistic organization because we are an organization of the people and the people have not given us any mandate to adopt pure, unadulterated socialism. We are just as socialistic as our numbers make us. When you vote Non-Partisan you vote for what the people want and not for what some clique may decide is good for them.'[69]

Just over a year later, at one of the crucial NPL-UFA debates, the 'objectives of the League' were read to H.W. Wood and others to demonstrate agreement on first principles. The principles relevant to participatory democracy inside and outside the movement organization preceded those dealing with economic change, and are impressive while not as demanding as the UFA's doctrine of delegate democracy:

The objectives of the League shall be:
1) To overcome partisanship:
    a) by the election of a truly people's government and the establishment of a business administration instead of a party administration.
    b) by educating our people to a higher sense of citizenship.
    c) by organizing them to co-operate in political action.
    d) by leaving the program of legislation to be enacted, and the financing of all elections, in the hands of the constituents.[70]

The No-Party League of Western Canada placed more emphasis on the need for grass-roots public education, the value of direct legislation, and the need for a non-partisan 'producers' government' than it did on its own democratic workings. None the less, its constitution insisted on complete local control over the affairs of each league branch, and stipulated a referendum-initiated procedure for changing the league's constitution.[71] At this point in his political career, E.A. Partridge was almost as concerned with promoting the principles of grass-roots democracy as he was with the policy objectives of the democratic struggle.

Both Saskatchewan's Farmers' Union of Canada and United Farmers of Canada were composed of a large number of locals that sent delegates to district conventions and the annual general meeting. This had a practical as well as ideological justification. In the FUC campaign for compulsory pooling, a centralized organization would have been of little value. When the UFC finally 'entered politics,' it accepted UFA principles regarding constituency autonomy, central-office prerogatives, candidate and MLA status as delegates, and the pre-eminence of the annual convention.[72] The organizational structure of the UFC(SS) was ready-made for this approach to political action, although amalgamation with the ILP in this year complicated matters somewhat.

The CCF's internal democratic structures, and their portrayal by movement spokespersons, are of greatest interest here. The structural aspect of the CCF's activities has been described in previous studies, particularly Englemann (1956), Lipset (1950), and Young (1969). To some extent, all three test the national CCF experience against Michels's 'iron law of oligarchy,' and all suggest that the Saskatchewan provincial organization provides the strongest Canadian exception to the 'iron law.'[73] Lipset's more detailed look at the Saskatchewan case establishes the sociological and historical validity of such an evaluation.

In Alberta, activists on the left of the UFA made much of the logical and substantive continuities between the UFA and CCF organizations. After the devastating defeats of 1935, the CCF leadership slowly came to recognize that their loosely federated structure was a liability, with its separate UFA and Canadian Labour party locals and CCF clubs.[74] An integrated provincial CCF organization was finally formed in 1940; well before this, CCF annual conventions featured condemnations of Social Credit autocracy and inaction. *The People's Weekly* printed regular attacks on Aberhart's style of rule, and insisted on the CCF's structural and ideological appropriateness as a democratic alternative. Editor William Irvine was especially emphatic in this regard, to the point that during 1937 he characterized Aberhart's methods as Fascistic. The 1938 CCF constitution enshrined traditions of delegate democracy as guarantees of faithful representation of all affiliated groups,[75] but the 1938 UFA convention decision to withdraw from the CCF ensured that these commitments were politically irrelevant.

The Saskatchewan CCF assigned the same importance to internal democracy as its UFC(SS) predecessor. Membership numbers provide a concrete indication of the extent of participation: party membership went from 4,460 in 1941, to 9,813 in 1942, 25,925 in 1944, and 31,858 in 1945.[76] As Lipset demonstrates, CCF delegates and local leaders came overwhelmingly from actively contested elections in intensely participatory rural community organizations.[77] The CCF thus had practical as well as ideological reasons for establishing a party structure that developed and channelled the participatory urges of Saskatchewan citizens.

CCF portrayals of its internal democracy during the 1930s and early 1940s tell us a good deal about the party's self-understanding. The first CCF publication distributed in Saskatchewan emphasized the new party's origins in like-minded organizations. The authors underscored the CCF's federated character, with provincial councils composed of affiliated group delegates and a national council. They emphasized the provincial origins of CCF policies; delegates 'came with definite mandates from conventions of their associations, and none of the decisions conflicted with the previously adopted programmes of the Farmer and Labour organizations represented at the conference.'[78]

At early conventions of the Saskatchewan Farmer-Labor Group, much was made of the decision to send proposed platform changes to all locals for discussion prior to the next convention. Advertising during the 1934 provincial and 1935 federal elections attempted to deflect Liberal and Conservative red-baiting and warnings concerning CCF 'dictatorship' by emphasizing old-party connections to 'big interests,' and how all Farmer-Labor Group policies had been discussed and endorsed by their district and annual conventions. By 1938, a chastened and more defensive Saskatchewan CCF felt the need to preface a pamphlet on its new land policy with an insistence that the whole CCF program was drawn up by delegates elected by ordinary Saskatchewan people. 'So it is not a question of what the CCF will do for the farmers, – but the question is what the farmers will do through the CCF government which the farmers themselves have pioneered, financed and will elect.'[79]

The pamphlet goes on to outline the new 1936 land policy, which 'had come from the people themselves.' When besieged by adverse press, old-party, and popular responses to the use-lease land policy, the CCF altered the policy and attempted to legitimize both old and new policies with reference to their democratic origins. This strategy was not as commonly adopted in provincial literature as one would expect, especially when one considers its popular appeal within the UFA. Perhaps the Saskatchewan CCF believed that its penetration into rural community organizations would produce a widespread recognition that CCF policy was the authentic expression of the popular will.

One indication that CCF leaders and advocates did not give internal democracy a key place in their public appeal can be found in the 1934 Farmer-Labor Group *Handbook for Speakers*. It employs a question-and-answer format to explain policies in a folksy manner, but says nothing about membership control over policy matters in the new political force. Land tenure and related economic issues were undeniably paramount for suffering farmers, but political traditions of support for popular democracy had not died. Noting that CCF leaders and activists employed an overly rationalistic model of voter behaviour may help to explain why the prairie CCF relied so heavily on policy presentation at the expense of appeals to popular-democratic traditions.

One of the most cogent and well-crafted appeals of this kind to come through official CCF channels was in *Make This Your Canada*. The irony is that co-author Lewis was the quintessential Michelsian party oligarch,[80] and Frank Scott is well remembered for his highly centralist view of federalism and party activities. None the less, chapter 9 includes a lucid and uplifting account of 'how democracy works' in the CCF. The account gives special attention to the 'faith in the people' underlying the participatory and decentralized party structure, the provisions made for policy creation and discussion by the rank and file, and the low-budget but popularly based party financing. Adding to the irony is Walter Young's demonstration of the high degree of élite dominance in the national organization as compared to provincial organizations, Saskatchewan's in particular.[81] Thus, while it may be true that democracy within the CCF organization was virtually an 'end in itself,' as Young says,[82] this belief was not systematically expressed in CCF popular appeals. To the extent that participatory democracy did feature prominently in the CCF's public discourse, it was primarily in proposals for reforming economic institutions.

In this broad set of concerns, the CCF broke little new political ground. We have already seen that E.A. Partridge used co-operative organizations, the No-Party League of Western Canada, his many articles and letters in the agrarian press, and his *A War on Poverty* (1926) to campaign for socialized, democratic control over economic life. Partridge's early campaign to increase the power of the grain growers' co-operatives and associations *vis-à-vis* the Winnipeg Grain Exchange can be seen as an attempt to provide the basis for a democratic producers' control over the western grain economy. His later advocacy of publicly owned grain elevators and public control over grain-marketing activities was partially justified in terms of organized producer control of their industry.

In the realm of formally political institutions and processes, Partridge joined most agrarian activists in promoting direct legislation, but unlike many crypto-Liberals, Partridge was no monomaniac on this matter. In the 1913 No-Party League Manifesto, he spoke of direct legislation as 'the first legislative step towards the establishment of the rule of the people – the workers.'[83] In *A War on Poverty*, however, his passion for highly participatory economic and political democracy is less evident. Assuming a coincidence of interests between citizens and government officials in the classless co-operative commonwealth, Partridge felt no need to develop a proposal for participatory structures in the public economy and political system.

We have already seen the positive participatory objectives promoted by the Non-Partisan League. Like Partridge, NPL activists supported direct legislation as a means of implementing the popular will. Yet this proposal was not connected to clearly defined proposals for participation by 'the people' (primarily farmers) in a democratic economy. The relationship between grain producers' co-operatives and elevators and state-owned flour mills and railway lines was never addressed except in terms of how it would benefit workers and farmers. Nor was the non-partisan 'business administration,' the NPL alternative to party government, ever explained in terms that demonstrated how popular control of government would enhance the expected efficiencies and responsiveness of the new state model. Such discussions were almost always conducted in issue-specific or abstract terms. One has to wonder if this was because the new structures of political democracy would not depart significantly from parliamentary norms, or because NPL leaders and activists believed that relations between popular organizations and the state would change unproblematically following socialization of the economy.

Non-Partisan League vagueness about economic and political dimensions of participatory democracy was ultimately not a problem for prairie social democratic populism. The organization was assimilated by the United Farmers of Alberta, which continued some of this vagueness in their own discourse. In Saskatchewan, many one-time NPL members found their way first into the Farmers' Union of Canada, then into the UFC(SS). Both of these organizations promoted their members' visions of enhanced democracy almost exclusively through struggles for the wheat pool and then the 100 per cent compulsory pool. Most of their members gave low priority to changes in political structures. Until 1931, only a vocal minority wanted to combine a form of group government with a socialized economy. By the time the UFC 'entered politics,' their political agenda was still dominated by economic issues. Democratization of the key public institutions thus meant 'social ownership and co-operative production for use.'[84] Participatory democracy within the organization would continue, and ensure the responsiveness of the organization's legislative representatives to membership opinion and decisions. However, between 1932 and 1944, comparatively few suggestions for democratizing formal governmental structures came out of the UFC's successors in Saskatchewan.

Surprisingly for a loosely structured federation of many radical organizations, the early CCF gave expression to few of its member groups' previous concerns with political institutional change. The only exception was in the Alberta CCF before 1936. The exception is more apparent than substantial, because in that province no integrated CCF organization emerged before 1938. The UFA from 1932 to 1935 continued to endorse delegate democracy and group government proposals, but with markedly reduced enthusiasm.

The Regina Manifesto and Woodsworth's 1933 presidential address in Regina express an only tangential concern with 'participationist' political reform. Several suggestive phrases can be found in the Manifesto: capitalism is to be replaced by a social order free from domination and exploitation, 'in which genuine democratic self-government based upon economic equality will be possible'; the CCF appeals to all who support 'a far-reaching reconstruction of our economic and political institutions'; and workers' organizations 'will be indispensable elements in a system of genuine industrial democracy.'

While elaboration on these themes is not to be expected from a manifesto, some concrete proposals for provisional institutional reform would not have been out of place. Such proposals would have provided a valuable reference point for future discussions about democratic control of public life. The only institutional reform proposal was for the abolition of the senate ('one of the most reactionary assemblies in the civilized world').

In his 1933 presidential address, Woodsworth raised the issue of institutional reform for popular-democratic purposes, then abandoned it. He advocated a distinctively Canadian socialism: 'we in Canada must work out our own salvation in our own way. Socialism has so many variations ... why not a Canadian type?' Yet, he continued:

'Democracy' – the rule of the people – is a much discounted word. Little wonder. The democracy which we have known in this country has been government of the people by party machines for the profiteers. The parliamentary machine is antiquated and its procedure obsolete. Government has functioned largely in the interests of the exploiting classes. The untrained masses are quite unfitted to pass judgement on the complicated problems that face modern executives. But having said this, I must confess that I still believe that the will of the people should prevail. This may appear a hang-over from the high-sounding but empty doctrine of Liberalism. But fundamentally it is sound. An intelligent and alert citizenship is the only guarantee of freedom. Attempted short-cuts, however alluring, offer no real solution.[85]

An 'antiquated' parliamentary machine would seem to require substantial change, especially from the perspective of a uniquely Canadian socialist movement. Woodsworth none the less eschews any proposals along these lines in favour of a mass educational campaign, following which the 'will of the people' would finally coincide with the interests of the people, and government would respond accordingly. Changes to the elected institutions of political decision-making seem to be lumped into the category of 'short cuts' incapable of offering 'real solutions' to the democratic problem. (In fairness, I should add that the short-cuts to which he referred were probably those advocated by the increasingly popular Communist Party.)

The Manifesto does propose non-elective institutional additions to the structure/process of public policy making. Paramount is a National Planning Commission, with responsibility for economic planning and overall co-ordination of the social services. Various boards managing newly created public enterprises were also prescribed for all three levels of government. The only hint of popular-representative input into this elaborate planning structure comes with the vague claim that workers in the new public enterprises 'must be given the right to participate in the management of the industry.'[86]

What can account for the absence of substantive proposals in the Manifesto for popular input into government policy determination? Perhaps the prudent leadership of the as yet unconsolidated CCF wished to avoid contentious proposals lacking well-considered support amongst federation affiliates. The economic-crisis environment of the CCF's founding may be the major reason. Proposals for political 'tinkering' might have been perceived as trivial and unnecessary for the millions suffering from the economic collapse. Bold departures in economic policy, however, would have a compelling character in the public mind. One is also tempted to conjecture that the League for Social Reconstruction's influence on the final shape of the Manifesto would have discouraged the inclusion of any unorthodox proposals for political reform. However, the absence of such reforms in the 1932 Calgary Program[87] suggests that this has limited explanatory value.

Woodsworth had a surprisingly mixed record on the question of unorthodox political reforms – surprising, that is, in view of his 1933 Address and the Manifesto. A 1935 article echoed Woodsworth's earlier support for the principles of group government, proposing occupational representation as one of several reforms that might make parliament more responsive to public opinion and interests. Proportional representation was another suggestion, again one that Woodsworth had made with the ILP in Manitoba from 1919 to 1932. Direct legislation did not find a place in the 1935 proposals. It was unconstitutional, and CCF representation of the people's interests seemed to hold more promise as a democratic corrective to parliament's failings.[88]

Woodsworth's most unorthodox proposals for the extension of democracy in Canadian public life applied not to parliament but to economic life. In his House of Commons speeches throughout the 1920s and 1930s, one can find scattered suggestions for representative public control of the workplace, regulatory and planning boards, and substantial expansion of co-operative enterprise.[89] Woodsworth and the CCF made their most systematic and influential contributions to Canadian political discourse in their advocacy of 'economic democracy.'

In institutional terms, economic democracy would entail two types of democratic control. One was the public's, through their elected and appointed officials, over state-owned enterprises. This would include innovations in the representation of various occupational-group organizations on various boards and commissions responsible for planning in certain sectors of the economy. The other type of economic democracy would operate within the 'socialized' and expanded co-operative sector. The Regina Manifesto merely reflected over a decade of farmer organizations' demands when it called for 'the encouragement by the public authority of both producers' and consumers' co-operative institutions ... through appropriate legislation and the provision of adequate credit facilities.'[90]

The State and Technocratic Thought

The state figured prominently in the social democratic vision of economic democracy. In this section we will focus on the negative and positive images of the state, and the discussion of state structures as vehicles for 'democratic ends' in this discourse.

Negative Images of the State

Negative images of the state had two sources: various socialist accounts of the relationship between class power and state power, and the agrarian hinterland perspective of the prairie resident. The most general aspect of the socialist analysis of the state was that it was directed by those with corporate power. The negative hinterland image of the state was quite compatible with this line of analysis, because the general distinction between those possessing, and those adversely affected by, state power ('the people/the power bloc') was a constant in all populist hinterland perspectives. Many on the academic left have seen agrarian-hinterland consciousness as an insuperable barrier to the development of socialist ideology and political direction. It is, none the less, undeniable that Canadian social democracy benefited greatly from the widespread prairie suspicion of the national government's class bias. This 'popular democratic tradition' of opposition to the state as an instrument of class power was a crucial foundation of prairie social democratic populism, as it had been in the populism of Patrons in Ontario a generation earlier.

There are many examples of social democratic populist characterizations of the link between dominant class interests and state performance. E.A. Partridge made it the central theme of the first issue of *The Grain Growers' Guide*, in his one experience as its editor. Fourteen years later, Partridge contrasted the existing state with the state in the new social order he envisioned: 'the old fashioned State functioned as the maintainer of property rights and class rule; the new one, to be, will employ itself in advancing the well-being of all its deserving citizens by whatever means appear advisable to employ.'[91]

When Partridge discussed class rule since confederation in his *A War on Poverty*, he spoke of 'the minions of Mammon who rule at Ottawa.' Partridge's folksy references to the class/state relationship influenced many Saskatchewan farmers who wanted their reform in larger doses than those offered by the SGGA and provincial Liberals.

William Irvine's Non-Partisan League journals were full of references to the class character of federal government legislation, as was *The Farmers in Politics*.[92] But however much it had been an instrument of dominant class interests in the past, the state could be refitted for progressive purposes. In fact, Irvine believed that only successive reforms could make the necessary changes. Sounding very Fabian, Irvine declared in 1917 that 'we must save the State through the State.'[93]

The negative image of the state in social democratic populist circles was primarily the result of their characterization of it as sustainer of a capitalist society. The prairie West suffered from national state policies, so agrarians and workers in the West were necessarily the exploited cogs in the capitalist productive machine. Perhaps the most sustained analysis along these lines came from J.S. Woodsworth. Throughout his political career, Woodsworth argued that concentrated economic power – especially finance capital[94] – effectively controlled legislatures and other arms of the state. Woodsworth contended that this situation would continue as long as concentrated economic power remained in private hands. Public or social forms of ownership were the only antidotes to capitalist direction of the state.

The state's negative image was portrayed in other ways. George Williams argued in *Social Democracy in Canada* that 'in our modern age 90 per cent of our laws revolve around the protection of invested capital.'[95] Speaking for the federal party leadership in 1943, David Lewis and Frank Scott claimed that laws in capitalist society only provide marginal relief to the 'socially wounded,' and do nothing to eliminate basic inequalities and the economic struggle stemming from them.[96]

Most prairie socialists included the constitution in their critique of the role of law in a class-biased regime. In doing so they were accepting the centralist assumptions of CCF constitutional criticism at the 1933 Regina meeting, as voiced by CCF leaders as different as Angus MacInnis[97] and Frank Scott.[98] A regular contributor to the *Western Producer's* letters-to-the-editor section provided a hard-edged, grass-roots perspective on the Canadian state's capitalist bias. W. Ganong from Sturgis, Saskatchewan, argued: 'We as workers and farmers cannot expect anything from the present parliamentary system of government. It is a rich man's institution and functions in the interests of the rich, lots of legislation in the interests of the capitalist, very little in the interests of the worker. A workers and farmers government would function in the interests of the workers and farmers, and could be used as an effective instrument in dispensing with the capitalist system.'[99]

The Positive Image of the State

The positive image of the state in prairie social democracy was shaped by several factors. One was the generic populist feeling that regardless of what the state's role should eventually be in civil society, the power of the state had first to be used to counteract that power of industrial, financial, and commercial monopolies ('the big interests'). Populists were also deeply suspicious of the state as a repository of concentrated power that threatened popular democracy. But populists placed little emphasis on the negative side of this healthy ambivalence when the focus was on the power of private monopolies in the western grain economy. Social democratic populists were thus on solid ground when they proposed government action to reduce the power of private monopolies such as the CPR, financial institutions, or the Winnipeg Grain Exchange.

A second source of the positive image of the state was an evolutionary theory of social development, articulated by Fabians, the Independent Labour Party, and virtually all left-wing thinkers in the United States and Britain. This theory posited the inevitability of public ownership of 'natural monopolies' in the capitalist economy. What was inevitable was also morally desirable, given the alternative of private monopolies exacting tribute from average citizens. Since only the state could ultimately defend the rights of the public against the power of the few, this protection was to be extended to legislation encouraging and protecting co-operative enterprises. The state thus acquired a positive image because social evolution made it the principal guarantor of 'the public interest.'

A third factor shaping the state's positive image was increasing complexity of economic life and social organization. Social democrats insisted that this made economic planning imperative. Given the desirability of distributing the benefits of such planning as equitably as possible, and given the history of corporate planning, the obvious agent was the state. State institutions would be subject to at least a modicum of public control, in the presence of representative assemblies, political freedoms, and the 'sovereignty of public opinion.' The social evolution that created the need for rational economic planning also necessitated co-ordination of such planning. Increased legitimacy for the state would be a condition of its democratic and rational planning in the future.

Finally, the positive image of the state-to-be was premised on the notion that the organized political vehicles of the people would eventually achieve political success in the 'democratic class struggle.' A positive image and enhanced legitimacy in the eyes of the people would help to sanction the new policies and programs formulated by the people's representatives in the legislature(s), and to encourage popular contributions to the new state's policy process. The likelihood of capitalist sabotage to the 'people's state' would also necessitate a high degree of public support for the state.

Social democratic populists usually made the positive case for the state quite simply, with references to the benefits that would accrue to the people from state activity in a certain sphere of public life. The state was depicted as a principal player in the creation of a truly social democracy. This idea was neatly expressed in one of William Irvine's principal pieces of booklet-length propaganda, *The Political Servants of Capitalism*. 'The State under democratic government,' Irvine asserted, 'is not something that controls the people, it "is" the people in control of themselves ... or at least the State which the Co-operative Commonwealth recognizes is the people.'[100]

Social democratic prairie populists thought of the relationship between state power and democracy in two basic senses. First, properly applied state power led to an equitable distribution of citizen welfare. The redistributive function of the state promoted democracy by advancing the old socialist ideal, equality of condition. Other extensions of democracy were contingent on successes in the redistributive realm. Progress towards equality of condition would both lead to an increasing equalization of power between citizens and provide all citizens with the wherewithal and incentive for meaningful participation in political life. Advances towards equality would develop rational and efficacious political actors. Thus, in what seems a paradox to the liberal, a more active and interventionist state enhances the participatory, power-equalizing character of public life.

The most characteristic and politically important proposals for enhanced state control and regulation of the economy are relatively well known. Some of the earliest proposals for 'democratizing' state action came from E.A. Partridge. His 1913 Manifesto of the No-Party League of Western Canada demanded the popular single tax and a wide extension of state-owned public utilities.[101] We have seen that these demands were also featured in the quintessentially crypto-Liberal 'New National Policy' program of the Canadian Council of Agriculture several years later. However, while both Partridge and the CCA leaders both argued for these innovations as supports for a structure of popular government and enhanced agrarian welfare, Partridge took the rationale one step farther. He portrayed both reforms as building blocks for control of the state by 'workers' and other 'genuine producers,' and thus gave a social democratic purpose to otherwise merely agrarian welfare-enhancing nostrums. The same rationale was evident when the Dominion Labour Party in Saskatchewan and Alberta endorsed these two reforms in the early 1920s, and the Independent Labour Party in Manitoba endorsed them from the late 1890s onwards.[102]

The Non-Partisan League in Saskatchewan and Alberta agitated for public ownership in the natural resource, industrial, financial, and commercial sectors of the Canadian economy. Both groups were inspired indirectly by British socialism, and directly by North Dakota's Non-Partisan League program. In Saskatchewan, league contacts with the urban labour parties were minimal, yet the two had similar proposals for state ownership of financial institutions, natural resources, public utilities, and various supply and processing operations in the grain trade. The Alberta Non-Partisan League had close ties with the Labour Representation League, and later with the Dominion Labour Party, through William Irvine. The 1917 Labour Representation League 'Platform of Principles' advocated 'public ownership and control of all the means of wealth production and distribution,' with special emphasis on natural resources, 'the means of transportation and communication,' and banks, as well as steep taxes on income, corporation profits, and 'unimproved land values.'[103] By 1919, the Alberta NPL constitution identified government ownership and control 'of all natural resources and fundamental industries feasible to government control' as 'objects of the League.'[104]

At a UFA district convention in 1919, Irvine emphasized the long-term character of this program, and insisted that the public would not be ready for government ownership to the degree advocated in the NPL program until 'the people own the government.'[105] A year earlier, he had drawn a distinction between simple government ownership and collective ownership. Government ownership would not be collective ownership (i.e., democratic) 'until the Government represents collective society.' The superiority of collective ownership would only be evident when it yielded maximum service at minimum expense while providing 'adequate protection for the labourers employed in the operation.'[106]

Like virtually all prairie social democrats, Irvine believed that collective ownership outside of the 'co-operative sector' had to be based on state ownership, even when the economic environment was predominantly capitalistic. As he argued in 1917, 'There has been great extension of Public functions during the last century. The Postal System, Public Schools, Libraries, Art Galleries, Bureaus of Research, Hospitals and municipal ownership of light, of water and of transportation. These are socialized institutions growing up in Capitalist society. Any lasting social reform today must be nursed at the breast of capitalism.'[107]

This essentially Fabian account of the gradual transformation of a privately owned economy was a staple of Canadian social democracy. Abandoning the 'parliamentary road to socialism' was culturally illegitimate, and the social democratic left joined virtually all educated opinion in perceiving an inherently progressive and democratic logic in social evolution. So while we may now scoff at their acceptance of Fabian logic, prairie social democrats should not be be dismissed as naïve 'liberals in a hurry.'

The social democratic conception of 'democratic results' to follow increasing state ownership was not constant over time or across organizations in the prairies. Irvine's career is representative. In his earlier association with farmer and labour organizations, he emphasized the connection between popular control of elected representatives and increased state ownership in the economy. He also tied reduced economic inequalities to increased total wealth and increased levels of popular participation in political decision-making and industrial control. The promise of social democracy was to be realized in both equality and participation.

The participatory dimension had a less prominent place in his period of social credit advocacy[108] and his years as a CCF leader on the prairies. When the problems engendered by economic crisis became more pressing, social democrats attended less to the participatory deficiencies in Canadian public life. They gave almost exclusive attention to the need to minimize hardships and reconstruct the economy. National planning and state ownership would enhance 'economic democracy,' seen primarily in terms of a welfare-maximization strategy. Equalizing economic power meant primarily equalization of consumption abilities, and secondarily equalization of public input into economic planning and other policy development. Judged by past Canadian practice, these social democratic objectives for state economic action are undeniably radical. Judged by their own broader philosophical commitment to a socialization of democracy, however, the ordering of these objectives is problematic.

We can now examine the types of 'state intervention' supported by prairie social democrats, and note the democratic rationalization provided for each. At the most general level were proposals for rational – and primarily national – economic planning. Before the Depression, the case for economic planning had three goals: 1 / eliminating economic institutions that yielded unacceptable profits for capitalists and exploited farmers and workers; 2 / expanding economic returns from the country's natural resources (i.e., translate potential into actual abundance); and 3 / redistributing resources to create a much greater material equality among individuals and classes, regardless of how much potential wealth had been realized as actual wealth.

The viability of the second goal of state planning had been demonstrated to social democratic populists by the range of planning activities successfully undertaken by Allied governments during the Great War. For prairie grain producers, federal government handling of wartime grain sales overseas was an especially pointed illustration. Social democrats had promoted the first and third-noted objectives of state planning before the war, but they assumed that if the second goal had been proved to be obtainable, then the other two were clearly within reach. The fact that these latter goals were, for social democrats, morally necessary, made them even more legitimate.

The Depression added a new dimension to the case for economic planning. Creating an economy of abundance was no longer the issue; the priority became minimizing hardship for 'the people.' The collapsed capitalist system had demonstrated its fatal unworkability in addition to its manifest immorality. Economic planning would satisfy both the moral and 'system-maintenance' requirements of a rational social and economic order.

The urgency of economic planning was clearly articulated in the Regina Manifesto. It asserted that some form of planning was necessary to counteract and replace 'the disintegrating capitalist system' with 'the most equitable distribution of the national income' and 'the most efficient development of the natural resources.'[109] The same priority can be readily seen in the UFA, Saskatchewan Farmer-Labor Group, and ILP-CCF programs and literature after 1930. In Robert Gardiner's presidential address to the 1934 UFA convention, delegates were told that they could 'find grounds for pardonable pride in the fact that the [Regina] program in all essential matters is identical in purport with the program which our association, as a result of action in successive Annual Conventions, has agreed upon.' He then commented that the CCF program 'in some respects is less advanced than our own.'[110] We can assume that he was referring to the absence of an explicit endorsement of group government and delegate democracy in the Manifesto, an absence that gave it a more technocratic tenor.

The Saskatchewan Farmer-Labor Group gave prominence to the idea of national (and provincial) economic planning at the 1932 convention. Statements on economic policy at federal and provincial levels had a common preamble and statement of objectives: .

Preamble: In the opinion of the organized Farmer-Labor group in Saskatchewan, the present economic crisis is due to the inherent unsoundness of the capitalist system, which is based on private ownership of resources and the capitalistic control of production and distribution.

Objective: The social ownership of all resources and the machinery of wealth production to the end that we may establish a Co-operative Commonwealth in which the basic principle regulating production, distribution and exchange, will be the supplying of human needs instead of the making of profits.

These policy statements listed as their first objective 'the establishment of a planned system of national economy ["social economy" in the provincial program] for the production, distribution and exchange of all goods and services.' All subsequent economic proposals implied a key role for the unspecified planning mechanisms noted in the first proposal.[111]

Two years later, ex-UFC president George Williams emphasized the planning appeal in his election literature. His platform committed the Farmer-Labor Group to state planning and public ownership of 'Natural Resources and key industries,' partly as the soundest way of alleviating unemployment.[112] Similarly, the 1936 Manitoba ILP-CCF platform proposed 'a program of social planning for Manitoba, to the end that the wealth-producing resources of the provinces shall be used for the benefit of the people, and the income of the province shall be more equitably distributed.' A CCF government would appoint an economic council to survey the 'resources of the province, and the requirements of its citizens' and assist the government in 'organizing these resources through public ownership, co-operative management, state regulation and control, so that they may be used to meet public need.'[113]

The social planning concept was popularized within prairie CCF circles through the League for Social Reconstruction's *Social Planning for Canada* (1935). As the first sustained socialist analysis of Canadian society and public policy, its influence should not be surprising.[114] Not all of the League's analysis and proposals met with approval among prairie CCFers. Its criticism of social credit economic theory was not appreciated in Alberta, and some Saskatchewan CCF activists objected to the extreme centralism of the league's plan for reconstruction.[115] However, by rationalizing a plausible program of state planning, *Social Planning for Canada* had a critical impact on prairie social democrats. Their socialist and anti-capitalist training had taught them that public planning would be superior to existing 'capitalist planning,'a belief given an apparently scientific vindication by the book. It is not difficult to imagine the comfort and strength provided to prairie social democrats by an account that promised greater freedom for all through expert planning responsive to the needs of the many rather than the privileged few.[116] This was of great value to the new movement, at a time when the argument concerning the democratic benefits and nature of planning by governments was a key weapon in the social democratic populist arsenal.

By the late 1930s, CCF candidates and leaders moderated their pitch for state ownership in response to public opposition to rapid and extensive 'conversion' of the private economy. Increasingly, the idea of planning as the principal task of government was presented as the major innovation of future CCF governments. State ownership was not rejected, but its urgency and scope were diminished in public appeals, especially in Saskatchewan.[117] In 1938 voters were told that a CCF government would work towards a new social order, in which 'the principle regulating production, distribution, and exchange will be the supplying of human needs.' This would require a substitution of 'social planning in the place of the ruthless competition now practiced under capitalism,' and 'a sane policy of Public Ownership, of governmental assistance to the needy, governmental regulation of Big Business, and governmental assistance in creating publicly owned co-operative institutions.'[118]

In the new CCF appeal, state ownership was to be an instrument of social planning, rather than *vice versa* (as is especially clear in *Social Planning for Canada*). Virtually all academic commentators on the CCF have interpreted this proposed role for state ownership either in terms of the pragmatism and ideological good sense of the democratic socialist tradition in Canada, or, less sympathetically, as a characteristic expression of the debilitating liberalism and/or *petit bourgeois* populism at the core of CCF political thought. It is important to recognize, though, that a combination of electoral experience and increased confidence in the ameliorative power of state planning *per se* was leading all Anglo-American democratic parties of the left away from an unqualified faith in massive state ownership.

The notion that systematic state planning was the central element in the whole process, rather than a simple corollary of extensive state (and other social) ownership, was not widely accepted in social democratic populist circles until roughly the mid-1930s. The Depression led many social democratic populists to perceive the national (and international) economy as a much more delicate mechanism than they had before. Many went to the extreme of seeing the social economy almost exclusively in terms of the mechanistic metaphor. They were thus quite susceptible to proposals featuring 'economic mechanics' as the saviours of the mechanism.

Giving a priority to planning yielded positive results for social democrats, especially where they maintained a strong participatory tradition, as the case of the innovative Saskatchewan CCF government demonstrated. It was elected on a platform heavily weighted towards planning and regulation in the agricultural sector, the natural resources sector, and the social service area. Administrative and planning innovations were quickly undertaken and eventually well regarded across the country.[119]

To better appreciate the social democratic position on state intervention, we can examine two public policy areas of special concern to prairie socialists. The socialization of credit and financial institutions, and measures designed to assist Canadian farmers, through guaranteed prices, state marketing efforts, state insurance schemes, and financial/legislative support for co-operatives, were given priority on their public agenda from the First World War to at least 1945.

The second plank of The Regina Manifesto committed the national CCF to socialization of banking and credit institutions. In the 'Calgary Program,' the prairie socialists' concern with this policy was even more striking. The second plank in the 1932 program called for 'socialization of the banking, credit and financial system of the country, together with the social ownership, development, operation and control of utilities and natural resources.'[120] In 1933 and 1934, convention-sanctioned UFA policy on monetary and credit reform was even more prominent than in the Calgary Program. The 1933 'Declaration of Ultimate Objectives' placed nationalization of currency and credit in the forefront of steps to be taken towards a co-operative commonwealth, as the key condition of viable social and economic planning.[121] The 1934 UFA convention adopted a detailed 'statement of policy on the control of finance' that elevated social control of finance above all other forms of transformative state action, and presented money and credit reform in Douglas-inspired but socialist-inclined terms.[122]

As we have seen, prairie agrarian organizations drew attention to the power of finance during the First World War, while calling for socialization of banks and financial institutions generally. The Non-Partisan League in Alberta was the first to do this aggressively, followed by the left wing of the UFA organization in 1921, and the Farmers' Union of Canada (Saskatchewan Section) shortly after. By the mid-1920s, C.H. Douglas's underconsumptionist economics had been integrated into the social democratic critique of Canadian capitalism in Alberta and Saskatchewan.

Some Alberta MPs and UFA activists became virtually obsessive about Douglasite analysis and nostrums. Even William Irvine had difficulty keeping his socialist bearings clear to the public during much of the 1920s.[123] Several prominent social democrats in Saskatchewan also had this difficulty, including J.W. Robson[124] and Harris Turner, editor of the *The Western Producer*. Even a casual examination of this farmers' organ shows how much the average reader was deluged with credit and finance socialization propaganda, especially between 1924 and 1932.[125] *The UFA* performed this same function for Alberta's politicized farmers, especially from 1930 to 1935.[126] In both organs, the case for socialized credit and financial institutions supported social ownership of other key sectors of the economy. In Alberta, those on the left of the farmers' movement never felt the need to choose between socialism and 'social credit.'[127] The latter was simply a tool, albeit a very crucial one, available to governments moving towards socialism as they understood it.

In Saskatchewan and Manitoba, the most influential social democratic leaders also saw finance capital as a crucial target of socialist reform.[128] However, they were unwilling to endorse the Douglasite version of credit reform as the obvious means of providing for public and democratic control of money and credit.[129] Rank-and-file support for Douglas social credit in the UFC and Farmer-Labor Group was, none the less, quite high.

The social democratic populist case for socialization of banks followed two lines. Either could be used by those impressed with social credit theory or by those who saw it as a confused distraction from the socialist analysis and alternative. The first argument was simply a variation on the more inclusive theme of the primary virtues of planning and social ownership. Socialization of finance would lead to a more efficient and productive economy. The resulting material benefits could then be allocated more equitably across the national population. Increased purchasing power for the average citizen would enhance individuals' powers of self-development, while improved social services and access to educational and cultural facilities would further enhance these powers.

This line of argument was expected to appeal to all western farmers and consumers who had experienced firsthand the extractive power of chartered banks and mortgage and loan companies. It did, in fact, have considerable appeal, as is illustrated in resolutions condemning the banks and the credit-regulation policies of Canadian governments, passed year after year in prairie farm organizations' annual meetings. Scholars have shown that farmers in a regional 'debtor economy' were a natural constituency for this type of appeal during the nineteenth and twentieth centuries across both Europe and the United States.[130] The history of the Independent Labour Party in Britain from roughly 1925 to 1935 also demonstrates, however, that an underconsumptionist and explicitly Douglas-inspired program could appeal to industrial workers, without seeming to challenge the socialist elements of their program.[131] ILP and other socialist organizations' concern with underconsumptionist theories was given considerable attention by farmers' journals, UFA MPs, and even J.S. Woodsworth,[132] who insisted that state control of finance would maximize the productive potential of Canadian industry.

The second line of argument concerning the democratic socialization of financial institutions demonstrates even more clearly why this connection was of special concern to prairie social democrats. It begins with the assumption that economic democracy requires that producers control the key dimensions of productive activity, either indirectly (*via* elected representatives and their administrative 'servants') or directly (as with either democratically run producer co-operatives or genuine 'industrial democracy' for wage labour). Socialization of financial institutions thus becomes a specific case of the more general demand for state responsiveness to 'the people.' In the prairies, social democrats argued that only state ownership could assure responsiveness of financial institutions to the specific needs of agricultural producers.[133] When social credit analysis was mixed with this, state control of finance was seen as a way of providing all with sufficient income to buy the goods and services that the economy could produce. The 'cultural heritage' and potential abundance would become public property, rather than the private property of financial and industrial interests.

This second approach was more likely to be attractive to those who already accepted much of the radical democratic theory of representation and government practice. Democratic control of functional group representatives could be expanded to cover the activities and policies of financial institutions. In Alberta, this extension of the group government logic to control of money and credit was easily effected within the UFA organization (to the distress of H.W. Wood).

In Saskatchewan, socialization of finance was also linked to the argument for effective social democracy. By 1931, however, UFC and ILP leaders George Williams and M.J. Coldwell accepted neither social credit analysis nor occupational representation theory. Their support for socialization of financial institutions was premised on more conventional social democratic arguments. These were stressed in their support for the Regina Manifesto's second plank.[134] The difficulties experienced with the Social Credit challenge in 1935 and 1938 elections drove the Saskatchewan CCF leadership even farther from the Alberta-style argument for socialized money and credit. The publication of *Social Credit or Social Ownership* by Manitoba CCF leader S.J. Farmer in 1936 indicated a similarly conventional social democratic approach to the finance question in that province.

The other aspect of the social democratic agenda to receive particular attention on the prairies concerned protection and support of family farmers. Socialization of financial institutions can easily be seen as a specialized albeit important component of this concern.[135] We can get a good sense of the overall argument by considering a 1933 Calgary radio address by UFA vice-president and CCF national secretary Norman Priestly.

The address began with a review of the transformation of farm conditions on the prairies since 1900. 'The great majority [of farmers] every year witnessed an increase in their indebtedness, even in comparatively prosperous times.' Farmers now realized 'that the decay of the present system is proceeding with such rapidity that the slow processes of voluntary cooperation cannot meet the immediate need.' More obvious than ever was the need to 'bring about great changes by Parliamentary action, in order to clear the way to the co-operative state of the future.'[136]

Priestly went on to deal with several aspects of the CCF's 1932 Calgary Program especially relevant to farmers. The first concerned the commitment to support 'all co-operative enterprises which are steps to the attainment of the Co-operative Commonwealth.' The second dealt with a proposal for legislation to guarantee farmers 'security of tenure,' which, while not exactly revolutionary, would 'enable the farm people to carry on while the present system lasts.' Priestly referred to recent UFA amendments to the Alberta Debt Adjustment Act, which restricted foreclosure proceedings and seizures of personal property and land by private creditors to those sanctioned by the Debt Adjustment Board. Priestly presented this legislation as typical of the agrarian relief measure introduced by governments across the prairies, designed to provide farmers with 'job security.'

Priestly's account then turned to the UFA's 'use-lease' land policy. This would involve voluntary surrender of land tenure, not state confiscation of land title, for those farmers threatened by foreclosure. The 1931 UFA policy, he claimed, was 'intended to provide for the farm people a maximum of security.' Further, 'the officers of the United Farmers of Alberta, who are elected by and responsible to the organized farm people, can be depended on to see that security of tenure shall remain ... the watchword of the movement.'

So attractive was this policy, Priestly claimed, that 'there is every reason to believe it will be the land policy of the CCF when its permanent program is adopted.' The UFA policy began on an apparently radical note. At the 1931 convention, the membership supported a resolution favouring the public ownership of natural resources, public utilities, and land. But as *The UFA* editor noted in 1934, 'the sponsors of the resolution made it clear that the expropriation of farms in individual farmer's hands was not contemplated; that the intention was rather to retain in public ownership land which had not been alienated from the crown.'[137] The 1932 convention did little to clarify matters, with its definition of the co-operative commonwealth: 'a community freed from the dominance of irresponsible financial and economic power, in which all social means of production and distribution, including land, are socially owned either by voluntarily organized groups of producers, or ... by public corporations responsible to the people's public representatives.'[138]

By 1934, criticism by press, other parties, and business lobby groups, confusion within UFA ranks, and perhaps national CCF executive pressure led the convention to amend the above definition. The sensitive phrase 'including land' was replaced by 'including all unalienated land and land that may revert from time to time to the Crown.'[139] As Smith explained in his 1934 article, the CCF in Regina had avoided stating a policy on land ownership, deciding instead to leave each provincial affiliate to establish its own. The implied land policy of the federal organization was, however, support for individual producers' retention of the 'Torrens title.' The section on agriculture in the Manifesto, 'in its main features the work of the representatives of the UFO,'[140] began with a proposal for 'security of tenure for the farmer upon his farm on conditions to be laid down by the individual provinces.' Later in the section, however, 'the family farm' was clearly identified as 'the accepted basis for agricultural production in Canada.'[141]

The relative conservatism of the UFO, and the political perceptiveness of both CCF leaders and convention delegates, assured that even a perceived assault on the culturally unassailable institution of the family farm would not become national party policy. The new party did not need such a millstone around its neck. Endorsement of a 'use-lease' land policy, such as was adopted by the UFA, and the UFC and the Farmer-Labor Group in Saskatchewan, would have cost the national CCF support among otherwise sympathetic constituencies.

The problematic character of the use-lease land policy was borne out in the experience of the Farmer-Labor Group in Saskatchewan, which contested the 1934 provincial election with the use-lease proposal intact. Liberal party campaign tactics deftly portrayed Farmer-Labor land policy as undemocratic, arbitrarily confiscatory, and menacingly communistic.[142] Attempts by George Williams and M.J. Coldwell to justify the use-lease policy as the only alternative to mass foreclosure and corporate farming were unsuccessful. CCF delegates retreated from their land policy in the 1936 convention.

Several commentators, including Lipset, Hoffman, and Sinclair,[143] have portrayed this policy change as a retreat from socialism for purposes of electoral success. The problem with this interpretation is that little can seriously be said to hinge on a change more cosmetic than substantial. The use-lease plan was never intended as a prelude to collectivization of agriculture, or to creating primary-level agricultural industries run as public utilities. It was only meant to be an instrument of provincial support for the family farm, consistent with a vision of a socialized economy that preserved a special place for the family farm alongside public control of potentially exploitive economic institutions. This meant that financial institutions, industrial and non-agricultural resource enterprises, and the principal transportation and utility services of the country would be state-owned and -operated. A well-integrated system of agricultural producers' and consumer co-operatives would round out the 'socialized' economy. From the agrarian social democratic perspective, this overall structure would allow individual farmers to securely produce foodstuffs.

Is leaving so much productive property in private hands 'truly socialist'? The theoretical Marxist position on this is well known: private property carries within itself the seeds of capital accumulation, and consequently an inevitable exploitation of a propertyless mass of tenant farmers or agricultural wage labourers. The practical Marxist position on this issue has usually varied from this theoretical position. In all countries where a Marxist-oriented government has been elected, and in most where a 'popular revolution' has established a purportedly Marxist regime, respect has been paid to small holders' and peasant farmers' preference for private ownership of agricultural land. In countries with social democratic governments, collectivization of land has never been seriously suggested by government or social democratic party leaders.[144] For these social democratic parties and governments, as for prairie social democrats, private ownership of agricultural land by individual producers was not seen as 'capitalistic' or antithetical to social control of the economy (including many aspects of the agricultural economy).

The social democratic populist position on state intervention in agriculture is nicely illustrated in Saskatchewan Farmer-Labor and CCF agricultural policy proposals from 1932 to 1944, when the controversial 'use-hold' land policy attracted the most attention. As reiterated in the 1932 and 1933 Farmer-Labor Group Economic Policy pamphlets, the proposal involved: 'Security of tenure to be obtained by institution of perpetual "use hold" on home and lands instead of patents or Torrens' Title. Substitution of perpetual "use hold" for home and land titles when and if requested by the present registered owner, or dispossessed owner who now occupies under a lease. The prevention of immediate foreclosures, due to arrears of mortgage instalments or purchase agreements with mortgage, land and investment companies and private individuals, by an exchange of provincial non-interest bearing bonds or equity based on actual economic value of the land and homes, and not on their speculative price.'[145]

M.J. Coldwell told the 1933 Farmer-Labor Group convention that 'no policy has been so misrepresented and closely criticised by our opponents as our land policy ... and yet the more I talk about it, the more I am convinced that, while we may have to change some details of this policy, we have in that policy the only possible method to giving security to our people in their farms and homes.' The choice was between 'being reduced to a system of collectivization under a system of capitalism instituted by the mortgage and loan companies' and 'security of tenure through the social ownership of this land.' Even 'the small minority of producers who now have clear titles'[146] would eventually support the use-hold concept. Coldwell insisted that the provincial government was constitutionally empowered to implement this scheme.

Shortly after the 1933 Farmer-Labor convention, George Williams addressed the national CCF convention on the Saskatchewan Group's agricultural policy. Williams spoke of the 'inalienable right' of all Canadian farmers to 'security of tenure on the farm which they have created.' He lambasted the Liberals for lying about CCF intentions in its agricultural policy, and then went on to provide a folksy explanation of the Saskatchewan Group's land policy. A Saskatchewan CCF government would provide mortgage and insurance companies with an 'arbitrated payment' for the land they wished to obtain through foreclosure, then turn the land over to the indebted farmer. The perpetual use-hold title would guarantee that the land would be turned over to next of kin ('son John').

Williams insisted that there was no necessary connection between 'the title' and socialism: 'the reason we give the use-hold title is to give security of tenure, not to bring about Socialism.' Neither nationalization nor collectivization of land will automatically lead to socialism, as the examples of the CNR and 'mortgage company collectivization' prove. Instead, socialism in agriculture would come with socialized credit, marketing boards, and 'pegged prices' that returned a decent income for the farmer's labour. 'Through the use-hold title we guarantee to the agriculturalist a home, a job – the job of producing wheat – and we guarantee to him through the marketing board an adequate wage.'[147]

Williams provides a representative social democratic populist account of the problem of 'socialization of agriculture.' He accepts the tradition of individual farm ownership, rejects collectivization, and rationalizes both in terms of the way state policies could be implemented to put farmers on a par with labourers. In one respect, however, his address is unrepresentative: he did not stress co-operatives in agriculture as instruments of its 'socialization' and democratic control.

The argument that permanent lease-hold agreements were preferable to tenancy on corporate farms[148] was unsuccessful. The 1936 CCF convention substituted a policy promising protection of the farmer from 'unjust foreclosure' and seizure of the whole crop, the use of a moratorium on high debt repayments, and effective crop failure insurance. The party retained this policy through the 1944 election. In the 1938 election, the party stressed the need to use social ownership of transportation, grain trade, milling, implement industries, and mineral and timber resources to decrease farmers' costs and increase public control over the economy. One 1938 pamphlet stated that socialism 'will give the farmer not only publicly-owned markets, but publicly-owned transportation facilities, and machinery made at the labor cost of production.'[149]

By 1944, the emphasis was more on security of tenure, increased income and better living conditions (e.g., electrification) on farms, guaranteed prices, effective marketing boards, and government encouragement of the co-operative movement. The new CCF government's efforts and achievements in these areas were quite substantial.[150]

Several things can be said of the intentions behind CCF agricultural policies in the 1930s and 1940s. First, it is clear that a major concern of this policy was retaining the family farm as the cornerstone of agricultural life in Canada. However, simply to call this a typically *petit bourgeois* concern would be misleading. We have seen that social democratic populists prior to and within the CCF were concerned with a redistribution of economic and political power among classes in Canada. A part of this goal was to provide security and a guarantee of 'just rewards' to the farming community. This was not detached, however, from a concern with justice to urban workers and the lower middle class, even though, as Lipset shows, these constituencies were not given much programmatic attention until the early 1940s in the Saskatchewan CCF.

That CCF agricultural policy can appear, in retrospect, to be politically pragmatic does not mean it was conservative. Using the state to restructure the non-primary spheres of the agricultural economy, as well as much of the non-agricultural resource and industrial economy, was always a CCF proposal. Agricultural producers were to benefit from these policy departures, perceived as radical then and now by the majority of the public. One cannot consider these 'pragmatic' agricultural policies in isolation from the overall economic program. Farmers may have been concerned most with policies likely to affect them directly, but they were by no means unaware of the other policies advocated, or the 'old party' and establishment press response to these.

The standard of 'radicalism' in agricultural policy often invoked by recent left-wing critics of the CCF is very close to that provided for the Farmers' Unity League (FUL) by its Communist Party superiors.[151] The league proposed a collectivization of agriculture.[152] The FUL portrayed farmers as industrial workers in hayseed's clothing, bitterly attacked 'the capitalist Wheat Pool,' and accused all other farmers' political movements of having 'prevented the struggle for socialism and served only to make the farmers more helpless under the dictatorship of finance capital.'[153] It made no concessions to the prevailing culture or popular-democratic traditions of the prairies. Consequently, it had only a marginal impact in poor districts of northern Saskatchewan and Alberta.[154]

Criticism of the socialist credentials of CCF agricultural policy and agrarian appeals is too often based on the 'impossibilist' criteria laid down by the FUL. North American socialism could not and cannot be politically viable without making substantial concessions to the institution of the family farm. The CCF would have simply deprived itself of an agrarian constituency if it had adopted land policies similar to those of the Farmers' Unity League. If the response is that nothing short of collectivization of agriculture brings socialism to a rural society, then the argument is over – but by definitional fiat. If this response is not chosen, then the argument concerning the 'petite-bourgeoisification' of the CCF must be conducted with more reference to the full program(s) promoted by, and the known intentions of, CCF leaders.

Technocracy versus Democracy

Previously, I argued that some populists' technocratic inclinations clashed with crucial assumptions about participatory democratic practice. The same contradiction existed in social democratic populist thought, largely because social democratic populists viewed 'social' or state planning as a positive force in itself, with both scientific credentials and automatic equity-maximizing results. To the extent that they perceived greater equalization of welfare among classes as a means and end of democracy, they understood planning to be inherently democratic. Political conflicts over alternative policy proposals, by contrast, could be evidence of irrational political and economic structures, and ideological or uninformed political practices. To the extent that rationality and equity are reciprocally dependent, technocratic decision-making would be fair and morally defensible.

Any socialist analysis of a capitalist polity will assert its unfairness and irrationality on more or less technical economic grounds. The capitalist economy is inefficient because it does not maximize the aggregate returns from available factors of production (land, labour, and various kinds of capital). Poor utilization of natural resources, technologies, and human capacities are endemic to the system. One reason for this is that the distribution of rewards to the various factors of production – especially labour – is inequitable and inefficient. People work better, and produce more, when they receive more equitable rewards for their effort. One such reward is the power to co-determine working conditions and the objectives of economic activity.

It follows that socialists insist on state-implemented changes in both economic organization and political direction of the economy. The state could make such changes in two ways: by responding to suggestions for institutional change made by organized social groups or by formulating a plan of change through its employees (civil service) and senior political strategists. The two are not mutually exclusive strategies. Analytically, however, they can be identified as opposite points on a continuum.

At one end of the continuum is a pure type of democratic state; at the other, an ideal type of technocratic state. These pure cases do not entail any assumptions about equitable distribution of the social product. Thus, unless it can be demonstrated that the democratic state will enhance productivity by distributing enhanced non-material rewards to citizens (in the form, especially, of enhanced power), the technocratic state can be expected to maximize and equalize consumer utilities as easily as the democratic state. More simply put, the rational individual valuing only personal consumption and material equity has no *prima facie* reason to choose the democratic state over the technocratic state.

The obvious response to this simplified dichotomy is that no self-respecting socialist would accept either this picture of the rational individual or the idea that productivity would remain the same under each state model. None the less, social democrats have always been inclined to accept assumptions making a version of the technocratic state attractive. As the discussion above suggests, one reason is the social democratic tendency to see a rapid increase in the aggregate of material goods as the single most important – and politically necessary – effect of social change. Socialists go farther, of course, and attach conditions of equitable distribution to the increased social product resulting from state reorganization of social institutions. The state's planning capacities should accommodate both the distributive and aggregate maximization goals: only state-enforced redistribution from rich to poor will make the distributive goal realistic and the aggregate-enhancing goal politically and socially feasible.

To reject these as desirable goals, or to deny that the state has a major role to play in achieving them, would be to reject socialism. However, believing that they are goals of state action does not guarantee that one is a socialist, because they imply nothing about the means to be employed. Planners can design state policies to achieve these goals independently from input by organizations representing the subordinate classes.

Realistically, however, the relevant cases of technocratic state action under social democratic governments involve planners establishing both priorities and methods that have a 'higher authority' than those presented by popular organizations of 'the people.' This is not to suggest that social democratic governments suspend elections or ignore party programs. Rather, the 'higher authority' of the planners is connected with definitive standards set for determining policies.

To locate a technocratic strain in social democratic populist thought, we will look at statements indicating the nature and value of planning for the socialist project. We will also note that social democrats considered qualifications and reservations regarding 'the planning function.'

William Irvine's *Co-operative Government* foreshadowed some later social democratic thinking on planning. His 1929 proposals for a 'Bureau of Statistics' and national planning agency showed that Irvine did not value them for their capacity to channel functionally defined group opinion. They were commended for their purported ability to 'collect the facts' about economic and social life; these facts would then 'speak for themselves.' These facts were to demonstrate the unacceptability of capitalism and illuminate the need for social ownership and social credit. Carefully administered by expert social scientists, resulting policies would fully utilize Canada's resources while creating social equality. Proposals for policies offered by popular organizations would be judged by the standards revealed by 'the facts,' and administered by experts.

The technocratic tendency implicit in social democratic planning was expressed more frequently after 1930, although seldom with Irvine's unqualified assurance. A sense of the urgency of planning increased, however, and more rank-and-file support for powerful planning commissions and instruments was evident in organizational resolutions and programmatic statements. In the previous section we saw how this was expressed in the Regina Manifesto, in Saskatchewan Farmer-Labor Group programs, in Manitoba ILP/CCF literature, and even in the 1932-5 UFA statements. It is worth returning to the Manifesto for a moment. The first plank, entitled 'Planning,' recommended 'the establishment of a planned, socialized economic order, in order to make possible the most efficient development of the national resources and the most equitable distribution of the national income.' To this end, the first step would be creation of 'a National Planning Commission consisting of a small body of economists, engineers and statisticians assisted by an appropriate technical staff':

The task of the Commission will be to plan for the production, distribution and exchange of all goods and services necessary to the efficient functioning of the economy; to co-ordinate the activities of the socialized industries; to provide for a satisfactory balance between the producing and consuming power; and to carry on continuous research into all branches of the national economy in order to acquire the detailed information necessary to efficient planning.

The Commission will be responsible to the Cabinet and will work in co-operation with the Managing Boards of the Socialized Industries.

... The CCF will provide that in Canada the planning shall be done, not by a small group of capitalist magnates in their own interests, but by public servants acting in the public interest and responsible to the people as a whole.[155]

The second plank, on the socialization of finance, proposes that the 'unused surpluses of production' be mobilized and directed 'for socially desired purposes as determined by the Planning Commission.' The third plank, on the socialization of industries and services, proposes their operation 'under the general direction of the Planning Commission by competent managements freed from day to day political interference.' Each state enterprise was to be run by competent boards established to 'conduct each particular enterprise on efficient economic lines.' This plank concluded vaguely that workers in these industries 'must be given the right to participate in the management of the industry.'

These proposals were quite consistent with Irvine's of 1929, and paid equally marginal attention to the role of democratic organizations' inputs into the planning process. Also interesting in this regard are House of Commons speeches on Woodsworth's 1 February 1933 resolution on the co-operative commonwealth, by Woodsworth and other federal CCF members. Woodsworth contended that 'in recent days we have the technicians pointing out not only the feasibility of fundamental changes in our social order, but the absolute necessity of such changes if our civilization is to persist.'[156] Irvine twice introduced criticisms of capitalism's inefficiency and injustice with the phrase 'we are told by technocracy that.'[157] His whole argument was based on the technocratic rejection of 'scarcity' as a limiting condition of economic activity. National life had but to be efficiently and knowledgeably planned for the people to benefit from the abundance of material resources.

The League for Social Reconstruction's *Social Planning for Canada* did not trade so heavily on the theme of 'abundance.' It did, however, elaborate on the Manifesto's skeletal recommendations for a national planning commission. Chapters entitled 'The Logic of Planning' and 'National Planning in Practice' articulate virtually all of the arguments made since by Canadian social democrats in favour of 'national planning.'

The league account of planning is self-consciously defensive concerning the democratic characteristics of their scheme, to an extent often lacking in prairie advocacy of centralized state planning. In one instance, they contended that planning must be responsive to a 'modified but democratic parliamentary system' and thus to public opinion, and that 'the prime assumption upon which this book is based is that it is possible for a democracy to control economic policy intelligently: not the abolition, but the improvement, of the functioning of democratic government, is the purpose of the reforms proposed.'[158] The two chapters did not, however, present any proposals for integrating organized popular group or party inputs into the planning process.

This should not cast doubt on the LSR's commitment to parliamentary democracy and 'a truer personal liberty than we have as yet achieved'[159] for 'the people who are planned for.'[160] However, the LSR's concern for the priority of 'expert rationality' over popular democracy is clear.

Later CCF publications provided additional evidence of prairie social democratic faith in expert state planning. A 1938 Calgary CCF study group publication entitled *The Way of Reason* referred to *Social Planning for Canada* as 'one of the finest documents ever written in this country,' with 'both an expert diagnosis of our economic ills and eminently sound and practical suggestions as to remedy.'[161] Like the LSR study, this pamphlet advocated a federal government planning commission, which 'should be an expert thinking body, intimately in touch with the political ministers of the state, but free to the extent its important function demands, that of formulating a national economic policy in its detailed and technical aspects.'[162]

The Educational Committee also recommended that all socialized industries 'be placed under the control of a small group of experts who will act as trustees for that unit.' Unlike the LSR document, this proposal specified that 'not less than half of these experts will be appointed by the Trade Union concerned.'[163] While proposing expert commissions to deal with internal and external trade, and distribution of the social product, the committee stressed the need for 'self-government' within each industry. This was a long-term proposition, but necessary to a co-operative commonwealth in which 'established democratic organization of industry will gradually come to parallel democratic forms of government.'[164]

In addition, private MPs were to be 'co-opted' to assist government ministers, to enable them to consider legislation more intelligently and discuss government policies with constituents 'with some degree of assurance.' 'In all,' they claimed, 'this plan brings the people into closer contact with the problems of government.'[165] Thus, along with the faith in state planning we find a serious concern for enhanced popular democracy. However, they do not address the possibility of a clash between industrial democracy and state planners. They assume that the considered judgments of popular organizations will virtually always concur with the decisions of state planners. Such an assumption had to be made to justify the great power given to expert planners in the CCF proposals.

In Saskatchewan the attractiveness of planning to social democrats was especially evident after 1930. The 1933 *Handbook for Speakers*, which outlines the Farmer-Labor Group's federal and provincial programs, proposes 'under a planned system of National Economy to thoroughly plan all activities in our national life and to balance production with distribution by means of our currency system.' Referring to a proposed provincial planning board the authors claim that: 'The Government ... might select a man of the calibre of G.D.H. Cole – an economic expert, who would understand the results of economic actions. To assist him statisticians and technical experts of proven worth in their respective fields would be employed. All these would work in conjunction with people representative of our agricultural and workers' associations.'[166]

These comments on planning parallel those made two years later by the LSR. Unlike the Calgary Educational Committee, the Farmer-Labor Group felt no need to outline co-ordination of inputs by experts and 'the people's representatives' in the planning process. Once again, priority was given to the experts, with little consideration for the policy-making role of popular organizations. A decade later, Saskatchewan CCF president Carlyle King addressed the objectives and methods of economic planning in his nationally circulated pamphlet *What Is Democratic Socialism?* A Planning Commission would 'fit the various departments of commerce and industry together for the efficient operation of the entire economic system. [The] expert staff of economists and statisticians [will] gather information about every part of the national economy and receive opinions and suggestions from those actually engaged in the day to day work of factory, field or mine. Then, using this material in the light of principles laid down by the people's representatives in parliament or congress, they will make plans for the co-ordinated production of the required goods and services.'[167]

King's commitment to popular participation in the planning process is not in question; he was, in fact, the architect of a legislative advisory council that kept the Saskatchewan CCF cabinet and party organizations abreast of each others' thoughts on past, present, and future government policy from 1944 to 1964. We should not minimize the significance of this innovation as a democratic check on state planning. None the less, there is still something of a technocratic flavour in King's 1943 depiction of the planning commission. He portrays the national economy in almost mechanistic terms, such that conditions allowing for its optimum efficiency could be determined by the planning commission's expert staff almost independently of popular involvement. Popular contributions and 'the principles laid down by the people's representatives' would ensure government accountability and responsiveness, but King's vision did not imply policy co-determination.

Mechanistic imagery in discussions of planning in the Canadian economy was not restricted to prairie social democracy. It was also evident in both *Democracy Needs Socialism*[168] and *Make This Your Canada*.[169] Both refer to the need for industrial democracy and popular organizational inputs into the planning process. However, the only guarantees for these inputs are vague suggestions for grafting representative boards and councils onto existing parliamentary and civil service structures.[170] These suggestions come at the end, rather than the beginning, of the discussion of planning functions and policy objectives.

Prairie social democrats were not completely unaware of the problems posed by central planning for participatory politics. Explicit rejections of a purely technocratic approach to policy-making, and expressions of support for some decentralization in the federal system, indicate that prairie social democrats gave some thought to this difficult matter.

The CCF in Saskatchewan printed a series of 'group study courses' for local organizations' use in 1930s. In one course lesson, J.S. Woodsworth said of the Regina Manifesto: 'Like the Technocrats we believe in planning. But instead of a theoretical Chart of the Future we advocate Boards of competent experts, working closely with those "on the job" under the control of a government responsible to the people. No Fascism for us!'[171]

While not wanting to deny the value of planning to his party's program, Woodsworth did wish to distance his party from whatever undemocratic connotations the technocratic 'movement' had acquired during the decade. George Williams had essentially the same intention in a letter to *The Western Producer* in 1938. He argued that

There is every indication that Technocracy will be the next form of insanity in Saskatchewan ... Technocracy deadens the effect of the progressive forces by asking people not to exercise their franchise at all ... Technocracy is based on the illusion that if people do nothing about the present situation it will ultimately destroy itself, and then by some strange alchemy the engineers and technicians will remake the system. It is a fairy tale ... like Social Credit ... The object of Technocracy is to ensure the control of Capitalism a little while longer by persuading enough people to refrain from exercising their franchise so as to make Democracy unworkable. It is of course obvious that the only hope of attaining economic change without chaos and revolution lies in the Social Democratic Party.[172]

Williams felt that he could discredit Technocracy by associating it with capitalism and anti-democratic forces. He does not really explain how it would promote undemocratic political and social relations, however, and one has to wonder why. Was it because he felt slightly uncomfortable with the high level of expert planning advocated by other CCF leaders? It is noteworthy that in his 1939 pamphlet *Social Democracy in Canada*, he devoted little attention to the party's planning proposals. He defined socialism in terms of 'production for use' and public ownership of goods and services needed by all, with little reference to planning.[173]

Several years earlier, the *CCF Research Review*[174] had printed an article entitled 'What about Technocracy?' The article was written in 1936, following a visit to Regina by Technocracy, Inc.'s American leader, Howard Scott. *Review* editor Jack King was highly critical of Scott's analysis and proposals. He reserved special scorn for its lack of class analysis and democratic principles, and for Scott's contempt for radical social movements. King worried that it was at least possible that 'a technocratic coup might result in a form of society acceptable to radicals.'[175] Granting the 'confused state of mind and human frailties of the mass,' King insisted that 'we still stand to gain infinitely more for ourselves and our fellow men by standing shoulder to shoulder with those whose aim is a classless society based upon the principles of true democracy.'[176]

The *Review* thus rejected the technocratic state in no uncertain terms, making explicit what was too often only implicit in the social democratic populist appeal: the need for popular control of the state. Like most other prairie social democratic analysis, however, it did not suggest how socialist planning could be reconciled with this popular control. None the less, it rejected planning divorced from a recognition of class inequalities and a democratic reconstruction of class relations. This was an important advance over the rather naïve belief in planning *per se* in Canadian social democratic circles. The *Review*'s pointed attack on Technocracy, Inc., shows that some CCFers thought critically about the technocratic tendencies in their own movement.

Prairie socialist perceptions of federal-provincial relations provide another measure of their technocratic leanings. There is no necessary connection between support for a strongly centralized state system and acceptance of a technocratic planning mentality. We have seen that social democrats' strongest response to the appeal of planning came in a period of economic crisis, and in recognition of the daunting economic and political forces arrayed against 'the people.' Thus a predilection for centralized state authority in the economic sphere did not mark its proponents as centralizing technocrats. They could have believed, for example, that federal authority over labour legislation would promote development of a strong, democratic working-class political movement.

With these qualifications in mind, we can note the centralist bias in prairie socialists' federalism. J.S. Woodsworth's 1935 article 'Political Democracy' characterized the BNA Act as 'a blank wall against which I run every day,' and 'the first refuge of a prime minister who does not wish to act.' He cites the case of the Dominion government's signing of the treaty regarding (ILO) labour conventions, and its subsequent abandonment of responsibility in these matters to the provinces, where a 'strong lobby ... appeal[ing] to local fears or prejudices' can confute national purposes and urgent needs. Reflecting national and most provincial CCF opinion, he insists that 'in the complicated and highly specialized industrial, commercial, and financial life of today, [the BNA Act] is hopelessly out of date.'[177]

The same logic shaped both the Regina Manifesto's statement on the need for constitutional reform and similar proposals in UFA, Farmer-Labor, and Manitoba ILP/CCF programs from 1932 to 1936. The argument was made in greater detail in the LSR's *Democracy Needs Socialism*,[178] Scott and Lewis's *Make This Your Canada*,[179] and Coldwell's *Left Turn, Canada*.[180] On the question of the desirable federal distribution of powers, most prairie social democrats followed their national executive's lead. Logically and practically, they had no real choice once they had accepted the reconstructive virtues of national planning.

This support for national planning gave expression to one side of a characteristic populist ambivalence towards central state structures. While social democrats identified federal state agencies as agents of the hated National Policy, they none the less believed that these agencies were essential to combat concentrated economic power and class inequality. Federal regulation of this concentrated power was desirable, since it would lead to extensive state enterprise. It would also encourage social control through co-operative enterprises protected by the state from capitalist sabotage. Federal governments' responsibility for policies that decisively structured the prairie economy – in national economic development, transportation, international trade, land and resources (until 1930), and financial institutions – garnered them a large amount of prairie reformers' attention. Thus social democratic populists granted more importance to federal state structures when addressing the larger reform picture, even though they were more likely to control provincial governments.

Oddly, *Make This Your Canada* conceded the importance of municipal and provincial planning bodies' contributions to the determination of the national plan. Lewis and Scott also argued that provincial governments' role in economic development could be greatly expanded.[181] By 1943, national CCF leaders had realized that the emphasis given to federal government planning could easily be a political liability. This realization had come earlier to CCF leaders in Saskatchewan.

The 1933 Farmer-Labor Group *Handbook for Speakers*, issued before the Regina Manifesto, included the argument: 'We can do a great deal of economic planning right in this province if we will, and we have that included in our platform ... it would be perfectly feasible in this province to set up an economic unit in the Dominion of Canada to supply ourselves with almost everything we require. We have the raw material in this province to set up a large number of secondary industries ... In the Province of Saskatchewan, we have a great opportunity of building up along these lines ... A Farmer-Labor Government in Saskatchewan would endeavour ... to begin planning for the use of our entire resources on a planned economy basis.'[182]

Six years later, CCF leader George Williams reiterated this argument, insisting that 'the extent of our Provincial powers is not generally known.'[183] Williams thus foreshadowed innovative efforts by the first CCF administration to plan, regulate, and develop the regional economy. Saskatchewan social democrats had experienced local control through their co-operatives, and believed that local control was inherently more democratic than regional or national control, so they were more likely to look for ways of extending this through the provincial state than were most CCFers outside the province.

This experience suggests that prairie social democrats were likely to step back farther from centralized technocratic planning when federal-provincial distribution of powers was at issue. They may have supported enhanced federal powers to deal with regional disparities, economic crisis, and social inequality, as T.C. Douglas and M.J. Coldwell did, but this did not reduce the importance of local control. It is still true, however, that Saskatchewan social democrats did not feel the need to ask tough questions about the quasi-technocratic justification of enhanced federal planning power that the national CCF leadership advanced. They assumed rather naïvely that national planning by sympathetic experts would not collide with local planning objectives or interregional conflicts.

The potential tension between the participatory democratic and technocratic orientations is greatest in the populism most committed to democratization of decision-making in all social relations: social democratic populism. American and British left-wing thinkers[184] had done much to convince prairie socialists of the power of science and technology to continually translate machine power into the greatest good for the greatest number, and eventually into material abundance. Almost all British socialists from 1880 to 1930 shared this idea, including people as opposed to Fabian utilitarianism as William Morris.

To many prairie social democrats, these insights and critiques explained their own 'poverty in the midst of plenty,' and vindicated their moral critique of Canadian capitalism. Their healthy contempt for the orthodox practitioners of 'economic science'[185] and federal bureaucrats did not prevent social democratic populists from believing that the technological sciences could be adapted to 'the people's' needs and interests. Social engineering by a corps of progressive state bureaucrats was expected to play a decisive role in the creation of the co-operative commonwealth.

In accepting technocratic social engineering as a primary means of fighting external corporate and financial power, social democratic populists were endangering the extension of their participatory political culture. By willing the (apparently necessary) means of their own vision of a socialist society, they were potentially denying a large part of its end. This denial was more likely if they failed to recognize the Fabian/technocratic antipathy towards popular participation in determining public policies. Heavy reliance on 'top-down' decision-making would unavoidably be contrary to political resocialization and development of participatory institutions. The example of the CCF government in Saskatchewan shows that, even with the best of intentions and vigorous interchange between populist party and government administrators, a Fabian/technocratic approach to 'socialist planning' can reduce democratic aspirations and commitments in movement organizations.

Were prairie social democrats aware of tensions between democratic ends and technocratic means? We have seen that they gave only passing attention to these tensions in proposals for economic reform and socio-political transformation. The reasons for this were political – why undermine a political project's viability and attractiveness for the public? They were also ideological, including a notion that a benign planning state would seldom collide with popular organizations on questions of state policy. There was no sustained discussion of how representative mechanisms might keep planners in their place. While this is politically understandable, it also tells us something about the social democratic populist vision of the good society

The Co-operative Commonwealth: Co-operation, Abundance, and the New Social Philosophy

Ideas about the good society expressed social democratic populist hopes for a socialization of democracy and their expectations of state planning and social ownership. Their vision of the good society thus contained the tension between democracy and technocracy inherent in their reform proposals. The vision contained a good deal else as well, but we will consider only factors and beliefs having a clear bearing on the two orientations.

Social Democracy and Co-operation

The theory and practice of co-operation were undeniably closer to the centre of social democratic thought on the prairies than in British Columbia, central Canada, or the Maritimes. Given the importance of co-operative institutions to the prairie economy, this is not surprising. In agrarian organizations, successful utilization of producer co-operatives was often the major political and politicizing issue. Thus the rank and file had their political visions shaped by their co-operative experience, and organization leaders recognized the need to link their political platforms and projects to this co-operative experience. For social democratic populist activists and leaders, this meant tying the co-operative movement culture's anti-capitalist and democratic traditions to a socialist analysis and vision, while demonstrating that socialism and co-operation shared fundamental values and objectives.

Demonstrating the anti-capitalist and expansively democratic character of the co-operative experience was the first step in countering crypto-Liberal claims about the political significance of co-operation. Establishing the incompatibility of co-operation and capitalism was a common objective. Social democrats occasionally argued that co-operative enterprises did not yield a profit like capitalist enterprise, because patronage dividends did not flow from exploitive working relations or from unequal competitive positions.[186] Co-operation and competition formed an 'antinomy' in the social democratic populist argument, and competition was identified with capitalism. As William Irvine said in a 1933 CCF pamphlet, 'there is no co-operative institution that ever existed or could exist under private property, and surely no co-operative institution ever existed on a competitive basis.'[187]

Economic co-operation was also anti-capitalist because it was directed towards 'production for use, not profit.' This argument appealed to prairie producers' sense that their productive activity met fundamental human needs, and thus served a higher calling than many other private enterprises. Because co-operatives protected producers' economic security and livelihood, their social justification easily surpassed economic enterprises, which threatened these for the sake of mere profit.

Co-operative enterprise could meet the needs of both producers and consumers, which meant both farmers and workers. In this sense it was anti-capitalist, because capitalist enterprise, in its various forms, sought to pit farmers against workers and to exploit both classes while doing so. Support for the anti-capitalist objectives of co-operative economic institutions was thus presented as a rational strategy for all of 'the people' as economic actors. This was a common theme in prairie CCF literature for many years.

Social democrats regularly championed co-operatives as inherently democratic forms of economic activity, and as key training grounds for the democratic citizen. Demonstrating socialist support for and roots in co-operatives helped counteract the contention that socialism would lead to state regimentation. Both their internal democratic procedures and their long-range commitment to economic democracy would help to stem the tide of centralized decision-making in modern society.[188]

To ease the transition from support of co-operation to support for social democracy, CCF publicists and politicians had to establish clear linkages between their philosophy and objectives. By any standards, they were remarkably successful. As S.M. Lipset observed, 'anyone listening to CCF speeches or reading CCF literature by 1944 would think that he was asked to vote for the co-operatives party.'[189]

In 1932, the Saskatchewan Farmer-Labor Group identified 'the encouragement of all co-operative enterprises which are steps towards the achievement of the Co-operative Commonwealth' as an 'immediate measure' for both levels of government.[190] The same pamphlet cited the UFC's 'ultimate objective' as 'social ownership and co-operative production for use, ... the only sound economic system.' A 1938 pamphlet contended that 'socialism is a system of co-operation in which the things produced will be used, enjoyed and owned by the workers.' The sane alternative was to 'co-operate for the common good rather than fight with one another in the fierce capitalistic battle of competition and profit seeking.'[191]

Socialism would thus replace the destructive capitalist logic of competition with its own logic of co-operation. A 1938 Calgary CCF publication claimed that co-operation was 'no mere theory; it is the most important fact of modern life, but as yet it lacks unity,' which it is the task of socialism to furnish.[192] Socialists reared in the UFA environment could hardly be expected to say anything else; for socialism to build on existing popular-democratic traditions, it had to be presented as the grail of the co-operative quest.

The desire for local autonomy and democratic control in economic activity had been crucial to producers' co-operatives in the prairies. Social democrats realized that prairie co-operators might view a heavy emphasis on central planning and state ownership as a denial of these objectives. The social democratic response to this was threefold. One was defensive: capitalism had stifled co-operation, exploited farmers and workers, and brought on a depression. It was thus contrary to the people's interests, more so than any system of public ownership and state planning could be. The positive reaction involved two strategies: an admission of the need for the decentralizing and democratizing presence of co-operative institutions in the socialist order, and, a lavish use of the word 'co-operative' as either a synonym for socialist, or a way to characterize the co-operative commonwealth's political system.

Regarding the first of the positive responses, social democratic populists on the prairies were quite willing to claim the decentralizing concern of co-operatives as their own. Thus we find Norman Priestly arguing, in a 1934 commentary on the Regina Manifesto: 'The Co-operative Commonwealth will provide against the too great dominance of the state by the use of co-operative associations of citizens grouped as producers and as consumers. While the planned economy will be the principal focus of interest, the State Planning

Board itself ... will encourage co-operative association within the general plan as a means of providing for individual initiative and our inherited genius for local self-government ... Local self-government in the economic as well as the political spheres will without doubt be one of the characteristics of any Anglo-Saxon co-operative commonwealth of the future.'[193]

In *Socialism and Co-operatives*, a Saskatchewan CCF pamphlet of the early 1940s, Carlyle King made the same kind of argument about CCF support for co-operatives as bulwarks against overcentralization. He asserted that the modern trend towards concentration and centralization of power would threaten a socialist society as much as any other. A crucial safeguard was thus 'to have economic power and authority spread out as much as possible.' The obvious mechanism, for King and his audience, was 'a widespread, vigorous, and constantly expanding co-operative movement.'[194]

Weyburn MP T.C. Douglas linked co-operatives, democratic local control, and socialism many times in his parliamentary career. In his reply to the 1943 federal budget speech, Douglas outlined the CCF's four favoured forms of social ownership: national, provincial, municipal, and co-operative. He claimed that the CCF saw co-operative ownership as 'the most important of all, hence the name Co-operative Commonwealth.' It would 'avoid bureaucracy and give to the individuals vitally concerned the responsibility for using their own initiative and developing their own economic processes.' The CCF believed that 'the co-operative movement is the basis of economic democracy'; such a belief proved that 'we have never advocated regimentation or bureaucracy or state socialism.' The CCF objective was, rather, that 'the common people, the workers and the farmers, should have an opportunity of owning, controlling, and operating the facilities by which they live.'[195] Thus Douglas articulated the CCF concern for economic democracy in a fashion complementary to the co-operative movement's objectives.

Characterizing socialist political objectives in terms of co-operative methods and values became increasingly common in CCF public appeals through the 1930s and early 1940s.[196] The political and ideological value of this approach in the prairie setting is obvious. It was not simply a response to the red-baiting techniques of old-line parties and their daily press supporters. UFA and UFC(SS) speakers' substituted the term 'co-operation' for 'socialism' in the late 1920s and early 1930s because they believed that the two terms were virtually interchangeable. Thus Carlyle King's *Socialism and Co-operatives* pamphlet merely expresses the beliefs of a generation of prairie socialists.[197]

King claims that both movements seek to maximize ordinary people's purchasing power, and that both see community ownership as the appropriate method. He quotes a 1941 joint statement by the Alberta and Saskatchewan wheat pools to demonstrate that co-operators joined socialists in seeing 'democratic planning' as the necessary alternative to capitalist economic activity. King goes on to assert the similarity of the co-operative and socialist movements' social principles: each advocates a pluralistic democratic political life, equality through abolition of class distinctions, equal opportunities for participation and human development, and an ethic of 'comradeship.'

In the most crucial part of the four-page pamphlet, King attempts to prove that each movement needs the other. He contends socialism needs co-operatives: because co-operatives are one basic means of realizing the socialist objective of popular control over production and consumption, because co-operatives are 'one of the most practical training grounds for democracy,' where 'democracy means running our own affairs'; and, because, as noted earlier, co-operatives guard against over-centralization. Co-operatives need socialism, he argues, because: co-operatives by themselves cannot transform the social structure in an egalitarian and democratic direction; only socialist governments will provide consistent support for a dynamic co-operative movement, by removing the obstructive power of capitalism from the movement's path; and, co-operatives cannot control heavy industry and finance, and only sympathetic socialist administrations can transform these sectors in ways that promote co-operatives and the interests of the average citizen. King concludes by noting the prominence of CCF members in the co-operative movement, and the consistent support given by CCF MPs and MLAs to Wheat Pool and other co-operatives' proposals.

King's pamphlet neatly summarizes a broad range of claims made by prairie social democrats concerning the relationship between socialism and co-operation. Few went so far in translating the objectives and approaches of each movement into mutually acceptable terms. Nor did all social democrats present co-operatives as precocious socialist organisms.[198] None the less, to be a prairie social democratic populist required a commitment to co-operatives as central institutions in the transition to and future of socialism.

The emphasis on co-operation in this socialist discourse concealed the ultimate conflict between the local control, anti-statist impulse in the co-operative movement and the strong statist central planning orientation of more conventional social democracy. A crude version of this potential contradiction was more obvious to the population at large, bombarded as it was by the anti-socialist campaign of press and parties.

This is not to say that co-operatives would not flourish under social democratic administrations. The Saskatchewan experience proves this conclusively. However, it is clear that CCF leaders and publicists never faced squarely the extent to which co-operators' traditional antipathy to compulsive state action would have reduced their support for CCF governments. This oversight leads us back to the question concerning the trade-off between popular control and technocratic planning. One has to wonder whether the majority of CCF supporters in Saskatchewan would have found the party so attractive if they had appreciated the concessions that the co-operative movement might have to make to technocratic rationality. Perhaps the perception of larger and more damaging concessions to 'capitalist rationality,' such as foreclosure, reduced job security, or corporate monopoly in the markets, made co-operative partisans less wary about the prospects of social planning and expanded state power. Co-operators' fears would have been further reduced if they believed that the new CCF administration would treat co-operatives and their members as preferred customers. This, of course, was an important part of the CCF appeal and achievement.

Understanding the social democratic populist case for the compatibility of socialism and co-operatives requires reference to its basic values, its conception of human nature, and its use of the idea of 'abundance.' The impact of the 'social gospel' on the value structure of prairie social democracy is well known. Many CCF leaders across the prairies (and nationally) cut their radicalizing teeth on doctrines of secularized Protestant reformism. The influence of the social-gospel message was felt well before the CCF was established, most notably in the prairie grain growers' organizations. Social-gospel appeals for brotherhood, co-operation, equality, 'positive freedom' through equalization of opportunity, a secular version of the hereafter in the form of a co-operative commonwealth, and even state ownership of industry were common features of prairie politics from at least 1910. By 1933, J.S. Woodsworth was speaking confidently to the delegates in Regina when he stated that 'if our movement is to be successful it must bear – as we think it does – something of the character of a religious crusade.'[199]

The integration of the social gospel into morally grounded CCF appeals by several provincial leaders shows that this approach was crucial to more than Woodsworth's and the national party's message. It was a crucial element in their anti-capitalist, pro-democracy, pro-co-operatives arguments. However, the social-gospel justification of the CCF position also had the effect of drawing attention away from inevitable trade-offs between popular democracy and technocratic planning in the future commonwealth.

Louise Lucas was one of the most popular social democratic orators. Her presidential addresses to the Women's Section of the UFC in the early 1930s demonstrate the folksy, social-gospel appeal made in community halls and churches across the rural prairie region by CCF activists. Her 1932 address was typical. She interpreted the UFC platform in these terms:

the capitalist system ... has been devised by man to bring the multitude to worship at the shrine of the golden calf; but we can not serve ... God and Mammon ... Everyone who contributes something for the good of society is entitled to a decent standard of living, because a good Creator provided us with a bountiful supply of natural resources that would allow everyone to enjoy well-being, if only we carried out in public life as well as private, the command, 'Love the Lord thy God,' and 'Love thy neighbor as thyself' ... when [women] recognize that socialism does not mean atheism, but a fuller conception of the Kingdom of God, then I shall have no fear for the future ... The Kingdom of God is at hand. To me it means a Co-operative Commonwealth.[200]

Louise Lucas included a larger social-gospel element in her CCF propaganda than many, but even George Williams, who cannot be considered a social gospeler, felt the need to trade on the popular tradition linking socialist objectives to Christian ideals. Thus in 1939, Williams claimed in a widely distributed booklet that 'what the world really needs is Socialism, which is the economic reflection of the spiritual gospel of the Brotherhood of Man.'[201] Socialism was truly Christian because 'under Socialism the duty of mankind would be Brotherhood and mutual self-help, not competition and self-seeking, so that neighbour-loving would become possible, indeed inevitable.' Such claims demonstrate more clearly than any made by T.C. Douglas the integration of the social-gospel appeal into prairie socialism.

William Irvine made one of the most concerted attempts to link the ethics of Christianity to the objectives of the CCF between 1932 and 1940, long after he had left the church for the job of political conversion. Much of his argument is found in an address he gave to the 1934 UFA Convention, 'The Ethical Implications of the CCF,' in which he made an extended case for the claim that 'capitalism cannot be successfully defended on the basis of Christian ethics.'[202] He insisted that religion and ethics cannot be separated from economic and social life, and that capitalism and its political supporters produced results that cannot be reconciled with Christian values. The CCF program, however, 'is the embodiment of Christian ethics in the economic, political and social life of the nation,' because of its attempt to 'establish that brotherly relation in human affairs which religious leaders have always advocated and foretold but which so far no one has ever attempted to bring about.'[203] Because the CCF aimed to create a society of freedom, equality, and economic security, a vote for the CCF contributed to creating 'an environment in which each human soul may have a chance to be the best that its potentialities will permit.' This, according to Irvine, 'is one of the chief ethical implications of our movement.'[204] While he admitted that the animating purpose of the CCF was to provide economic security for 'the disinherited masses,' it was 'ethical in that it seeks the highest good for all through the joint efforts of all.'[205]

Irvine repeated this argument in a series of pamphlets in the early to mid-1930s.[206] *Can a Christian Vote for Capitalism?* included a glowing foreword by Reverend Salem Bland. Bland praised Irvine's argument that 'Christianity and the present economic system are as essentially and incurably incompatible as ever were Christianity and slavery.' He observed that 'until the present competitive, profit-motivated system is replaced by a co-operative system in which service is the incentive, unemployment, exploitation and unrest will continue.'[207]

This social-gospel argument did not have the desired effect, relative, at least, to CCF ambitions. Most early CCF leaders and activists assumed that the church-going prairie community would find socialism acceptable because of its secularized Christian character, if they had not already seen the value of the CCF program on other grounds. The injustice and un-Christian character of capitalism were so manifest to CCF leaders, especially those with clerical backgrounds, that the 'argument from Christian authority' appeared to be as compelling as any the CCF could marshal. As election results in the prairies demonstrated, however, a majority of self-proclaimed Christians voted CCF only once before 1950. And there is no way of proving the impact of the social-gospel appeal on this outcome.

What we can say is that this appeal reduced the perceived need for making a positive case for either popular control or expert planning. The ethical critique of capitalism, as a justification for socialism, was a negative case for popular democracy. Capitalism prevented equality and free human development, thereby reducing popular political activity and influence; thus, socialism would enhance these because it removed capitalism. Similarly, a negative case was made for state planning: capitalism produced suffering because it was driven by profit-greed and refused to plan the efficient use of all available resources. Socialist planning was rational and would produce security and abundance for all; it was uniquely compatible with ethical service of human needs.

The problem here is that ascribing ethical, Christian results to planning and state ownership *per se* can reduce the perceived need for popular control of the overall planning process. Social-gospel sanctification of 'co-operation' as the Christian alternative to competition is only partially compensatory in this regard: co-operation in economic and political affairs implies joint decision-making, but perhaps at no more enhanced a level than is found in corporatist arrangements. Such, at any rate, might be the case when economic security is the principal goal of planning.

As one would expect of an ideology of the left, the social democratic conception of human nature was an important source of faith in the possibility of the good society. All prairie socialists believed that man's 'higher nature' and telos suited him to such a project. As a Saskatchewan CCF pamphlet proclaimed, 'human nature has changed from savagery to barbarism, then to civilization. It will change to socialism, and come to measurable perfection just like the sour crab apple became, under proper care, a big mellow pippin.'[208]

This homey metaphor grants socialism a natural ordering principle one associates with natural law doctrines. Comments by prairie CCF intellectuals provide more evidence as to the social democratic position on human nature. *The Way of Reason's* authors argue that 'it is not human nature that stands in the way of Socialism, for the latter is in truth itself an expression of the former asserting itself against an inhuman economic system ... Socialism, appealing as it does to our truer and better selves, would certainly give human nature a better chance.'[209]

Carlyle King takes up the idea that co-operation is central to 'true' human nature in *What Is Democratic Socialism?* He summarizes evidence that suggests human nature changes over time, in response to environment, and changes progressively when 'co-operation or mutual aid' becomes a key factor in the evolutionary process. He concludes this discussion by saying:

there does not seem to be anything necessarily fixed or unchangeable about human character and behaviour. The evidence shows that men's attitudes and behaviour have varied enormously according to time, place and circumstance; that ... men have been able to deal justly, live peaceably, and work co-operatively with their fellows; and that when they have been able to do so, they have had life more abundantly. It is for us to draw more heavily upon the fund of human good, to develop our ... natural human resources. The faith of the socialist is this: in spite of all his 'hoggish, cheating, bedbug qualities' (to use Walt Whitman's phrase), man does desire liberty, equality, and fraternity. There is within him, potentially, enough intelligence and good will to make a better world than this.[210]

Despite living in 'an acquisitive society,' the average man is at least as concerned with doing useful work, while belonging and participating with his fellows in a co-operative endeavour, as he is with acquiring money. The socialist society will build on this concern to contribute, by restructuring education to emphasize the value of functional work for mutual benefit. 'It can and must appeal to the powerful hunger in men to work together for common ends,' and thus 'appeal to men's desire to co-operate, to men's desire to be comrades.'[211]

King's theme was central to prairie social democratic discourse: men are naturally co-operative, but fully so only when conditions, training, and social relations conducive to its development are established. Thus we find resolutions calling for teaching of co-operation in schools in virtually all UFC(SS) and UFA conventions after 1930, as well as in those of the early CCF.

One also sees in King's booklet a hint of the common social-gospel idea that man's dual nature was not simply a product of environment. Co-operation and camaraderie were at war with competition and selfishness in every man's bosom. The triumph of the higher qualities was not automatic; training and opportunity were required to tip the balance in the proper way. This could only be provided in the co-operative commonwealth.

The theme of potential but unrealized abundance was crucial to social democratic populist thinking about the good society, particularly as it affected their position on technocratic planning. It was most evident in the common phrase 'poverty in the midst of plenty.' This concise indictment of the capitalist economy had been issued by generations of British socialists and American populists before it became common in prairie CCF circles. Both A.A. Heaps and William Irvine addressed Woodsworth's 1932 resolution on the co-operative commonwealth by insisting that the 'problem of production' had already been solved by the great advances in the 'machine age' over the last century, and that Canada had sufficient resources and technology to 'satisfy all our human requirements.'[212] Irvine went farthest in this direction, contending that justifying capitalism with the concept of scarcity was no longer valid. Consequently, socialism was at last a practical proposition, free to solve the 'problem of distribution': 'We can begin our new system by laying down the cornerstone of the co-operative commonwealth on the bed-rock fact of abundance.'[213] In *Co-operation or Catastrophe* (1934), Irvine asserts that 'when the great fact of plenty has been fully accepted, individualism and competition will yield to social ends achieved by co-operation, ... an entirely different technique of production and distribution will evolve, and the objective will be the general good instead of private gain.'[214]

Irvine continued to emphasize this theme for more than a decade.[215] This emphasis was atypical of CCF propagandists, but not the acceptance of its basic truth. The same argument was common to the messages of George Williams,[216] M.J. Coldwell,[217] and T.C. Douglas.[218] It was often buttressed by references to unsold goods stacked on factory warehouse shelves, or elevators jammed with unsold grain. *The CCF Goal*, a 1938 Saskatchewan campaign pamphlet, illustrated the kind of mass appeal CCF leaders expected this argument to have. 'It is our duty,' the authors claimed,'to take up the torch of scientific knowledge and carry it further ... to ensure us that Canada can produce

PLENTY and to spare for all of us; ... we know bitter POVERTY because we lack only the right social institutions to distribute that PLENTY with which applied science and skill has endowed us.' Social co-operation and a CCF government implementing its program would ensure 'the proper distribution of that leisure and abundance into the general life of all Canadians.'[219]

The CCF Goal was not an atypical piece of social democratic propaganda. On the eve of the CCF victory, Tommy Douglas assured his radio audience that 'whether we know it or not, science has opened the door to a new world of infinite possibilities.' Saskatchewan people were 'standing on the threshold of a scientific era in which the ingenuity of man has made possible prosperity, security and abundance.'[220] Douglas's projection of Saskatchewan's potential abundance was preceded by E.A. Partridge. In *A War on Poverty*, Partridge had confidently asserted that western Canadians lived 'in a land of potential plenty for ten, yes twenty times the present population.'[221] No wonder a separate western Canadian commonwealth seemed viable to him.

What is the significance of the abundance axiom? At one level it seems to have discouraged serious thought about the problems the state, co-operatives, and all other organizations would encounter in the transition from artificial scarcity to the commonwealth of abundance. Arguing that 'real' plenty exists easily leads one to assume that its proper distribution requires no great sacrifices by any class. Only unreasonable people would refuse to accept the scientific plan for imminent leisure and abundance. In effect, too much emphasis on the 'fact of abundance' tends to depoliticize precisely what is most political: the sacrifices and rearrangement of responsibilities among social classes required by the scientific 'plan for plenty.' In addition, the standards of judgment in this extremely complex enterprise are removed from politics and granted to those with scientific knowledge.

Under these circumstances, merely political concerns could easily be seen as hindrances to the goal of plenty. Problems previously requiring democratic determination could too easily be defined into insignificance by positing imminent abundance. In the co-operative future, with 'rational' forms of social and economic organization in place, the state and civil society would seem to run on 'automatic pilot.' Democratic politics and public life suffer serious setbacks whenever what are perceived as major social purposes (security, abundance) appear achievable primarily by technocratic means.

CCF leaders and activists did not intend to surrender to technocratic determination of social priorities. They were sincerely committed to extending power to 'the people.' However, their emphasis on imminent abundance did little to encourage democratic development in the movement, while increasing supporters' expectations about state planning.

To some degree, the same can be said of their account of the 'co-operative rationality' inherent in human nature, although here the case is more complex. The problem is that while encouraging people to believe they have co-operative capacities is crucial to movement-building, it can also have the effect of inclining people to regard the 'co-operative ethic' as the primary requirement of the new social order. This could be especially likely for those whose perspective was influenced by the social gospel, and whose experience of social conflict was 'at one remove' from direct confrontation. The CCF farmer had no trouble co-operating with fellow grain growers, but saw his class antagonists only from afar (banks, grain exchanges, implement and consumer goods producers). Co-operation with other economic actors he knew was easy enough: why could not co-operative rationality be extended to political and economic relations generally? The promise of co-operative human nature reduced attention to social and political obstacles to co-operative relations between producers, while encouraging the 'socialist farmer' to think abstractly about the application of human reason (co-operative rationality) to the task of social reconstruction.

The rationalist element in social democratic populism provided a much needed *esprit de corps*. It did little to enhance a realistic appreciation of the strength of popular support for the prevailing social system. It also placed undue responsibility for managing the co-operation on the same group responsible for abundance: scientifically knowledgeable planners. Co-operation was a laudable principle for the good society, but social democrats have since learned that it is not a force inherent in Canadian political and social evolution.

In this section we have focused on sources of optimism concerning the compatibility of participatory democracy and state planning as instruments of the co-operative commonwealth. Such a focus unavoidably creates the impression that social democrats on the prairies were more confused and self-delusive in these regards than socialists or radicals elsewhere. This is not the case. Combining decisive state-directed social transformation with methods of popular control over such state action has posed a challenge to all egalitarians since Rousseau, who attempted to resolve it with the *deus ex machina* of the Legislator. Most socialists in power have relied on technocratic methods to reduce the power of those opposed to social change, and to provide immediate material benefits to 'the people.' Such moves are not self-consciously undertaken to undermine the power of the popular movement *vis-à-vis* the state in matters of policy determination. However, without clearly developed structures for co-determination of policy by 'the people' and state planners, this is often an unintended effect.

Social democratic populism on the prairies actually had a stronger commitment to popular democracy than many other left-wing movements, by virtue of its emphasis on the place of co-operatives in the good society. Co-operatives' internal democratic structures and principles, and distrust of compulsive state action in the economy, imparted to prairie socialism an anti-technocratic inclination lacking in, for example, the League for Social Reconstruction's view of political life. Often, however, the ambivalence about the state developed without any conscious recognition of the inherent tension. In the inter-war circumstances, economic crisis and the apparent potential for abundance distracted attention from the inconsistency.

Our earlier discussion of the participatory dimension of prairie socialist thought showed how these social democrats conceived of their mass organizations as the epitome of democratic practice. They applied their emphasis on co-operation from this experience to the image of the state in the co-operative commonwealth, as the name suggests. Problems involved in altering the state to incorporate the democratic dynamic of popular organizations have to be taken very seriously. However, prairie social democrats tended to assume that co-operative mechanisms in the 'new state' would emerge naturally with the achievement of social ownership, abundance, and a widespread 'co-operative rationality.' Capitalism was on the way out, and the new social order would produce its own institutions of democratic co-operation – inside and outside the state – almost as a matter of course. By definition, the co-operative commonwealth would eliminate policy conflicts between state and the new moral, rational order. The state would not wither away, but it would become the natural extension of a co-operative society. During the period of transition, one would have to give the state the benefit of the doubt – that is, assume that its planners worked in the interest of the people.

The problem with this image of the co-operative state is that it assumes the existence of something which could only be created by developing a whole new set of institutions guaranteeing close popular control over planners, administrators, and elected officials. Parliamentary institutions available may have been amenable to transformation in this direction, but prairie social democrats never devoted sustained attention to how they might be adapted. Typically, they assumed that the federal state would become the co-operative state. They thus avoided the problems of 'the transition' that would highlight the tensions between popular-democratic and technocratic policy determination.

The good society of social democratic populism was not and is not unique in containing an expression of the unresolved problems of its practical political program. Of the populisms examined in this study, however, it does provide the most chastening illustration of popularly based democratic thought which aimed at a relatively well-defined economic and social target, and then failed to find the political mark implied by its own critical standards. The magnitude of the stakes involved in the enterprise make this failure understandable. Its partisans can take consolation in the fact that these problems have bedevilled all democratic left-wing political organizations and governments during the twentieth century.

5   Social Credit and Plebiscitarian Populism

Most literature on the Social Credit experience in Alberta deals only superficially with its democratic thought, the obvious exception being C.B. Macpherson's *Democracy in Alberta*. For Macpherson,'plebiscitarian' referred to the Social Credit attempts to transform political competition into plebiscites or demonstrations of a 'general will for results.' Plebiscites in the Western world have tended to be tools of regime legitimation and mass manipulation in the hands of charismatic leaders,[1] and have thus acquired a bad name among most twentieth-century democratic theorists.[2]

Macpherson argues that plebiscitarian democracy is one of several ways to obscure class tensions,[3] which becomes the obvious form of democratic politics once delegate democracy fails to achieve its objectives in a quasi-colonial, predominantly *petit bourgeois* society. Neither of these claims is integral to 'plebiscitarian populism' in this chapter; instead, the phrase draws attention to the Social Credit League's anti-participatory pattern of democratic thought and practice.

If plebiscitarianism is the distinguishing feature of a fourth prairie populism – to which credit reform nostrums, a passion for decentralization, and antipathy towards socialism were only contingently related – then William Aberhart's Social Credit League is its sole important case. One could perhaps make a case for including the urban quasi-populism of Herridge's 'New Democracy' in this category,[4] but it was too short-lived and uninfluential to warrant separate attention, as were the diminutive prairie cells of Technocracy, Inc. Social Credit provides more than enough grist for our mill.

The People

'The people' in Social Credit appeals connoted less regionalism and less physiocratic content than did the same crypto-Liberal phrase, while offering a more confusing picture of prevailing social antagonisms. Although English Social Credit founder C.H. Douglas[5] contended that 'the sovereign people' should rule by expressing a 'general will' for 'results' or goals, he did not use the term 'the people' often in his writings. This is not surprising, since his vehement anti-collectivism was founded on a contempt for the rationality of the common man. While some of these notions found their way into early Social Credit League leaders' perspectives, they were not prominent in Alberta Social Credit circles until the 1940s. By this time, the rhetoric of 'the people' was solidly entrenched in Social Credit discourse.

It was only natural that Aberhart and his lieutenants should translate their appeals and nostrums into this indigenous political language. The UFA impact on the provincial political culture had created 'the people' as an indispensable rhetorical category for any political appeal. Reference to 'the people' was also natural for an evangelical preacher, which Aberhart was, and sounded 'right' to the many Alberta members of Protestant sects.[6]

At the most general level in Social Credit discourse, the people included all small producers, small businessmen, and 'little people' who had produced but not adequately benefited from 'the cultural heritage.' Aberhart followed C.H. Douglas regarding the promise of material security and leisure that modern technology held out for all citizens. In a 1943 speech, the premier argued that 'as these vast power-driven machines make it possible to produce more and more, with less and less effort, everybody should be better off. The people generally should reap the benefit.'[7]

Social Credit speakers also identified 'the people' with consumers. In the famous *Social Credit Manual*, Aberhart claimed that 'as the people have no purchasing power, they cannot get the goods that are piled high in the factories and warehouses.'[8] The people are all those suffering from underconsumption. However, one social category is not included in 'the people': 'men known as "The Fifty Big Shots of Canada" ' who had 'selfishly manipulated and controlled' the province's natural resource wealth. This wealth, he claimed, was the 'cultural heritage' of all 'bona fide citizens of Alberta.'[9]

This ambiguous identification of the 'enemies of the people' is expected by post-Hofstader[10] analysts of populism. An ideological appeal trading on an unorthodox explanation of poverty could also be expected to identify the people as debtors. The per-capita private debt in Alberta was in fact the highest in Canada by 1935,[11] and fell especially heavily on farmers and small merchants. In a way conveniently consistent with Social Credit theory, the people were thus 'seekers after freedom from financial tyranny,' as a 1937 government pamphlet put it.[12] Freedom would be theirs when various Social Credit remedies allowed them their share of the cultural heritage.

Macpherson shows how Aberhart adopted Major Douglas's idea that the people were a homogenous group in the one political sense that counted. They all wished to end poverty, desired the benefits of the cultural heritage, and should thus join together to give Social Credit a broad mandate to achieve these results. On the eve of the 1935 provincial election, Aberhart contended that while all voters had their own wishes and hopes, 'their united will – the will of the People – is not difficult to interpret.'[13]

The UFA had contended that all group interests could be reconciled in the future. By contrast, Aberhart argued that Alberta lacked any politically significant basis for intraprovincial conflict of interests. Thus, 'the people' had no legitimate reasons for pursuing different political paths: they all had an equal interest in supporting the 'general will.' Those who believed otherwise were either mistaken (as Rousseau claimed) or not part of the people.

Not surprisingly, then, politicians – those who tried to steer the people's will along politically distinct paths – were not considered part of the people. Social Credit politicians could be part of the people, however, since supporters of the people's will could not be politicians. Social Credit leaders, press, and government publications from 1935 to 1945 regularly advanced this anti-politician theme. Given the antipathy towards politicians generated by the UFA movement, this was a clever strategy in Alberta.

UFA and Social Credit critiques of politicians *per se* shared some common assumptions, but parted company on the relationship between politicians and the expression of popular power. To the UFA, politicians frustrated the clear expression of delegated and distinctive group wills; in Social Credit thought, politicians frustrated the expression of an undifferentiated general will. This key difference could be lost on an audience habituated into suspicion of politicians and made desperate by the Depression.

Another effective way of identifying the people was through the religious terminology common to most Protestant sects. Whether God had chosen them and thus given moral sanction to their struggle,[14] or whether they had chosen God and the right moral path, 'the people' were those working in association with God and against 'the iron hand of the oppressor.'[15] This evangelical identification of the people had been fundamental to Reverend Aberhart's radio broadcasts well before he integrated the Social Credit message into his Sunday sermons. Although such an approach would not have appealed to Major Douglas, Aberhart made the transition with ease. Biblical injunctions against money-changers and usury helped link the Social Credit crusade to God's endeavours to free his people in Alberta from oppression. We need not doubt Aberhart's sincerity to acknowledge that luck was on his side.

The social analytical content of 'the people' in this discourse is best appreciated by identifying the people's antagonists. Social Credit speakers most often lined up the people against financial interests, government planners and bureaucrats, and political parties.

The most natural and successful of their rhetorical contrasts was 'the people versus the money power.' As Mallory has said of the 1930s in Alberta, 'the dominant political issue was the clash of interest between a class of debtors who lived in the midst of economic ruin, and a class of creditors most of whom did not.'[16] The money power and the financial interests were synonyms for 'plutocracy,' which in radical democratic and social democratic populism had referred to a much broader range of business power. One might find Aberhart or writers in the *Alberta Social Credit Chronicle* attacking either plutocracy or even 'capitalistic interests'[17] as stiflers of the people's will, but the context virtually always identifies these as financiers and their minions.

One of the clearest brief statements of this antagonism came in a 1940 Bureau of Information pamphlet, *Premier Aberhart on Agricultural Reform.* As part of a larger case for establishing a 'Union of Electors' to defeat 'The Money Power,' Aberhart argued: 'the money system is being operated to divest the farmers of the fruits of their labor. As the financial interests, who now control the money system, are the chief beneficiaries of this arrangement, it is quite certain that they will resist any change by every means within their power ... This, like every other social issue, is centred in a conflict between the People and the Money Power. At present the people are divided and unorganized, thus being easily manipulated by the powerfully organized financial interests.'[18]

By 1943, a defensive Aberhart continued to portray the fundamental social antagonism in these terms: 'Not having the constitutional power to change the financial system, we were faced with the choice of either obeying the demands of the people or the demands of the financial interests, [and] chose to obey the people.'[19]

Aberhart usually left inflammatory attacks on bankers to others, but occasionally indulged himself. A warning about public debts contained this colourful prose: 'Do you not realize that unless we make definite plans for dealing with this slimy octopus which is wrapping its clammy blood-sucking tentacles around every man, woman and child in this Canada of ours, we shall find ourselves bound in abject slavery to the lords of finance who, by this iniquitous swindle have gained such power that they are virtually super-dictators to whom democratically elected governments have to go cringingly, cap-in-hand, to obtain permission to carry on?'[20]

The drawing of battle lines involving the people did not end at a financial conspiracy. As in many populisms, the people were portrayed as unremittingly opposed by political parties and politicians in general.[21] This theme was important to the Social Credit campaign in 1935,[22] and again in 1940, when the league's propaganda claimed all party opposition was financed by the banks and their political heelers.[23] Other party candidates were hopelessly corrupt, but the Social Credit League, acting in the interests of the people, would put forward a new kind of candidate: 'reliable, honorable, bribe-proof business men who have definitely laid aside their party politic affiliations.'[24]

Parties were also indicted for intentionally distracting the people from their desire to work towards justice and prosperity. The UFA had developed a complex argument to show how omnibus parties could not represent citizens' group–generated rational contributions to public policy, but Social Credit insisted that parties confused the people by proposing different policies for them to consider. As Macpherson demonstrates,[25] Alberta Social Crediters were inconsistent in this regard. They accepted Major Douglas's claim that electoral competition should eliminate policy debate, since 'the people' were capable only of stating their general desire for results. Party critics of Social Credit in 1935 were accused of attacking 'the Douglas System of Social Credit ... over which they thought they could bring about the most confusion, consequently they commenced on Major Douglas' famous A plus B theory ... which the average person ... cannot refute or confirm.'[26]

Aberhart contended that 'since party politics had arisen and usurped authority by rather questionable means, the people have found it very difficult to express their policy.'[27] The obvious solution was to 'refuse to be misled by claptrap and the platitudes of party politicians,' and 'vote for emancipation.'[28] From the moment the league appeared until at least 1945, Social Credit leaders and press enjoined the people to vote for results – i.e., for the Social Credit League – rather than for political parties instructed by 'the interests' to confuse the people with policy discussion.[29]

However, Aberhart still discovered that supporters were dissatisfied if fed only abstract arguments. He thus devised his own plan for Alberta, involving credit houses, dividends, and 'non-negotiable certificates,' most of which appeared in *The Social Credit Manual*. Aberhart appeared to have no choice but to speak about 'methods' as well as 'results,' and credited part of his 1935 victory to the league's detailed plan.[30]

Social Credit speakers regularly insisted that their movement owed nothing to politicians. In rhetoric reminiscent of the UFA, the Social Credit organ contended that 'if any reform is going to better the people it must come from ourselves, not from politicians; [if] any movement ever originated with the people, Social Credit in Alberta has, and we ought to be thankful that politicians have had nothing to do with it.'[31] Unlike past 'money barons' and 'political bosses with their heelers,' Aberhart's motives had nothing to do with a desire for power and glory; 'he has everything to lose, and nothing to gain, his victory will be a victory for the people.'[32] As Irving has demonstrated, the Social Credit press and faithful attributed a suprapolitical character to Aberhart's mission.[33]

Although Aberhart and the Social Credit press attacked planners, centralizers, and the bureaucratic state in the early years of the movement, it was not until 1937 that this became a centre-piece of their appeal. 'Bureaucracy,' representing planning, centralization, collectivism, and a whole host of related evils, was eventually presented as the people's principal antagonist.

Following the federal government's disallowance of Alberta legislation regulating the banks, Premier Aberhart made public the text of a letter he had sent to Prime Minister King. Aberhart accused King of being in league with the people's enemies in a very direct way: 'The fact is your advisers are chiefly bankers and lawyers, who, unfortunately, too often think that THE PEOPLE are made for the system and not the system for THE PEOPLE.' He further accused King of having a bureaucratic view of social problems: 'Your attitude now which exalts the institution above the individual is fraught with danger — not only to THE PEOPLE in this province, but to all Canadians.'[34] He couldn't resist linking the federal government to the banks: 'Banks, through charters engineered for them by political satellites are able, like the slave owners who preceded them, to batten and fatten on the enforced servitude of men and women, who are compelled to put up with anything that bankers think is good for them because YOU shield these bankers.'[35]

The Case for Alberta portrayed the federal government as meddlesome and regressively interventionist (largely relative to its 1937 disallowance action),[36] but was a far cry from the shrill anti-statist line taken in 1943. Aberhart then spoke of portents of totalitarianism on a world scale, such as compulsory unemployment insurance schemes, the purchase of agricultural land by financial institutions, and a variety of regulations issued by the federal government. In a series of 1943 radio broadcasts, he warned:

Any post-war reconstruction worthy of the name must come out of the people themselves. It cannot be imposed upon them by planners and schemers working behind closed doors.[37]

Our battle at the moment is against state socialism, regimentation, and the control of the many by the few. It appears to me that State Socialism is creeping right into the very life of the Canadian people ... No one can be free to live his life in his own way if control and power are allowed to become concentrated, socialized and centralized in a bureaucracy.[38]

... if the people sit back and allow their representatives ... to be chased around and bullied by a lot of bureaucrats with the mentalities of dictators, and still re-elect them, then we have no right to expect democracy to work.[39]

... to obtain any benefits under a [compulsory unemployment insurance] scheme the individual is forced to conform to a mass of regulations and conditions which are arbitrarily imposed upon him by some State bureaucracy. In short it is a system of centralized control of the many by the few, involving regimentation and domination of the people by a State authority. It is a retreat from democracy and a step towards the servile state of financial bureaucracy ... that is the kind of new Post-war order that is being established in this country.[40]

By 1943, Social Credit rhetoric of 'the people' and its antagonists presented a paranoid vision of financiers, central planners, the federal government, and state socialists creating a 'general scheme of State-dominated bureaucracy – an autocratic control over the lives of every citizen.' Much the same analysis, with even grander conspiracies (involving Jewish bankers), was found in the annual reports and other publications of the Social Credit Board from 1940 until 1947.[41] There was a good deal of C.H. Douglas in this,[42] but Aberhart did not sanction their racist excesses. Presentation of the people and the state as antagonists was a post-1937 development; in 1935, promises of dividends, just prices, state-controlled credit, protection from foreclosures, and expanded social services obviously precluded this approach.

Aberhart was not alone among North American populist leaders in counterposing 'the people' and large, distant institutions symbolic of average people's powerlessness. In a recent study of the careers of Huey Long and Father Charles Coughlin, Alan Brinkley has shown how each of these Depression demagogues generated startling popular support by contending that 'the people' had lost touch with their neighbours, their governments, and the institutions of private power. Long garnered considerable support for the 'decentralization of wealth,' a program to bring social, economic, and political control back to communities.[43] Like Aberhart, Long and Coughlin were promoting contradictory measures. State power was to be expanded into civil society to defend the middle class, while the power of corporations, central state institutions, and bureaucracies was to be reduced. All three portrayed a sinister entente between a centralizing federal government and a parasitic, exploitive financial sector.

John Irving was the first to identify the broad range of Social Credit support in 1935. He notes that Aberhart's Prophetic Bible Institute broadcasts acquired a large religious following[44] including the urban lower-middle class, rural small producers, and a good cross-section of small-town people.[45] He also notes organized labour's support for Social Credit proposals and movement,[46] the attraction of small-town small businessmen to the movement (after fifteen years of exclusion by the UFA), the political inexperience of Social Credit candidates (and yet their 'representativeness' in occupational terms),[47] and, in general, the 'surging response from ordinary people' in the early movement.

Jean Burnet's earlier study of social organization in Hanna, Alberta suggested that Social Credit support was from the less–well-off businessmen, farmers who had previously been socially and politically unintegrated, a good number of old UFA supporters, and many non–Anglo-Saxon voters in both town and country.[48] J.P. and L.M. Grayson's account of Social Credit's urban voting base in the 1935 elections shows that the Social Credit party received roughly one-third of its provincial and federal popular vote from the urban areas,[49] and more support from smaller than large towns. Unemployment was more highly correlated with voting for Social Credit than membership in a fundamentalist sect,[50] while urban people of British origin were more likely than others to vote for the new party.

Finally, recent scholarship has modified the long-standing impression that Social Credit support was primarily rural and/or *petit bourgeois* in the early years. Larry Hannant and Alvin Finkel[51] have demonstrated that many skilled and semi-skilled workers supported and participated in the Social Credit movement, particularly in Calgary, as early as 1933. The high rate of urban working class unemployment, the appeal of the $25 dividend, Aberhart's talk of poverty in the midst of plenty, and the pathetic state of the Canadian Labour Party and the CCF, all contributed to a substantial working-class base for the new movement. Working-class perspectives did not, I believe, have a decisive impact on the early Social Credit ideology, but this working-class support was still important for Aberhart's cross-class appeal and electoral victory.

Compared to the UFA before 1935, and to the Alberta CCF after 1935, the Social Credit movement drew a broad cross-section of 'the people' to its 1935 campaign in 1935. Many farmers, small merchants, urban unemployed workers, and even middle-class professionals saw Reverend William Aberhart, BA, as the most attractive alternative. His appeal extended well beyond the rural *petit-bourgeois* electoral backbone of the province to other classes, including the CCF's expected stronghold, urban workers.

Like Huey Long and Father Coughlin,[52] Aberhart appealed to many relatively prosperous workers and middle-class people whose fortunes had declined precipitously with the Depression and who therefore were experiencing anxiety about status, financial security, and the inability of 'average folk' to influence public life. Aberhart's crusade for 'the people' may have built on ambiguity, doublespeak, and policy contradictions, but it was attractive. Meaningful popular participation in plebiscitarian democracy was a different matter.

Democratic Methods in Plebiscitarian Populism

To consider the democratic rhetoric and experience of the Social Credit movement is to deal with a remarkable political and ideological contradiction. While other countries have produced mass movements with anti-participatory, authoritarian dimensions, few of them succeeded a popular movement whose appeal centred on a compelling theory of participatory democracy. The Social Credit success[53] can be partly explained by the Social Credit approach to democratic practice, as revealed in its prescriptions for a 'real democracy,' and in the early practice of the Social Credit government.

The political and ideological contradiction referred to above can be stated generally. On the one hand, the Social Credit crusade gained a mass following by promising a genuine popular sovereignty and relief from economic suffering, followed by transition to an age of plenty. On the other hand, the movement was very leader-dominated and manipulative, providing participatory opportunities only in propaganda dissemination and organization-building. The contradiction between promise and delivery was even greater when measured by the standards and achievements of the UFA. Examining two crucial elements of the Social Credit promise of popular democracy – decentralization and the critique of party – will demonstrate how the league's leaders traded on the province's popular-democratic traditions, substituting rhetorical surrogates for democratic practice.

Advocacy of decentralization and the critique of party politics in Social Credit discourse were both 'tailor made' for Alberta's political environment. This was especially true of the critique of party, since the UFA experience 'left a people confirmed in their repugnance to the party system, and distrustful of party machines.'[54] Albertans 'knew' by 1935 that the old-line parties served the will of 'the interests.' Aberhart and his movement spoke to this understanding with the imprecise, integrated-enemy rhetoric that has given populism a bad name.

August 1935 issues of the *Alberta Social Credit Chronicle* typify this approach. They spoke of the 'big financial interests' throwing dust 'in the eyes of the people,' Father Coughlin and Mr. Aberhart trying 'to save the world from the Communism that high finance, unfair big business and unscrupulous party politicians are driving it into,' and the upcoming provincial election as proof that Albertans 'have decided they will no longer be hoodwinked by the old political parties who have proven themselves just servants of the capitalist.'

Incumbent politicians, including sitting UFA legislators, were 'merely puppets of the financial and profiteering oligarchy from whom they get their corrupting contributions to debauch the electorates ... and broadcast lying statements to discredit Social Credit and to libel and slander our honored leader, William Aberhart.'[55]

This message built effectively on UFA traditions of 'party-bashing.' The United Farmers was a party dominated by financiers and politicians, in Social Credit eyes, because they had not adopted Social Credit remedies for the problems of poverty in the midst of plenty.[56] Only an organization above partisan concerns and obeisance to financiers could solve this problem, and Social Credit was it. Between 1934 and at least 1945, Social Credit speakers regularly used this approach to justify their movement and government activities, and to attack their opponents.[57] The Social Credit League refused to characterize itself as a party for well over a decade after gaining power.[58]

We saw earlier that parties were criticized for confusing 'the people' as to their real desires and proper expectations of governments, and that the Social Credit response here was inconsistent. When convenient, policy debate and discussion by party politicians was castigated for its obfuscating character, or because it would pre-empt the work of 'the experts' to be selected by a Social Credit administration. In a 1934 lead article in the *Alberta Social Credit Chronicle*, Aberhart spoke in orthodox Social Credit terms: 'We need hardly point out that no definite plan should be formulated until after a government favorable to [Social Credit's] introduction has been elected. The citizens must declare themselves desirous of its introduction by electing favorable representatives before any steps in this direction would be in order. Once the citizens had thus expressed themselves by their ballots, the problem of introduction would involve five steps.'[59] Four of the five steps involved the explicit use of 'experts' of one kind or another.

Aberhart also forbade his campaigners from engaging in debate over 'methods' or Social Credit theory during the 1935 campaign. Irving's study documents many refusals to respond to criticism with anything except ridicule, personal invective, virtual libel, or silence.[60] This rejection of debate during the campaign was consistent with the idea that only parties would debate issues. The true purpose of a campaign was to mobilize and show the people that what they had wanted all along – economic security, freedom from 'wildcat exploitation,' and the ability to consume what society could produce – would be theirs if they united in expressing their will for these results.

The problem with this generous interpretation of Aberhart's strategy is that the Social Credit League did provide a set of plans through Aberhart's *Manual*, his *Chronicle* articles, and his Bible Institute broadcasts. His responses to critics involved homey reiterations of claims, promises, and schemes that emerged in the summer of 1934. The hypocrisy of his critique of party did not appear to reduce popular support from a population more concerned with escaping the Depression than theoretical consistency.

Macpherson has sketched Social Credit's anti-party line after the 1935 victory,[61] noting its tendency to focus on the federal Liberals as the obstacle to implementation of the Social Credit plan, and the threat posed by CCF socialism to freedom. This line was not required by any theory, but was instead a matter of convenience for a regime that could not 'deliver the goods' on the grand scale promised in 1935. It was, like the earlier anti-party line, a matter of trading on popular traditions of antipathy towards central Canadian interests and parties – or, in the case of the anti-CCF line, a matter of supplementing an old grievance with a new bogey. In neither case did a coherent positive case, such as the UFA's, underlie the critique. The closest that Aberhart's movement came to producing a positive case came in two forms: the argument for decentralization of economic and political power, and the concept of a general will expressed through plebiscitarian representation.

For Aberhart, as for Douglas, the financial system's centralized character was a major part of its evil. Banks exploited consumers because they were not subject to community control. Such control would allow sufficient credit for citizens to purchase goods equal to the value of those they could produce. In the absence of community control over money and credit, underconsumption and underproduction were inevitable, since bankers had an interest in restricting output and money/credit to maximize profits.

This and considerably more 'technical' evidence had convinced Aberhart that decentralization of control over credit was necessary in Canada. As 'a sovereign province' with 'complete control over its own affairs within its own boundaries,'[62] Alberta was an obvious political unit to control its own credit system.

Major Douglas had predicted that western polities would experience either a complete centralization or radical decentralization of power, depending on action taken regarding the 'monopoly of credit.'[63] However, there is little evidence that Aberhart took this view seriously before 1937. One finds the occasional endorsement of decentralized power in the pre-election materials, but they almost always applied to economic rather than political power. A typical example of this comes in the question-and-answer section of the *Social Credit Manual*: '53. What will be your attitude toward the development of gas and oil fields? ANSWER – Social Credit stands for the decentralization of power. It would, therefore, support all individual effort and remove the monopolists control of the large companies.'[64]

It is typical of Social Credit talk on this issue that it did not translate the decentralization theme into positive account of the virtues of local self-determination and community development, as one found in the UFA arguments for decentralization.

Decentralization became more important to Social Credit political discourse following federal and Supreme Court rejection of Social Credit legislation regarding credit regulation in 1937. Aberhart justified his attack on centralized power by claiming he had no choice, given Albertans' suffering and will for self-improvement. 'No power known to man can force on 750,000 people operating within their own clearly defined borders, laws which they have made up their minds they will not endure – and that is the position I have to deal with here.' This excerpt from a public letter to Mackenzie King in August 1937 typifies his case against 'centralization of power,' where the villains were the federal government and the banks, denying Albertans 'the right they have always possessed to deal with their own credit in their own province, in their own way individually.'

Accompanied by claims about the 'spirit of the Constitution' and the lack of federal government authority to confer 'credit monetization powers' on the banks, this argument was developed by the future attorney general of Alberta in a widely reproduced speech in the legislature in August 1937.[65] It featured the notion that the province had a duty to look after its own people by providing them with economic liberty. The Alberta government had no obligation to heed the federal disallowance because the federal government was contravening 'divine law' by preventing the province from carrying out this duty.

In retrospect, it is clear that little more than Social Credit frustration with its inability to implement 'social credit' legislation, and a desire to get maximum political mileage out of their defeats, was behind their case for decentralization. Thus people in the province were encouraged to rally behind their government, strenuously 'demand results' from their government, and thus hasten the transition from the 'concentrated power over the social organization' and 'tyrannical financial rule' to 'democratic social organization.'[66] The message's essentials did not change through the late 1930s and 1940s, although new bogeys – state socialism, compulsory unemployment insurance, and welfare-state planners – became agents of centralization and threats to 'true democracy.'

Despite the transparency of rhetoric about decentralization, there is no denying that federal government inaction regarding credit crises, deflation, unemployment, and burgeoning agricultural debts left prairie provincial governments without the option of 'standing pat.' Debt moratoriums were soon introduced by the Saskatchewan and even the federal governments. Most commentators on the Social Credit government express some sympathy with its actions, in view of federal government acceptance of the bankers' campaign to escape the financial burdens of the period.[67] However, the objective need for government debt relief is not the same as a substantive case for decentralization.

To be convincing, a case for democratic decentralization must show its superiority in stimulating and acting on local responsiveness. Smaller-scale communities know what they want, but also lend themselves to a more easily co-ordinated and self-sustaining system of self-government. To speak of self-government without reference to some degree of popular control over policy-making procedures and administration is a contradiction in democratic terms. Yet this is precisely what Social Credit did. In the 1937 publication cited above, for example, the Bureau of Information and News declared: 'The matter can be put in a sentence: In democracy all matters of policy, i.e., deciding results should be controlled by The People and all matters of administration, i.e. methods, should be centrally controlled, subject to such administration yielding the results demanded by democracy.'[68]

If all means of achieving 'results' are to be centrally controlled, and if policy is equated with expression of mass support for prosperity and 'economic liberty,' the case for decentralization as self-government evaporates. There remains no reason to decentralize political authority except that the central government is not acting in the desired way. Provincial control over credit is rationalized by default rather than on the basis of the positive merits of decentralization *per se*.

Aberhart's Plebiscitarian Leadership Style

Observers of the Social Credit experience have expressed amazement, dismay, and detached appreciation of William Aberhart's organization and leadership of the Social Credit League.[69] Aberhart's first academic biographer overstated the case when he said that 'his leadership and organization ... provided the basic ingredients for the Social Credit victory at the polls in 1935.'[70] Yet it is true that a leader with fewer organizational and leadership abilities would not have harnessed the possibilities for radical electoral change. Our interest here is with the implications of Aberhart's leadership and organization for Social Credit's 'democracy in action.' We will examine three aspects of the leadership style and organizational approach: the appearance of intensive and meaningful popular participation, Aberhart's authoritarian style and organization, and the portrayal of leadership and organizational activity as transcending the sordid world of 'politics.'

The Social Credit crusade mobilized unprecedented popular support in Alberta from 1933 to 1935. On the eve of the election, the Reverend Mr Aberhart was broadcasting to more than 300,000 listeners in southwestern Saskatchewan, northern Montana, and most of settled Alberta.[71] Over 32,000 registered Social Credit League members[72] and approximately 1800 'study groups' had emerged in Alberta.[73] The study groups were crucial to the movement-building and election effort; Irving referred to them as the 'dynamic nuclei in almost every city block or rural district,' and the 'principal media through which funds were raised for the movement.'[74] One of the earliest indications of organizational possibilities came in early 1934. During a brief campaign spearheaded by Aberhart's radio pleas, 53,000 Albertans signed a petition urging the UFA government to bring Major Douglas to Edmonton. The large gap between the plurality that returned the UFA to power in 1930, and the majority that toppled them in 1935[75] is additional evidence of the magnitude of Social Credit popular support.

Several factors produced a widespread sense of the Social Credit crusade as a 'people's movement' with genuine popular input. Aberhart's audiences were not merely huddled around radios in the homes of the zealous or curious; they also attended 'monster' rallies and Sunday picnics that made even early UFA equivalents pale by comparison. Aberhart 'stumped' the province during the summer of 1934, a good half-year before he announced the organization's electoral intentions. He did so again in the spring and summer of 1935, speaking to gatherings of as many as 20,000 wildly enthusiastic supporters.[76] At these meetings he commonly called for 'voice votes' on general 'results' desired by the people, such as an end to insecurity, the advent of prosperity through enhanced purchasing power, or an end to the reign of the 'fifty big shots' of finance. Thousands of people offering this mandate in unison could not help but feel that they were contributing to achieving the crusade's goals.

Aberhart's weekly broadcasts from the Calgary Prophetic Bible Institute also engendered this feeling. By personally welcoming groups of the faithful who had travelled to see their leader, announcing study-group meetings, and responding to questions received in the past week's mail, Aberhart gratified supporters and promoted 'boosting' of Social Credit.[77] After covering the 1940 campaign, a prominent newspaper reporter declared that because Aberhart was 'the only Canadian politician to realize and exploit the possibilities of radio,' he was 'closer to the people than any other public man in Canada.'[78]

Aberhart's ability to impart a sense of crusade participation had striking parallels with efforts by Father Charles Coughlin and Senator Huey Long to the south. However, Aberhart faced no competition from a national leader widely regarded as a serious reformer, nor did he fail to follow up his radio work with systematic organizational work 'on the ground.' He did not, like

Long and Coughlin, make 'the relatively passive process of listening to the radio the dominant activity of their followers, [thereby ensuring] that their movements would never become what the populist movements had once been: a constantly visible presence in the lives of communities.'[79] Indeed, as Irving shows, when complemented by a provincial network of speakers and study groups, Aberhart's radio work maximized ego-involvement and conversion by his movement's participants.

Irving also illustrates Aberhart's ability to convince his radio audience that they were being consulted about the conduct of his campaign, when he was orchestrating support for a predetermined course of action. The best example is his success in inducing constituency and district associations in April 1935 to pass resolutions 'telling' him not to comply with the UFA government's request to construct a detailed Social Credit plan for Alberta.[80] Aberhart was able to achieve two ends simultaneously. He avoided the potential embarrassment of having to produce a plan – something he was not capable of doing, he believed and said, because he was not an 'expert' and had not compiled the necessary 'facts.' His supporters also believed that they were sharing direction of the movement in their organizational activities, since he was both leader and servant of the people. One could not ask for a better example of how to 'run' a popular movement.

The faithful often perceived their participation in the movement's organizational, study-group, and proselytizing activities as spiritually meaningful. They were contributing to a crusade for relief from misery, and perhaps a 'new social order.' We should not condescend to the participants by writing off their convictions as the result of mass delusion. Irving's social-psychological account of the movement shows that the value of the Social Credit gospel could not be reckoned in terms of dividends.

Participation in the Social Credit movement offered the individual a dynamic purpose in life, and the person of Aberhart became the living symbol of the purpose ... thousands of people who had been frustrated by the depression achieved a renewed self-confidence, greater in many instances than they had ever previously experienced ... Participation in the life of the groups was the elementary source of satisfaction that most people obtained from the movement ... Aberhart helped his followers to achieve ego-enhancement by insisting on their direct participation in the activities of the Social Credit movement. Through incessant personal effort, a new orientation was given to their lives and ... many of them exhibited surprising qualities of local leadership. In addition, the movement appealed to their feelings of self-regard in that it promised a restored, a redefined, or a greatly improved status for all of them should victory be achieved.[81]

Intense participation was thus crucial to Social Credit movement-building and electoral success. However, it was a limited participation, notably distinct from that in radical democratic social democratic and crypto-Liberal organizations on the prairies. Whatever ego-enhancing and quasi-spiritual benefits Social Credit participation conferred, it was restricted to the activities of mass education in Aberhart's formulas and slogans, and in the activities of organization *per se*. People were not given the wherewithal to critically assess their problems, or to develop their own solutions within a general ideological framework. Instead, their popular-democratic traditions were compressed into a psychologically unassailable and ideologically exclusionist vision.

This vision was not inherent in social credit monetary and credit reform proposals. Rather, it was the result of Aberhart's organization and proselytization, his acceptance of Douglas's political strategy, and his authoritarian and demagogic leadership style. All were consistent with the idea that the role of 'the people' in democratic action is simply that of 'demanding results.' Only the form and some of the psychological benefits of participation remain, without the substance – at least when compared to the integration of form and substance in radical democratic populism.

It is important to consider how Aberhart's authoritarian style complemented the technocratic orientation of Social Credit thought. Macpherson has indicated that an application of Douglas's political strategy entailed an authoritarianism approach to movement-building, election-contesting, and governance. Aberhart's philosophy of instruction in secular and religious schooling,[82] combined with the remarkable devotion he sought from all movement leaders and followers (until at least 1937), led him from authoritarianism to demagoguery.

One example of this demagoguery comes from Aberhart's proposal for a candidate selection scheme giving him ultimate control. He bluntly informed his followers: 'If you are not going to let me have any say in the choice of my supporters, you will not have me as your leader.'[83] The convention resolution sanctioning this scheme stated that Aberhart's direction was necessary to prevent disguised old-line party candidates from using 'wire-pulling tactics' and deception to undermine Aberhart's Social Credit plan.[84] A convention resolution 'instructing' Aberhart to lead his forces through the campaign offers further evidence of his demagoguery: 'Whereas, William Aberhart, despite the fact that he has repeatedly declared his personal aversion to political office and has constantly refused to enter the field of political office, is, nevertheless, recognized as the one responsible for the social credit movement in Alberta, and the individual best qualified to lead to victory the thousands whose hopes for economic security through his educational campaign ... Be it resolved that this convention ... demand that Mr. Aberhart complete the work that he has begun by assuming the active leadership of the social credit forces of this province, and furthermore, we insist that he regard this resolution as the mandate of Southern Alberta social credit supporters whose hope he has aroused.'[85]

To us this merging of delegate democracy and plebiscitarian mandating appears transparently loaded in the latter direction. It did not to participants in the movement. *The Alberta Social Credit Chronicle* contributed to their self-deception. In a typical and contradictory editorial, the *Chronicle* said of the Southern Alberta convention that produced these resolutions:

Hard thinking men and women attended this convention with a definite purpose, that was to support wholeheartedly William Aberhart and his Social Credit principles, and to get 100 per cent behind the suggested platform, they did what they set out to do [*sic*]. Carefully analysing each and every proposal, giving thought to the speakers and their addresses, they weighed every point before they gave a decision.

It was no 'Yes' convention, it was no follow the leader meeting, but a convention of men and women who were out for one main purpose – to settle that great problem of today – POVERTY IN THE MIDST OF PLENTY.

William Aberhart ... has studied Social Credit from every angle, he has come to the conclusion that it is the only system that can forever do away with 'Poverty in the midst of Plenty,' and when he has come to that conclusion it is safe for everyone of us to get right behind him 100 per cent ... [86]

Such ritualistic concession to democratic self-respect, combined with democratically unbecoming deference to the inspired leader, was typical in Aberhart's movement. The passage demonstrates how the plebiscitarian spirit had fused with his leadership style.

In 1940, when Aberhart used these same methods for candidate selection, the party was officially silent, but Aberhart's candidate inquisition was roundly condemned by the daily press, other parties, several rejected incumbent MLAs, and a good number of dissatisfied voters.[87] In the same year, Aberhart had insisted on control over selection of 'New Democracy' candidates in his uncooperative 'alliance' with W. Herridge's short-lived splinter party.[88] By extending the same strategy to the Social Credit campaign in the Saskatchewan provincial election, he reduced popular support for the party in its competition with the struggling CCF.[89] Aberhart's contempt for provincial party autonomy provided another indication of how little he trusted his followers to demand the correct results.

Some of Aberhart's plebiscitarian techniques have already been noted here, such as the use of 'voice votes' at large rallies and the 'instructed' refusal to construct a social credit plan for the UFA government in the spring of 1935.[90] Each technique gave Aberhart a blanket endorsement for his recent decisions and activities, as well as a clear mandate to proceed as he chose. In addition, each created the impression that the involvement of the followers was decisive for the overall direction of the movement. Both of these results were crucial to movement participants' sense of meaning-in-action, and to their belief that their leader was genuinely responsive.

Aberhart realized the importance of this sense of involvement to his project as early as 1933, when he circulated petitions on his first provincial speaking tour. They demanded that the provincial government investigate, then implement, Social Credit proposals. By late 1934, a second tour, increased press coverage, a movement organ, and a massive growth in study groups had brought Social Credit to the centre of political discussion. Aberhart initiated a petition requesting the UFA government to import Major Douglas as architect of a Social Credit plan. This petition, with its 54,000 signatures, was easily the largest to date in the province.[91] Aberhart could thus claim that his request was only an extension of widespread desire, and that 'the people' had collectively forced the government to follow their will.

Related techniques included the 'straw ballot,' platform-construction management, and voters' pledges. After the 1935 victory came MLA's covenants, an appeal for member support during the 1937 MLA insurgency, and some of the crudest anti–federal government propaganda seen before 1980. The straw ballot was systematically conducted through constituency associations.[92] Presented as a test of constituencies' support for Social Credit candidates, it was also intended to give supporters a sense of movement-building and to indirectly endorse Aberhart as leader. The ballots' impressive results accomplished all three objectives.

Calgary Social Credit headquarters distributed a draft platform to local associations shortly after these results appeared. Its contents were endorsed virtually unaltered, and sent to the Calgary and Edmonton conventions as the organization was put on a battle footing.[93] In plebiscitarian fashion, the election platform's preamble claimed that its contents were 'the findings of the two General Conventions ... for the purpose of formulating the planks of the Social Credit platform.'[94] While formally true, this claim misrepresented the actual process, since the intended audience had learned to take such claims seriously from the UFA.

The voters' pledge came shortly after the platform and was based on C.H. Douglas's electoral strategy. It involved voter support for dividends to conquer poverty, for only '100% Social Credit candidates,' and punishment of incumbent MLAs, to teach them that 'true democracy enjoins obedience to the will of the people.'[95] Once again, we find two ingredients of the plebiscitarian technique. The pledge is presented as an expression of the will of the people, and is intended to enhance the individual's sense of contribution to the crusade. The pledge also implicitly grants the leader of the '100% Social Credit candidates' an open mandate to pursue his own path once in power, since he initiated the campaign and divined people's needs in the first place.

Aberhart's successful attempts to neutralize the 1937 insurgency through plebiscitarian appeals to constituency associations for support, and MLA's 'covenants,' have been covered well by Macpherson and others.[96] The MLA's covenants (or 'agreements of association') subordinated them to the Social Credit Board as formal representatives of 'the people's will.' There was also an indirect but clear resubordination by MLAs to Aberhart. The board was only temporarily and ineffectually 'above' Aberhart and his cabinet. Radio appeals to constituency associations for a further broad mandate after the passage of the first credit legislation were even more blatantly plebiscitarian. Mandates via elected constituency representatives were politically unreliable, especially during the insurgency, so Aberhart circumvented the legislature by reaching the people directly over the radio.

The plebiscitarian style was also employed in Social Credit's anti–federal government propaganda. The attack was mounted by the provincial government's 'Bureau of Information,' a group of Social Credit activists calling themselves 'United Democrats,' the weekly movement organ *Today and Tomorrow*, and, of course, Aberhart's weekly broadcasts from the Bible Institute. They presented the federal government as self-conscious tools of the bankers, intent on frustrating the 'sovereign will' of Albertans. Premier Aberhart was, by contrast, the people's saviour; the people were thus adjured to 'let yourselves be seen and heard in support of Mr. Aberhart's policies.'[97] Aberhart's adroitness at making the federal government the scapegoat for his own failures owed much to his ability to present his fight as something mandated by 'the people' in Alberta. This produced a wider space within which his actions could be legitimized and sustained a strong sense of popular participation in the crusade.

These objectives were also furthered by the oft-used argument that implementing Social Credit measures was 'beyond politics,' specifically party politics. Acceptance of the contention that the crusade was educational and spiritual was important to the movement-building process from 1933 to 1935.[98] In November 1934, for example, the *Chronicle*'s readership was assured that the way to create a government devoted to 'full liberty and freedom to enjoy the bountiful fruits of nature' was to 'forget politics completely and vote a straight No. 1 for the Social Credit candidate in your constituency.'[99] In the last issue of the *Chronicle* before the election, Aberhart associated politics with unscrupulous tactics: 'Why have the smartest politicians and spell-binders been imported to coax and scare and ballyhoo you once again ...? Are you for sale?' Aberhart promised to be led by the people's wishes, with 'the word of a man whose word has never been doubted, and if Social Credit does not work or is not allowed to work, he will resign. Did you ever hear a politician promise that?'[100]

This kind of appeal did not end after the election. The Social Credit nostrums and crusade were continually presented as above politics, beyond mere party wrangling. By itself, this appeal is not plebiscitarian in character. The Social Credit approach transformed it by making Aberhart and the 'sovereign people of Alberta' martyrs to the cause of human freedom, and by adopting a rigid approach to political co-operation. A 1939 government publication entitled *Democracy Denied* insisted that

During the past three years there has been a most deliberate and unjustifiable attempt to block every measure designed to relieve the suffering and want which exists throughout the Province ... The People elected the Government to achieve a certain objective, but every possible obstacle has ... been used to thwart the Will of the People of Alberta ... We have answered the destructive criticism of old party politicians with the mellowed tones of sound reasoning; we have answered the mailed fist of money dictatorship with the padded glove of peaceful fellowship ... Even the old party leaders are now telling us they, too, believe we are right in our demands. If we enter the fight with their hands clean, we welcome them. Social Credit is not a party issue and we must never allow it to become a political party football. We are prepared to welcome people of every political creed into our ranks, but they must take up the fight on our terms and according to our rules.[101]

In the absence of survey results gauging Social Credit members' responses to this appeal beyond politics, it is impossible to judge its success. The decline in membership (from 36,000 in 1936 to 24,142 by 1939)[102] and the reduced popular vote in the 1940 election do suggest that this appeal had lost some credibility. The brush with the 1937 insurgents and the high-decibel campaign against the federal government were apparently seen as political by a good number of 1935 faithful. At the same time, the divided opposition, with its overdrawn portrait of Aberhart as a crypto-Nazi[103] and its negative campaign, must have appeared highly political to many of the 1935 supporters. Subsequent Social Credit administrations portrayed their objectives and performance as non-political, but this was increasingly less important to their overall appeal. After Aberhart, the plebiscitarian dimension in this appeal declined markedly.

Social Credit on Representation

Plebiscitarian political theory is primarily about how representation can achieve certain broad goals and legitimize approaches to political leadership and policy development. Consequently, the general concept of Social Credit representation is simply rendered. Representation expresses a broadly based desire for 'results' – the elimination of poverty, and the material delivery to the people of society's technological capacity to produce goods – and, very secondarily, a means of ensuring that those responsible for delivering these results respond to this demand. The people demand results, representatives facilitate delivery of results, experts deliver results by selecting and applying appropriate methods. Nothing beyond this formula suggests strict guide-lines for or limits on what representatives should do to 'facilitate' results, except that they should not prescribe 'methods' to those actually making policy decisions. In this sense, the Social Credit concept of representation lacks what Pitkin calls a 'substantive' dimension.[104] Yet there is a vague set of conditions that underlie this approach to representation.

At first glance, nothing in the nature of the basic social conflict Aberhart identified necessitated this type of representation. Just because the people were in conflict with the financial-politicians conspiracy, it did not follow that the people were best served by plebiscitarianism. However, when one considers several other Social Credit assumptions, the conflict can be seen to have implied a good deal about representation. These were the supposed existence of a general will for results, the incompetence of those ('the people') willing them, and the technical complexities of choosing and implementing 'methods.' Adding all of these factors together, the mode of representation required a large degree of what Pitkin calls the 'authorization' dimension.

Macpherson demonstrated how the idea of a 'general will' for several goals originated in C.H. Douglas's writings and was plausibly defended by Aberhart.[105] Aberhart was particularly blunt about this: all of the people suffered because financiers manipulated the system of money and credit, and all wished to end this suffering through increased purchasing power. For Aberhart, the conclusion was simple: 'democracy says, if you have any intelligence, you must ask and say it with one voice or else get out.' Democracy was in trouble because of a 'lack of cohesion' among the people.[106]

Thus for the 1935 election the issue was obvious: 'If we as a people do not keep steady and pull together, where may we expect to get?'[107] The conflict between the money power and the people demanded that the people speak with one voice, demanding the good life that Social Credit could provide. Aberhart proposed a folksy social contract to express a general will: 'You know, in the old days, the people used to sign covenants one with another. They said we shall stand by one another through thick and thin. We have a common purpose so we shall sink petty differences and press on for that which will benefit all rather than the few. These covenants have been carried through many years. I wonder if it will be possible for each group to have an honor group of 100% social creditors signed up. Head it something like this, "I covenant with all who sign below to cooperate in every way possible and reasonable to break this horrible depression and poverty in the midst of plenty. I believe in this and shall be loyal to the Alberta Social Credit Group."'[108] Such a covenant was necessary because the 'financial tyranny' had eliminated all important differences among the people.

While Douglas unambiguously portrayed the people as incompetent on all matters of policy, Aberhart could not emphasize this theme in Alberta. Following the UFA experience, supporters were accustomed to actively examining new reform proposals. In such an environment, lecturing the people about their analytical shortcomings would incite antagonism. The trick was to assure the people that they could assist in their own salvation, to allow supporters to puzzle over the mysteries of Social Credit, and then to restrict their activities to organization. Indirectly, Aberhart and Social Credit leadership contended that the people were incompetent in all but articulation of sloganized desires.

Aberhart and his advisory board's selection of candidates from a list sent by the constituency association was an astonishing denial of member's ability to recognize good candidates.[109] The proscription on instruction of convention delegates regarding specific resolutions, and on specific policy resolutions themselves, also demonstrated that the people had a very limited role in the overall process of representation. (This ban was not lifted for several years, but even in 1935 some delegates and constituency groups insisted on discussing or promoting 'methods' through resolutions.)

Aberhart's practice of dismissing criticism by telling his listeners to leave experts to settle the technical questions was another indirect slight to the people's intelligence. When pressed on the constitutionality of his credit-reform proposals, for example, he told his audience that his critics were simply 'arguing and putting up this criticism only to delude you and confuse you.' The answer? 'Leave that to the lawyers to settle. Let them do the work.'[110] After his election, Aberhart found this approach particularly convenient, especially as the dividends and other promised benefits did not materialize. At a post-insurgency picnic, Aberhart told supporters that he was working hard to meet the people's demands. As a reporter from *The Albertan* recorded the proceedings: 'The people need not bother how these aims might be accomplished, he stated, but could leave that to the experts chosen to do it. "Don't let details bother you, ask for results," he stated. "For goodness sake, don't get the inferiority complex," the premier continued. "You cannot get anything if you don't think you can get it. How? That is something you don't need to bother about. You go ahead with your farm work."'[111]

A 1943 broadcast vividly demonstrated Aberhart's inclination to see ordinary people's political life as essentially passive. In an extended argument against 'compulsory state insurance schemes,'[112] Aberhart repeated Douglas's definition of freedom. 'Freedom is the right to choose or refuse any proposition which is placed before you, without interfering with the same right of everybody else.'[113] People were to feel politically fulfilled if enabled to vote in plebiscites drawn up and interpreted by leaders and experts.

Popular consideration of policy was singled out for attack by professional propagandists in the new administration after 1935. They produced two striking examples in 1937: *A Sovereign People Demand Results*, by G.F. Powell, and *And This Is Democracy*, by the provincial government's Bureau of Information and News. Powell was one of the official experts sent from Douglas's directorate in London, and is predictably faithful to Douglas's claim that the people are essentially 'a mob,' incapable of any useful thoughts on policy.[114] Powell argues that 'THE PEOPLE are quite unable to govern; are quite unfitted in every way to say HOW things should be rightly ordered.' Such matters, he insists, are 'so technical that relatively few are able to understand even so little as the meaning of the words with which each METHOD has to be discussed.' It follows that 'if we desire efficiency in our democratic mechanism, we must never ask the electors anything other than "What results do you desire?" and "In what order do you want them?" That is the only answer which it is within their competence to answer.'[115]

The Bureau of Information's account of democracy presents the distinction between results and methods in terms of the scientific division of labour required of a modern social organization. The people's rightful function is to demand results by voting: 'By teaching The People to use the power of their political vote to demand the results they want, and to steadfastly refuse to vote for methods, programs, parties and all the other devices used to render democracy futile, the Government is enabling Albertans to establish political democracy. [With both political and economic democracy], we shall be the first democratic community in the world – a community organized to enable its individual members in association to demand and get the results they want and thus realize their social credit.'[116]

The final two factors conditioning plebiscitarian representation are closely related. Both 1937 publications, Powell's in particular, illustrate the Social Credit leadership's insistence on the technical complexity of all aspects of policy considerations. As official expert and true believer, Powell had a clear interest in spinning a web of pseudo-scientific mysticism around the policy process. This was not merely an expression of contempt for the masses. It was also designed to minimize popular expectations of short-run achievements, and deprive people of standards for measuring Social Credit achievements. Perhaps most important, this mysticism would discourage Social Credit supporters from insisting on participation beyond 'demanding results.'

Characterizing public policy as the natural preserve of scientific experts was a necessary part of creating a political environment conducive to plebiscitarian representation. It excluded precisely what the radical democratic variant required: critical, informed communication and accountability between voters and representatives. The UFA approach to policy construction was to begin with certain goals, then refine and adapt them in specific policy directions as the democratic organization developed citizenship abilities. While the UFA approach began with certain goals, Social Credit supporters' democratic efforts were to end with the same general goals with which they began.

Attending to the results demanded through the people's vote was to be a non-political process. The Social Credit account of this process inevitably involved pseudo-scientific discussion of organizations, the natural social division of labour in policy matters, and the technical mysteries of the economic system. We have seen that Douglas, and then Aberhart, attacked parties and competitive politics generally because they raised policy alternatives the public were unfit to assess. A logical extension was to insist that 'the question of social organization is a science,' and that 'smoothness and efficiency ... in achieving the purpose for which it exists' are wholly dependent on a scientific division of labour between those who demand satisfaction and those capable of meeting these wants. In such a felicitous division of labour, the people 'must be provided with an effective system of stating their wants and having these satisfied.'[117] This system would be effective only if demands were not distorted or frustrated by 'political' interference, and if those qualified to engineer satisfaction were allowed free rein. 'Specialization in methods ... the outstanding factor in the progress of civilization' must be allowed to operate unfettered by political considerations in the policy realm.

Curiously, another rationalization for this rejection of politics in policy decision-making was open to Alberta's Social Credit, but it conflicted with

Aberhart's authoritarian rejection of popular participation. The UFA had argued that the genius of the group-delegate system of representation was that representatives could, in a sense, become the experts that their vision of social transformation seemed to require. Social Crediters in Alberta could have incorporated the attractiveness of this UFA approach by saying that many experts could be found in the province and their movement.

Aberhart did not encourage this line of thinking, but it was advanced cautiously in an August 1935 *Chronicle* editorial entitled 'Where Are the Experts?' The division between the people and the experts is removed in this isolated piece, but the notion of policy-determination as 'supra-political' remains: 'Social Credit does not require jugglers of figures, they require clean honest men and women, who are beyond bribery and corruption, and surely in Alberta can be found these people. There are thousands of experts of all classes of work living in Alberta today, professional and otherwise, who detest the nefarious methods of old political trickery and would be only too willing to give their services for an upright and honest cause of the people ... Of course we have clever scholars and experts in every line ... RIGHT IN THE RANKS OF OUR HONEST SOCIAL CREDITORS.'[118]

These experts would be above the dirty world of politics, and would have the virtue of being local people. However, such a message could open the door to a demystification of Social Credit 'techniques,' and possibly even encourage greater popular input into policy. Thus this approach to the relationship between people and experts was not popular in subsequent Social Credit discourse.

These factors conditioning Social Credit representation produced a modified version of what Hanna Pitkin calls a 'formalistic authorization' concept of representation. Three expressions of the Social Credit representation formula can demonstrate its relationship to Pitkin's category. Each endeavours to legitimize the distinction between 'results' and 'methods' to guide people's expectations of representation. In the first, Aberhart congratulates the 1935 Calgary Social Credit convention's rejection of resolutions binding candidates to support specific legislative measures. 'A democracy,' he announced, 'can suggest but it has not the power to execute, and that is what anybody would be doing when you start to decide what your government should and should not do when it is elected. Don't try to tell your government everything they should do. The minute you start to talk or interfere with the policing of the country you are out of order.'[119]

Aberhart then assured his followers that the 'methods' they were considering in these resolutions were of such small importance to their own role in the representational process that they should disregard criticisms of Social Credit from non-believers. (He had already issued a ban on debate with other parties' supporters or sceptics, which was to apply throughout the campaign.)[120] As he put it, 'if any man differs from you in opinions, don't let that bother you, we can smooth that out, just let the voice of the people be the guide for all of us and everything will be all right.'[121]

One of the most concise versions of the representation formula came in *And This Is Democracy!* Accountability is introduced into the formula, but in a way that implies nothing concrete or demanding of the representatives' relations to the voters: 'the people in a democracy are concerned solely with results, and not methods. Methods should be left to those qualified to provide the results and they should be held responsible for securing those results ... The political machine should be used by democracy to demand results, results dealing with their relationship with their fellow men and women. This can be achieved by The People electing representatives whom they instruct as to the results in these respects required. These representatives should then use their authority to see that those qualified to devise proper methods are charged with giving The People what they want.'[122] This passage seems to suggest a kind of instructed delegation in the representational process, but the last sentence assures that both instruction and accountability are to be deprived of anything but psychological value.

Finally, we can note the distinction between methods and results in a widely circulated pamphlet justifying the 1945 Alberta Bill of Rights, a public display of support for the privately abandoned Social Credit reform agenda. In the foreword, anonymous government authors caution Albertans to concern themselves only with the broad objectives of the act ('social and economic security with individual freedom'), lest the people be 'led astray into purposeless arguments on the technical aspects of the methods proposed in Part II, thereby losing sight of the objectives set out in Part I.' They argue:

It is always important to distinguish results from methods. In all spheres of human endeavour the people generally are concerned primarily with results. The detailed technical knowledge and training necessary to put into operation methods of obtaining those results is something with which the people generally are not concerned. For example, only a few men in any community are expert chemists or qualified architects or electrical engineers, yet the results of their technical skill are enjoyed by large numbers and are the concern of all. The citizens of a democratic society cannot all be expected to acquire the technical knowledge and training in economic matters necessary to enable them to devise and implement methods which will successfully reform the economic system and make it produce definite and satisfactory results any more than they could be expected to know the technical details of building highways and bridges or running a power station to provide electrical energy.

However, the people individually and collectively do know the results they want in each of these different spheres. The economic sphere is no exception. If the results which the people want in the economic sphere are physically possible, it is the duty of their elected representatives to obtain men with the necessary technical qualifications to devise and put into operation in the economic sphere methods which will produce those results. The people can judge whether the methods used are satisfactory by the results they obtain.[123]

Typically, the authors jump from claiming that the people are not trained economists, which is indisputable, to claiming that the people can only support economic security with individual freedom, and can pass judgment on methods only indirectly and in the indefinite future. Even then, their judgment will only involve 'authorizing' a new set of representatives, who would then cede all authority over policy development to experts. As Macpherson has shown, this was a misrepresentation of what elected officials in Aberhart's cabinet actually did,[124] but by depriving MLAs of a meaningful role in policy deliberations, the Social Credit argument reduced the already meagre role of the voter in the overall process. If the representative was merely to represent mass desire to the technicians and take their ability to produce results on faith, the voter's role could not extend beyond almost meaningless mandating. Even Joseph Schumpeter, the famous theorist of elitist democracy ('Democracy means only that the people have the opportunity of accepting or refusing the men who are to rule them'),[125] would have found this unsettling.

What Pitkin calls the formalistic authorization mode of representation[126] is easy to spot in the above three cases. Social Credit representation was conceived in terms of formal arrangements preceding and initiating the representation, including the tacit covenant made by all Social Credit voters in the act of voting. They agreed to demand only results and not interfere with methods, and to judge the Social Credit government's performance on this basis only.

Pitkin claims that formalistic representation is silent on the act of representation itself – i.e., on what the representative does to translate supposed or stated public choices into government action. Having said something about the 'duty' and 'responsibility' of representatives to choose experts, Social Credit representation remained in the formalistic category, because the representative and the represented were given no criteria for choosing or judging experts, except whether they produce results. This gave no real responsibilities to anyone except the government leader. Yet the leader's broad mandate strips his representative function of specific parameters. The relationship between represented and representative was already so highly skewed in favour of the latter that, when these authorizations were added, virtually anything could count as representation. As Pitkin says, once the formal conditions are met (in this case, the vote, tacit covenant, and deference to experts), the representative is free to represent according to his interpretation of the mandate.[127] However, since representatives are deemed incapable of making 'technical' policy decisions, the vote becomes at least as important as an admission of the arcane nature of policy as it is a mandate for elected representatives – especially the party leader – to carry the crusade into the legislative arena.

Once again, Joseph Schumpeter's élitist democratic theory comes to mind. Three of his six 'conditions for the success of democracy' are implicitly fulfilled in the Social Credit understanding of representation: 'that the effective range of political decision should not be extended too far,' that there be a 'strong and independent bureaucracy,' and that citizens exercise 'democratic self-control' by not instructing either representatives or bureaucrats on the substance of their activities.[128] These conditions are, in fact, fulfilled with a vengeance, since Schumpeter did not propose reducing responsibilities or activities of voters or representatives to the level of symbolic performance advocated by Social Credit.

One important qualification of our classification of Social Credit's concept of representation as 'formalistic authorization' would appear to result from its 'accountability' dimension. The accountability view of representation, Pitkin says, is 'usually intended as a corrective to theories or examples of representation which, like the authorization view, give the representative authority and new rights but place no obligations and controls on him.'[129] In the Social Credit case, two views of accountability emerged. The first was quite orthodox: voters were encouraged to hold the UFA to account for not easing suffering or implementing social credit measures. This latter was Aberhart's official reason for Social Credit's 'going into politics': the UFA annual convention had rejected Aberhart's social credit 'plan' for Alberta.

The inclusion of a 'recall' plank in the Social Credit platform was a more interesting expression of the accountability approach . The program approved by the Calgary district conventions promised that 'Every Social Credit Candidate must agree to submit to the Voter's Right of Recall if he fails to carry out the proposals made prior to the election.'[130] Two weeks later, at the northern Alberta convention, this plank was toned down to request a Social Credit government to pass legislation 'empowering recall of all candidates.'[131] The final platform, however, combined the two previous planks to suggest that candidates submit themselves to the 'voters' right of recall' if election proposals went unfulfilled.[132] This recall plank became law in April 1936, shorn of the suggestion that voters use the mechanism if their representatives failed to deliver. With two-thirds of the eligible voters' signatures and a report from the chief justice acknowledging that all formal requirements had been met, a recall procedure could unseat an MLA.[133]

Macpherson portrayed the 1936 recall legislation and the 1935 promise as instances of the 'commonplace technique of mass leaders to insist that they are utterly the servants of the people and readily dismissable by the people.'[134] The editor of *The Alberta Social Credit Chronicle* was more enthusiastic, arguing that 'the recall plank in the Social Credit platform gives the people the right to withdraw any elected member if he or she is ever found wanting.'[135] However one views it, the promise was a temporary deviation from the authorization approach. Neither Aberhart nor his publicists emphasized it in the Social Credit campaign, despite its presumable appeal to converts from the UFA.

The recall provision was not consistent with the rest of the Social Credit package. Recall provisions only make sense if their proponents assume that the people are capable of judging not just results but also methods. Why should the intricate plans of technical planners be exposed to disruption so soon after Social Credit had received a mandate? Ordinary people's opinions on whether 'proposals made prior to the election' were being carried out were almost certain to be wrong. In any case, how could a Social Credit representative fail to represent the mass desire for security – was not the mere fact of being a Social Credit MLA sufficient evidence that this representative function was being performed? Recall did not fit in with Social Credit assumptions about the capacities and functions of the people or their representatives.

This inconsistency did not prevent a segment of the Alberta population from using the 1936 act in a most irreverent manner. Aberhart's own Okotoks–High River constituency seemed well on the way to harvesting the required number of recall signatures shortly after the 1937 insurgency by MLAs impatient with the slow pace of Social Credit reform. These constituents were acting in the UFA tradition, rather than remembering Aberhart's earlier advice to 'please, when you put your candidates in, give them a chance to carry out the will of the people.'[136] The premier moved quickly to pass legislation repealing the recall act in October 1937. As Mallory charmingly put it, 'Mr. Aberhart's sense of mission was stronger than his belief in popular sovereignty.'[137] In practice then, Aberhart discovered and acted on what is clear in theory: meaningful accountability was not consistent with Social Credit representation. What began as a qualification of this representation quickly became an embarrassment.

Even if the recall legislation had remained, Social Credit representation would not have promoted appreciably greater accountability. The problem with the accountability perspective, according to Pitkin, is that it fails to have any predictable effect on the quality or substance of representation, because it does not furnish criteria to assess the work of the government officials.[138] The threat of dismissal in the recall provision does not incorporate clear critical standards unless the preceding steps in the representational process go beyond formalistic, mandating authorization. In the 1937 Okotoks–High River case, the constituents believed that the Social Credit program had done this, with talk of dividends, just prices, credit houses, and the like. From 1936 on, Aberhart and his government argued that they had made no such specific undertakings and that, in any case, their culpability was all but removed by the federal government's rejection of its measures. Even if this latter excuse had not conveniently arisen, the Social Credit administration could – and did – fall back on the argument that the people were using the wrong standards to judge the government, and were expecting too much too soon.

Ultimately, the only thing that Aberhart considered subject to accountability was whether there was evidence that the government wished to end poverty, vanquish the financiers and their federal government allies, and provide economic security. Since the plebiscitarian schema required representatives only to transmit the general will for these results, evidence of this kind could be provided through a constant flow of government rhetoric on the goodness of the desired results and the evil of the obstacles thereto. This was amply supplied by Aberhart's government and party. At this level, Aberhart was happy to be held accountable. When his constituents clamoured for more accountability, the premier was unable to accommodate.

This discussion of Social Credit representation sheds light on some unorthodox features of the Social Credit political experience. We can locate its leadership style and organizational activity within a tradition of democratic theory that has its roots in Hobbes.[139] The plebiscitarian mandate, and use of the movement organization to promote such a mandate, are instances of an approach to representation that severs the tie between represented and representatives after authorization has been granted. The achievement of the Social Credit variant, of course, was that the appearance was quite the opposite. People believed that the economic remedies would heal their wounds, but also that the movement, the league's anti-political rhetoric, and continual reference to their own sovereign will signified intimate ties with Aberhart and his candidates. Authorization theory, when filtered through movement-based plebiscitarian populism, can serve its political time when crisis combines with charisma and class insecurity.

Applying the concept of authorization to the Social Credit case also complements an understanding of its democratic theory as an instance of 'general will' ideology. To have the legitimacy required to give it real power, a mandate cannot be transparently and narrowly class-based. The mass desire for security and prosperity is, by definition, something all classes desire. During a serious depression, it would have been surprising if large numbers of people from all classes had not found Social Credit nostrums at least superficially attractive. There was a seductive degree of truth in Aberhart's claim that, in the face of the misery brought on by the Depression, political differences between 'the people' were petty. There was, then, a kind of general will to end poverty and achieve economic security. A skilful use of Social Credit economic analysis, combined with an idiosyncratic application of authorization theory, tapped the political potential underlying this general will. People wanted to believe that they shared common political interests stemming from a common plight, and wanted to believe that they could, in fact, become sovereign over their own destiny. The social environment and history of UFA-engendered hopes for popular democracy made these beliefs especially strong in Alberta, as did the tendency of rural people to believe in a non-class specific popular will.[140]

What gave the plebiscitarian variant of authorization theory some of its credence, however, was an acceptance of the idea that economic experts could deliver the people from evil, and that the surest way to allow them the chance to do so was to elect those most willing to let the experts do their job. In post–eighteenth-century representative democracies, authorization theory has not usually gone this far. Even though John Stuart Mill believed that parliamentary representatives had a limited role to play in policy-making, he did not go so far as to give appointed officials exclusive power in this regard.[141] Neither Joseph Schumpeter nor his epigone in the school of American 'democratic élitism' was willing to deprive the elected representatives of policy input opportunities once their election 'authorized' them to represent. Contempt for the people and politics as public decision-making was restrained enough to preclude the full technocratic option. In neither case (Mill or Schumpeter et al.) was the notion of a general will given credence. But when the assumption of a general will provides transitive authorization (i.e., through representatives) for scientific production of results, the orthodox liberal democratic limits on who and what are authorized in elections fall away. The plebiscitarian mandate of Social Credit theory is thus the extreme form – almost the reductio ad absurdum – of the formalistic authorization concept of representation.

The degeneration of political life and contempt for the conventions of parliamentary practice in Aberhart's regime[142] can also be seen as an extreme expression of the authorization concept of representation. As we saw earlier, the formalism of this approach renders it silent on the substance of representation. Aberhart's treatment of his caucus as cheerleaders, his avoidance of participation in legislative debate (once before 1940), his assumption that the weekly Bible Institute broadcasts were a suitable surrogate for both political dialogue and public accountability, and his conferral of sweeping powers on the Social Credit Board are all evidence of his having taken advantage of the open-endedness of the authorization inherent in the 1935 election. Each of these practices could be rationalized, within this framework, as either facilitating 'results' or answering to the sovereign people.

The only understanding of the state that would sit comfortably with this approach to representation was highly technocratic, informed by a conspiratorial view of social forces, and unorthodox by North American standards. That the Alberta Social Credit view of the state also had a social reform cast was a contingency and stemmed from its Depression environment, and the nature of reform appeals *per se*, but was not a necessary feature of the plebiscitarian view of the state.

The State and Technocracy in Plebiscitarian Populism

The Negative Image of the State

Social Crediters' indictment of the state shared much with those of other prairie populists.[143] The major point of continuity and convergence was that the state (usually referring to the national government) was portrayed as the agent of 'the interests' – in the Social Credit case, the financial interests. From this, it followed that state institutions were staffed by persons with perspectives and interests contrary to those of 'the people.'

As we have seen, part of the Social Credit remedy to this conflict between the people and the state was an altered system of representation, to assure that the 'people's' interests would displace the financiers' as the motive force behind government policy. Representatives would install experts who saw through financial systemic flaws and could design monetary and credit systems to realize material abundance and foster both political and economic democracy. While the remedies proposed were somewhat unusual,[144] the intention of removing 'the interests' from the driver's seat in government was orthodox by prairie populist standards. Like social democrats, Social Crediters believed that replacing existing government staff with sympathetic and unorthodox experts would transform the state into a positive force.

Another common denominator was distrust of the federal government (and consequently the two 'government parties') as author of the regional subordination implicit in the National Policy. There was surprisingly little attention paid to this in the pre-governmental phase of the Social Credit experience, but it became a key basis for rallying support once controversial legislation began in 1937.

Social Crediters, radical democratic populists, and crypto-Liberals, all viewed the state as an institution enforcing compliance rather than facilitating community-based, voluntary activity. As in many other cases, Social Credit theory and practice on this issue were inconsistent. Douglas was a staunch individualist to whom the state was a necessary but untrustworthy agent of economic and political reform. This belief was reflected in his insistence that credit institutions be controlled by the community rather than the state, although he never specified the mechanisms of such control. Aberhart differed from Douglas on this score, even though his later rhetoric suggested a simplistic Victorian liberal apprehension of the compulsion-oriented state.[145] One could also point to the philosophical basis of Social Credit remedies for underconsumption and economic insecurity, which rejected 'collectivist' action in favour of subsidies to individuals' incomes and equated economic freedom with enhanced spending power.

The practical problem was that such adjustments required state redistribution of income from one group of creditors to a much larger group of debtors or low-income earners. While intended to increase individuals' economic freedom (i.e., enhance their status as consumers), such interventions did not look consistent with an anti-statist individualism to the *Financial Post*, the daily press, and other defenders of contemporary business liberalism. Nor did the 1937 Press Bill, or 1937 legislation preventing individuals employed by financial institutions from using the right of appeal in the courts, seem designed to defend individuals from the arbitrary use of state power. The 1936 'registration drive' was equally suspect, with the provincial government soliciting 'covenants' from citizens, pledging 'complete co-operation' with unspecified government actions to implement Social Credit. This was not the stuff of genuine non-compulsion.[146]

The Social Credit attack on bureaucracy and planning provides further evidence of the inconsistency noted above. *The Social Credit Manual* assured readers that Social Credit 'makes the individual supreme ... [and] bends all its efforts to protect his rights,' thus implying an opposition to bureaucratic power. But the theme was not developed, and even within the *Manual*, this contention is undermined by a discussion about allocation of dividends. These were not to be issued in proportion to 'work done,' but were, rather, to be given 'as a bare support of citizenship, loyalty to the State and the best interests of the country.'[147] Little was made of this claim in the context, but it might well have seemed ominous to critics who later characterized Aberhart as a Fascist.[148]

The anti-bureaucratic theme was almost entirely absent from *The Alberta Social Credit Chronicle*, except indirectly when the weekly noted that the 1935 platform demanded that 'every Department of the Government needs to be reorganized and to be put on a business basis to eliminate the present enormous waste of taxpayers' money.'[149] This promise was not tied to any uniquely Social Credit reform, and was thus simply a variation on the crypto-Liberal demand for 'efficient, business-like administration.'

When the federal government began to frustrate the Alberta government's financial reform intentions, the anti-bureaucratic theme became more prominent. At one level it was used to reinforce a perceived opposition between 'the people' and the federal government, as we saw earlier. Social Credit spokesmen regularly denounced the Rowell-Sirois Commission and its advisers as sympathetic to financial interests. Privately, Social Credit MLAs suspected Alberta government bureaucrats of sabotaging implementation of Social Credit plans.[150]

The attack on the federal government did not really display a serious antipathy towards bureaucrats *per se*. One might argue that compared to the CCF program of public employment and economic restructuring, the Social Credit option of income supplementation through free credit, dividends, and 'non-negotiable certificates' indicated an underlying antipathy towards bureaucratic power. But Aberhart's program was anything but non-interventionist. To take an example from the 'plan' outlined in the *Manual*, Credit House Inspectors were to be given powers to 'warn the citizen that he was abusing his rights and privileges and that it must be stopped or he would lose his dividends.'[151] As anyone who has thought about policing welfare recipients can attest, such an administrative proposition would entail extensive bureaucratic discretion and employment. The same could be said for the 'just price commission,' the decentralized system of state credit houses, and the work required to calculate the 'unearned increment of association' for which all bona fide citizens qualified. While all of these things may have been desirable, they would not reduce the role of the bureaucracy in public life.

It should also be obvious that if elected representatives were to surrender virtually all policy-making power to experts, one cannot speak of a consistently anti-bureaucratic theme in the Social Credit appeal. While these experts might successfully 'eliminate the present enormous waste of taxpayers' money' by implementing effective prosperity-creating programs, their technocratic regime would be antithetical to the anti-bureaucratic orientation of the elected politicians. The anti-bureaucratic inclination of the early years was very selectively applied to a federal government at odds with 'the Alberta experiment.' By briefly describing the likely mechanisms of Social Credit in Alberta, Aberhart exposed the contradictions in Social Credit's ambivalent attitude towards the state.

This contradiction could be disguised only by downplaying the public commitment to government by experts. This strategy became attractive, indeed necessary, when the prospect of implementing the Social Credit plan provincially disappeared and an alternative means of generating popular support was required. By 1940, it was clear that the federal government would abide no provincial tinkering with the financial system. Also, the CCF posed the most serious challenge to Social Credit as an alternative to the two old parties in the provincial and federal arenas. Thus arose the opportunity to revive dormant anti-statist tendencies in Social Credit thought. The cost was rejection of an important part of the plebiscitarian formula – i.e., transferring great power to planners and experts. The gain was new support from orthodox élites within the province, continued support from a now-conservative rural population, and retention of power for another generation.

Two illuminating examples of anti-bureaucratic, anti-statist thinking in the post-1940 Social Credit experience came in 1943. Premier Aberhart's *Post-War Reconstruction Broadcasts* offered the following typical comments:

We say we are fighting for our Christian principles and democratic institutions. But what does that mean? ... Are we fighting to keep away from oppression by tyrants and bureaucrats? Did you say 'Yes'? [37]
... there are two great opposing elements in the world warring against each other ... democracy versus totalitarianism, individual freedom and economic security versus regimentation and socialization ... [37]
... the people sit back and allow their representatives to go down to Ottawa and pass laws which permit the nation to be ground down in degrading poverty and debt bondage, and to be chased around and bullied by a lot of bureaucrats with the mentalities of dictators. [45-6]
[compulsory state insurance schemes] all involve compulsion and regimentation. Some central planning body decides by how much everybody's wages and salaries are to be reduced by compulsory deductions ... the individual citizen is forced to conform to a mass of regulations and conditions which are arbitrarily imposed upon him by some State bureaucracy. In short, it is a system of centralized control of the many by the few, involving regimentation and domination of the people by a State authority. [57-8]
... Those of you who are keeping abreast of the times know that Government bureaucracy is quite the opposite of democracy, and should be thoroughly eliminated. [64]

... Social Credit makes no suggestion of taking over the present efficient production system, and handing it to a vast State Bureaucracy, with the inevitable inefficiency, and regimentation which would result. [80]

A conference on post-war reconstruction organized by the Social Credit League in December 1942 featured warnings of an even closer connection between bureaucracy, 'state socialism,' and totalitarianism. One of the resolutions passed by the conference, then reprinted in a league publication, read: 'be it resolved that we oppose as anti-democratic the national socialist policies being advocated and adopted (under the cover of a professed adherence to democratic principles) for increasing the arbitrary power of a vast government bureaucracy to dominate and regiment the people, thereby crushing initiative, destroying free enterprize and robbing the individual citizen of his rightful liberties and privileges under our democratic constitution ... And be it further resolved that the people be aroused to the peril of this trend towards a totalitarian national socialist state before it becomes entrenched as the basis of the post-war order.'[152]

This anti-statist rhetoric was occasioned by the Beveridge Report and other proposals for social-welfare schemes. In fact, as the 1940s progressed, such rhetoric was central to attacks on the CCF. For Social Credit Board extremists, the rhetoric exposed a world plot linking the Jewish bankers to world communism and all traces of 'state socialism' in the expanding Canadian welfare state. Planning itself became synonymous with financier-socialist conspiracies in the 1943 to 1947 Social Credit Board annual reports.[153] While Premier Manning dissociated himself from and eventually dismantled the Social Credit Board, he did nothing to boost the old Social Credit faith in achieving results through expert planning. By the time the pragmatic and conservative Manning had inherited the mantle from his old teacher, technocracy's high profile in Social Credit's public teachings had been quietly eliminated. If the provincial government could not engage in technocratic reform and administration of the polity, then no one should – especially not the federal government, which was assumed to be in league with financial interests and socialist-centralizers.

The Positive Image and Functions of the State

Social Credit was supported in an electoral stampede largely because of, not in spite of, the positive purposes Aberhart assigned to a Social Credit state. At the grandest level, these purposes involved abolishing 'poverty in the midst of plenty' and providing economic security and freedom for all. As Aberhart told a mass rally in May 1935, 'speak in one voice as to what we want done, and then hold on, and have your men do what you want done, and everything will be alright and the Depression will be solved.'[154] Social Credit speakers were not bashful about suggesting that this required considerable state intervention.

Although one can easily get the impression that Social Crediters were monomaniacs for the nostrums of monetary and credit reform, it is important to recognize that most activists and supporters saw these as means to a larger end.

'It is the duty of the State through its Government to organize its economic structure in such a way that no bona fide citizen, man, woman, or child, shall be allowed to suffer for lack of the bare necessities of food, clothing, and shelter in the midst of plenty or abundance.'[155] So read the first paragraph of Aberhart's classic 1935 *Manual*, under the heading 'Our Basic Premise.' Such a claim belongs to a strongly interventionist approach to state functions. Juxtaposing suffering with actual abundance implies the potential of state action to elevate the standard of living tremendously. We can consider the importance of this assumption of abundance to the whole conception of the state later. Here, it is worth stressing the large responsibility for social-welfare enhancement Aberhart accords the state. Also evident is the magnitude of mandate requested, and the burden of salvation placed on a few social credit solutions offered by the leader.

The 1935 Social Credit solutions included the famous $25 annual dividend for each adult citizen, the provision of free (or at least 'cost' priced) credit to producers, merchants, and consumers through a network of state credit houses, a complementary local control over credit policy, a system of 'just prices' and 'just wages,' and the circulation of a provincial currency-substitute ('non-negotiable certificates'). Each scheme was to increase purchasing power for the average consumer, thereby stimulating new production and employment. Each was premised on the belief that the actual wealth of Alberta could be 'monetized' to facilitate expanded credit and the various direct subsidies to consumers. The potential wealth was called the 'cultural heritage,' created and thus deserved by all citizens of the community.

State-owned credit facilities, annual dividends, just prices and wages, and even free credit were not necessarily tied to Social Credit reform. The CCF had called for a nationalization of banking and credit facilities in 1932, in the tradition of left-leaning agrarian political organizations since the early 1920s. Dividends could be seen as a kind of incipient welfare-state subsidy to consumers, although the universality in Aberhart's plan was rejected by groups urging the federal government to move in such a direction. 'Just prices' were not a new idea, nor were regulated wages, but their integration into Aberhart's overall plan was unique, since they did not require a sacrifice on the part of the merchants or employers. Like previous proposals for 'just' prices and wages, they were advertised as fair compensation for the labour of all working people (so that farmers were promised, in effect, 'parity prices'),[156] and as a means of protecting consumers from 'excessive prices.' The just price and wage system was in fact portrayed as a means of eliminating exploitation of labour.[157]

Even free credit was not a new promise: North American agrarian organizations had advocated it since at least the mid-nineteenth century. However, only the Social Credit no-interest proposals were to involve no fundamental redistribution of resources within the polity. Social Credit was based on the idea that sufficient purchasing power for all would come from a 'monetization' of the 'real credit' accumulated over generations of economic and technological development. Social Credit planners would tap the unexploited reserve of credit and purchasing power previously suppressed by a flawed system of accountancy, a conspiracy of financiers and their willing political puppets. This new credit was simply there for the taking, given the right combination of political will and scientific policy.[158]

There is no need to detail these basic Social Credit mechanisms for replacing poverty by plenty.[159] Aberhart's doctrinal differences with Douglas were inconsequential, except on the question of state ownership and control over financial institutions. Douglas viewed state operation of financial institutions as a marriage of the two most oppressive factors in modern society.[160] Aberhart rejected this concern in 1935, and proposed a system of state credit houses and inspectors as institutions of community controlled credit.[161] What is worth noting about Social Credit policy proposals is their model of individuals' relations to the state, and their promotion of generous social-welfare benefits to individuals. Regarding the first point, Aberhart was quite explicit: 'The State shall be viewed by its citizens as a gigantic joint-stock company with the resources of the province behind its credit. The bona fide citizens are each and all shareholders entitled to basic dividends sufficient to provide the bare necessities of food, clothing, and shelter for each individual and his family ... These dividends are not to be given on a basis of so much work done, but as a bare support of citizenship, loyalty to the State, and the best interests of the country.'[162]

Macpherson demonstrates the compatibility of this conception of the state with the limited rights of citizens in the plebiscitarian representational system: citizens' rights are effectively 'reduced to the one right of receiving a dividend,' and their control over the 'joint-stock company' is limited to 'the right to change directors and experts.'[163] The latter is undeniably true. However, the rest of the *Manual*, and *The Chronicle*'s continual discussion of the good things to accompany free credit, just prices, and so on, suggest that Macpherson has attributed too small a welfare-supplementing intention to Aberhart's joint-stock company state. During its crusade, Social Credit presented dividends and all other income-enhancing proposals as the universal entitlements of a properly managed cultural heritage and modern technology.

Even though Social Credit leaders spoke of the people as consumers and shareholders, whose rights to effect the 'firm's' policies were almost completely formal, the overall Social Credit plan did promise a substantial return on investment to the people. Since the broad promise of economic security would end the threat of foreclosure on the homestead, or prevent small-town business bankruptcies, and protect workers' homes and jobs, such a return on an investment of one vote was attractive to many Albertans.

The 'joint stock company' metaphor also connotes a trusteeship relation between citizen and state. With its suggestion of decision-making by proxy (i.e., by experts selected by elected representatives), of plebiscitarian legitimation of the 'firm's' activities, and of the passive receipt of dividends by citizens, the metaphor encourages a perception of the state as the trustee for a largely helpless population.

Hanna Pitkin's account of how trusteeship has served as an analogy for representation and, by extension, for the role of the state is useful for our purposes here. She notes that

the analogy suggests that the powers of government may be thought of as property, to which the representatives have title, but which they must administer for the benefit of others. Thus it might be their duty to preserve the national wealth, employ the income from it in certain ways, or divide it among the beneficiaries. [Representatives] are under no obligation to consult their beneficiaries or obey their wishes ... Often the notion of trusteeship is linked with the idea that the beneficiary is incapable of acting for himself, or at least that the trustee is far more competent than he ... it evidently has no necessary implications about accountability to the government or responsiveness to their wishes, although it obviously has implications about looking after their welfare ... The implications of calling government a trusteeship are by no means democratic ones.[164]

Fitting the Social Credit case into the category this passage describes requires some adjustments. The trustee, for example, is only formally and partially the elected representative; experts are charged with employing the 'national wealth' (cultural heritage) in ways that promote citizens' interests. The experts' accountability to the 'beneficiaries,' as we have seen, is indirect, formal, and infrequent. The MLA's connection with the beneficiaries was superficially direct, but because the MLA was to be trustee of the public's 'demands for results' or the supposed general will, the theoretical functions of MLA as decision-making trustee were seriously limited when compared to those of other formal trustees. (In practice, the limits on this aspect of the MLA's activity were more a result of their deference to Aberhart's leadership, political inexperience, and simple confusion as to how the 'plan' could be implemented.)

With these qualifications noted, however, striking similarities remain. The Social Credit regime promised great gains in total and individual incomes in Alberta. The Social Credit message conveyed the impression that the additional purchasing power and prosperity its experts could deliver was a kind of property that all citizens had a right to, through dividends and just prices. The message also emphasized that this property was accessible only if powers of decision-making regarding 'methods' were granted to those experts. The implications of such an arrangement, as we have seen, were far from democratic. And finally, imputing a dimension of trusteeship to the citizen-state relation was credible primarily because it was to 'look after their welfare' with results that Albertans could then only dream about.

The welfare to be looked after by a Social Credit state was not exclusively reckoned in terms of purchasing power or economic security. The citizen-shareholders of Social Credit, Inc., were also promised a variety of 'group benefits,' in ways which appealed to prospective shareholders' class identities and regional sensibilities, emphasizing the idea of equity. This was especially clear in the notion of a 'just price.' The just price appealed simply in terms of material benefits, but for Albertans who had paid high prices on commercial goods, and received low prices for their labour, a sense of fairness denied was strong. Social Credit promised to redress this injustice. Aberhart explained how the just price would accomplish some of this task: 'The commission of experts appointed by the government would investigate the price spread and fix an equitable, just price for all goods and services ... fair to the producer, manufacturer, and distributor, and which did not exploit the purchasing power of the consumer ... The farmers today are obligated to sell their goods below the actual cost of production ... there could probably be a reduction of 10 to 15 per cent on groceries ... The same applies to many other lines. This also would give the small businessman a fair chance with the larger departmental or chain stores.' Aberhart even promised married women a better position in the social economy: 'Surely it is time that women were uplifted and made more independent. Women would no longer have to consider marriage from the present economic insecurity angle ... Do you think it would hurt the wife to have her own income with which to purchase her own clothes and not have to ask her husband when she wants anything? I am persuaded that Social Credit would tend to happier homes.'[165]

The Social Credit League's 1935 election platform emphasized the just price (planks 1 and 5) as an equity-generating measure. 'Ten Planks Make One Platform' also promised changes in the Debt Adjustment Act and introduction of interest-free loans, which were to reduce the power of 'financial interests' over Albertans. Equity of a sort was also promised in plank 7, which pledged 'satisfactory health attention for people in all parts of the Province' and 'the ultimate introduction of State Medicine into the Province.' Finally, 'amendment of the present Compensation Act with a view to just compensation to all workers' was put on the new government's legislative agenda.[166]

The new government continued to promise equitable distribution of the imminent abundance after the 1935 election. In a 1940 pamphlet, the premier argued: 'Closely bound up with the plight of agriculture is the need for social justice, without which a victory in this war would be still quite ineffective ... Adequate wages and just working conditions; security in the home and the business; security against destitution in old age, in sickness and in unemployment; adequate health and educational services – all these are vital issues.'[167]

In other government publications of the late 1930s and early 1940s, much is made of attempts to reduce debt payments, provide for home-owner security, and generally protect a debtor population.[168] Many of these were disallowed or declared *ultra vires*. Progressive changes to legislation covering minimum wages, hours of work, trade union security, labour-management arbitration procedures, and a new Industrial Relations Board, were all legislated in the first Social Credit administration.[169] High levels of urban working-class support for Social Credit between the 1935 and 1940 elections[170] suggest that these changes were expected and appreciated by working people in Alberta. The changes did not deliver benefits or equity on the scale promised in the pre-election discussion of 'just wages,'[171] but they were generous by the standards of contemporary Canadian governments. Indeed, the market interventions Aberhart's government attempted during its first term made it look very welfare-statist compared to the federal state.[172]

Even when Aberhart and the Social Credit Board began a shrill campaign against the welfare state (including previously endorsed state medicine),[173] they retained a rhetorical commitment to equity in the 'new social order.' We thus find Aberhart explaining in a 1943 broadcast that a Social Credit monetary commission 'would see that incomes were distributed in such a manner that the security and leisure made possible by the abundant production would be available to everyone on an equitable basis, thus removing the fear of destitution from unemployment, disability, sickness or old age, without bureaucratic State regimentation.'[174] The Social Credit state would deliver all of the supposed benefits of socialism with none of its drawbacks.

Anti-capitalist rhetoric peppered the speeches of Aberhart and Social Credit spokesmen from the 1935 campaign up until 1940. The broad implication was that the Social Credit state would act as an anti-capitalist 'agent' on behalf of the people. This message was normally qualified to establish a safe distance from the presumed approach of socialist nationalizers, but still retained the anti–big business tone characteristic of western Canadian populism. A passage from the *Social Credit Manual* is typical: 'Social Credit is not based on any confiscation scheme by which we take the wealth of the rich or well-to-do and give it to the poor. Social Credit recognizes individual enterprise and individual ownership, but it prevents wildcat exploitation of the consumer through the medium of enormously excessive spreads in price for the purpose of giving exorbitant profits or paying high dividends on pyramids of watered stock. [But] people who have bank deposits or insurance policies with cash surrender value need not be alarmed in any way.'[175]

An anti-capitalist message emerged in other places in the *Manual*, as in the answer to the question, 'Is it the intention under Social Credit to limit the income of the citizens to a certain maximum?' Appearing to contradict the earlier denial of redistributive plans, Aberhart replies: 'Yes, it is, for no one should be allowed to have an income that is greater than he himself can possibly enjoy, to the privation of his fellow citizens.'[176] Aberhart also pledged that a Social Credit regime would 'remove the monopolists' control of the large companies' in the oil and gas industry.[177]

On other occasions in the 1934-5 campaign, Aberhart or his official organ criticized the negative effects or characteristics of capitalism. In October 1934, Aberhart asked: 'Is it not time we forgot this business of getting rich by immense profits, and began the true object and purpose of production, *viz.*, to produce for use, consumption or enjoyment?'[178] In a July 1935 editorial, the *Chronicle* editor threatened that 'the Capitalist parties are going to use every strategic method, fair or unfair, to bring defeat to Social Credit,' then commended the work of H.H. Steven's Reconstruction party. Stevens and Aberhart made 'a hard combination for the exploiters of labour to battle with.'[179] The next week the editor claimed that Albertans 'desire a change in the rotten system under which they are at present living, they desire to free themselves from the bonds of the Financier and Capitalist.'[180] Post-election editorials referred to 'opposing capitalistic forces' and 'the war against capitalistic injustice.' One could be forgiven for believing that Aberhart's government did intend to carry the battle against capitalism farther than was authorized by a loose credit, dividend-creating, just-price scheme.

This belief was undoubtedly a factor in urban labour's support for Social Credit, which was strong despite the UFA connection to Canadian Labour Party affiliates of the CCF.[181] The opportunistic and organizationally unattractive character of the Labour Party, and sheer economic desperation, were probably more important.[182] Most important of all, for urban labour as well as for farmers and small businessmen, was the promise of rapid economic recovery, and economic security through a range of surrogate welfare-state measures. An interventionist state to deal immediately with the worst aspects of the Depression was an important part of the Social Credit program's attractiveness.

Surprisingly, Social Credit speakers used the popular-democratic tradition of anti–central Canadian feeling sparingly until 1937. Traces of this in *The Social Credit Manual* are quite unconnected to the overall case, and found almost no echo in other propaganda before the 1935 victory. It was tactically important to emphasize Albertans' ability to provide for their own needs under a Social Credit government, rather than to emphasize federal government or eastern financiers' responsibility for their plight. Thus, whereas the Canadian Council of Agriculture's 'New National Policy' focused on regional dimensions of old National Policy injustice, *The Social Credit Manual* began with a 'demonstration' of Alberta's potential wealth and ability to fend for itself.[183] This approach heightened the already impressive sense of political efficacy in the Social Credit movement.

Within a year of the Social Credit victory, emphasis on provincial abilities declined, and accusations of federal government culpability for Alberta's plight increased dramatically. The campaign against the federal government and central Canadian creditor interests peaked from 1937 to 1939, with federal disallowances of provincial credit legislation and the creation of the Rowell-Sirois Commission as major targets.

The State in Theory and Practice: Centralization, Decentralization, and Technocracy

On matters relating to federalism and technocratic rule, the Social Credit understanding of the state was internally inconsistent but instructive. A campaign for decentralization of power, its actual concentration, and the leadership's qualified technocratic orientation became key features of this plebiscitarian populism.

Much has been written about the Social Credit government's clashes with the federal government and Supreme Court. We are interested in how these confrontations were viewed from the Social Credit side, and how they shaped a previously inchoate image of the federal system. What emerges is a naïve and radically decentralist picture of the federal state system in response to perceived antagonism from the federal state.

Considering the furore his government's legislation was to cause in the federal system from 1937 to 1943, William Aberhart was remarkably blasé about federalism before the 1935 election. He began to mention the federal distribution of powers in 1934, only after orthodox Douglasites in Calgary, UFA MPs, and eventually the UFA provincial government denied that his social credit plan could be implemented provincially. In *The BNA Act and Social Credit*, he argued that any constitution of moral value would not prevent reforms designed to benefit the public's welfare enormously. However, in this short pamphlet he insisted that this consideration was beside the point, since neither the BNA Act nor the Bank Act contained anything that would prevent provincial action on Social Credit proposals.

His scheme was thus morally and legally vindicated to his satisfaction. But in a passage foreshadowing later events, Aberhart rhetorically asked whether a democratically legitimate majority in Alberta would allow their will to be blocked and their suffering continued 'by loosely-jointed constitutional machinery, overstepping its proper functioning through influences of a sordid nature brought to bear upon our good governments.'[184] By 1937, these 'influences' had taken a concrete form – institutions in the Canadian financial establishment – and the federal government and courts were using the 'loosely-jointed constitutional machinery' of disallowance, reservation, and *ultra vires* rulings to fulfil Aberhart's prophecy.

During the year preceding August 1935, Aberhart regularly applied the standards of plebiscitarian democracy to the 'constitutional problem.' By late 1934, the whole province knew his position that Social Credit dividends, just prices, and so on would not interfere with the federal power over currency.[185] He mixed legal, moral, and democratic arguments again in a November 1934 issue of the *Chronicle*, contending that the province could implement the Social Credit plan because the Canadian constitution 'gives to it complete control over its own affairs within its own boundaries, provided that in the carrying out of these rights and privileges it does not interfere with the rights and privileges of others. Once the principles of Social Credit are understood, it is self-evident that their application to Alberta would in no wise interfere with the other provinces of the Dominion; nor with the present monetary system which is under the control of the Federal Government. It is the right of Democracy to dictate its economic policy, and then to employ experts to see that its wishes are carried out. The united voice of 650,000 people demanding the introduction of Social Credit could not possibly be ignored in a British country under Canadian constitution.'[186]

Aberhart and the *Chronicle* repeated this optimistic reading of the constitution throughout 1935, despite C.H. Douglas's rejection of, then equivocation on, Aberhart's position[187] and a solid front of denials coming from the UFA government, UFA MPs, and professional economists.[188]

Aberhart's approach to the constitutional question involved other curiosities. He presented possible constitutional problems in terms of a fight between loyal British subjects 'revolting against slavery' and 'the financial dictators of the world.'[189] He minimized the seriousness of the constitutional question by referring to the BNA Act as 'Brownlee's National Anthem,' and by assuring listeners that if they expressed a solid will for Social Credit results, the arguments presented to delude them could easily be countered by expert lawyers[190] – even if the constitutional problem turned out to be less simple than he had insisted. Arguments regarding federal and provincial powers were tied closely to plebiscitarian representational theory when not based on specious quasi-legal reasoning. However, Social Credit preferences regarding the federal distribution of power had not been clarified by the provincial election.

Despite the howls of alarm from the financial press and central Canadian dailies following his election victory, Aberhart had reason to be cautiously optimistic about federal non-interference for a short time. During the federal election campaign in September 1935, Mackenzie King assured western audiences that 'the best course is to give the Alberta government every opportunity of testing out their plan, and if it is successful it will spread like wildfire throughout Canada.'[191] King was also clever enough to present himself as the scourge of the 'big interests' during the campaign, in a way that would undercut both the CCF and the Social Credit campaigns. In Saskatoon, he insisted: 'Canada is faced with a great battle between the money power and the people, a battle which will be waged in the new Parliament. I plead for a sweeping Liberal victory to carry out my policies of Public control of Currency and Credit. Until control of currency and credit is restored to the Government all talk of sovereignty of Parliament and democracy is idle and futile.'[192]

Such rhetoric did not induce Aberhart to support King – he did, after all, hope for a national Social Credit party. It is still probably safe to say that Aberhart found such talk reassuring while his government puzzled over how to deliver on their promises.

The first indication that Aberhart would stake out a stubbornly provincialist position came in early 1936 when he rejected a proposed federal government loan council to approve all provincial government loan requests and external borrowing plans.[193] At the time, this merely put him in the company of Hepburn in Ontario; it was not seen as a portent of escalating provincialism by federal authorities. Only with the abrupt introduction of orthodox Social Credit legislation in the summer of 1937 did the Alberta position become clear.

This legislation may have been precipitated by the 'back-benchers' revolt,' and its accompanying rationale may have been designed for a government under pressure to 'deliver the goods.' It none the less marked the official beginning of a long attack on federal powers over credit and financial affairs. This campaign featured a level of decentralist rhetoric and Ottawa-bashing unmatched in English Canada until another Alberta government responded to the National Energy Policy in 1980.

The 1937 disallowances provided the Social Credit government with an opportunity to integrate its official position on the constitution and popular democracy with its critique of concentrated financial and political power. In a stream of public statements, letters, and pamphlets, Aberhart, his cabinet colleagues, and 'Social Credit experts' from London elaborated on the true moral and legal basis of provincial autonomy. They also did much to supplement Aberhart's contention that federal interference could be attributed to 'the thumb-screws applied by the financial barons,'[194] as Social Credit political theory had led them to expect.

With the federal government in the enemy's camp, an approach to federalism favouring the Alberta government had to be produced rapidly. The resulting denunciation of the King government's disallowances disputed the federal government's legislative powers over credit, rejected the federal power to disallow any provincial legislation, and stressed the immorality of responding to bankers' interests rather than to the needs of Albertans.[195] Shortly, the 'will of the people' and the 'Sovereignty of Alberta' were used to make a positive case for the sweeping reinterpretation of provincial powers implied in the 1937 legislation. The establishment of the Royal Commission on Dominion-Provincial Relations in August 1937 provided a new impetus for developing the positive case for provincial rights. A year later, the provincial government released *The Case for Alberta* as an unofficial contribution to the commission's deliberations.

The Case for Alberta delivered the Social Credit view of the federal state with little plebiscitary and moral rhetoric. By prairie populist standards, Part I of *The Case* was an orthodox account of the Alberta economy's resource base, performance, and problems. Part II included a Social Credit analysis of Canada's economic structure, complete with two chapters outlining Social Credit teachings on the nature of money, credit, underconsumption, the famous 'A plus B' theorem, and the unholy alliance between financiers and the state. The last two chapters of Part II addressed the nature of and solutions for problems of Canadian federalism.

Chapter V of the *The Case*, entitled 'Democracy and Confederation,' begins with an argument that both 'democratic' and 'centralized' forms of organization have functions in the state's activity. Through a series of specious analogies and claims about the federal character of Canadian society, the authors conclude that only a massively enhanced provincial autonomy in the economic policy sphere could produce a democratic division of power within the federal system. They refer to Canada as 'a union of nine separate social groupings,'[196] and contend that 'the people of each province must be sovereign in regard to policy as it affects them individually and collectively within their provincial borders.' Failing this, 'the basis of confederation is destroyed.'[197] The chapter admits that the Dominion government could exercise 'centralized authority' over matters affecting provinces where central administration is more efficient. However, their examples of such cases are not in the realm of fiscal or monetary policy, and they insist that central authority should be exercised only in response to 'the result which has been decided by the people of each province.'[198]

In effect, this reduces the role of the federal government to implementer of the consensus of provincial governments. The authors emphasize this by rejecting federal government participation in attempts to sort out constitutional and economic problems.[199] A provincial veto power is implicit in the suggestion that the Dominion government be granted 'jurisdiction over administration of provincially and democratically decided policy in all matters which affect each province and in respect of which it has been agreed by each province that Dominion administration is desirable.'[200] The logic of these proposals and contentions makes the 'Gang of Eight's' position in the 1981 constitutional negotiations seem almost centralist, and is reminiscent of the rationale attributed to the Meech Lake constitutional accord by Pierre Trudeau and other critics.

The Case for Alberta illustrates the idiosyncratic Social Credit interpretation of constitutional terms in several other ways. In attempting to square section 91 of the BNA Act with the plebiscitary democratic theory, its authors claim that 'provincial jurisdiction over civil and property rights under Section 91 recognizes the basic principle of democratic social organization that sovereign control of policy must belong to THE PEOPLE. The primary civil right of a democracy is its right to decide policy – that is to decide what results shall be provided by the social organizations which exist to serve its individual members.[201]

If the BNA Act were found to 'contravene the principles of democracy,' 'no serious difficulty would arise in gaining general agreement as between all provinces for its amendment.'[202] The federal government, apparently, need not be a party to constitutional change, since confederation was simply a union of nine provincial 'social groupings.'

The final chapter, 'Recommendations for Social and Economic Reconstruction,' extends the case for provincial dominance in chapter 5. We are told that 'democracy in the correct sense of the term requires that policy (in particular policy in the economic sphere), shall be decided by the people of the provinces concerned, except in regard to matters affecting the relations of the Dominion with other countries, in which case it should be decided by all of the people of all provinces collectively.'[203] As participatory as this sounds, this is code language for direction of federal policy by provincial cabinets. The first recommendation to 'the sovereign People of Canada and their Governments' states the general proposition regarding provincial rights: 'It is submitted that provincial Governments should take early action to establish the sovereignty of their people within the boundaries of their own province to control policy – i.e. to obtain the results they desire – in respect of all economic and political arrangements within their provinces, provided that the same right of the people of any other province is not thereby subjected to interference.'[204]

Other recommendations regarding financial adjustments and taxation involved provincial governments administering Social Credit panaceas. The panaceas were not new, but before the 1937 disallowances Social Credit had not proposed excluding the federal government from so broad a range of its traditional economic functions. One must conclude that the plebiscitary theory rationalized a decentralized federal state because the Alberta government was frustrated with its own slow progress. Once initiated, the argument linking plebiscitary democracy to the radically decentralized state performed yeoman service. The provincial government could denounce anticipated[205] and actual Rowell-Sirois Commission recommendations as part of a plot to marginalize provincial governments and abet the centralization of financial power in Canada.[206] The provincial government even found itself condoning the Social Credit Board's warning that implementing the commission's recommendations would 'be a complete denial of the basic principles of democracy and indicates a trend towards totalitarianism.'[207] The commission's ominous proposals could not have come at a more convenient time for the Aberhart party and government.

Provincial government practice in Social Credit's early years, and their theory regarding the role of experts in government, were each seriously inconsistent with the crusade for decentralized power. In each case, centralization rather than decentralization was the reigning principle.

Centralization of power within the Social Credit regime was entirely consistent with the plebiscitarian and technocratic orientations in the organization's philosophy. This centralization took several forms, some noted above in other contexts. The most obvious form was in Aberhart's unabashed dominance of his party, cabinet and caucus. Less obvious, but still revealing, was the creation of the Social Credit Board, with its enormous delegated powers and policy responsibilities. The board not only rendered a large portion of the government caucus redundant; it also provided legislative authorization for selection and policy-making activities of 'Social Credit experts.' The board's creation and its selection of the Provincial Credit Commission[208] were central to the vastly diminished legislative power implicit in Social Credit statutes from 1937 to 1945.[209]

Other institutional changes during Aberhart's rule indicate a less than passionate commitment to decentralization of power. Against the wishes of 10,000 elected school trustees, 3,750 local school districts had been forced to amalgamate into 50 administrative units by 1939.[210] By 1943 local government in rural areas had experienced a less drastic but similar 'rationalization.'[211] *The Case for Alberta* had argued that centralization was justified when certain efficiencies could be achieved, or when determining 'matters which are common to all' of the 'social groupings' affected. Aberhart employed this vague rationale in relation to the school district reorganization during his first speech to the Alberta legislature. The larger school units were 'proving very satisfactory ... in most cases the total cost of education in the larger school units has been slightly less than the total cost under individual local school districts.'[212]

It is not surprising that during the Depression an administration would attempt to cut costs. However, to reduce community control over so important a local institution as the school required a more compelling argument, especially from one who benefited from the old policy of community control as a high-school principal and educational 'innovator.' The same might be said of the local government reorganization. One would not expect major centralizing changes to the 'bedrock of democracy' to be undertaken while the battle for decentralization was being waged in federal-provincial relations. Yet at virtually the same time that municipal reorganization was going on, the Social Credit Board and senior cabinet ministers were insisting on decentralization of power in all social organizations.[213]

Oddly enough, *The Case for Alberta* had offered a more theoretically satisfying rationale for such centralizing moves. While explaining the distinct yet complementary purposes of 'democratic' and 'centralized' organization, the authors illustrate how 'democratic organization, while it must provide the basis for a national order of society, has its limitations.' Suppose a group of individuals associate to build a bridge. How do democratic and centralized methods of organization combine to satisfy these individuals?

Every one of them ... are [*sic*] the greatest living authorities on the subject of *what results* they want, [and] they freely enter into association with the others to get what they want. However, if each of them had to decide also on *how* the bridge should be built, the unity of purpose would soon be shattered by arguments on the methods to be employed. Every one would have different ideas and possibly the one person who had a real knowledge of bridge building would have this view subjected to criticism and amendment by those who knew nothing about the technique, and the results would be disastrous to all. The obvious procedure to adopt in order to attain their objective would be for democracy to provide inducements by which the person who has the necessary knowledge of bridge building would undertake the task, the group holding him personally responsible for the results. Thereafter they would adopt the centralized form of organization, placing themselves under the administrator and taking instructions from him. Should he fail to produce the desired result, however, or should he bungle the work in the process, they should be able to remove him.

The foregoing example illustrates the strength and limitations of democratic organization, and the place which the alternative form of centralized organization should occupy in a natural social order – the social order which we know as democracy.[214]

Thus 'in a democracy, every aspect of the social organization employed, and every institution and other mechanism devised to enable society to fulfill its purposes should conform to these basic principles.'[215] These principles could easily be applied to rationalization of local government and school administrative structures; superficially, one could still argue that by voting every four of five years, people could democratically 'judge' the results and thus 'control' the rationalized structures. But the problem that is logically entailed could not have cheered the Social Credit government. If this argument justifying centralization of school and local government structures is sound, why could the same rationale not be applied to the federal system? Why not cede all decision-making powers, especially in the economic realm, to federal 'experts,' who are, after all, equally accountable to the people's occasional verdict? There are a variety of answers, but all undermine the facile division of responsibility between democratic and centralized organization offered in *The*

Case for Alberta. The real answer, of course, was that because only Alberta had a Social Credit government, the division of powers had to be altered to maximize its impact on public policy and the common weal.

What does emerge in the long analogy quoted above is an argument for technocratic determination of public policy, qualified with only a minimum of democratic control. The people were faced with their own limited competence, and the realization that their participation in shaping 'methods' might prevent a solution by 'the one person who had a real knowledge.' The only sensible approach would be adopting the 'centralized form of organization,' and taking instructions from the administrator. Citizens would have a democracy of the last resort, voting him out should he 'bungle the work in the process.' This provides a colloquial formula for Social Credit's desired technocratic state, in which decentralization of power is not a factor.

The bridge-building metaphor reveals a key assumption of the technocratic perspective. Bridge-building lends itself to an unambiguous, technical solution. Far from being typical of the problems encountered in the complex world of contending forces and interests, bridge-building is typical of the socially detached and post-political problems that scientists and technicians believe themselves to be addressing. The example is clearly chosen because all rational people can presumably agree on the need to obtain the result.

If the desired results of public-policy development are economic security and human freedom, the metaphor remains appropriate only if social conflicts are presumed to present no obstacle, or if some *deus ex machina* removes the basis for such conflicts while simultaneously facilitating the results. In Social Credit thought, the latter role is accorded to a set of credit and monetary cures, as chosen and administered by experts. These experts will build bridges[216] to the era of abundance, thereby eliminating the basis of existing economic and social conflicts. State-employed experts will facilitate a future democratic on several counts: individuals will be free to pursue their own objectives, economic exploitation will be impossible and unnecessary, and most important for the plebiscitarian case, the people will get the results for which they had expressed a desire by voting for Social Credit.

Identifying experts' roles in a Social Credit administration was not central to Aberhart's early movement-building. This lack of attention can be attributed to several things, most important his faith in the feasibility of converting potential into actual wealth and a perceived necessity to mobilize the popular will for prosperity. There was no need to explain what experts would do – even if he himself had a developed idea of their role – if Social Credit theory and measures were so obviously the solution to the problem of 'poverty in the midst of plenty.' As leader of a movement based so largely on faith, enthusiasm, and repressed despair, he could see no sense in trumpeting the centrality of an unidentified set of experts to the crusade's success. None the less, Aberhart provided some indication of their role and character during 1934 and 1935.

As we have seen, Aberhart addressed the division of labour between results-demanders and methods-producers in the fall of 1934. That November, he elaborated on the experts' function in an article on 'The Problem of Introduction.' Denying that a 'definite plan' could be constructed before the election of a 'government favorable to its introduction,' he none the less outlined six steps in the introduction of Social Credit, involving three kinds of experts.[217]

A 'body of expert constitutional lawyers' was deemed necessary to formulate a 'Social Credit Act,' suggesting that Aberhart was not entirely confident his plans squared with the BNA Act. A second set of experts, 'Social Credit efficiency experts,' were to be trained in Alberta's universities and technical schools to 'handle the work of the credit houses' and 'assure a smooth operation of the system.' These experts served two purposes in the political appeal of Social Credit. They required 'special training' to assure supporters that the arcane details and application of the theory were sufficiently technical that mere supporters could not appreciate them. The mystique surrounding 'methods' had to be maintained for the cure to retain a miraculous aura.

At the same time, the Alberta supporters of Social Credit were sufficiently sophisticated that such methods had to be comprehensible to some of their number after proper training. Their curiosity about methods forced Aberhart to 'reveal' many more details about the salvational package than he (or Major Douglas) wished. Social Credit supporters therefore wanted to believe that they or their children could become experts, or at least Social Credit technicians. Aberhart was careful to promote this belief, insisting that university and technical school graduates, and a 'large number of capable men' within the province, could render valuable service to Albertans. More assurance was provided in the proposal for a 'Just Price Guild,' to be composed of two commissions staffed by 'experts from every branch of industry.' The potential Social Credit supporter, sceptical of rule by a coterie of 'eggheads,' could find solace in the promise of functional representation in two key commissions. (This person might be Mallory's typical Social Credit supporter, who was 'likely to have both a distrust of, and a faith in, experts and expert knowledge.')[218]

It is also possible that the technocracy of a Just Price Guild appealed to old UFA supporters, who believed occupational representation would develop expert views on the negotiations between classes. While not democratically selected or educated by UFA standards, members of the guild would none the less represent groups whose problems and perspectives they would understand. Aberhart thought enough of functional representation among experts in the Social Credit administration that he referred to it in *The Social Credit Manual*.[219]

Functional representation in and training of local talent for a Just Price Guild and state credit houses[220] were reassuring, and meshed well with the just price, credit house, dividend, and other proposals Aberhart offered the method-hungry public. With the general framework for implementing Social Credit policies apparently already worked out, the degree of discretionary power left to experts seemed smaller. Thus those inclined to fear unnamed experts could console themselves that while experts would perform a key function in the new regime, they would not actually be exercising greatly enhanced power. Locally trained experts working within a well-conceived general plan could make important, but clearly still technical, decisions on policy matters.

Another factor reduced popular concern for the elevation of the experts. In Social Credit writings on the cultural heritage, the unearned increment, and the possibilities of a leisured existence, power to do good was always associated with science and the mastery of technique. Power to do evil was employed by party stooges in political life, and by scheming usurers in financial circles. If technicians of the Social Credit school could operate in a suprapolitical environment, free from the machinations of high finance, their power to do good would be untainted by politicians' and financiers' power to sustain domination. Experts could be trusted because they were not politicians or financiers, and because their natural work was the production of plenty.

While this account may exaggerate the consistency of the case for experts that Aberhart offered voters, it finds support in Social Credit literature. A *Chronicle* editorial insisted that virtually all of the experts required by 'the plan' could be found 'right in the ranks of our honest Social Creditors' and 'in all classes of work living in Alberta today, professional and otherwise.'[221] When experts appear so familiar, preparing the political system for experts to supervise the realization of plenty seems to pose little threat.

Presenting experts as ordinary folk trained in the verities of Social Credit had its drawbacks for Social Credit leaders. For those steeped in the UFA tradition, it would enhance popular expectations about participation in political life, as well as expectations about the delivery of Social Credit promises. The former expectation became evident when constituency associations stubbornly offered policy resolutions at annual conventions for several years after the election.[222] The very fact that average folk could become experts suggested that the overall plan was foolproof. According to the *Chronicle* editor, the Social Credit plan could 'explain definitely all and every detail and question, an impregnable armour of solid facts.'[223] Taken seriously, this belief would generate the idea that solutions would appear almost immediately after the plan's trustees took office.

The Social Credit government never introduced formal functional representation in its expert bodies, and did little to transform well-educated young Albertans into cognoscenti of the Social Credit theory. The latter was pointless, since the theory could not be sensibly applied, and the federal authorities blocked Aberhart's belated attempts to do so.

After the 1935 election, the outwardly confident but inwardly confused regime ceased to talk about experts as ordinary people. They reverted to the idea of experts as an intellectually privileged and mysterious group deserving implicit faith. As Macpherson shows, the attempt to solicit expert advice from C.H. Douglas was a fiasco, largely because Aberhart refused to cede authority to the founder of the system.[224]

Attention to the role of experts waxed again following the passage of some bona fide Social Credit legislation. The Alberta Social Credit Act of 1937 included rhetoric about the appointment of 'suitable persons as Social Credit technical experts' by the Social Credit Board, and the strong suggestion that Board members were themselves experts.[225] The board was to appoint a 'Provincial Credit Commission,' which would in turn employ experts to determine levels of just prices, dividends, credit offerings, and so on. So much detail concerning their responsibilities was offered in the act, including formulas for calculating price discounts and dividends, that experts would have their activities tightly circumscribed.

Shortly after the proclamation of this act, the Social Credit Board and its experts from the London Douglas Secretariat began to deny that their duties could or should be precisely identified by the government. One of the most striking variants came in a pamphlet by G.F. Powell. He repeated the standard argument concerning the inability of the 'mob' to do anything except 'feel,' and the consequent need to distinguish between methods and results. Elected representatives should 'confine themselves to being experts as to the RESULTS the electors in their constituencies desire.' Governments (i.e., cabinets) had a higher responsibility, but were not fully capable of decisions regarding methods either: they 'need be expert only in seeking out and choosing those best qualified to devise means whereby THE PEOPLE can get what they want and in securing timely detection and dismissal of the incompetent among such experts.' Thus 'THE PEOPLE, the Legislature, Cabinet Members and Technicians are confined, in their responsibilities, pronouncements, and activities, each strictly within their respective competence,' ensuring that 'no one part of a democratic mechanism for government interferes with the other.'[226]

This rendering may have accurately reflected the orthodox Douglas position, but it accorded poorly with the environment Powell found himself working in as senior expert in the Aberhart government. The board and its experts had only a momentary tenure as formal superiors to the Alberta cabinet, and even this was more illusory and rhetorical than real.[227] The real purpose of this temporary loyalty to Douglas's doctrine of technocratic rule was the same as all other efforts in this direction: it took pressure off the beleaguered cabinet and premier, and reduced expectations of the Social Credit faithful.

As soon as the constitutionally invalid Social Credit legislation met with rejection by the courts or the federal cabinet, the experts and their elected proponents (especially in the Social Credit Board) acquired a new defence. They alleged that federal politicians and their financial cohorts were preventing Social Credit experts from employing their scientific skills pursuant to the mandate of the Alberta people. This was to be a staple of Social Credit rhetoric until well into the 1940s. Aberhart's masterful oratory, the partial truth of the case against the federal government and central Canadian financial interests, and a widespread desire for new credit and 'welfare' policies made the new wrinkle in defence of the experts surprisingly acceptable in the province.

The relationship between technocratic orientation and an assumption of abundance was a key part of Social Credit thought. In placing the possibility of 'plenty' at the centre of his case, Aberhart was being faithful to Major Douglas,[228] and responding skilfully to a compelling popular democratic tradition on the prairies.[229] Put to moderate use, the belief simply assured that those who worked hard in the bountiful land would make a good living, if not stymied by external political and economic forces. In its more utopian forms, this tradition became a belief that the whole nation could revel in leisured abundance, justice, and equity. As we saw, this was integral to the social democratic vision of the co-operative commonwealth.

William Aberhart believed that such a situation could be established with little disruption through Social Credit economic engineering. He contended, following Douglas, that 'the machine had solved the problem of production,' but that because 'the whole financial system is designed for an Age of Scarcity, drudgery and hardship,' poverty in the midst of plenty would continue unless experts redesigned it.[230] In a distortion of the Douglas theory, he claimed that the basic dividends would, by themselves, accomplish much of the work involved in realizing plenty: 'the payment of dividends ... is returning to [our people] their rightful share of the value which their Social Credit has given to the products of industry' and will result in 'poverty and privation [being] abolished forever from our land of plenty and abundance.'[231]

Achieving this great prospect required Albertans to abandon 'politics,' which had maintained an artificial scarcity, and allow Social Credit scientists to calculate dividends, just prices, and credit circulation. Having replaced financiers and their political puppets, Social Credit officials would facilitate freedom in abundance rather than conspire in unnecessary domination and enforced scarcity.

The assumption of potential abundance was crucial to Social Credit supporters' acceptance of a model of benevolent technocracy. Having lost faith in established solutions to their desperate economic condition, they were more likely to believe that only Social Credit experts could 'produce the goods.' Many had accepted the UFA doctrine concerning the ultimate compatibility of class interests, so a solution to their problems that was 'beyond' politics did not seem particularly foreign. For those with faith in Social Credit remedies, a vision of imminent abundance rendered an impoverished democratic practice much less objectionable.

Had the promise of plenty through Social Credit science seemed less compelling, the anti-participatory character of Aberhart's proposals would have appeared offensive to many more in 1935. However, this promise implied that contemporary democratic mechanisms – including, apparently, those of the UFA movement – were more than ineffective, or a disguise for the real government by financial oligarchs. In addition, the implication was that participatory political life was largely unnecessary, even if it could live up to its own billing. For why would people need or want to concern themselves with other people's business, when it is apparent that all are well attended to in the scientifically arranged land of abundance? The Age of Plenty, or even a reasonable approximation of it, would not require an extensive public life, especially if simplistically conceived security, freedom, and leisure are life's principal goals.

Despite their failure to produce even the $25 monthly dividends, the rhetoric linking experts to the provision of plenty did not disappear from Social Credit propaganda. As late as 1943, Aberhart promised that a national Social Credit monetary commission 'would see that incomes were distributed in such a manner that the security and leisure made possible by the abundant production would be available to everyone on an equitable basis, thus removing the fear of destitution ... without bureaucratic State regimentation.'[232] Aberhart's confrontation with the real world of fallible 'experts,' an uncooperative federal government, and an increasingly sceptical provincial population, had dimmed the utopian light in his picture. Experts and prosperity were none the less still linked within the positive image of the Social Credit state.

In the absence of any real Social Credit achievements in technocratic economic change, it might be thought that the emphasis on technocracy in this chapter is misplaced. However, this dimension of Social Credit discourse was central to a process within Alberta that eviscerated popular democracy and undermined opportunities for its future rebirth. Urbanization, demographic diversification, eventual prosperity via the oil boom, and the narrowing of North American political horizons were also important in this regard. But the rapid demise of support for popular democracy in Alberta cannot be explained without appreciating the Social Credit campaign for plebiscitarian technocratic rule.

Co-operation in Social Credit Discourse

Unlike other prairie populisms, Social Credit did not seriously attempt to integrate the values of indigenous agrarian co-operatives into its social philosophy.[233] In the Social Credit vocabulary, 'co-operation' was almost exclusively a code word for a part of the political strategy designed to acquire and retain governmental office.

Social Credit theory and rhetoric in Alberta almost completely ignored the radical and social democratic populist conception of co-operation as the true moral principle of social interaction. One could occasionally find passing reference to or indirect endorsement of co-operation as moral behaviour, but such concessions to social gospel and other popular Christian teachings were never seriously tied to systematic reform proposals. Co-operation was not regularly identified as an intrinsic moral good.

The Social Credit position on co-operation as an economic 'third way' between capitalism and socialism was slightly more confusing, but still far removed from the positions of radical and social democratic populism. The confusion arises because the core idea of Social Credit – as something arising from a community's belief in its ability to produce as required, and hence to generate its own credit – could be presented in such a way that co-operation was crucial. Thus in 1943 we find Aberhart saying that 'the Democracy we have, has not been functioning as it should, because we have refused to allow Social Credit, I mean the belief and the ability of the people to produce co-operatively, to place at the disposal of the people generally the benefits that are the result of our Common Cultural Heritage.'[234]

This comment may appear to call for a different system of economic relations, but Aberhart is only claiming that the same set of property and power relations would produce more if dividends, just prices, and cheap credit were available. In testimony to the Alberta legislature's Agricultural

Committee hearings on Social Credit almost a decade earlier, C.H. Douglas had claimed that 'we have a co-operative commonwealth,' that 'the whole productive system is a co-operative system,' and that 'what we have not got is the proper means of drawing from that co-operative commonwealth which exists at the present time underneath our very noses.'[235] Understood in this sense, the economics of co-operation would entail no changes to the social relations of production. Aberhart was saying exactly this, and despite efforts to get political mileage out of the word, his meaning of 'co-operation' was far from that of the UFA or CCF in this regard.

Co-operation as a strategy for building then retaining political power for 'the people' was the only form to which Social Credit discourse paid much attention. Earlier discussions of 'the people,' and of themes in democratic action, suggested the place of co-operation in this rhetoric. We saw that the 1935 campaign promoted expression of a 'united will for results,' to overcome divisions within the people, then drive parties and their financial masters from the halls of power. The themes of 'united democracy' and a neo-Douglasian 'Union of Electors' were well utilized between the constitutional defeats and the 1940 election. Aberhart articulated the idea of co-operative political action in a 'Union of Electors' in a 1940 pamphlet on agricultural reform: 'At present there are several farmers' organizations. The old age pensioners have their own organization. Wage earners are organized under their own unions. Business men are organized in various organizations – and so forth. Separately these various unions representing different interests are weak. They can be played off against the other. But united for a common, definite purpose, as a non-party Union of Electors, they would be able to achieve their worthy objectives ... before which the Money Power would have to bow in obedience.'[236]

Several years later, Aberhart warned what fate might befall progressive people who failed to constitute themselves as a solid, 'co-operative' bloc for political purposes. Germany fell to Hitler because Germans 'became divided into numerous groups and political camps. They lost the spirit of co-operation and democratic unity. That is our first danger ... Do not let us be blinded by all these political labels. Rather let us unite in support of the results that we want.'[237]

'Co-operation' thus became the code word for popular unity behind the platform and actions of the Social Credit leadership. It was an invitation to avoid 'party politics' and provide a plebiscitarian mandate to the incumbent premier. During Aberhart's regime, co-operation in Alberta ceased to signify moral social relations to replace the competitive ethic. The co-operative vision was removed from the centre of political debate, even though Social Credit legislation in the late 1930s and early 1940s provided assistance to co-operative enterprises in the province.[238] Isolated from other politically complementary activities, this legislation had no impact on provincial attitudes towards democratic politics.

By reducing the democratic dimensions of the concept of co-operation to the level of transparent regime-building and -maintenance, Social Credit hastened conservatization of the co-operative movement, and populist action, across the prairies. Given the participatory implications of co-operatives' organizational 'self-government,' it is not surprising that Aberhart and his associates were not anxious to emphasize the co-operative movement's politicizing potential. The CCF did so in Saskatchewan, thereby helping to retain an ideological environment conducive to social democratic populism.

Social Credit and the Good Society

It is impossible not to be struck by the other-worldliness of Aberhart's vision of the 'new social order,' and by the enthusiasm with which many Social Credit voters embraced it in 1935. One may dismiss this vision as a species of evangelical fantasy, or even as a 'Canadian Cargo Cult,'[239] but the $25 monthly dividend was widely perceived as merely the tip of the iceberg of abundance in depression-wracked Alberta.

My discussion of the Social Credit view of the good society will not cover Aberhart's personal theology and eschatology, which were undoubtedly key factors in Social Credit's appeal to many Albertans.[240] Aberhart's evangelical Christianity did little to alter the overall structure of Social Credit democratic thought. Perhaps his theology encouraged a more authoritarian form of leadership, and his predilection to believe in miracles and cataclysmic change may have heightened his faith in the power of experts to hasten a secular utopia. These and related possibilities have been pursued elsewhere.[241] In my opinion, such relationships between democratic thought and theology were not decisive for the plebiscitarian populism of Social Credit. None of the elements discussed below required anything more than a basic Protestantism for their moral footing and legitimacy.

The secular side of Douglas's Social Credit vision of the good society included production primarily by technology rather than human labour, a leisure-filled existence, economic security and material satisfaction for all, elimination of economic class-based social conflict, and freedom for individuals from domination by centralized institutions of the state and the financial system.[242] John Finlay has emphasized an anti-political, quasi-anarchistic tendency in Douglas's political and social vision which is only partially at variance with a characterization of Social Credit as a technocratic doctrine.[243]

Most of these elements found their way into Aberhart's presentation of Social Credit's promise. Aberhart and writers in the *Chronicle* proclaimed the ability of 'the industrial machine' to produce the goods required for a comparatively leisured existence. As we saw earlier, Aberhart contended that Social Credit would remove the blight of class conflict, and provide a solid foundation for expression of a general will for 'results.' Financial domination of the people would end, thanks to a victory over the conspiracy between 'the fifty big shots' and their political party flunkies. Domination of the people by state employees was thus not to be feared. Employees of the Social Credit state were either benevolent experts consumed by the scientific challenge of realizing plenty or administrators of the cheap credit, dividends, or just prices ensuring popular enjoyment of this abundance. Individual freedom was to find expression in the realm of material consumption, and in regular opportunities to vote for or against elected governments.

More important than anything else for the Alberta electorate in 1935 was the promise that Social Credit would provide equitable economic security for all. For impoverished farmers, nearly bankrupt small-town merchants, and urban unemployed heeding Aberhart's call, economic security was the prerequisite to all else in the good society. Just prices, just wages, monthly dividends, and ready access to credit were to furnish this security. The faithful were casually promised that these mechanisms would almost immediately produce the society of plenty.

Alberta's Social Credit vision gave much more emphasis than Douglas's to its inherent egalitarianism and social justice. Social justice was an important element in the utopian image of all other prairie populisms. In the Social Credit case, Aberhart used the concepts of the cultural heritage (on which all had an equal claim), the just price (which would provide more equity in the realm of personal purchasing power), and unconditional monthly dividends for all Alberta citizens to broadly imply an egalitarian distribution of the benefits of Social Credit policy. He also communicated an egalitarian tone by insisting that potential abundance would be made actual under the new regime.

As Macpherson notes, the major nostrums (just price and dividends) depended on the assumption of realizable abundance. The assumption of potential plenty also removed the need to deal with immediate obstacles to a more equitable distribution of social wealth and opportunities. If plenty is easily realized, Social Crediters could contend that the questions socialists and other reformers ask about redistributing present benefits, burdens and power are simply beside the point. In the Social Credit view, once power is removed from financiers and corrupt party politicians and given to technical experts, the question of redistributing power among social classes simply does not arise. It was this aspect of the Social Credit approach that so angered the CCF in Alberta and elsewhere. Social Credit could appear to be criticizing the powerful business interests, but was not, in the CCF view, proposing structural changes to deprive them of their inordinate power.

Avoiding the question of which groups should bear the short-run burden of social reform was characteristic of the Alberta Social Credit appeal. Yet Aberhart did feel obliged to add to the story for an audience raised on the rhetoric of more demanding changes to 'the power system.' Thus he assured readers of *The Social Credit Manual* that Social Credit would eliminate 'wildcat exploitation' and would save Albertans natural resources from the 'Fifty Big Shots of Canada.'[244] Aberhart even proposed limiting Albertans' income 'to a certain maximum ... for no one should be allowed to have an income that is greater than he himself and his loved ones can possibly enjoy, to the privation of his fellow citizens.'[245]

Aberhart's injection of an egalitarian dimension into the league's appeal showed that he knew an audience bitter about immediate injustices would not be satisfied only with promises of an equitable and abundant future. The Social Credit government's aid to beleaguered Alberta debtors indicates that his commitment to social justice was not hollow. In a sense, Aberhart was willing to take on 'the fifty big shots,' and at least temporarily 'confiscate' the wealth derivable from loan collections. While this plan was eminently sensible in political terms, limiting incomes within the province was not, and was never attempted.

Issuing dividends based on the 'credit of the province' would have been unsurpassable as a means of securing popular support for the new regime. It would have definitively demonstrated the peculiar Social Credit commitment to social justice. Practical difficulties and federal intervention prevented the government from delivering on this promise. Since this failure, political opponents and academic analysts have almost unanimously characterized the notion of Social Credit dividends as a crankish pipe-dream. However, in some polities untouched by Social Credit movements, the idea of a social dividend has been taken quite seriously, especially as means of increasing worker-controlled investment. Danish Social Democrats introduced a plan with dividends in 1973.[246] While it differs markedly from the Social Credit plan, it shares several important features, such as the idea that average citizens' economic power should be increased because they have contributed to the present economic 'machine,' and that all citizens should receive dividends irrespective of their individual wages and tax contributions.

The point is that the Social Credit idea of dividends need not be rejected out of hand. It is true that it was based on fallacious economic reasoning, and related to a view of society as a collection of atomized consumers whose freedom would consist in making consumer choices with adequate purchasing power. The idea of dividends, however, did carry a germ of egalitarianism and fulfilling human development that enhanced the appeal of Social Credit's image of the good society.

Of the anti-political, technocratic, and essentially anti-participatory dimensions of Social Credit discourse, only the former was honestly portrayed in the Social Credit utopian appeal. The technocratic theme was strong but disguised by the personal popularity of Aberhart and the spectacle of mass mobilization in support of the new leader and his plan. The anti-participatory logic of the Social Credit polity was also well hidden by this movement-building, and was denied by those who equated popular democracy with plebiscitarian leadership and mandated popular sovereignty.

As we saw earlier, the anti-political and technocratic aspects of Social Credit thought were logically tied to the assumption of abundance. The possibility of abundance made political meddling undesirable, since past politicians had assisted financiers' maintenance of an artificial economy of scarcity. Plenty also necessitated technocratic economic intervention, since only scientific experts were capable of 'delivering results' according to the popular mandate. The reality of abundance, however, would provide another rationale for 'doing away with politics,' since material prosperity would eliminate the economic and social conflicts on which party politicians preyed. In the absence of such conflicts, and with leisure and material satisfaction achieved, politics would sensibly be reduced to occasional plebiscites on experts' results.

Any other politics, like popular participation in public policy development, would be simply irrational. At this point in the Social Credit scenario, there was no practical contradiction between the technocratic and the anti-political, anti-participatory elements in the doctrine, because the political ends of facilitating economic engineering and eliminating artificial conflict would have been achieved. State intervention in the economy could then decline, and the realms of public life and public policy could be almost self-regulating. (This scenario conveniently overlooked the extensive activity involved in state credit houses, and just price and wage determination, but such an oversight was unimportant to those who could see immediate benefits flowing from the credit houses.)

Underpinning the belief that politics could be excised from public life was a very simplistic sense of how society functions. Especially in Social Credit Board publications, but even in early movement propaganda, one finds claims about how society, government, and economy would work smoothly if organized properly. As a 1937 publication states, 'This question of social organization is a science, as indeed is all organization ... The test of any organization is the smoothness and efficiency with which it operates in achieving the purpose for which it exists. So it is with social organization. A natural social order would be one which was functioning vigorously, yielding complete satisfaction to its individual members ... Its individual members in association would, in the main, be getting what they wanted. This would be democracy if the form of organization was designed to achieve this result.'[247]

The author continues that since 'specialization in methods is the outstanding factor in the progress of civilization,' and since the people at large cannot be expected to be expert in all specialized methods, the people must simply express demands for results. 'Those qualified to provide the results' will do the rest, with the proviso that a government will supervise their actions and 'insist that they yield those results.' By combining political and economic democracy, this would establish 'the first democratic community in the world – a community organized to enable its individual members in association to demand and get the results they want and thus realize their social credit.'[248]

Such an argument is technocratic and anti-political not just because of the role assigned to experts, but also because all problems of social life are assumed to be scientifically and unambiguously resolvable. Once experts determine the only answers to these problems, the people cannot object because these solutions will be obviously correct. Such anti-political fantasy neglects the very real class, sexual, racial, and other conflicts preventing unanimously approved solutions to most questions in public life. And yet, a belief in readily established solutions for perplexing social and political problems was central to the UFA theory of group government. Their approach relied less on the magic of experts and more on a recognition of contending economic and social interests, but none the less aided the emergence of a Social Credit utopian vision.

With the UFA movement in mind, we can turn to a final point regarding the Social Credit image of the good society. Unlike the UFA, or for that matter the CCF or the Progressives, Social Crediters lacked a sense of what 'the citizen' was to be. Individuals were to be materially satisfied, and thus free to pursue their own personal development. But with public life characterized as an unnecessary and functionally improper dimension of individual activity – except at election time – what became of citizenship? As we saw earlier, citizenship was reduced to a formal category, to correspond to the representative process favoured by Social Credit. Citizens were individuals who demanded results and, when and if the technicians worked their magic, collected dividends and other monetarily reckoned benefits.

For a political philosophy purportedly working towards 'the first democratic community in the world,' directed by the first scientific theory of democracy, these were rather tawdry promises. The satisfaction of individual participation in and collective contributions to political life was denied these citizens, except when their efforts were needed to build and sustain the political vehicle of technocratic rule. Had this been clear from the outset, it is unlikely that even materially deprived Albertans would have supported the Social Credit alternative in 1935.

According to W.L. Morton, Social Credit in Alberta was the chief example of western utopianism in a period of utopianism (1925-55).[249] This characterization correctly draws attention to Aberhart's widely accepted promise of plenty, and to the magical solutions purportedly productive of plenty, but it overlooks the centrality of participatory, popular democracy in the utopian vision of other prairie populisms and its merely rhetorical presence in the Social Credit variant. This omission invites a very one-sided appreciation of what most popular organizations in the West were ultimately aiming for. Prosperity, equity, and even technologically provided leisure were certainly important, but if one neglects the passion for popular democracy, the peculiarity of Social Credit thought and success is easily minimized.

6   Conclusion

In this analysis I have explained prairie populist ideologies between 1910 and 1945 as four distinct variants of democratic thought. My examination of six themes in prairie democratic thought focused on problems and conflicts typically encountered by mass-based movements or reform organizations. Comparative analysis of prairie political concerns and experiences demonstrated the logic and ideological unity of the populist discourses. This analytical framework also helped to test an important proposition: that while the long-term objectives of each populist organization possessed a class-based character, this class basis did not exclusively define its extended conception of democracy. Class attachments do not necessarily produce all-embracing class logics. The similarity of many prairie populist proposals to those of contemporary North American and European labour organizations suggests that the class basis of an organization should not be granted inordinate explanatory power.

While particular patterns of democratic thought provided an ideological unity for each prairie populism, contradictions or inconsistencies also existed. Indeed, I argued that each populist ideology, possessing simultaneously commitments to some kind of popular democracy and to technocratic socio-economic engineering, was unable to avoid a tension between participatory democracy and technocratic governance. This tension was not unique to prairie populism; it has bedevilled virtually all post–eighteenth-century movement-based regimes and reform movement organizations.

This tension does not eliminate a popular ideology's unity; instead, the particular way the tension is addressed or avoided indicates a good deal about the unique and populist character of the ideology. Using the language of 'popular-democratic traditions,' populists appeal for a redistribution of power from 'the power bloc' to 'the people.' Thus populism contains proposals promising to 'return' state control to the people, while creating a vague new repository of suprapopular power, namely 'the experts.' Such proposals create an inevitable dilemma for the politics of social transformation and popular democracy.

Reducing all differences between CCF, UFA, Social Credit, and Progressive organizations to a broad common denominator – such as 'hinterland protest' or *'petit bourgeois* agrarian politics' – has appeared plausible to many Canadian academics. In this study, I have reproduced many passages from movement literature to demonstrate that the nature and logic of particular populist appeals often varied significantly from those of their competitors. Comparative comments are scattered throughout the analysis, but an overview of the salient distinctions and general orientations is still required.

Prairie Populisms in Review: Six Themes, Four Patterns

Crypto-Liberalism, radical democratic populism, social democratic populism, and plebiscitarian populism were distinct ideological frames of reference and languages of political discourse. In reviewing the character of six democratic themes within each, we can see how these populist discourses could retain an overall logic, yet still merge with other discourses on specific issues and in particular political strategies.

The People

One can go as far back as Aristotle's *Politics* to discover the importance of an understanding of 'the people' for any distinctive body of democratic thought. Identifying which parts of the *demos* should rule and accounting for how their interests are frustrated by ruling forces distinguished the democratic ideology of popular movements from ideologies of predecessors and competitors. These two rhetorical aspects of 'the people' indicate clearly how such movements' actors understood their political projects, whom they perceived as their major enemies, and, indeed, why the movements and companion ideologies were created. In addition, political rhetoric about the people's interests and their antagonists uses what Laclau refers to as 'popular-democratic traditions' in movement- and ideology-specific ways. The popular movements and ideologies thus demonstrate their populist credentials in a manner that assists comparative analysis.

A general pattern is discernible in the four cases discussed in this book. A positive relation exists between 1 / the degree of specificity used to identify particular groups and relations within 'the people,' and particular features of the power structures preventing rule by the people, and 2 / the degree of a populism's radicalism. With regard to the former, specificity in such analysis may carry fewer radical implications if it simply singles out one characteristic of an otherwise undifferentiated 'people' or focuses obsessively on a single aspect of the people's foes. Thus Social Credit conveyed limited radicalism by insisting that financiers were imposing an artificial cash shortage on all consumers – the people.

Social Credit rhetoric of 'the people,' however, implied a populism more radical than that of crypto-Liberalism. Crypto-Liberalism defined a more precise constituency as 'the people' – agricultural producers – but this discourse was less specific when identifying the economic and political forces and institutions blocking 'the people's' agenda. Crypto-Liberal politicians were also closer to and less suspicious of the exercise of power than were Aberhart and his associates, and demanded less redistribution of economic power between classes than Aberhart did in the 1930s.

From a contemporary perspective, radical democratic populists' critique of political institutions may appear chiliastic. It was, none the less, consistently principled and well developed, as was best illustrated in the UFA account of an antagonism between the people and the party system of political representation. Insofar as the theory of delegate democracy and group government was explicitly intended to maximize popular democracy, this populism deserves high marks as a radical populism. The obvious qualification, made famous by C.B. Macpherson, is that the UFA offered a vague account of the system of economic class power limiting their members' political possibilities. Their economic radicalism, while occasionally merging the social democracy of William Irvine, Robert Gardiner, or E.J. Garland, was usually limited by the parameters of H.W. Wood's 'co-operativist liberalism.' It was, by the standards of the time, anti-capitalist and clearly reformist, but it did not reject the crypto-Liberal acceptance of prevailing property institutions. Their political radicalism – expressed in rhetoric regarding 'the people' – was none the less a frontal attack on an élite-dominated political process.

In social democratic populism we also found a radical rhetoric of the people, involving more emphasis on the economic than the political bases of 'the people's' subordination. Participatory democracy was still a key objective of social democratic populists, but less for its own value than for the egalitarian purposes to which an anti-capitalist people would apply it, via a socialist administration. Social democrats argued much more insistently against capitalism than they did against the party and political systems they claimed had perpetuated class power. They used popular-democratic traditions to stress the common interest of the people – workers, farmers, and those performing a socially useful function – in social ownership and social planning. Social democratic populists contended that major ills of the political system could be cured by extending formal political democracy into the economic realm.

Prairie populist rhetoric of 'the people' also expressed an antagonism towards political life, and especially towards politicians. This feeling was weakest within the leadership circles of crypto-Liberalism, and strongest in plebiscitarian populism. The crypto-Liberal antipathy towards politics and politicians was based on frustrations with central Canadian domination of the two major parties, and on the influence of the non-partisan, anti-statist orientations of the co-operative movement. The people had been duped by the old parties, and should pursue their economic objectives through collective organization as producers.

Many rank-and-file supporters of the Progressives, and even some early grain growers' association leaders, also advocated circumventing unscrupulous politicians and parties to achieve political objectives such as prohibition, the single tax, and female suffrage. The vehicle for achieving these objectives was to be direct legislation, which attained widespread popular support in the prairie provinces but had limited legislative successes. Local control over candidate selection, campaign financing, and political agenda-setting revealed an anti-politician, anti-élitist orientation in the West, and was given considerable attention in crypto-Liberal speech about 'the people.'

Condemning politicians and politics generally was integral to Aberhart's contention that only Social Credit could serve the people's needs. The plebiscitarian assurance that 'the sovereign people' would rule was based on a promise that political agents of financial interests would be replaced by 'bribe-proof businessmen' representatives and Social Credit experts. Politics was simply confusion, manipulation, and broken promises, so the Social Credit leader and administration would have nothing to do with politics. Only in circumventing politics, by demanding such 'results' as security, material plenty, and freedom, could the people recover control over governments.

A brief glance at such an appeal makes it difficult to understand what is attractive or threatening in the Social Credit contraposition of 'the people' and politicians. However, this antinomy was not just an innocuous extension of the radical democratic critique of party and state. In chapter 5, I argued that this rhetorical tactic was psychological preparation for a plebiscitarian, pseudo-participatory politics. It was also intended to increase faith in Social Credit experts' ability to realize the potential of technology. The Social Credit attack on politicians in the name of the people was central to Aberhart's overall political strategy.

Radical democratic populists used the people/politicians antinomy to good effect, but with intentions almost the opposite of Social Credit's. UFA spokespersons anchored their case against politicians in a systematic critique of the party system. They intended to demonstrate that party politics blocked development of an informed, organized citizenry capable of self-rule. Social Credit speakers, having savaged party politics, transferred the decision-making burden and process to experts. By contrast, radical democratic populists argued that decision-making should be transferred to a dynamic, educational, and self-governing system of occupationally defined citizen groups. In terms of the extension of popular democracy, then, the radical democratic critique of politics and politicians had an inherently positive agenda. Social Credit manipulated existing popular-democratic traditions regarding the negative side of politics to stand the UFA objective on its head.

Social democratic populists also found themselves heir to legacies of anti-politician sentiment. Their challenge was to translate these into a popular rejection of the relations between business élites and old parties, and to establish that these relations were intrinsic to capitalism, the primary cause of 'the people's' woes. Simultaneously, however, this critique of politics had to be redirected to prevent the people from losing faith in the state and political life as such. The ability of the people's politicians and organizations to force the state to pursue progressive purposes could not be seriously questioned. Thus, while sowing seeds of discontent about élites' uses of political institutions, they had to make political action by a united people appear realistic and attractive. Waging such a campaign in the face of an anti-socialist political culture was not easy. It led to state power only in Saskatchewan, where the CCF became widely viewed as the political expression of co-operatives' objectives. Elsewhere, social democrats could not convince enough voters that they were politicians unlike the others, committed to the people's interests.

The modern legacy of the prairie populist disposition to see politicians as the people's foes is mixed. Prairie residents have changed dramatically since the 1940s – they are now much more urban, generally more prosperous, and less inclined to participate in social movements and politicized economic organizations. As Roger Gibbins argues,[1] they are demographically closer to the Canadian norm. Nevertheless, prairie residents remain deeply suspicious of federal politicians and politics, and often still believe that their provincial politicians, having lost touch with 'the people,' are too similar to federal politicians. This belief can spell trouble for incumbent governments where credible opposition parties exist. The Saskatchewan and Manitoba elections of 1981 and 1982 demonstrate this clearly; to a lesser extent, so does the Alberta election of 1985.

Prairie residents' suspicion of politicians has not yet reached the level found in the United States, but one can still see shades of the people/politicians dichotomy in current prairie political rhetoric. The dichotomy is implied in everything from the Saskatchewan government's rationalization of extensive 'privatization' and welfare benefit reduction to the right-wing critique of the Alberta government's 'state capitalism,' to the demand for entrenchment of private-property rights in the constitution. In one case, it surfaces very clearly – the Western Canada Concept and Reform Party of Canada have insisted on recall and referendum statutes as part of their anti-statist program.

Prairie Populism and Advocacy of Popular Democracy

One striking intergenerational political comparison germane to this study is the contrast between the prairie populist preoccupation with methods of popular democracy and the virtual absence of these concerns from political discussion in Canada today.[2] All prairie populisms condemned the absence of true democracy in Canada, emphasized the need to remedy this problem, and strenuously debated prescriptions for a democratic body politic.

All prairie populists agreed that 'the interests' of central Canada were in some sense responsible for the sad state of Canadian democracy. All also believed that established political parties were the interests' instruments. Prairie populists all proposed new political vehicles and methods to translate popular demands into public policy.

These common denominators may appear to justify the conclusion that differences in populist approaches to problems of democratic politics were ultimately insignificant. We have seen that this judgment is insupportable. There was much substantive disagreement over analysis of and alternatives to the Canadian political economy. Claiming that all of this was simply variation on a *petit bourgeois* theme trivializes the novel efforts and experience of two generations of prairie residents, while establishing impossible criteria for what 'really counts' as radical or distinctive political thought.

We can briefly characterize the different stances taken within prairie populist thought regarding what prevented, and was required for, true democracy. Crypto-Liberals believed the national Liberal party's capture by tariff-protected business interests, and the party's consequent centralized and anti-agrarian character, were the essence of the problem. Their solution included direct legislation, to circumvent their old party while it remained the tool of eastern interests. Their solution also involved greater internal democracy and local autonomy within the alternative political organization – the Progressives – established to represent western interests in the federal parliament. Support for both direct legislation and greater grass-roots control was more in evidence among crypto-Liberal and grain grower activists than at the apex of the Progressive organization.

Departures from conventional Canadian democratic practice advocated by crypto-Liberals may have seemed radical to Tories, the Liberal establishment, and the Lords of the Judicial Committee of the Privy Council.[3] These departures did not constitute either a well-developed theoretical or radical alternative when compared to those found in the other three populisms. Crypto-Liberalism did, however, 'stir the pot' and encourage prairie residents to reconsider Canadian democracy seriously. The 1921 election of sixty-five Progressives surprised many westerners, and led them to believe that they could develop improved techniques of popular rule, especially because this election followed on the heels of the UFA victory in a previous Liberal stronghold. However, after 1921 the momentum for exploring new democratic horizons passed quickly to radical democratic and social democratic populists.

Led by H.W. Wood and William Irvine, radical democratic populists pressed the anti-party and class-organizational beliefs of some crypto-Liberal activists into a demanding new mould. This featured the complementary theoretical forms of delegate democracy, group-based citizenship, and group government. The overall framework was shaped by an incisive account of the political party as a failed form of popular-democratic action. The anti-party position of United Farmers organizations in Alberta and Saskatchewan provided a standard of criticism of 'politics as usual' to which all competing and successive populisms had to make at least rhetorical concessions.

The distinctiveness of the UFA argument for popular democracy was their theoretical embrace of the participatory implications of their critique of party. By mixing these with a functionalist theory of social organization and relations and a class-based theory of citizenship, the UFA produced the only explicitly non-parliamentary theory of democratic politics and government to gain widespread acceptance in Canada. As Macpherson demonstrated, the irony of this accomplishment was that it could not be practised in the very province where it had achieved such approval. A theory marrying co-operative political action to pluralist occupational representation and governance could not operate in an environment of party competitiveness, interregional class inequality, and provincial agrarian dominance.

Social democratic populists were committed to extending political democracy into the economic realm. Since they saw more clearly than radical democrats the obstacles to this inherent in capitalism, their proposals were more realistic than those based on the co-operative vision of Henry Wise Wood. However, prairie social democrats did not progress much beyond vague commitments to developing industrial democracy, establishing close relations between co-operatives and the state, or integrating other structures of economic democracy with structures of political democracy. With the notable exception of radical democratic 'hybrids' such as William Irvine, E.A. Partridge, and Robert Gardiner, social democratic populists expressed surprisingly few reservations about the adaptability of parliamentary forms to a system of effective popular democracy.

This caution owed much to the British socialist notion that economic democracy involved equitable distribution of the social product much more than new structures for workers' control. Social democrats were also concerned that prospective supporters of their policies might feel uneasy about striking departures from the traditions of Anglo-Canadian political life. The backlash against radical labour parties in the West just after the Great War had given prairie radicals ample reason for strategic caution.[4]

Prairie social democrats often attacked government by old parties as critically as the UFA, but almost never rejected party government *per se*. Even William Irvine eventually agreed that only a party – albeit popularly based and internally democratic – could mobilize enough of 'the people' to challenge the Liberal-Conservative hegemony. Irvine and most other leading prairie social democrats suspended the problem of creating new forms for democratic action until the new party had achieved national power. If they had novel blueprints for the creation of popular democracy, they were well hidden after 1935. Social democrats' commitments to participatory democracy were complicated by their technocratic orientations.

In plebiscitarian populism, this compromise took an extreme form, as one would expect from the logic of its position on popular democracy. Social Credit promotion of its mass but highly circumscribed movement activity used concepts of citizenship and representation antithetical to those of radical democrats. The Social Credit approach to 'rule by the sovereign people' was informed by a contempt for democratic decision-making within the mass movement, and prescribed that only experts in the mysteries of Social Credit techniques would contribute to public policy. Aberhart deftly mixed religious feelings with carefully reconstituted popular-democratic traditions (of opposition to parties, politicians, and plutocrats) to produce the appearance of a radical critique and a people's movement.

While his appeal spoke to farmers' concerns for security and independence, it tapped the same feelings in a broad cross-section of urban and rural middle-class and working-class Albertans. Aberhart's claim to represent Albertans' general will in 1935 was not entirely specious. Extension of this to claim democratic credentials for his movement – in the spirit of the early UFA, no less – undoubtedly was. He used the 'argument from abundance' to distract attention from such considerations; material plenty could be achieved only if Social Credit solutions were applied.

When combined with the argument that all party governments were servants of financial institutions, Aberhart's attack on the existing regime shifted voter attention even farther away from democratic deficiencies in his movement and theory of representation. No demonstrably successful economic technique existed for solving the paradox of 'poverty in the midst of plenty,' or for ending a patently undemocratic distribution of the economy's benefits and burdens. In the absence of these, Social Credit's plebiscitarian technocracy received a level of support in the previous stronghold of radical democratic populism that stunned the rest of the nation.

Democratic Problems and Technocratic Solutions in Prairie Populism

We saw that William Aberhart's approach to democratic public life employed the orthodox Douglasite distinction between results, which the people demanded, and methods, which the experts chose and implemented. The premier partially usurped the role of expert for himself and several other trusted colleagues, but otherwise clearly intended the technocratic imperative to regulate division of labour between the people and the state.

The purposes of popular-democratic action were to be so circumscribed and manipulated that in theory no tension existed in the relation of democracy to technocracy or people to experts. The purported existence of a scientific economic doctrine assured that a benign technocratic state would deliver results willed by the people. Once the appropriate political vehicle had been parked in the stalls of government, the job of creating the new order of plenty was above politics. If the people were guaranteed abundance, they would not wish to meddle in a political, unscientific, even irrational, way with the scientific designers of economic freedom and security.

Social Credit's negative conception of the state shared much with other prairie populisms. The state had been the instrument of privileged business interests – financial interests, to be precise. In its Social Credit incarnation, the state would regulate distribution of credit and the price system to provide all with an equitable share of the 'cultural heritage.' Like that of other prairie populisms, the Social Credit agenda for state action was considerably more interventionist (on the side of 'the people,' and against business élites outside the prairie community) than that of contemporary Liberals and Conservatives. But unlike other prairie populists, Social Crediters argued that the benefits of state intervention were to come in the form of annual dividends, 'just prices,' and essentially free credit. While there was to be a redistribution of power between creditor and debtor interests, capitalism was to be put right, not rejected by the Social Credit state. Unaccustomed to unsympathetic treatment by a Canadian government, the Canadian business establishment none the less responded with an indignant roar to Aberhart's mildly confiscatory debt legislation.

Finally, we should recall that Social Crediters gave rhetorical support to the idea of a decentralized state system. The campaign against a stronger federal government was initiated following reservation, disallowance, and Supreme Court *ultra vires* rulings on Social Credit legislation. It was accompanied by an increasingly shrill argument about a parallel, government-supported campaign of financial centralization. In practice, however, Aberhart's government and movement featured unambiguously centralist approaches to decision-making. These were more consistent with the plebiscitarian and technocratic logics that informed Social Credit political strategy and state action.

Social democratic populist thinking on the state contained an underlying tension between technocratic and participatory democratic orientations. Such a tension is unavoidable for any political body recognizing the necessity of forceful state intervention and long-range state planning for the success of reform objectives. However, I argued that social democratic populists' 'blind spot' in this area reveals both the shortcomings and relative caution displayed in their conception of participatory democracy. One sees another instance of the more general dilemma faced by democratic socialists in working out a strategy of transition to a democratic social order.

The prairie social democratic understanding and critique of the existing state was not particularly novel by socialist standards. Canadian political history was seen as a story of close relationships between old parties and party governments, senior levels of the civil service, and the central Canadian capitalist class. Social democrats thus perceived the Canadian state as a class state, operating to the continuing disadvantage of ordinary people in town and country. The state could be transformed into an agency of social progress and equality if enough people voted for a socialist-oriented people's party.

At such a time, the state could move rapidly to organize an economy based on social ownership, social planning, and 'production for use, not profit.' In the interim, state intervention would reveal the benefits of planning and public ownership. As governments responded to the growing political strength of the social democratic political organizations, social-welfare benefits to lower- and middle-income citizens would increase. Canadian social democrats were so hopeful of an imminent political breakthrough that this interim scenario was not seriously re-examined from the late 1920s to the early 1940s.

Their concept of social planning was the unrecognized fly in the ointment of expanded democracy prescribed by prairie social democrats. Social planning could mean planning for society, or planning by and for society. While its context usually implied the latter, well-developed accounts of what this democratic planning would entail are rare in prairie social democratic literature. Instead, one finds assertions about the more democratic, or equitable, outcomes to result from well planned production, and no acknowledgment of the damage that Fabian paternalism might do to their movement's dynamism and to development of a more democratic culture.

It is also useful to relate the scientistic certainty of this Fabian perspective to the triumph of secularist social science over traditional theology in the Canadian Protestant community.[5] In the prairies, as elsewhere, this triumph transferred the burden of salvation from scriptural interpretation to social planning. It seemed that as the need for salvation increased, conflicts between planning and participation were less readily recognized.

In addition, and consistent with the above myopia, social democrats' discussion of planning was pervaded by an unrealistic sense of the harmony of social interests. They seemed to assume that once the right political forces acquired state power, serious conflicts between state planners' decisions and the people's wishes would virtually disappear. Informed by social and technical scientists, the state could solve those disputes that did arise. From this perspective, distinctly political disagreements within the population would possess little legitimacy in relation to the findings of planners.

This perspective posed no problem for Social Crediters, but social democrats should have found it unsettling. Yet social democrats seemed unwilling to admit this was a potential problem requiring careful consideration of how to make planning democratic and well-integrated into democratic relations within and between different industrial sectors.

Some rural social democrats contended that agrarian co-operatives could serve as a model for extending and integrating economic and political democracy. We ought not to shrug this off as a *petit bourgeois* delusion. But the co-operative experience, while in some ways instructive for these purposes, could not carry so heavy a burden. To my knowledge, the only attempt to elaborate on this suggestion came from E.A. Partridge in *A War on Poverty*. This explicitly utopian tract introduced so many additional ideological and theoretical foundations for the co-operative democracy of 'Coalsamao' that it likely left most prairie readers more confused than enlightened.[6]

As in the Social Credit case, the assumption of potential abundance strengthened the social democratic predilection to entrust public policy matters to planners and 'experts.' Social democrats believed scientists could design an economic system that would eliminate scarcity. This enhanced their belief that many bases of social conflict would disappear in the plentiful future, even though they presently required democratic resolution by the interests involved.

The expectation that scientists could perfect 'rational' forms of economic organization drew attention away from the need for democratic, participatory forms of social conflict resolution.

The tension between democratic and technocratic techniques thus showed up as much in what social democrats left unexplored as in their proposals. One cannot deny that their vision of an equity-producing state and economic democracy was challenging in its day. Yet by the standards established in their critique of existing governments and structures of power, the same social democratic vision left technocratic options too large an opening. This becomes especially clear if one notices their acceptance of proposals for substantial centralization of the federal system.

Some argue that technocracy is a uniquely *petit bourgeois* ideological excrescence because its approach to social policy questions obscures perception of classes. It is more realistic to acknowledge the integration of technocratic perspectives into western industrial liberalisms, to the point that technocracy now works more powerfully in the service of all dominant ideologies. However, during the Depression years, technocratic proposals often seemed to pose a serious threat to the existing system of class power. This was especially true for many political activists and intellectuals concerned with people's suffering in what seemed to be a disintegrating economic order. Social democratic populists found value in technocratic critiques of capitalism, but most shrank from its political implications when these directly contradicted the social democratic vision.

UFA theorists Henry Wise Wood and William Irvine provided the most revealing indications of radical democratic thinking on the state and the role of experts therein. Both argued that the Canadian state was flawed because it had served the interests of plutocracy and autocracy. Both argued that this was so because inherently undemocratic political parties acted as intermediaries for 'the interests' in their direction of the state. Minor reforms to these parties would not solve the problem; a whole new structure and process of representation and governance was required to democratize the state.

Radical democratic populism insisted that delegate democracy would have to link a pluralism of organized economic group interests to a co-operative, group government. To become democratic, the state would have to transform at least its legislative branch into an extension of the functional pluralism of occupational groups. Democratic citizenship would be channelled from economic activity directly into legislative activity, rather than have its potential for well-informed, creative, and co-operative contributions scuttled by the medium of party activity. The state would thus become amenable to democratic control, and less expressive of its essence as a 'false divinity,' as Wood called it.

Irvine's British socialist background left him less suspicious of the state *per se* than Wood, who was raised in Missouri. But from 1916 to 1935, Irvine still maintained that democratic governments must reject partisanship for occupational organization and representation. Irvine's extensive rationale for group government identified socio-economic pre-conditions of the co-operative commonwealth and its group government. While Wood spoke vaguely about the coming victory of democracy over autocracy, Irvine spoke plainly about eliminating the capitalist basis of economic and social life. Neither Irvine nor Wood spoke clearly about extending the decentralist logic of their delegate-group system to the division of powers within the federal system.[7]

With its emphasis on highly organized and intensively democratic control over the state, technocratic orientations in radical democratic populism are hard to find. A plausible case for their existence hinges on appreciating the importance of radical democratic claims about the existence of objective social laws, the rationality-enhancing powers of co-operation, and the ability of group representatives to resolve conflicts in a way that virtually transcends politics. The character of state decision-making implied by these claims created a theoretical opening for an unusual technocratic dimension within the radical democratic future, rather than the existence of blatantly technocratic proposals.

Briefly, my argument is as follows. Wood, Irvine, and other UFA speakers often referred to 'social laws,' especially in their discussion of the historical dialectic between competition and co-operation. These social laws were often granted the epistemological status of natural laws, which was an old Anglo-American radical tradition.[8] Such status was also encouraged by the recent secularization of Protestantism; some basis for cosmological certainty was still required. Natural laws provided a solid foundation for the creation and operation of democratic social institutions and relations. Successful decision-making within the polity required a development of the 'highest intelligence of citizenship' in occupational group organizations, and elimination of exploitive relations between such groups. From this framework a new rationality of enlightened self-interest could emerge, based on intergroup (and intragroup) co-operation.

This natural-law–guided system of group representation would feature policy deliberations that were above politics. Each group's representatives would have an expert yet practically based knowledge that came from the organization of well-defined economic interests. Together in legislative deliberation, groups' representatives would be aided by the higher rationality of co-operation. For lack of a better phrase, this whole process involved a kind of 'popular technocracy,' in the sense that group representatives were responsively connected to their group bases, while conducting their deliberations without political or ideological motivation (in the pejorative senses then ascribed to the terms).

A scientifically ordered democratic process would allow group representatives to transcend a thoroughly disgraced political realm. Representatives were to be democratically sanctioned by both a delegate process and the natural laws that legitimized this process. Once they entered legislative chambers, they would cast lowly politics aside and act as co-operative technocrats. As we saw, Irvine went even farther, proposing a primary role for government social scientists in the policy process. They would gather 'the facts,' and 'let the facts speak for themselves' in passing their policy recommendations to group representatives for approval. Wood had reason to be cautious in endorsing *Co-operative Government*, Irvine's forum for these ideas.

The tension between technocratic and democratic values emerges in the assumption that a democratic system can be so scientifically designed and operated that conflicts could be virtually eliminated from its highest levels. This assumption, in turn, depends on the idea that the basis for conflict between various social interests ('classes') could be largely eliminated by the spirit and practice of co-operation.

The major difficulty with this line of reasoning was that radical democrats simultaneously argued that expression of distinct class interests was so natural as to be entrenched in representative structures. Who, then, would co-ordinate the co-operation and harmony forecast by Wood and other radical democrats? No answer was directly offered, although Irvine's account of the role of social scientists in discovering solutions suggests a partially technocratic resolution to this knotty problem.

Another problem arises when one considers that insisting on 'science' and 'natural laws' as the standards of public policy choice would eventually stifle the politics of educational and effective mass participation. Here radical democrat populists exposed themselves to dilemmas similar to those of social democratic populists. But UFA theory built in a crucial safeguard that prairie social democrats chose not to pursue or develop an equivalent for. Radical democrats insisted on the importance of structured, non-partisan, producer group representation in processes of political mobilization and policy deliberation. To them, this was the only guarantee of responsiveness to and democratic cultural growth within people's organizations allied with the new state.

The technocratic impulse and concept of the state in crypto-Liberalism can be presented simply. Most crypto-Liberal leaders approached these questions in ways reminiscent of contemporary Canadian liberalism (excluding curiosities such as Mackenzie King's 'liberal corporatism').[9] Rank-and-file Progressives tended to stray farther from this safe ground, but were either too suspicious of major deviations from parliamentary government, or too suspicious of state ownership, to accept radical democratic or social democratic views of the state.

Crypto-Liberals tended to see the Canadian federal state as an arbiter between economic interests. The state that showed anti-agrarian biases through the National Policy could become responsive to their interests without major institutional or social-structural reform. Even crypto-Liberal support for direct legislation reflected less alienation from prevailing structures of power than other prairie populisms. To some degree, this was the result of the entente between Manitoba and Saskatchewan grain growers' organizations and Liberal governments. We saw how these administrations emphasized 'sound business administration' in representing themselves to the public. 'Brackenism' characteristically expressed technocratic values of North American governmental practice. Following the prevailing norms in this regard obviated a good part of the rationale for popular democracy, with the result that crypto-Liberal provincial governments clashed with the grain-grower campaign for a more participatory style of public policy determination.

The crypto-Liberal rank and file also differed from their leadership over the scope of state intervention in the economy. Whereas Crerar and other national leaders were only slightly reconstructed free-trade liberals, grain grower rank and file urged substantial state intervention to adjust the terms of trade more in their favour. Crypto-Liberal provincial administrations were thus pressured into legislating for the defence of co-operating grain growers. Schools, highways, public utilities, and other services for rural populations also emerged quickly. Organized grain growers demanded and received special treatment from prairie provincial governments. An activist state that reduced the imbalance between eastern business and western farmer did not offend these crypto-Liberals. Prairie farmers have continued to ask for this kind of provincial assistance ever since, regardless of their political affiliations or the party flags flown in provincial capitals.

The continuity in provincial government responses to agrarian demands for assistance has led some commentators to suggest that self-proclaimed political and ideological differences among agrarian organizations were largely superficial.[10] Our review of populist perspectives on the state and technocratic practices should demonstrate that significant differences did exist in this aspect of prairie democratic thought. One finds considerably greater variation within the prairie populist spectrum on such basic political questions than is available in current political dialogue between Canadian political parties. It seems that the *petit bourgeois* political imagination of the prairie past is considerably more fertile than that of present Canadian society. It is no coincidence that current public discussion of the state's role in Canada takes place without reference to distinctive paradigms of democratic political life.

One final comment on prairie populist views of the state is appropriate. With the exception of Alberta Social Credit, prairie populists engaged in remarkably little discussion of the federal division of powers. It is true that prairie governments and populist leaders lobbied for transfer of powers over national resources. So, however, did the Conservative parties in each province. The CCF in all three prairie provinces followed the national organization's line on the need to grant many provincial powers over economic activity to the federal government, but this was not a source of contention between the provincial populist competitors outside Alberta.

This relative inattention to matters of federalism is interesting for two reasons. One is the populists' simultaneous commitment to decentralization of political and economic power, which would now appear strangely inconsistent to most Canadians. The other basis of curiosity is the agitation for a rearrangement of powers and institutions within the federal system that has characterized western Canadian politics since the early 1960s. Westerners still keep a high national profile expressing dissatisfaction with the political system's central Canadian bias.

However, the stated objectives and underlying agendas of the two eras' complaints are in striking contrast. Current western expressions of dissatisfaction with the political system are dominated by power-jealous provincial regimes, and virtually never go beyond the question of redistribution of powers among governments within this system. What is missing is that to which all prairie populists once devoted so much attention: commitments to redistribute power from the corporate/state power nexus to 'the people.'

With the exception of Social Credit, prairie populists were not as concerned with which level of government formally held power in particular areas of legislation as they were with how all governments could be made more responsive to their citizens. They were thus not interested in debating new roles for the senate, or constitutional amending formulas, or federal-provincial conferences and agencies to reduce intergovernmental conflict. They were concerned with refashioning relations between organized civil society and the state so that social and economic conflicts harming 'the people' could be drastically reduced. They may have been naïve in devoting so little attention to the intricacies of the federal system, but there was limited reform energy available. The prairie populist emphasis on rearranging structures and relations of power in the national political economy demonstrated their concern for democratizing Canadian society in ways that current federal-provincial wrangling has never intended.

Co-operation and Prairie Populism

Virtually all politicians pledge to achieve greater co-operation between social groups, economic classes and organizations, regions, and governments. Spurious political copyrights on the idea of co-operation are as ubiquitous as patronage. But prairie populisms were the only significant Canadian political discourses to place co-operation at the centre of their appeals. The exception to this was the plebiscitarian populism of Social Credit, although even it attempted to trade on co-operation's positive connotations.

Beginning with the radical democratic populist case, we can recall just how central the theory and practice of co-operation was to prairie politics. For Henry Wise Wood, co-operation ('the true social law') would become the directing principle in all aspects of economic, political, and social life. This meant that the farmers' experience in producers' co-operatives should be extended to and integrated with agrarian political activity. Beyond such integration, farmers' co-operative experience should be adapted to the organized economic and political life of all producers' groups, and then to the operation of the political system – with its pinnacle in group government. Wood's preferred political strategy, however, involved little practical co-operation between organized producers before their combined forces won a decisive victory over the forces of autocracy.

Wood and other radical democratic leaders stressed the inseparability of co-operative economic and political activity. The UFA organization had designed its internal operations to ensure this close integration of democratic practice. For rank-and-file agrarian radical democrats, then, the virtues of parallel political and economic co-operation, and the ethic of co-operation, had been proved in the life of their movement. The movement culture's co-operative backbone was not an artificial implant, but a carefully nurtured part of its anatomy. The radical democratic critique of economic and political competition had its natural complement in movement activities merging economic and political concerns.

William Irvine was the best-known hybrid radical-social democratic populist, advocating an explicitly anti-capitalist co-operative political strategy for agrarians and other labouring classes. An interventionist state would establish wide-ranging public ownership outside of farming, as a necessary support for and complement to the extension of co-operative 'social ownership' in agricultural and several other sectors of the Canadian economy. In each case, such proposals were made within the context of support for intra-organizational democracy and eventual group government, and were accompanied by a blistering critique of 'partyism.' Principled advocacy of these basics made Irvine and his fellows more than social democrats *manqué*. Their differences with Wood involved extension of the logic of co-operation, so as to defeat the combined forces of capitalism and achieve the co-operative commonwealth.

Regardless of how sceptical one might be about applying the 'rationality of co-operation' to government operations, the group government scheme demonstrates that radical democratic populism was thoroughly committed to modelling political and social relations in accordance with the principles of co-operation. William Irvine's claim that 'the key to the political philosophy of the United Farmers is co-operation' was not just rhetoric.

Social democratic populists also featured co-operation in their political discourse. Their logic of co-operation did not entail a reconstituted legislative assembly, however; nor did it preclude rhetorical and practical attempts to organize 'the people' for political action across class boundaries. Finding no ineradicable flaw in the structures of party and legislative representation, they saw no reason to segregate class political activity as a means of ensuring full development of 'citizenship strength.' Thus social democratic populists advocated close political co-operation among all elements of 'the people' as the most effective way of countering old-party and business power.

The political vehicles of social democratic populism were sociologically dependent on agrarian co-operatives and their 'interest-group' homes. With the indigenous prairie institutions implicated in the new social democratic federation, socialism and co-operation were, of necessity, defined in terms of each other. This reciprocal definition was manifested in portrayals of co-operatives as exemplary forms of democratic 'social ownership.' Social ownership featuring state control would enable the fullest extension and development of co-operative ownership. Promotion of collective control mixed with private ownership was crucial to social democracy's appeal in the prairie community. Without this accommodation to popular-democratic traditions, a challenge to prairie liberalism would have been inconceivable.

Finally, we should recall the role of the co-operative ethic in prairie social democratic ideology. Even those not known as social gospellers used social-gospel language to demonstrate the moral deficiencies of the established order, and to link CCF programs to the new social order. They presented the ethic of co-operation in terms of a higher dimension of human nature and the long-awaited brotherhood of man. This social-philosophical glue bound together short- and long-run proposals.

Social democratic populists may have appeared sanctimonious in arguing that only their political package took seriously the social prerequisites of a truly co-operative society. When combined with pragmatic appeals for state aid to beleaguered grain growers, this approach none the less expanded the social democratic constituency beyond those committed to a socialist vision. In Saskatchewan, where the United Farmers had eschewed direct political action provincially since 1921, social democrats were able to claim the political copyright to the co-operative ethic within a decade of their first electoral contest.

The rhetoric of co-operation was considerably milder and more narrowly focused in crypto-Liberal discourse than in that of its radical democratic and social democratic competitors. One would expect that the less penetrating critique and less demanding vision of crypto-Liberalism would incorporate less of the democratic logic of co-operative enterprise. As past or present executives in grain growers' associations, crypto-Liberal leaders could be counted on to lobby for their members' specifically commercial interests. Despite *The Grain Growers' Guide*'s espousal of the 'co-operative way,' crypto-Liberal leaders' promotion of producer co-operatives implied few major departures from prevailing economic and political practice, as is clear from the careers of Thomas Crerar, John Bracken, and Jimmy Gardiner.

The major departure originated at the grass-roots level, and involved an enhanced suspicion of partisan politics imparted by the co-operative tradition to prairie producers. This suspicion was translated into support for direct-legislation statutes, a call to 'clean up' party financing and patronage practices, and a temporary foray into 'independent politics' via the Progressive organization. Collectively, these developments helped to shape an environment in which unorthodox prairie populisms could emerge and contend. At the same time, the crypto-Liberal failure to extend the co-operative promise beyond interest-group politics and regionalist economics did much to open the door for other populisms I have discussed.

Aberhart's plebiscitarian populism was alone among prairie populisms in attempting to remove the co-operative vision from the centre of political discussion. This attempt was not made by directly attacking Henry Wise Wood's co-operative humanism, or by legislatively restricting the accomplishments of co-operative enterprises such as the Alberta Wheat Pool. Instead, Aberhart virtually ignored these legacies of the co-operative experience and substituted new concepts of co-operation.

In the economic sphere, co-operation became a vague synonym for the interdependent activity that had produced the cultural heritage and a technical potential for abundance. Having proved the existence of this plenty, Social

Credit economic analysis required a complementary political co-operation. Co-operation in the political sphere was simply a part of the correct division of labour between the people and the experts; it would allow Social Credit experts to distribute benefits to all citizens. The people – all those who had been victims of the financial interests – were instructed to ignore their social differences, and join together to demand the results that they all wanted: security, freedom, and leisure in abundance. A united will could allow the experts to deliver these results to the people.

Past this electoral co-operation the combined political efforts of citizens must not go, lest the balance be upset between people's and experts' contributions to the new era of plenty. Co-operation in consideration of 'methods' to achieve abundance was explicitly rejected in the Social Credit argument. In short, co-operation in the Social Credit discourse represented a clear shift away from the participatory dimension of prairie co-operation. The superficially extensive popular involvement in the Social Credit movement, masterfully organized and presented by Aberhart, disguised rejection of the co-operative movement's democratic legacy. The irony of this happening where co-operation had been the byword of the UFA's participatory democracy is obvious.

Social Credit's rhetorical manipulation of co-operation raises the question of whether co-operation was merely ideological obfuscation in the other prairie populisms. Was co-operation simply an attractive way of disguising *petit bourgeois* grain growers' pursuit of maximum profits? Was it based on a delusory belief that the economy could be made satisfactorily equitable while still operating on the foundations of liberally conceived private property? Was it a form of special pleading for those who refused to give up the privileges of private ownership while advocating state-controlled 'social ownership' in other economic sectors? Did its political extensions rest on a naïve understanding of class conflict and the power of capital?

There is no one answer to these questions applicable to all prairie populisms, which suggests why we should locate their understandings of co-operation in a larger framework of democratic thought. We can best respond to these questions in considering what each populism comprehended as the good society.

The Good Societies of Prairie Populism

Writers as different as Walicki and Hofstader[11] have argued that populism is characterized by chiliastic longing for a simple society that somehow supersedes modern industrialism while retaining pre-capitalist moral codes. Such ahistorical utopias merely confirm the analytical naïveté and ultimately regressive essence of a political anomaly unable to come to terms with either modern liberalism or modern socialism. Populism is thus a retreat from reality at three levels: it romanticizes the past, misconstrues the present, and projects hopelessly idealized social scenarios into the future.

To what degree were each of the prairie populisms guilty of such charges in their portrayal of 'the good society'? The answers we provide will build on the other dimensions of populist democratic thought already reviewed, and will help us to see that Canadian prairie populisms deserve no more ridicule on these grounds than the more mainstream political ideologies of their era. In some cases, prairie populists were surprisingly prescient of post-1960 participatory democratic thought.

The crypto-Liberal utopian vision was the most mundane and uninspiring of all prairie populisms. Most thoroughly affected by central Canadian traditions, it was thus radicalized least by the currents of unorthodoxy that ran across western Canada. The 'received culture' of Anglo-American politics was most restrictive upon populist visions in the crypto-Liberalism of Manitoba, as the figures of Crerar and Dafoe demonstrated. They viewed Progressive politics as an exercise in modified interest-group pressure on a reformable Liberal party. This precluded a markedly different vision of the future than that of their temporarily estranged Liberal associates. Still, crypto-Liberal future hopes were not simply those of displaced Liberals – Grit or otherwise. Geographical location, regional economic and social structure, and various tides of reform sentiment contributed to a distinction between even the mildest of populists and their orthodox political cousins.

Geography and an agricultural environment encouraged a marked physiocratic orientation among crypto-Liberals, and led to what Gerald Friesen has called 'the idea of a western mission.'[12] Agricultural production was not just the most important aspect of the Canadian economy, it was also the most 'natural' calling – especially when contrasted with 'artificial' industries protected by the hated tariff. In the good society, the state and its citizens would duly recognize this fact, by allowing the morally superior culture of honest agrarian communities to guide the nation past the distractions and inevitable corruptions of urban culture. The Arcadian idyll was not defiantly promoted, but it became implicit in the popular-democratic tradition contrasting debased eastern city life with a more egalitarian, class-harmonious prairie community.[13] This tradition was appropriated by all subsequent or contending prairie populisms.

Crypto-Liberals also believed that national acceptance of the superiority of the farm-centred economy would reduce class conflict. To some extent, this belief was predicated on the idea that fewer protected industries would mean fewer labour-capital disputes and less antagonism between Canadian manufacturers and western grain producers. Crypto-Liberalism was in numerous company articulating its conflict-reducing intentions and nostrums, but of all prairie populisms, it was least clear or iconoclastic in its account of how such a desirable outcome could be achieved.

To make their conflict-reducing intentions seem more plausible, crypto-Liberals proposed extension of co-operatives associated with the agricultural sector.[14] Co-operation between different economic and social groups in Canada was supported in *The Grain Growers' Guide*, crypto-Liberal leaders' speeches, and grain growers' association conventions. However, practical proposals or application of this ideal beyond agriculture were rare. Participation in co-operative enterprises by grain growers probably enhanced the average farmer's sense of his distinctive class interest. Partly because their cause with respect to central Canadian business and parties was defensible, we are still not inclined to see co-operative enterprises as covers for narrowly conceived economic interest. Co-operatives trained members for a participatory culture, and educated their participants on wider questions of social justice, women's rights, and even international affairs.

Insofar as they were institutions of agrarian self-defence, prairie co-operatives were unavoidably vehicles of class self-interest, which had to accept most of the terms of the capitalist market competition. Having said this, however, we must add that this is an equally appropriate characterization of this era's Trades and Labour Congress. There is nothing distinctively *petit bourgeois* about organizing to protect class members' interests against the power of capital. What can be said of the crypto-Liberal approach to co-operatives and co-operation, however, is that the rhetoric of co-operation was not backed up by an account of how defensive, class-based co-operative activity could be extended to inter-class co-operation.

A final reminder on the crypto-Liberal vision of the good society concerns its anti-political tendencies and consequent view of the future democratic state. Crypto-Liberals' support for direct legislation expressed their suspicion of 'politics' and politicians. Administration of the National Policy by both major parties had engendered high levels of distrust concerning conventional politics and state action. Many prairie farmers with previously Liberal affections consequently insisted on their own locally controlled farmer candidates and platforms. Many crypto-Liberal farmers redirected their political energies into the co-operative movement after the 1921 Progressive electoral achievement.

The point is that the cumulative scepticism concerning traditional politics and the national government strengthened an anti-statist dimension within the crypto-Liberal vision of the good society. The agrarian tendency to exaggerate both the virtues and potential independence of their rural communities accentuated their anti-political vision. And while these crypto-Liberals had identified flaws in the existing market, many retained a residual nineteenth-century liberal faith in its magic. If the current market was not equitable because it had been tampered with by a state too solicitous of business interests, then the solution would be to remove state protection for these interests and let the 'natural' economy re-establish itself. In the short term the state had to be somewhat interventionist to remove government-fostered privilege; in the long term, such intervention would not be necessary.

Crypto-Liberalism extended a moderate critique of the existing order into a rather timid vision of the future. Guided by men such as Crerar, Dunning, and Dafoe, crypto-Liberals were faithful to the Liberal tradition of incrementalism. For those more dissatisfied with the pace of social change, other prairie populisms had something to offer.

UFA conventions and legislators joined Progressives and prairie Liberals in supporting a wide range of specific legislative acts. But radical democratic populism was driven by a utopian vision that immediately distanced it from Liberal and crypto-Liberal orthodoxies. In fact, one might complain that Henry Wise Wood's invocation of the good society was too compelling. It distracted UFA activists from considering existing economic obstacles in strategies for transition to the good society.

Radical democrats joined social democrats in calling the good society by a long-hallowed name in British and American left-wing circles: the co-operative commonwealth. Prairie radical democrats gave the co-operative commonwealth a physiocratic construction, for the same reasons the crypto-Liberal vision did. Following Macpherson, we might also add that H.W. Wood imposed an agrarian perspective on the social conflicts preceding the co-operative commonwealth. Thus most radical democratic populists failed to see that their experience in the political economy of contemporary capitalism was not characteristic of other economic classes, and was, in any case, not so independent of this political economy's conflicts as they believed.[15] These misperceptions had less impact on the analysis and prescriptions of left-wing radical democratic populists. Yet even they assumed that the good society would reserve a special place for agrarians and their co-operatives.

The radical democratic commonwealth was to incorporate non-exploitive economic class relations with mutually reinforcing political co-operation. Much more was said about the necessary conditions of intraclass political co-operation than of economic co-operation. Radical democrats were thus insufficiently attentive to the features of the capitalist economy that prevent non-exploitive economic co-operation. William Irvine was less guilty than Henry Wise Wood in this regard. Their utopian visions each contended that non-partisan, occupationally based participatory democracy and neutralizing the power of 'plutocracy' were minimum pre-conditions of the co-operative commonwealth. The genius of the UFA movement was that its internal operations were structured to demonstrate to members the value of their participatory goals. Frustrated in realizing other aspects of their vision, committed radical democrats could still see this substantial advance towards their good society.

The social democratic co-operative commonwealth shared much with the UFA's. Eliminating class exploitation, ending domination of the state by business classes, and creating a political framework for true popular democracy were thus high on the long-term agenda. So was achieving a mutually beneficial co-operation between economic groups, and a strong, semi-autonomous agricultural sector. However, social democrats parted company with radical democrats over crucial elements of their utopian visions.

Not surprisingly, most of these differences stemmed from social democratic perceptions of peculiarly capitalist obstacles to true democracy. This perception, in turn, led social democrats to contend that not just organized democratic action but also substantial state intervention, planning, and ownership were key solutions to problems separating prairie people from a democratic future. Social ownership and popular democracy could not fulfil their promise unless the state structured economic life.

Social democrats contended that economic equality was as much a part of the democratic goal as popular self-government. In fact, they were willing to emphasize 'material democracy' more in the short to medium term, hoping it would facilitate a more extensive political democracy in the longer run. This meant that the state, through its corps of benevolent social scientists and planners, had a heavy democracy-producing burden. Thus emerged a technocratic dimension in the social democratic strategy for fostering progress and abundance. Participatory democracy was by no means rejected, least of all within the movement organizations. In retrospect, we must say that it was rather sparsely conceived and related to proposed activities of the equity-oriented state.

Co-operation was none the less granted a privileged position in the social democratic good society. Political co-operation between those who rendered a legitimate service to the community was presented as the only way to turn society around. This was illustrated in a name: the Co-operative Commonwealth Federation. Replacing capitalist ownership in the major sectors of the economy with social ownership and planning would produce fertile Canadian ground for economic co-operation.

Such a transformation was not to require state ownership of farms. Co-operative organizations of prairie farmers would instead perfect their own form of social ownership. To social democrats on the prairies, the prevailing agricultural ownership was not capitalist, and was certainly not incompatible with state ownership in other sectors. The state might assist impoverished farmers by buying their land and then leasing it to them in perpetuity (as in the 'use-lease' schemes of the early 1930s). The state might also provide cheap credit, subsidize transportation for agricultural commodities, or assist in grain marketing and setting of 'parity prices.' Social democrats saw no need for the state to appropriate all agricultural land, and employ farmers as wage labourers, to achieve social control over agricultural production.

Did prairie social democrats' support for private property in the agricultural sector mean they were not socialists? Did their classification of co-operation as social ownership simply express a *petit bourgeois* outlook and agenda? The answers to these questions obviously depend on one's criteria for socialism. In chapter 4, I argued that if one accepts reasonably broad criteria, CCF support for the family farm cannot be the sole basis for an affirmative answer to these questions.

Briefly, two considerations seem crucial. First, consistency with prairie farmers' class interests and past traditions does not mean that these proposals are compatible only with their class perspective or interests. It is by no means obvious that small-scale private ownership of agricultural 'enterprises' entails a transfer of power[16] to their operators from other producing groups, especially if the planning and conduct of other economic sectors is democratic. When accompanied by co-operative institutions, equitable treatment by the state, limits to land acquisition by families, and a social democratic political culture, the agricultural sector need not generate excessively individualist, anti-social orientations among farmers. In short, private ownership of agricultural land and capital can be made compatible with an otherwise largely socialist economy. Those who follow Lenin in denying this possibility conceive too rigidly of a socialist economy, and tend to be less than honest about the experiences of many developing countries. I would also argue that they are also too pessimistic about the impact that a democratically structured national economy, and a democratic political culture, might have on an agrarian 'co-operative' economy.

The other point is simpler and less contentious. The successes and failures of political organizations in western democracies have indicated the importance of accommodating a class-based appeal to popular-democratic traditions of the polity. Political parties and populist movements are not shackled by these traditions; flexibility is usually assured, in fact, because traditions can be chosen, reconstituted, or embellished to support a current program and critique.

But concessions must be made, even if highly selectively and misleadingly. Thus neo-conservatives promise to retain the 'entitlements' of social-welfare programs for the 'truly needy,' and argue that tax reductions for the wealthy generate 'opportunity' and freedom for all. Whether the party faithful or leaders believe this scenario is almost beside the point. Successful contact with key popular democratic traditions of America has been made.

To return to more relevant ground: in modern competitive polities, all viable parties of the left have conceded something to established values and popular traditions. This is especially evident in countries with a large agricultural sector. In developing countries, the call is for land reform, in language that appeals to landless peasants. In industrialized countries, viable socialist parties offer a variety of farm-support programs, none of which are made contingent on eventual state ownership of farms. This is true of the Communist parties in Italy and France since the Second World War, all European social democratic parties, the British Labour Party since the early 1920s, the pre–Second World War Socialist Party of America, and, of course, the CCF in Canada.

Shall we call all of these parties' socialist credentials into question because they failed to insist on Soviet-style agriculture? Or should we recognize accommodations to prevailing cultural traditions and agrarian sentiments as the *sine qua non* of an appeal extending beyond militant labour? To the extent that each of these parties appeals across class boundaries to build an anti-capitalist coalition, it employs a populist technique. This does not mean that the parties in question abandoned their long-term goals of socialist democracy (however they understood it). They were showing that they took seriously one of the simpler rules for building towards power. This may have 'corrupted' or liberalized them – but what was the alternative? If alternatives did exist, they remained hidden in theoretical disputes beyond the margin of political relevance.

None of this should be taken to mean that prairie social democrats supported the family farm and defended co-operatives only because they smelled electoral success. The vast majority did believe what they said, and were more inclined to be suspicious of state ownership than their LSR colleagues in the CCF.

But they were not archetypal *petit bourgeois* agrarians, to be lumped together with crypto-Liberals and most Social Credit supporters. By reasonable standards – those sensitive to the history of North American politics and culture – CCF activists were socialists and populists, as reflected in their vision of the future. The social democratic critique of class-based exploitation in capitalist society made theirs the most radical of all prairie populist utopian visions.

The plebiscitarian Social Credit view of the good society shared some and rejected other elements of competing populist visions. Aberhart made some effort to link a physiocratic view of the economy to flaws in the existing credit system, but he seldom presented the Social Credit League as a farmers' political organization intending to create an agriculturally centred economy. The Social Credit constituency included all in need of credit, dividends, just prices, and security. Farmers needed no special assurances because they would require no special advantages once dividends and just prices were established.

Social Credit joined other populisms in promising a future free from class conflict and exploitation, where all citizens would co-operate to generate material abundance from the 'industrial machine.' We saw that the burden of this whole edifice of harmonious economic and social relations rested on three pillars: direction and administration of social credit mechanisms by experts, a minimum of popular participation in important public decisions, and transformation of potential abundance into actual abundance.

The first pillar shared a kind of technocracy with social democratic populism, but was far more mystically rendered, and far less amenable to contributions by organized economic groups. With its vision of a passive citizenship responding to plebiscitarian mobilization, the Social Credit utopia was easily distinguished from even the crypto-Liberal view. Aberhart and his associates were more explicitly optimistic about abundance than all but a handful of social democratic dreamers. Social Crediters also allowed the prospect of abundance to cut more substance away from the practice of popular democracy, in the present and the future, than any prairie socialist came close to contemplating.

The vacuity of public life contemplated for the average citizen in this vision indicates that Social Credit ideology also exceeded other prairie populisms in projecting frustrations with current politics into an antipathy towards 'politics.' The curious thing was that even though this attitude stemmed from a deep suspicion of the state, the Social Credit corollary to a public realm devoid of meaningful citizen activity was a powerful technocracy in the future. The experts' power was not to be 'political,' however; according to Aberhart and others, such power was to be an automatically benevolent, life-simplifying power of applied Social Credit science. If this suprapolitical power could be exercised, popular democracy concerned with anything but reciting 'results' was gratuitous in the land of plenty, and counter-productive during the voyage to this land.

One final comparison should be drawn in fairness to the reputations of Social Credit supporters. Especially from 1933 to 1935, Aberhart devoted considerable attention to the equitable effects of his scheme. In his 1935 campaign, he implied a kind of social-welfare program to save the people from ruthless creditors and their ilk. If one also considers Aberhart's attacks on financial interests, and his insistence that all citizens would benefit equally from the proposed system of dividends, just prices, and cheap credit, it is clear that he convincingly promised imminent social justice to Albertans. In doing so he joined other prairie populists, even though his explanation of who would pay the price of this justice, and how, left much to be desired.

Such a deficiency did not bother most Alberta voters. They had liked underconsumptionist explanations of poverty in the midst of plenty well before Aberhart offered his mixture of Major Douglas and evangelical religion. They saw no good reason to believe that Aberhart's prescription for social justice in the good society was not as good as or better than others. It was, after all, guaranteed not to upset the ailing social body, and claimed to pose no threat to dreams of security with independence. However quackish the diagnosis and cure may appear to us now, the promise of social justice was clearly responsible for much of Aberhart's appeal. As in other prairie populisms, this dimension of the utopian vision bonded other aspects of ideology and motivated rank-and-file activity within the movement.

Popular Democracy and Class Politics

By this point, I hope to have demonstrated the pervasiveness of democratic themes in prairie populist thought, and the existence of important variations within this regional discourse. Extensive quotation from and commentary on representative primary literature, and locating them in the context of contemporary debates and patterns of thought, allow us to better appreciate prairie populists' contributions to Canadian democratic thought.

Some will criticize this study for the absence of detailed attention to the specific class character of the movements and organizations observed. How can one evaluate the populist organizations and proposals unless they are more precisely located sociologically? Do not class interest and class consciousness play a larger role in structuring populist political thought than I have indicated? I have essentially two responses.

The first is simple: the objective class character of the organizations whose discourses I have examined is well established.[17] It is therefore not necessary to reiterate sociologists' findings, or to conduct new research in this area. However, this response begs a more important methodological question. If the class positions of populist organizations are clear, why did I not account for the specific claims, arguments, and dimensions of each populism in terms of its class character?

The answer to this question takes us back to my initial conceptualization of populism and popular-democratic thought. Popular-democratic thought and its practical expression, populist political action, are patterns of recognition and critique of existing social distributions of power. These include claims about the need to develop methods and political strategies to overcome certain aspects of the 'people/power bloc' antagonism that Laclau describes. The perception and reality of this antagonism extends across socio-economic class boundaries within the ranks of the people. In politically volatile circumstances, many economic and political organizations recognize the antagonism in their public discourses and activities. This recognition can occur without debilitating, class-alliance negating attention being paid to class divisions among 'the people.' The evolution of popular-democratic thought can thus be characterized by ideological cross-fertilization among economic and political organizations whose members see themselves on the same side of a conflict between the people and a power élite.

For *ex post facto* analysis of prairie populism, appreciating this pattern of development in popular-democratic thought is important. Focusing too much on the class location and presumed interests of prairie farmers between the wars inclines one to characterize populist ideas as simply *petit bourgeois*. What is lost thereby is a motivation to examine these ideas more closely. One then risks overlooking the impact on '*petit bourgeois*' democratic thought of many problems, and assumptions, in modern liberal and socialist thought. My study cannot demonstrate this conclusively; none the less, the problems encountered by prairie populists in their analyses, strategies, and visions of democratic politics have been shown to transcend a single class perspective. Their solutions did not bear non-transferable class copyrights. A policy proposal's consistency with one class's interest does not prove its inconsistency with other classes' interests.[18]

Class position and interests still influence organizations and movements in crucial ways. However, the influence provides long-term direction rather than molding each ideological element to predetermined and class-exclusive standards. One should thus not be surprised to find that political discourses from the same regional and class background differ in appeal, argument, and rhetorical allies. The democratic concerns, perspectives, and proposals examined in this study were not exclusively *petit bourgeois* in character, even though the organizations from which they emerged were predominantly of the agrarian *petite bourgeoisie*.

Several conditions on the prairies after 1910 enhanced the likelihood that unorthodox perspectives on democracy would circulate within agrarian organizations. A rupture with the national party system and organizations enlarged the space within which regional political differentiation could occur. A regional conflict with central Canada over the terms of the National Policy further expanded possibilities. So did the recently settled society of communities experiencing rapid growth from comparatively unencumbered beginnings. A widespread expectation of change following the First World War was especially evident in the prairie region, and seemed likely to develop when the wheat economy reeled in 1920. Having a highly educated farming community, imbued with both a sense of democracy's inevitable progress and a desire to read about and discuss how this might come to pass, was crucial to the West's pre-eminence in reform thought and action.

Perhaps the greatest single factor promoting political experimentation in the prairies was immigration: of large numbers of politicized socialists from Britain, of farmers' movement participants from the Great Plains states, and of many – especially teachers, ministers, and social-service workers – whose early adult lives had been affected by reform thought in Ontario. None of these groups saw the western Canadian extension of the national party system as natural. All brought rich traditions of anti-capitalist popular-democratic critique and vision to their new prairie homes. Support for direct legislation and the single tax, a view of the radical possibilities of co-operatives, support for state action and enterprise in the service of 'the people,' and moral commitments to some kind of 'economic democracy' were thus influential within the youthful region.

The combination of these conditions between the wars helped nurture considerably more differentiation among mass-based political discourses than that experienced by any other region of Canada. Ideally, this study would have integrated detailed popular intellectual history with agrarian organizational histories to help account for the internal variations within prairie populist democratic thought. Existing political biographies of key figures in the prairie populist experience are suggestive, but only scratch the surface of the intellectual history of prairie populism.[19] As one is inclined to say in a conclusion, much work remains to be done.

The Relevance of Prairie Populism

While demonstrating the complexity of prairie populist democratic thought, I hope to have suggested its relevance to Canada's political present as well as its past. It is appropriate to conclude by elaborating on this relevance.

The party system criticized by all prairie populists was altered but ultimately not fundamentally changed by their campaigns. Provincial competition for office has changed significantly in the West, but the political parties that dominated national politics from 1910 to 1945 do so today. They are not markedly more internally democratic or sensitive to non-élite social groups now than they were in 1920. Their connections with and service of the national corporate élite have not weakened appreciably. The politics of image and unaccountable policy practiced by the old parties[20] has incurred democratic deficits that no amount of convention hoopla and attitudinal surveying can balance.

Prairie populists have thus been vindicated in their insistence on the patently élitist character of mainstream partisan activity and intentions. Their calls for popularly based organizations that could supplement electoral and state institutions appropriate to a democracy are no less relevant today. While prairie populist alternatives to established party practice had their own shortcomings and blind spots – especially with regard to matters of sexism and Anglophone racist nativism[21] – all but the Social Credit variant had positive lessons for contemporary democrats. It is difficult to cut through the layers of cynicism and resignation that help to protect the current party system from effective public evaluation, but the lessons are there.

One lesson is that however much the major political organizations have succeeded in removing class conflict and class interests from the agenda of public concern, there are ways of re-introducing these in the service of political democracy. Populists employed languages of class conflict and interest that blurred some distinctions insisted on by Marxists. But they were still languages of class, in idioms that revealed social antagonisms preventing a more democratic society. As long as large numbers of 'the people' conceived of themselves as the victims of an undemocratic political economy, the populist project of democratizing society was not implausible.

The evidence since 1945 suggests that this project ceases to be viable when a generalized perception of antagonism between the people and some 'power bloc' disappears. For reasons too complex to consider here, labour organizations in Canada have only rarely and briefly served as the basis of a popular-democratic movement. Instances where unions have performed this role, such as the recent Solidarity experience in British Columbia, have featured a decidedly populist appeal and an alliance-building effort by organized labour. Using a language opposing the interests of the people to those of the Social Credit regime and its class supporters extended popular support for labour's objectives. One cannot offer a simple formula for success in the use of this 'quasi-class' appeal. It does appear to be necessary to popularly based political campaigns challenging the complacency of existing party politics. Prairie populists demonstrated the value of this quasi-class appeal more clearly than any other set of political actors in Canadian history.

A political discourse claiming to speak for the people against an élite sounds hollow to its constituency if it is not built on the action of the people. One of prairie populisms' most valuable legacies to the jaded and alienated Canadians should have been a recognition of the value of participatory democracy and decentralized control over economic and political power. This legacy has not been effectively passed on, partly because even the populist movement in Saskatchewan was adversely affected by the caution and technocratic force of government power. It is also true that organizational vehicles and cultural milieux receptive to populist messages of participatory politics have been only intermittently and locally healthy since the Second World War.

None the less, most promising signs in the development of popular power do unconsciously reflect the prairie populist idea that popular involvement and decentralized decision-making must be achieved. We can see this at neighbourhood and regional levels among the urban poor, outport fishermen, and the victims of government cut-backs. The political right has rather easily appropriated the decentralization theme for its own anti-popular designs.[22] This political twist can only be countered by a serious attempt to understand why decentralization and participatory initiatives have widespread appeal, and how they can be integrated into progressive political projects. 'The left,' and even left-liberals, otherwise risk even more facile ridicule as promoters of a sinister, paternalistic, and bureaucratic view of public life.

Prairie populists of all but the plebiscitarian variety recognized that the call for decentralization could not be made separately from the call for a participatory politics. This must be stressed even more today, when arguments from conservative western Canadian governments for a decentralized federal system are not just detached from but actually antithetical to popular democratic participation in 'province-building' adventures. There is no evidence that this pattern will change in the absence of sustained and widely based popular campaigns to reunite what were to populists the two complementary initiatives of decentralization and participatory politics.

In current circumstances of media-focused mass politics, high levels of political apathy and inefficacy, and the resurgence of conservatism, it seems utopian to talk of combining pressure for decentralization with participatory politics in mass-based, pluralistic organizations. But we have seen that all prairie populists employed something of a utopian vision, and received enhanced support from the rank and file inspired by this vision. It is true that the world of western politics then was more ideologically innocent than it is a half-century later. A utopian vision may seem more counter-productive than worthwhile in the 1980s. Such a vision is decidedly out of style in centrist liberal politics, and appears now to be almost feared by the democratic left in advanced capitalist societies.

It is worth remembering, however, that the political right has made a vision of corporate benevolence, consumer satisfaction, happy families, nineteenth-century values, and entrepreneurial dynamism compelling to many North Americans. Surely it is possible to counter this vision with one that speaks genuinely to the common desire for a democratic society and polity. If use of a utopian vision is conceded to the political right, democratic politics is destined to remain a historical echo. Many prairie populists keenly appreciated the need for such a vision. Their success in defining much of the agenda for regional political debate over several decades should be understood with this in mind.

The populist experience with utopian visions has not been entirely positive. Populists' faith in the magic of scientific technique demonstrates one of the pitfalls that democratic strategies can encounter. Present-day or future democrats in Canada can learn a good deal from prairie populists' over-reliance on technocratic solutions to problems of democratic process and class conflict, and from their underestimation of difficulties in democratic decision-making during social transformation. But prairie populists should not be faulted for utopian visions that failed to resolve dilemmas inherent in democratic politics.

Contemporary democrats must provide a less ambiguous place for participatory political and economic democracy in their future visions. This does not preclude compromises with competitive politics, but does indicate the need for precise commitments to participatory institutions. Recent NDP administrations in Saskatchewan and Manitoba have demonstrated the eventual political dangers of a technocratic approach to governance. Parties of the left should reconcile themselves to erring on the side of participatory awkwardness rather than technocratic efficiency. When the bloom falls from the economic development rose, a progressive government party can be left with too little to show in the way of a democratic vision and participatory progress. It will thus be left vulnerable to an anti-statist, superficially populist attack driven by neo-conservative values and goals.

Recent events in prairie political life experience raise another lesson of the prairie populist experience. The Saskatchewan Progressive Conservative party, along with the Western Canada Concept and the Reform Party of Canada, have been presented as appropriate heirs to the prairie populist tradition by most of the Canadian press. Our examination of the popular movement base, quasi-class analysis, and democratic visions of prairie populists between the wars should demonstrate the superficiality of this characterization. If the populist agenda for extending popular democracy had been more successful, such mis-characterizations would not be taken seriously. The development of a truly indigenous and distinctive group of democratic political ideologies was a tremendous achievement, from which one wishes Canadians had learned more than our current public life suggests.

The Farmers' Platform

(As brought up-to-date, 1921)

Drafted by the Canadian Council of Agriculture, 29 November 1918, and accepted by the member organizations, 1919.

1. A League of Nations as an international organization to give permanence to the world's peace by removing old causes of conflict. [*sic*]

2. We believe that the further development of the British Empire should be sought along the lines of partnership between nations free and equal, under the present governmental system of British constitutional authority. We are strongly opposed to any attempt to centralize imperial control. Any attempt to set up an independent authority with power to bind the Dominions, whether this authority be termed parliament, council or cabinet, would hamper the growth of responsible and informed democracy in the Dominions.

The Tariff

3. Whereas Canada is now confronted with a huge national war debt and other greatly increased financial obligations, which can be most readily and effectively reduced by the development of our natural resources, chief of which is agricultural lands;

And whereas it is desirable that an agricultural career should be made attractive to our returned soldiers and the large anticipated immigration, and owing to the fact that this can best be accomplished by the development of a national policy which will reduce to a minimum the cost of living and the cost of production;

And whereas the war has revealed the amazing financial strength of Great Britain, which has enabled her to finance, not only her own part in the struggle, but also to assist in financing her Allies to the extent of hundreds of millions of pounds, this enviable position being due to the free trade policy which has enabled her to draw her supplies freely from every quarter of the globe and consequently to undersell her competitors on the world's market, and because this policy has not only been profitable to Great Britain, but has greatly strengthened the bonds of Empire by facilitating trade between the Motherland and her overseas Dominion – we believe that the best interests of the Empire and of Canada would be served by reciprocal action on the part of Canada through gradual reductions of the tariff on British imports, having for its objects closer union and a better understanding between Canada and the Motherland and at the same time bring about a great reduction in the cost of living to our Canadian people;

Fosters Combines

And whereas the Protective Tariff has fostered combines, trusts and 'gentlemen's agreements' in almost every line of Canadian industrial enterprise, by means of which the people of Canada – both urban and rural – have been shamefully exploited through the elimination of competition, the ruination of many of our smaller industries and the advancement of prices on practically all manufactured goods to the full extent permitted by the tariff;

And whereas agriculture – the basic industry upon which the success of all our other industries primarily depends – is unduly handicapped throughout Canada as shown by the declining rural population in both Eastern and Western Canada, due largely to the greatly increased cost of agricultural implements and machinery, clothing, boots and shoes, building material and practically everything the farmer has to buy, caused by the Protective Tariff, so that it is becoming impossible for farmers generally, under normal conditions, to carry on farming operations profitably;

And whereas the Protective Tariff is the most wasteful costly method ever designed for raising national revenue, because for every dollar obtained thereby for the public treasury at least three dollars pass into the pockets of the protected interests thereby building up a privileged class at the expense of the masses, thus making the rich richer and the poor poorer;

And whereas the Protective Tariff has been and is a chief corrupting influence in our national life because the protected interests, in order to maintain their unjust privileges, have contributed lavishly to political and campaign funds, thus encouraging both political parties to look to them for support, thereby lowering the standard of public morality.

Definite Tariff Demands

Therefore be it resolved that the Canadian Council of Agriculture, representing the organized farmers of Canada, urges that, as a means of remedying these evils and bringing about much-needed social and economic reforms, our tariff laws should be amended as follows:

(a) By an immediate and substantial all-round reduction of the customs tariff.

(b) By reducing the customs duty on goods imported from Great Britain to one-half the rates charged under the general tariff, and that further gradual, uniform reductions be made in the remaining tariff on British imports that will ensure complete Free Trade between Great Britain and Canada in five years.

(c) By endeavoring to secure unrestricted reciprocal trade in natural products with the United States along the lines of the Reciprocity Agreement of 1911.

(d) By placing all foodstuffs on the free list.

(e) That agricultural implements, farm and household machinery, vehicles, fertilizers, coal, lumber, cement, gasoline, illuminating, fuel and lubricating oils be placed on the free list, and that all raw materials and machinery used in their manufacture also be placed on the free list.

(f) That all tariff concessions granted other countries be immediately extended to Great Britain.

(g) That all corporations engaged in the manufacture of products protected by the customs tariff be obliged to publish annually comprehensive and accurate statements of their earnings.

(h) That every claim for tariff protection by any industry should be heard publicly before a special committee of parliament.

Taxation Proposals

4. As these tariff reductions may very considerably reduce the national revenue from that source, the Canadian Council of Agriculture would recommend that, in order to provide the necessary additional revenue for carrying on the government of the country and for bearing the cost of the war, direct taxation be imposed in the following manner:

(a) By a direct tax on unimproved land values, including all natural resources.

(b) By a graduated personal income tax.

(c) By a graduated inheritance tax on large estates.

(d) By a graduated income tax on the profits of corporations.

(e) That in levying and collecting the business profits tax the Dominion Government should insist that it be absolutely upon the basis of the actual cash invested in the business and that no considerations be allowed for what is popularly known as watered stock.

(f) That no more natural resources be alienated from the crown, but brought into use only under short-term leases, in which the interests of the public shall be properly safeguarded, such leases to be granted only by public auction.

The Returned Soldiers

5. With regard to the returned soldier we urge:

(a) That it is the recognized duty of Canada to exercise all due diligence for the future well-being of the returned soldier and his dependents.

(b) That demobilization should take place only after return to Canada.

(c)   That first selection for return and demobilization should be made in the order of length of service of those who have definite occupation awaiting them or have other assured means of support, preference being given first to married men and then to the relative need of industries, with care to insure so far as possible the discharge of farmers in time for the opening of spring work upon the land.

(d)   That general demobilization should be gradual, aiming at the discharge of men only as it is found possible to secure steady employment.

(e)   It is highly desirable that if physically fit discharged men should endeavor to return to their former occupations, all employers should be urged to reinstate such men in their former positions wherever possible.

(f)   That vocational training should be provided for those who while in the service have become unfitted for their former occupations.

(g)   That provision should be made for insurance at the public expense of un-pensioned men who have become undesirable insurance risks while in the service.

(h)   The facilities should be provided at the public expense that will enable returned soldiers to settle upon farming land when by training or experience they are qualified to do so.

6. We recognize the very serious problem confronting labor in urban industry resulting from the cessation of war, and we urge that every means, economically feasible and practicable, should be used by federal, provincial and municipal authorities in relieving unemployment in the cities and towns; and, further, recommend the adoption of the principle of co-operation as the guiding spirit in the future relations between employers and employees – between capital and labor.

Land Settlement

7. A land settlement scheme based on a regulating influence in the selling price of land. Owners of idle areas should be obliged to file a selling price on their lands, that price also to be regarded as an assessable value for purposes of taxation.

8. Extension of co-operative agencies in agriculture to cover the whole field of marketing, including arrangements with consumers' societies for the supplying of foodstuffs at the lowest rates and with the minimum of middleman handling.

9. Public ownership and control of railway, water and aerial transportation, telephone, telegraph and express systems, all projects in the development of natural power, and of the coal mining industry.

Other Democratic Reforms

10. To bring about a greater measure of democracy in government, we recommend:

(a)   That the new Dominion Election Act shall be based upon the principle of establishing the federal electorate on the provincial franchise.

(b) The discontinuance of the practice of conferring titles upon citizens of Canada.

(c) The reform of the federal senate.

(d) An immediate check upon the growth of government by order-in-council, and increased responsibility of individual members of parliament in all legislation.

(e) The complete abolition of the patronage system.

(f) The publication of contributions and expenditures both before and after election campaigns.

(g) The removal of press censorship upon the restoration of peace and the immediate restoration of the rights of free speech.

(h) The setting forth by daily newspapers and periodical publications, of the facts of their ownership and control.

(i) Proportional representation.

(j) The establishment of measures of direct legislation through the initiative, referendum and recall.

(k) The opening of seats in parliament to women on the same terms as men.

(l) Prohibition of the manufacture, importation and sale of intoxicating liquors as beverages in Canada.

From W.L. Morton, *The Progressive Party in Canada* (1950), Appendix C, 302-5

Notes

Chapter 1

1 Ernesto Laclau makes this case well in *Politics and Ideology in Marxist Theory* (London: New Left Books, 1977).
2 W.L. Morton, *The Progressive Party in Canada* (Toronto: University of Toronto Press, 1950), 26
3 See Gerald Friesen, *The Canadian Prairies: A History* (Toronto: University of Toronto Press, 1984).
4 See ibid, chapter 15.
5 See especially John Richards, 'The Decline and Fall of Agrarian Socialism,' in S.M. Lipset, ed., *Agrarian Socialism*, rev. ed. (Berkeley: University of California Press, 1968); John Richards and Larry Pratt, *Prairie Capitalism: Power and Influence in the New West* (Toronto: McClelland and Stewart, 1979), chapters 5, 6, and 8; Evelyn Eager, 'The Paradox of Power in the Saskatchewan CCF, 1944-61,' in J.H. Aitchison, ed., *The Political Process in Canada* (Toronto: Macmillan, 1963); Evelyn Eager, *Saskatchewan Government: Politics and Pragmatism* (Saskatoon: Western Producer Prairie Books, 1980); A.L. Johnson, 'Biography of a Government: Policy Formulation in Saskatchewan 1944-61,' PhD dissertation, Harvard University, 1963; George Cadbury, 'Planning in Saskatchewan,' in L. LaPierre et al., eds., *Essays on the Left* (Toronto: McClelland and Stewart, 1971); Meyer Brownstone, 'The Douglas-Lloyd Governments: Innovation and Bureaucratic Response,' in LaPierre et al. See also Lewis H. Thomas, ed., *The Making of a Socialist: The Recollections of T.C. Douglas* (Edmonton: University of Alberta Press, 1982).
6 See Ramsay Cook, 'Tillers and Toilers: The Rise and Fall of Populism in Canada in the 1890s,' in *Historical Papers* (Ottawa: Canadian Historical Association, 1985).

7   See Louis Aubrey Wood, *A History of Farmers' Movements in Canada* (Toronto: Ryerson Press, 1924), chaps XX-XII; Brian McCutcheon, 'The Patrons of Industry in Manitoba,1890-1898,' in D. Swainson, ed., *Historical Essays on the Prairie Provinces* (Ottawa: McClelland and Stewart, 1970); Brian McCutcheon, 'The Birth of Agrarianism in the Prairie West,' *Prairie Forum*, vol. 1, no. 2 (1976), 79-94; 'James Moffat Douglas' and 'The Agrarian Movement in the 1890s,' *Saskatchewan History*, vol. 7, no. 1 (Winter 1954), 47-55; D.S. Spafford, ' "Independent" Politics in Saskatchewan before the Non-Partisan League,' *Saskatchewan History*, vol. 18, no. 1 (Winter 1965), 1-9; *Handbook Introducing Facts and Figures in Support of the Patron Platform and Principles* (Toronto, 1895), in Shortt Library and Archives, University of Saskatchewan, Saskatoon.

8   See Wood (1924), chapter XIV; Hopkins Moorhouse, *Deep Furrows* (Toronto: G.J. McLeod, 1918); H.S. Patton, *Grain Growers' Co-operation in Western Canada* (Cambridge, Mass.: Harvard University Press, 1928); Hugh Boyd, *New Breaking* (Toronto: J.M. Dent, 1938).

9   See R.D. Colquette, *The First Fifty Years* (Winnipeg: United Grain Growers, 1957), and Boyd (1938).

10   'The Newspaper Scrapbook,' *Saskatchewan History*, vol. 4, no. 1 (1951), 72, excerpted from *The Regina Leader*, 22 March 1894

11   A classic account, written when the ideas still had currency in Ontario political life, is Wood (1924; reprint ed., University of Toronto Press, 1975). Also contemporary is H. Michell, 'The Grange in Canada,' *Queen's Quarterly*, vol. 22, October 1914, 164-83. More recent are S.E.D. Shortt, 'Social Change and Political Crisis in Rural Ontario: The Patrons of Industry, 1889-1896,' in D. Swainson, ed., *Oliver Mowat's Ontario* (Toronto: Macmillan, 1972); Frank Underhill, 'Some Reflections on the Liberal Tradition in Canada,' 'Some Aspects of Upper Canadian Radical Opinion in the Decade before Confederation,' and 'Political Ideas of the Upper Canada Reformers 1867-1878,' in his *In Search of Canadian Liberalism* (Toronto: Macmillan, 1960); and Russell Hann, *Some Historical Perspectives on Canadian Agrarian Political Movements: The Ontario Origins of Agrarian Criticism of Canadian Industrial Society* (Toronto: New Hogtown Press, 1973).

12   The major early contribution came from the ten studies sponsored by the Canadian Social Science Research Council, directed and edited by S.D. Clark, and published by the University of Toronto Press, 1950 to 1959.

13   As representative instances, see Gary Teeple and R.T. Naylor, 'Appendix: The Ideological Origins of Social Democracy and Social Credit,' in G. Teeple, ed., *Capitalism and the National Question in Canada* (Toronto:

University of Toronto Press, 1972); Peter Sinclair, 'Class Structure and Populist Protest: The Case of Western Canada,' *Canadian Journal of Sociology*, vol. 1, no 1 (1975), 1-17; A.K. Davis, 'The Saskatchewan C.C.F.' in D. Roussopoulos, ed., *Canada and Radical Social Change* (Montreal: Black Rose Books, 1973); John Conway, 'Populism in the United States, Russia, and Canada: Explaining the Roots of Canada's Third Parties,' *Canadian Journal of Political Science*, vol. 11, no. 1 (March 1978), 99-124; J. Conway, 'The UFA and Social Credit Regimes in Alberta: Some Continuities' (paper presented to Canadian Political Science Association Annual Meetings, Montreal, 1980), and J. Conway, 'The Nature of Populism: A Clarification,' *Studies in Political Economy*, no. 13, Spring 1984, 137-44.

14 For a recent but partial account of what has occurred in this area, see R.J. Brym and R.J. Sacouman, eds., *Underdevelopment and Social Movements in Atlantic Canada* (Toronto: New Hogtown Press, 1979).

15 For the best account of this, see Lawrence Goodwyn, *Democratic Promise: The Populist Moment in America* (New York: Oxford University Press, 1976).

16 Friesen (1984), 348

17 See ibid, 365-6.

18 See Jean Meynaud, *Technocracy* (London: Faber and Faber, 1968), and Sheldon Wolin, *Politics and Vision* (New York: Little, Brown and Company, 1960), chapter 10, 'The Age of Organization and the Sublimation of Politics.'

19 See James Weinstein, *The Corporate Ideal in American Democracy* (Boston: Beacon Press, 1968), and Richard H. Pells, *Radical Visions and American Dreams: Culture and Social Thought in the Depression Years* (New York: Harper Torchbooks, 1974).

20 See essays by Donald Macrae, Peter Wiles, Kenneth Minogue, and Peter Worsley in G. Ionescu and Ernest Gellner, eds., *Populism: Its Meaning and National Characteristics* (New York: Macmillan, 1969), and Margaret Canovan, *Populism* (New York: Harcourt, Brace, Jovanovich, 1981).

21 A prominent exception to this is the Russian populism of the late nineteenth and early twentieth centuries. See Franco Venturi, *The Roots of Revolution* (London: Weidenfeld and Nicholson, 1960), and Andrej Walicki, *The Controversy over Capitalism: Studies in the Social Philosophy of Russian Populists* (Oxford: Clarendon Press, 1969).

22 This was strongly reflected in the indigenous fiction and periodicals of the period. See David C. Jones, ' "There Is Some Power about the Land" – the Western Agrarian Press and Country Life Ideology,' *Journal of Canadian*

Studies, vol. 17, no. 3 (1982), 96-109; and Gerald Friesen, 'Three Generations of Fiction: An Introduction to Prairie Cultural History,' in D.J. Bercuson and P.A. Buckner, eds., *Eastern and Western Perspectives* (Toronto: University of Toronto Press, 1981).

23 Peter Worsley, 'The Concept of Populism,' in Ionescu and Gellner (1969), 218

24 Much of the argument in this and the preceding paragraph is made by Laclau (1977) and John Richards, 'Populism: A Qualified Defence,' *Studies in Political Economy*, no. 5 (1981), 5-28.

25 For a much more perceptive account of how this leadership style counts as one minor type of populism – 'politicians' populism' – see Canovan, chapter 7.

26 Worsley (1969), 246 and 248

27 'Popular-democratic ideologies never present themselves separated from, but articulated with, class ideological discourses. Class struggle at the ideological level consists, to a great extent, in the attempt to articulate popular-democratic interpellations in the ideological discourses of antagonistic classes. *The popular-democratic interpellation not only has no precise class content, but is the domain of ideological class struggle par excellence.* Every class struggles at the ideological level simultaneously as class and as the people, or rather, tries to give coherence to its ideological discourse by presenting its class objectives as the consummation of popular objectives' Laclau (1977), 108-9 (author's emphasis).

28 Laclau, 172. E.P. Thompson's *The Making of the English Working Class* (London: Victor Gollancz, 1963; reprint, Penguin, 1968) vividly demonstrates the importance of late–eighteenth-century popular notions such as 'the free-born Englishman,' as well as a range of broadly anti-aristocratic and anti-authoritarian ideas generally, for the radical movements in Britain throughout the nineteenth and twentieth centuries.

29 Laclau (1977), 117

30 Ibid, 110-11

31 Ibid, 173-5

32 Laclau pays insufficient attention to this organizational component in the development of populist discourse – possibly because it has been overemphasized at the expense of explaining the dynamics of populist ideologies in most other accounts of populism. Whatever the reason for this lacuna, there is no incompatibility between his theoretical approach and a recognition of the importance of strong organizations to populist successes.

33 For examples of the ways in which organization has an impact on movement discourse, see C.B. Macpherson, *Democracy in Alberta: Social Credit and the*

Party System (Toronto: University of Toronto Press, 1953), S.M. Lipset,
*Agrarian Socialism: The Co-operative Commonwealth Federation in
Saskatchewan* (Berkeley: University of California Press, 1950), and John
Irving, *The Social Credit Movement in Alberta* (Toronto: University of
Toronto Press, 1959).

34 Laclau (1977), 176 and 194

Chapter 2

1 The best-known book-length studies are: W.L. Morton, *The Progressive
Party in Canada* (Toronto: University of Toronto Press, 1950); Paul F.
Sharp, *The Agrarian Revolt in Western Canada: A Survey Showing American
Parallels* (Minneapolis: University of Minnesota Press, 1949); Lewis G.
Thomas, *The Liberal Party in Alberta* (Toronto: University of Toronto Press,
1959); David Smith, *Prairie Liberalism: The Liberal Party in Saskatchewan,
1905-1971* (Toronto: University of Toronto Press, 1975); Louis Aubrey
Wood, *A History of Farmers' Movements in Canada* (Toronto: Ryerson
Press, 1924); Ramsay Cook, *The Politics of John W. Dafoe and the Free
Press* (Toronto: University of Toronto Press, 1963); and Walter D. Young,
*Democracy and Discontent: Progressivism, Socialism and Social Credit in
the Canadian West* (Toronto: Ryerson Press, 1969). A recent addition is
Charles M. Johnston, *E.C. Drury: Agrarian Idealist* (Toronto: University of
Toronto Press, 1986), valuable for its portrait of a key rural crypto-Liberal
in Ontario.
2 Morton (1950), 194, 200-1
3 See Barbara Cameron, 'The Transition from Whig to Reform Liberalism in
Canada' (paper presented at 1981 annual meeting of the Canadian Political
Science Association, Halifax, NS).
4 See Ramsay Cook, *The Regenerators: Social Criticism in Late Victorian
English Canada* (Toronto: University of Toronto Press, 1985).
5 The Liberals published the 1918 Farmers' Platform alongside their own 1919
platform in the *Speakers' Handbook* for the 1921 election. C.P. Stacey,
Historical Documents of Canada, Vol. 5: 1914-1945 (Toronto: Macmillan,
1972), 36.
6 Stacey (1972),'The Liberal Platform, 1919,' 36-40
7 Frank Underhill, *In Search of Canadian Liberalism* (Toronto: Macmillan,
1960), 41
8 Ibid, 1
9 Wood (1924), 109-58; Ramsay Cook, 'Tillers and Toilers: The Rise and Fall
of Populism in Canada in the 1890s,' *Historical Papers* (Ottawa: Canadian

Historical Association, 1985) and S.E. Shortt, 'Social Change and Political Crisis in Rural Ontario: The Patrons of Industry, 1889-1896' (1972)

10 See notes 7-11, chapter 1.

11 See Cook, 'Tillers and Toilers,' especially on the role played by George Wrigley, editor of the *Canada Farmers' Sun.*

12 On the significance of the social gospel orientation in such radicalism, see Cook, *The Regenerators.*

13 Shortt (1972), 222

14 See Morton (1950); David Smith, 'A Comparison of Political Developments in Saskatchewan and Alberta,' *Journal of Canadian Studies,* vol. 4, no.1 (1969), 17-25, and 'Interpreting Prairie Politics,' *Journal of Canadian Studies,* vol. 7, no. 4 (1972), 18-32; and Nelson Wiseman, 'The Pattern of Prairie Politics,' *Queen's Quarterly,* vol. 88, no. 2 (Summer 1981), 298-315.

15 Morton (1950), 14

16 With only 22 per cent of the popular vote, UFO candidates managed to win 40 per cent of the seats (45), while the incumbent Conservatives elected only 22 per cent of MPPs with 32.7 per cent of the popular vote. See Loren M. Simerl, 'A Survey of Canadian Provincial Election Results, 1905-1981,' in Paul Fox, ed., *Politics Canada: Fifth Edition* (Toronto: McGraw-Hill Ryerson, 1982), 655-93.

17 See David Hoffman, 'Intra-Party Democracy: A Case Study,' *Canadian Journal of Economics and Political Science,* vol. 27, no. 2 (May 1961), 223-35.

18 Ibid

19 See W.C. Good's autobiography, *Farmer Citizen: My Fifty Years with the Canadian Farmers' Movement* (Toronto: Ryerson, 1958). For an account of the 'anti-political' orientation in the Ontario farmers' movement, see Ian MacPherson, 'The Co-operative Union of Canada and Politics, 1909-1931,' *Canadian Historical Review,* vol. 54, no. 2 (June 1973), 152-74.

20 On the conservatism of the eastern Liberal faithful ca. 1919-21, see Morton (1950), 77.

21 There is an extensive literature relevant to this subject. One of the best treatments is Gerald Friesen, *The Canadian Prairies: A History* (Toronto: University of Toronto Press, 1984). A classic of economic history that sets the frontier experience in useful perspective is Vernon Fowke, *The National Policy and the Wheat Economy* (Toronto: University of Toronto Press, 1957).

22 Among other things, recent immigrants to the prairies would hardly have concurred with Patrons' opposition to the National Policy's prairie settlement program in the mid-1890s. Shortt (1972) cites one *Canada Farmers' Sun* editorial in 1895, which contended that 'trumping up

immigration out of the dissatisfied and ne'er-do-well class in any country is a business for which the people cannot afford to pay.'

23 For a discussion of the flow of American co-operativist ideas into Canada for the two decades following the First World War, see Ian MacPherson, 'Selected Borrowings: The American Impact upon the Prairie Co-operative Movement, 1920-1939,' *Canadian Review of American Studies*, vol. 10. no. 2 (Fall 1979), 137-51.

24 This position was exemplified in J.W. Dafoe's *Free Press* editorials in support of free trade from the early 1900s to the 1930s. In 1911, he put the democracy–free trade relation at the centre of the election: 'Canada comes to the crossroads on September 21. One is the road to democracy, to a larger and freer national life, to wider markets, to the greater happiness and prosperity of the plain people; to the application of the rule of government that the greatest good of the whole nation must outweigh the desires of any one class. The other road leads to privilege, to the administration of the country by a class in its own interests, to the exhaltation of ... certain special interests, to high protection, ... restricted markets and trust domination.' (*Manitoba Free Press*, 12 September 1911, editorial; cited in Gerald Friesen, 'Studies in the Development of Western Canadian Regional Consciousness, 1870-1925,' PhD dissertation, University of Toronto, Department of History, 1973). For more along these lines, see the classic writings of Edward Porritt.

25 See, for example, 'Oregon's Popular Government' (editorial) and 'Direct Legislation in Oregon,' *Grain Grower's Guide*, 14 September 1910.

26 These same instruments of direct democracy were promoted by the Patrons of Industry, and even the Independent Labour Party, in Ontario of the 1890s. See Shortt (1972), Cook, 'Tillers and Toilers,' and *Handbook of the Patron Platform* (1895).

27 See Friesen (1984), chapter 14.

28 Macpherson (1953), chapter 1

29 Morton (1950), chapters II and III

30 We will discuss particular elements of crypto-Liberal 'co-operativism' later in the chapter.

31 Wood (1924), part II. In 1893, the Patrons of Industry had roughly 100,000 members in Ontario (Shortt, 1972, 212). While most of these members were or wished to become members of co-operatives, most of these co-operatives were consumer rather than producer marketing co-ops (with the exception of co-operative creameries), and few were allied with any larger co-operative organization.

32 As Cook, 'Tillers and Toilers,' points out, electoral political activity by the

Patrons in Ontario in the 1890s was stimulated by the ceaseless calls to action of George Wrigley, editor of the Patrons' official organ, the *Canada Farmers' Sun*. When the *Sun* ceased to mobilize the rural constituency for political action, farmers tended to leave active politics. Which is cause, and which effect, is not altogether clear; the *Sun* stopped promulgating this message of independent politics after the federal Liberal victory, and Goldwyn Smith's purchase of majority interest in the paper, in 1896.

33 Lawrence Goodwyn, *Democratic Promise: The Populist Moment in America* (New York: Oxford University Press, 1976), xviii

34 Ian MacPherson, *Each for All: A History of the Co-operative Movement in English Canada, 1900-1945* (Toronto: Macmillan, 1979), 42-3

35 See Patrons' *Handbook* (1895); D.S. Spafford, ' "Independent" Politics in Saskatchewan before the Non-Partisan League' (1965), 'The Agrarian Movement in the 1890s' (1954), 50-4; and, Brian McCutcheon, 'The Patrons of Industry in Manitoba, 1890-1898' (1970).

36 Organized elements within the central Canadian working class felt that this regressive incidence was offset in their own case by the existence of a greater number of employment-offering 'infant industries' able to survive because of the protective tariff, and were thus, as producers, generally opposed to tariff reductions. This did nothing to endear prairie or Ontario farmers to their urban fellows, or *vice versa*.

37 This point was made in the Patrons' *Handbook* (1895), and all of the agitations by the Patrons in Manitoba and Saskatchewan in the mid- to late 1890s.

38 In 1894, Laurier told a Winnipeg audience: 'We stand for freedom. I denounce the policy of protection as bondage – yea, bondage; and I refer to bondage in the same manner in which American slavery was bondage. Not in the same degree, perhaps, but in the same manner. In the same manner the people of Canada ... are toiling for a master who takes away not every cent of profit, but a very large percentage, a very large portion of your earnings for which you sweat and toil' (*Manitoba Free Press*, 3 September 1894; cited in Edward Porritt, *Sixty Years of Protection in Canada*, 2nd ed. [Winnipeg: Grain Growers' Guide, 1913], 316).

39 *Sixty Years of Protection in Canada*; *The Revolt in Canada against the New Feudalism*; and 'Death of Edward Porritt,' *Grain Growers' Guide*, 2 November 1921, 7

40 'Agrarian Movement,' 56

41 Wood (1924), chapter 20; George Chipman, ed., *The Siege of Ottawa* (Winnipeg: Grain Growers' Grain Company, 1911). For an account of the

hopes hanging on the 'Siege,' see *Guide* editorials of 16 November, 23
November, 30 November, and 21 December 1910.

42 See Colquette (1957), Wood (1924), and Good (1958).

43 See especially *Handbook of the Patron Platform* (1895), 15-43 (two-thirds of
the *Handbook* is devoted to an attack on the tariff).

44 Morton (1950), 62

45 Fiscal responsibility was also a major concern of the Patrons in Ontario and
the West. It is important to appreciate that this did not reflect a *laissez-faire*
desire for a minimum state; as Cook, 'Tillers and Toilers,' points out, and as
one can see in the Patron Platform and Declaration of Principles in the
Patrons' *Handbook* (1895, 1-2), the economies being proposed by the
Patrons were all related to their perception that the urban business élite had
usurped political authority, and were living well, through scandalous
patronage and wasteful subsidy, at the expense of Canada's farming and
labouring population.

46 Morton (1950), 303

47 Once again, see Patrons' *Handbook* (1895) for extensive argument to this
effect.

48 In a 1921 *Guide* editorial, Chipman argued that 'the real issue' in the
upcoming election was 'whether the people or the politicians and the big
interests are going to govern the country.'

49 Canovan (1981), 294-5

50 See both Cook, 'Tillers and Toilers,' and Shortt (1972) on the physiocratic
element in Patrons' discourse in Ontario a generation earlier.

51 Morton (1950), Appendix 1, 297. For virtually verbatim parallel statements
by Patron leaders in Ontario, see Cook, 'Tillers and Toilers,' 13-14, and
Shortt (1972), 231-2.

52 Morton (1950), 298

53 'President's Address,' *Manitoba Grain Growers' Yearbook*, 1919, 25. William
Irvine took essentially the same position regarding the Platform in 1920
(*The Farmers in Politics* [Toronto: McClelland and Stewart, 1920], 222-3).

54 From August 1909 to mid-1910, the *Guide* was in fact entitled *The Grain
Growers' Guide and Friend of Labour*. Also significant were the friendly
relations between the Patrons and organized labour in Ontario between 1890
and 1896, which failed to result in political alliances, but appeared to be
premised on a similar populist critique of business power and the moral evils
of industrialized society. See Cook, 'Tillers and Toilers.'

55 Foster Griezic, 'The Honorable Thomas Alexander Crerar: The Political
Career of a Western Liberal Progressive in the 1920s,' in Susan

Trofimenkoff, ed., *The Twenties in Western Canada* (Ottawa: National Museum of Man, 1975), 114-15

56 Crerar, 'Confession,' 7

57 Ibid

58 Cook (1963), 109 and 116

59 On the ties of the Winnipeg business community with the UFM in 1922, see John Kendle, *John Bracken: A Political Biography* (Toronto: University of Toronto Press, 1980), 28.

60 'Liberal or Conservative, Which?' Liberal Party Literature file (Archives of Saskatchewan, Saskatoon)

61 As Duff Spafford, ' "Independent" Politics,' noted, 'the Liberals did their best to portray their government as a committee of delegates performing as a legislative arm of the farmers' organization – as a true 'farmers' government. They were good at playing out the role, and indeed circumstances never permitted them to consider any other ... The farmers insisted on a government that was responsive and accountable in a very direct way to the electorate.' (*Saskatchewan History*, vol. 18, 1965, 3). See also David E. Smith, 'James G. Gardiner: Leadership in the Agrarian Community,' *Saskatchewan History*, vol. 40, no. 2 (Spring 1987), 42-61, for the way Gardiner saw and presented the Liberals as the party of the people, and minorities, as against the provincial and federal Tories.

62 For anti-CCF and pro-CCF accounts of this, see W.L. Morton, *Manitoba: A History* (Toronto: University of Toronto Press, 1957), and Nelson Wiseman, *Social Democracy in Manitoba: A History of the CCF-NDP* (Winnipeg: University of Manitoba Press, 1984).

63 See Spafford, ' "Independent" Politics,' Cook, 'Tillers and Toilers,' and Martin Robin, *Radical Politics and Canadian Labour* (Kingston: Industrial Relations Centre, Queen's University, 1968).

64 This support was so great in Saskatchewan by 1913 that a resolution in support of direct political action at the Saskatchewan Grain Growers' Association annual meeting was defeated only because C.A. Dunning (future provincial and federal Liberal minister) tacked on an amendment claiming that direct legislation would be more efficient than party action in achieving the farmers' objectives. See Duff Spafford, '"Independent" Politics,' 8.

65 W.L. Morton, 'Direct Legislation and the Origins of the Progressive Movement,' *Canadian Historical Review*, vol. 25, no. 2 (1944), 284, 279-88; see also discussion later in this chapter.

66 Ibid, 285-6; Hon. Rodmond Roblin, *Sir Rodmond Roblin on Initiative and Referendum, a Socialistic and Un-British System* (Speech delivered in the Manitoba Legislature, 27 January 1913)

67 Morton (1944), 286-7
68 'President's Address,' *MGGA Yearbook,* 1911, 6
69 'President's Address,' *MGGA Yearbook,* 1912, 16
70 The *Guide* supported the direct legislation campaign in almost every 1909-11 issue, including a detailed account by Robert Scott in four successive feature articles (16, 23, and 30 November, and 7 December, 1910), and coverage of Oregon's experiments with direct legislation. A 14 September 1910 *Guide* editorial, 'Oregon's Popular Government,' argued that ' the corporations have more power than the people and the only way in which this can be overcome is through Direct Legislation, which will place the government completely and at all times in the hands of the people ... If the people of Canada wish certain legislation enacted and the legislature refuses to enact it, the people are powerless ... until [direct legislation] becomes a part of the statutes of each of the provinces.'
71 Elizabeth Chambers, 'The Referendum and the Plebiscite,' in Duff Spafford and Norman Ward, eds., *Politics in Saskatchewan* (Don Mills: Longmans, 1968), 77
72 *Manitoba Law Reports,* vol. 27, 'In re. Initiative and Referendum Act,' 13; cited in Morton (1944), 287
73 Morton (1944), 288
74 'The Confession' was one of the Progressive leader's two most complete statements of objectives to reach a mass audience (in *Maclean's,* January 1921, and reprinted in the *Guide,* 28 February 1921).
75 *The Guide,* 19 October 1921, 7-9. This may have simply been a pragmatic move, in view of the courts' rulings against such legislation. None the less, one still must wonder why Crerar made no mention of the issue, even if it would have been unreasonable to expect him to launch a full-scale campaign on its behalf.
76 Morton (1944), 286-7
77 In a *Guide* editorial of 20 September 1910, George Chipman argued that 'We need Direct Legislation in every province, and when it becomes a part of provincial statutes it will be much easier to secure the reforms which the people demand. Direct Legislation injures no party but places all power at all times in the hands of the people. Who else should hold that vast power?' No Liberal party would have endorsed this conception of direct legislation.
78 Shortt (1972), 219
79 Lewis G. Thomas, *The Liberal Party in Alberta* (Toronto: University of Toronto Press, 1959), 195
80 In 1920, a ten member 'P.R.' constituency was established in Winnipeg. Morton (1957), 374

81 J.P. Harris, 'The Practical Workings of Proportional Representation in the United States and Canada,' *National Municipal Review* (Supplement), May 1930, 365. Seventeen cities had taken up this option by 1922, although twelve had abandoned it by 1929 through popular votes or provincial ordinances.

82 Ibid, 367

83 For extensive accounts of this, see Morton (1950); Sharp (1949); Smith (1975); C.B. Macpherson (1953); Wood (1924); A. Ross, 'National Development and Sectional Politics: Social Conflict and the Rise of a Protest Movement; The Case of the Saskatchewan Grain Growers Association,' PhD dissertation, University of Toronto, 1978; Carl Betke, 'The United Farmers of Alberta, 1921-35: The Relationship between the Agricultural Organization and the Government of Alberta,' MA thesis, University of Alberta, 1971.

84 Smith (1975), 91-5

85 Morton (1950), 74ff

86 'Appendix I,' in H.A. Innis, ed., *The Diary of A.J. MacPhail* (Toronto: University of Toronto Press, 1940), 59

87 Once the SGGA opted for direct political action in 1922, constituency organizations were given control over the decision to field a candidate, and conduct of the campaign. See Smith (1975), 94-5.

88 'United Farmers in Politics,' *United Farmers of Manitoba Yearbook*, 1921, 18-9

89 The executive included UFA President Wood, and United Farmers of Manitoba President J.L. Brown.

90 Morton (1950), 269-70; Sharp (1949), 155-6

91 'Crerar's Manifesto,' *Guide*, 19 October 1921, 7

92 In 1919, Henders the MP was forced to resign the MGGA presidency in disgrace for not voting against a Unionist budget giving no tariff relief (see Morton [1950], 69-70, and the *Guide*, 'The Evolution of Mr. Henders,' 12 October 1921, 5). That he later became a rather egregious opportunist in grain grower politicians' ranks does not render his earlier critiques of partyism unrepresentative of grain grower sentiment.

93 'President's Address,' *MGGA Yearbook*, 1914, 13

94 See 'Introductory,' editorial of first issue of the *Guide*, June 1908, and 'To Whom It May Concern,' June 1908, 11-12.

95 See 1922 SGGA 'Educational Policy Report' by A.J. MacPhail and Mrs V. McNaughton, in Innis (1940), Appendix II, 62-4.

96 Smith (1975), 67

97 'President's Address,' *MGGA Year Book*, 1916, 20-1

98   Ibid, 17-18
99   Morton (1950), 171-2
100 The *Guide*, 2 March 1921, 7
101 *Guide* editorial, 12 October 1921, 6
102 The *Guide* was full of this during the fall of 1921.
103 *Handbook of the Patron Platform* (1895), 1
104 Shortt (1972), 218
105 See chapter 3, below.
106 Morton (1950), 301
107 Griezic (1972), 109-11. This judgment, and many others regarding T.A. Crerar, will be challenged in a forthcoming political biography by J.E. Rea. I do not wish to suggest that Crerar lacked integrity, only that his principles were often out of step with those of popular democracy in prairie farmers' movements.
108 Ibid, 125ff
109 See, for example, 'The Patronage System,' *Guide* editorial, 21 March 1921.
110 C.W. Mills and H.H. Gerth, eds., *From Max Weber* (New York: Oxford University Press, 1946), 224-30
111 The *Guide*, 'Crerar's Manifesto,' 19 October 1921, 7, my emphasis
112 Closely related to this concern was one for 'fiscal responsibility.' The Patrons had insisted on a variation of this in 1895, but one that would focus on elimination of unnecessary political appointments that led to meddling in properly local affairs. They argued that 'no reform is so urgently needed in Canada as a reduction in the cost of government in all three spheres, Federal, provincial and municipal. There is a swarm of departmental officials at Ottawa, and a still greater swarm of outside Federal officials, judges, customs and revenue officers ... and so on ... while high over all, amid their archaic state and trappings, sit the Governor-General and lieutenant-governors with their considerable retinue, the whole constituting a hierarchy of tax-handlers such as no other five million people on earth have to support out of moderate resources. It is not "revolutionary" for Patrons to declare that this immense edifice of officialdom ought to be reduced to a footing somewhat in keeping with our means and requirements' (*Handbook of the Patron Platform*, 1895, 13).
113 Kendle (1980) 24
114 Ibid, 30
115 Ibid, 31
116 Ibid, 35, 40, and 39
117 Smith (1975), 154. Smith notes that Dunning was more willing than Martin to admit his partisanship.

118 See Macpherson (1953), chapter 1; Morton (1950), chapters 1-3; Sharp (1949), chapters 1-4, and Friesen (1984), chapter 14.

119 James Anderson, 'The Municipal Reform Movement in Western Canada, 1880-1920,' in A.F.J. Artibise and G.A. Stelter, eds., *The Usable Urban Past* (Toronto: Macmillan, 1979), 79

120 Carl Betke, 'Farm Politics in an Urban Age: The Decline of the United Farmers of Alberta after 1921,' in L.H. Thomas, ed., *Essays on Western History* (Edmonton: University of Alberta Press, 1976), 179

121 Ibid, 185

122 For a fuller discussion of this, see chapter 3 below.

123 Morton (1950), 27-8

124 See J.H. Thompson, *The Harvests of War: The Prairie West, 1914-1918* (Toronto: McClelland and Stewart, 1978), Robert Craig Brown and Ramsay Cook, *Canada 1896-1921: A Nation Transformed* (Toronto: McClelland and Stewart, 1974), and Friesen (1984).

125 Once again, the Patrons of Industry had stressed this theme a generation earlier. See *Handbook* (1895).

126 Griezic (1972), 119

127 'My Confession of Faith,' 14

128 See cartoon in the *Guide*, 5 October 1921, 6, entitled 'Meighen's Class Government.' A farmer, horrified by the list of cabinet ministers, says to Meighen: 'This looks like a lawyer–corporation–big interests government. I thought you didn't believe in class government.' Meighen, dressed in the plutocrat's tails and top hat, answers: 'Of course I always except my own class and its clients. That's the class I believe in.'

129 See especially 23 November 1921 front-page editorial cartoon, featuring a lumbering Goliath with a right arm labelled 'Meighen Government,' a sword of 'subsidized politics,' a shield of 'protection,' a vest of 'special privilege,' and a club of 'wealth.' Organized farmers, the 'modern David,' are approaching Goliath, armed merely with 'the ballot' in a sling. Meighen was the prime minister responsible for killing the Canadian Wheat Board in 1920.

130 *MGGA Yearbook*, 1912, 17

131 The first two years of the *Guide* were full of articles praising public ownership, primarily of grain elevators and railways.

132 Morton (1957), 300

133 See Gad Horowitz, 'Conservatism, Liberalism and Socialism in Canada: An Interpretation,' *Canadian Journal of Economics and Political Science*, vol. 32, no. 2 (1966), 143-71. In Manitoba, the pre-eminent prairie Tory, Sir

Rodmond Roblin, introduced publicly owned telephones and hydro-power while premier.

134 H.V. Nelles, *The Politics of Development: Forests, Mines, and Hydro-electric Power in Ontario, 1849-1941* (Toronto: Macmillan, 1974)

135 See 'National People's Party Platform' (Omaha, 1892), in G.B. Tindall, *A Populist Reader* (New York: Harper and Row, 1966), 90-6; Goodwyn (1976), Appendix D, 'Ideological Origins of the Omaha Platform'; and Canovan (1981), 56-7.

136 According to Sharp (1949, 69), American agriculturalists were envious of the success with which Canadian grain growers had forced provincial governments to enact some limited 'single tax' legislation.

137 William Irvine endorsed both the CCA critique of tariff and its alternatives for revenue creation, in *The Farmers in Politics* (1920), 217-20.

138 MacPherson (1979)

139 This began with the first (June 1908) issue of the *Guide*, along with coverage of developments in the American co-operative movement.

140 The idea of a co-operative as an almost self-contained society, which provided a model for general social reform, was quite widespread amongst participants in the co-operative movement in Canada in the early decades. See MacPherson (1979), 27.

141 D.S. Spafford, 'The "Left Wing", 1921-1931,' in Spafford and Ward (1968).

142 MacPherson (1979), 46-7

143 Ibid, 47

144 Ibid, 78

145 'My Confession of Faith,' *Guide*, 23 February 1921, 28

146 'Cooperation is a religion pure and simple. It is something which all your senses recognize and long for in proportion to the good there is in you' (*Guide*, 18 October 1911, 20).

147 Morton (1950), 304-5

148 See D. Laycock, 'Political Neutrality and the Problem of Interest Representation: Co-operatives and Partisan Politics in Canada,' in Murray Fulton, ed., *Co-operative Organizations and Canadian Society: Popular Institutions and the Dilemmas of Change* (Toronto: University of Toronto Press, forthcoming).

149 As MacPherson puts it from the perspective of the co-operative movement, 'many cooperators, already exposed to the movement's a-political traditions, had their suspicions reinforced by the Progressive experience. Inevitably, these cooperators became more aloof from political activity, especially at the federal level, during and after the early twenties' (1979, 77-8).

150 See Richard Allen, *The Social Passion: Religion and Social Reform in*

Canada, 1914-28 (Toronto: University of Toronto Press, 1971), chapters 12 and 22.

151 See Cook (1985), McCutcheon (1970), and Spafford, ' "Independent" Politics.'

152 W.L. Morton, 'The Bias of Prairie Politics,' *Transactions of the Royal Society of Canada*, vol. 49, series III (June 1955), 63-5

153 Ibid, 64

154 W.L. Morton, 'A Century of Plain and Parkland,' in A.R. Allen, ed., *A Region of the Mind* (Regina: Canadian Plains Research Center, 1969), 174

155 For a good selection of examples of this aspect of 'country life ideology' in regional periodicals and fiction of the period, see David C. Jones, ' "There Is Some Power about the Land": The Western Agrarian Press and Country Life Ideology,' *Journal of Canadian Studies*, vol. 17, no. 3 (1982), 96-109; and Gerald Friesen, 'Three Generations of Fiction: An Introduction to Prairie Cultural History,' in D.J. Bercuson and P.A. Buckner, eds., *Eastern and Western Perspectives* (Toronto: University of Toronto Press, 1981).

156 This was the theme of most of Ralph Connors's popular stories about life in the new West. See F.W. Watt, 'Western Myth: The World of Ralph Connors,' in D.G. Stephens, ed., *Writers of the Prairies* (Vancouver: University of British Columbia Press, 1973), 7-17

157 Friesen (1984), 374

158 Morton (1950), 302

Chapter 3

1 However, *The Western Producer*, official organ of the UFC(SS), promoted a non-partisan line that supported the UFA position on involvement in partisan competition.

2 For the phrase 'left populism,' and a brief account of the Non-Partisan experience in North Dakota, see John Richards and Larry Pratt, *Prairie Capitalism: Power and Influence in the New West* (Toronto: McClelland and Stewart, 1979).

3 W.L. Morton, *The Progressive Party in Canada* (1950), 159

4 'The Price of Democracy,' *Guide* (cited in C.B. Macpherson, *Democracy in Alberta* [1953], 38). See also other early Wood speeches in the *Guide*.

5 Richards and Pratt (1979), 25-8

6 *Nutcracker*, vol. 2, no. 9, 1917, 7 (cited in Anthony Mardiros, *William Irvine: The Life of a Prairie Radical* [Toronto: James Lorimer, 1979], 56).

7 James Anderson, 'The Municipal Reform Movement in Western Canada, 1880-1920,' in A.F.J. Artibise and G.A. Stelter, eds., *The Usable Urban Past*

(Toronto: Macmillan, 1979); John Weaver, *Shaping the Canadian City* (Toronto: Institute of Public Administration of Canada, 1977)

8　More than 6,000 of the 19,000 UFA members in 1919 were also NPL members.

9　Mardiros (1979), 91

10　1923 UFA Annual Convention, *Minutes and Reports*, 26 (my emphasis)

11　Ibid, 3-4

12　'We Are Trying to Get All the People to Work in Harmony – Political Parties Seek Division and Discord,' *The UFA*, 17 June 1926, 10

13　Margaret Canovan, *Populism* (New York: Harcourt, Brace and Jovanovitch, 1981), 262

14　*The UFA*, 17 October 1925, 1 and 18

15　'We Are Trying ... ,' 11 and 14

16　1924 UFA Annual Convention, *Minutes and Reports*, 5

17　Irvine (1920), 59

18　'The Significance of Democratic Group Organization', Part II, *The UFA*, 16 March 1922, 16. This feature article in the first two issues of *The UFA* soon became a widely distributed pamphlet.

19　'Neither Farmers Nor Labour Can Break into the Plutocratic Classes,' address by H.W. Wood to East and West Calgary UFA district Association Convention, 7 October 1921 (issued as a pamphlet by the UFA, October 1921), 1

20　1921 UFA Annual Convention, *Report*, 11

21　1917 UFA Annual Convention, *Minutes and Reports* , 9

22　See, for instance, *The UFA*, 7 September 1925, 8; *The UFA*, 2 September 1924, 10; and *The Western Producer*, 30 April 1925, 5; and 25 March 1926, 11.

23　*Progress or Reaction*, an address delivered by Mrs Walter Parlby, during the Medicine Hat by-election in the Empress Theatre, 25 June 1921; reprinted in pamphlet form by the UFA, July 1921.

24　'The Significance,' *The UFA*, 15 April 1922

25　'The Cooperative Commonwealth Federation,' *Canadian Forum*, August 1932 (reprinted in *Forum: Selections from the* Canadian Forum, *1920-1970* [Toronto: University of Toronto Press, 1972])

26　See chapter 2 above.

27　'Women and Citizenry,' *The Nutcracker*, 2 December 1916, 5

28　'Life and Work: Non-Partisan Politics,' *The Nutcracker*, 17 August 1917, 8

29　Editorial, *The Alberta Non-Partisan*, 19 June 1919, 5

30　Mardiros (1979) makes this argument, which is only plausible if one is speaking of the full range of significant ideas raised in the UFA, but not if one is focusing on the unique – i.e., comprehensively radical democratic – dimension of UFA political thought.

31 Macpherson (1953), 40
32 Ibid, 41
33 See Crerar's letter of resignation as Progressive leader, and reply to H.W. Wood, in the *Guide*, 15 November 1922.
34 The Price of Democracy,' *Guide*, 20 June 1917
35 'Organized Farmers and Politics,' *Guide*, 19 September 1917, 10
36 'Significance ... ,' *The UFA*, 15 April 1922, 5
37 Irvine (1920), 160-1
38 'Political Action in Alberta,' *Guide*, 7 May 1919, 7
39 1924 UFA Annual Convention, *Minutes and Reports*, 71
40 W. Irvine, *Co-operative Government* (Ottawa: Mutual Press, 1929), 137
41 H.W. Wood, 'Presidential Address,' 1920 UFA Annual Convention, *Minutes and Reports*, 6
42 'Presidential Address,' 1922 UFA Annual Convention, *Minutes and Reports*, 8-9
43 Lawrence Goodwyn, *The Populist Moment A Short History of the Agrarian Revolt in America* (New York: Oxford University Press, 1978), xix.
44 *United Farmers of Alberta Provincial Platform* (Calgary: United Farmers of Alberta, 1921), 1
45 'Editorial,' *The UFA*, 2 July 1926, 3
46 'Forces of Cooperation and Harmony Remain Immune to Poison Gas of Divisionists,' *The UFA*, 2 July 1926, 1
47 Irvine (1929), 167
48 'The Vindication of the Alberta Farmers,' *The UFA*, 15 August 1930, 6-7
49 Ibid, 12
50 For one of the best discussions of this concept and its implications, see Hanna Fenichel Pitkin, *The Concept of Representation* (Berkeley: University of California Press, 1967), especially chapter 7.
51 *Re. the UFA: How Organized and Purposes* (Calgary: UFA Central Office, 1921), 2
52 Macpherson, 63
53 Ibid, 81
54 These three aspects of the subversion of delegate democracy are treated sequentially in Macpherson, 67-92.
55 Ibid, 67-70
56 Ibid, 75-6, 80
57 Macpherson, 82-4
58 Ibid, 91

59 Ibid
60 Irvine (1920), 152, 156, and 161
61 For an account of the opposite, existing situation, see ibid, 236-7.
62 Ibid, 174 and 181
63 Ibid, 251
64 Most pluralist theory attached to conventional forms of representative government has 'interest group' functions assumed but not built into the state system.
65 See chapter 4, below.
66 Ibid, 212
67 H.W. Wood, 'Significance,' *The UFA*, 15 April 1922, 5 and 25 (my emphasis)
68 Irvine (1920), 25-6
69 Ibid, 55
70 Irvine (1920), 78
71 Ibid, 164
72 Ibid, 187
73 The former phrase of endorsement, while strong, is vitiated (quite unintentionally, we must assume) by the latter phrase describing the guild project. However one understands the receptiveness of western farmers to alternative political methods and projects, they would not have been comfortable with a synthesis of the culturally and politically foreign political designs of Bakunin and Marx.
74 Irvine (1920), 188-9
75 Ibid, 180-3 (my emphasis)
76 Ibid, 210-11
77 Ibid, 138
78 Irvine (1929), 89
79 Irvine (1920), 90-1
80 Ibid, 141
81 See H.W. Wood, 'In Defence of Group Politics,' *Canadian Forum*, vol. 3, no. 27 (1922), 72-4.
82 Irvine (1929), 219
83 The most important are that political conflict in party politics is artificial and obscures genuine problems and interests of functionally distinct social-economic groups (classes); that representatives of genuine and 'group conscious' class organizations will be able to identify real interests and real intergroup problems/conflicts much more directly and helpfully; and that the 'spirit of co-operation' engendered in intragroup activities will naturally be extended to intergroup conflict resolution, because the spirit of co-operation

and a recognition of delicately balanced functional group interdependence are inseparable.

84 Irvine (1929), 97
85 Ibid, 237-8
86 Carl Betke, 'The United Farmers of Alberta, 1921-1935: The Relationship between Agricultural Organization and the Government of Alberta,' MA Thesis, University of Alberta, 1971, 71
87 Macpherson, 4
88 *House of Commons Debates*, 20 March 1922, 217
89 See W.C. Good, *Farmer Citizen* (1958).
90 Irvine (1920), 213-23
91 Ibid, 92-4
92 For a fuller account of NPL doctrines and proposals, see David Laycock, 'The Political Ideas of William Irvine: A Study in the Development of Western Canadian Political Thought,' MA Thesis, Department of Political Economy, University of Toronto, 1977; Mardiros (1979), Richards and Pratt (1979), and Sharp (1949).
93 See *UFA Directors' Bulletin*, no. 20, 18 November 1921, 'Some Opinions on the Causes of Agricultural and Industrial Depression.'
94 See Laycock (1977), chapter 5.
95 For a fuller account of the relation between Irvine's social credit and socialist ideas, see Laycock (1977).
96 'The Significance of Democratic Group Organization,' 5
97 'Is the UFA Plan of Cooperation Constructive?,' *The UFA*, vol. 1, no. 18, 25 November 1922, 1
98 For Britain, see E.P. Thompson, *The Making of the English Working Class* (1963); for America, see Staughton Lynd, *The Intellectual Origins of American Radicalism* (New York: Vintage Press, 1969).
99 See W.E. Mann, *Sect and Cult in Alberta* (Toronto: University of Toronto Press, 1955), and H. and T. Palmer, 'The Alberta Experience,' *Journal of Canadian Studies*, vol. 17, no. 3 (Autumn 1982), 20-34.
100 Irvine (1920), 7
101 Ibid, 24
102 Ibid, 99-100
103 Ibid, 101-02
104 Ibid, 147-8
105 Reg Whitaker, 'Introduction,' in *The Farmers in Politics* (Toronto: Carleton University Press, reprint, 1977), xxiii; Macpherson (1953), 37. See also Laycock (1977).
106 'The Great Adventure,' *The UFA*, 1 April 1927, 4

107 See below.
108 Consider, for example: 'Organized economic classes are now in competition in Canada ... as a result class war rages ... It is the economic question which goes to the very heart of our national problems' (147); 'Economic interests are always stronger and more determining in an organization than ideas. There are in every country organizations which may be said to be based on ideas, but the part they play in real life is almost nothing' (164); 'According to this [UFA] philosophy, economic and political questions are inseparable ... Politics to [the farmer] is but the direction of economic affairs' (189); in Irvine (1920).
109 'The Part of the UFA in a Constructive Cooperative Program,' *The UFA*, 16 September 1929, 6
110 'The Significance of Democratic Group Organization,' 5
111 1927 UFA Annual Convention, *Proceedings and Reports*, 4
112 See Wood, 'Are We Ready to Shoulder Responsibilities of Democratic Citizenship?' *The UFA*, 1 May 1926, 1.
113 'Political Action in Alberta,' *Guide*, 7 May 1919, 7 and 11
114 See Alvin Finkel, 'Populism and the Proletariat: Social Credit and the Alberta Working Class,' *Studies in Political Economy*, vol. 13, no. 1 (1984), 109-36; Betke (1971), and Warren Caragata, *Alberta Labour: A Heritage Untold* (Toronto: James Lorimer 1979).
115 See Laycock (1977), Whitaker (1977), and Mardiros (1979).
116 *The UFA*, 1 October 1925, 11
117 'Close Cooperation with Labor for Solution of Economic Problems Urged by Annual Convention,' *The UFA*, 16 February 1925, 4
118 See Garland's account of farmer and labor groups' common purposes in 'The Farmer's Group in Politics,' *Canadian Forum*, vol. 6, no. 69 (June 1926), 270-2.
119 'The Twenty-Fifth Annual Convention of the UFA,' *The UFA*, 1 February 1933, 6
120 For a concise account of this integration, see Garland (1926), 270-2.
121 Once again, Garland (1926) is a good example of this approach.
122 Irvine (1920), 191
123 'The Part of the UFA in a Constructive Cooperative Program,' 5
124 Ibid, 5
125 1931 UFA Annual Convention, *Proceedings and Reports*, 163
126 Wood's campaign against 100 per cent compulsory pooling demonstrated his suspicion of state-co-ordinated schemes. See W.K. Rolph, *Henry Wise Wood of Alberta* (Toronto: University of Toronto Press, 1950), 193-6, and Ian MacPherson, *Each for All* (1979), 90-1.

127   'Manifesto ... ,' 1931 UFA Annual Convention, *Proceedings and Reports*, 166
128   1935 UFA Annual Convention, *Proceedings and Reports*, 'Appendix,' 20-1
129   See Douglas Owram, *The Promise of Eden: The Canadian Expansionist Movement and the Idea of the West, 1956-1900* (Toronto: University of Toronto Press, 1979) for an excellent discussion of this.
130   For a fuller account of this influence on Irvine, see Laycock (1977), chapters 4. and 5.
131   See H.W. Wood's address to the 1926 UFA Convention.
132   *The UFA*, 2 January 1932, 6
133   Ibid

Chapter 4

1   For a list of the organizations where this populism had a significant impact, see chapter 1, above.
2   See Duff Spafford, ' "The Left Wing" 1921-1931,' in Duff Spafford and Norman Ward, eds., *Politics in Saskatchewan* (Don Mills: Longmans, 1968).
3   See A. Ross McCormack, *Reformers, Rebels and Revolutionaries* (Toronto: University of Toronto Press, 1977).
4   See Nelson Wiseman, *Social Democracy in Manitoba* (1984); Allen Mills, 'Single Tax, Socialism, and the Independent Labour Party of Manitoba: The Political Ideas of F.J. Dixon and S.J. Farmer,' *Labour/Le Travailleur*, vol. 5, spring 1980, 34-56; and McCormack (1977).
5   On labour politics in Alberta, see Warren Caragata, *Alberta Labour: A Heritage Untold* (Toronto: James Lorimer, 1979); Alvin Finkel, 'The Obscure Origins of the CCF in Alberta,' in J.W. Brennan, ed., *Building the Cooperative Commonwealth: Essays on the Democratic Socialist Tradition in Canada* (Regina: Canadian Plains Research Center, 1985); and Alvin Finkel, 'The Rise and Fall of the Labour Party in Alberta, 1917-1942,' *Labour/LeTravail*, vol. 16, Fall 1985, 61-96.
6   The league had exactly one meeting, held one day after the 1913 SGGA convention. Partridge organized the meeting in response to C.A. Dunning's successful attempt to reroute an SGGA convention body that seemed ready to adopt direct political action. The next day's league meeting endorsed a mass political education organization, rather than a third party, but the league was stillborn when Partridge left for Winnipeg shortly after. See Duff Spafford, ' "Independent" Politics in Saskatchewan,' *Saskatchewan History*, vol. 18, no. 1 (Winter 1965), 8-9.
7   *A War on Poverty* (Winnipeg: Wallingford Press, 1926), 144ff

8   *The Why of the Non-Partisan League* (Regina: n.p., 1917), 7
9   *Farmers' Educational League: Manifesto* (Saskatoon: n.p., 1927), 1
10 Partridge (1926), 50
11 *The Way of Reason* (Calgary: Alberta CCF Clubs, 1938), 27
12 David Lewis and F.R. Scott, *Make This Your Canada* (Toronto: Central Canada Publishing Co., 1943), 97
13 M.J. Coldwell, *Left Turn, Canada* (London: Victor Gollancz, 1945), 83 and 94
14 See, for example, *The Why of the Non-Partisan League* (1917), 7, and *The People's Weekly* (Edmonton), 5 August 1939, 4.
15 This was especially true within UFA and UFC(SS) circles.
16 See, for example, *Speeches on the Cooperative Commonwealth* (Regina: Farmer Labor Group, 1932), and George Williams, *Social Democracy in Canada* (Regina: McGinnis Brothers, 1939).
17 See M.C. Urquhart and K.A. Buckley, eds., *Historical Statistics of Canada* (Toronto: Macmillan, 1965), series C1-7, 59.
18 Such as the Farmers' Union of Canada and Farmers' Educational League of Saskatchewan, and Carl Axelson of the UFA.
19 See, for example, two of Axelson's many letters to the *The Western Producer*: 'The Producers Must Learn to Rule' (30 April 1925, 5), and 'A Word to Farmers and Workers' (25 March 1926, 11).
20 *The Why of the N.P.L.*, 1917, 5 and 14
21 *The Nutcracker*, 15 January 1917, 10
22 J.S. Woodsworth, 'The Non-Partisan Movement,' *Alberta Non-Partisan*, 12 September 1918, 11
23 W. Irvine, 'What We Mean by Democracy,' *Alberta Non-Partisan*, 27 September 1918, 13
24 *T.C. Douglas Budget Speech* (Regina: Saskatchewan CCF, 1943), 8
25 *Manifesto*, 1
26 *Speeches on the Cooperative Commonwealth*, 8
27 'Presidential Address,' CCF National Convention, Regina, 1933; reprinted in *C.C.F. Research Review*, Regina, August 1933, 2
28 League for Social Reconstruction, *Democracy Needs Socialism* (Toronto: Thomas Nelson and Sons, 1938), 108
29 Ibid, 115
30 Lewis and Scott (1943), 91-110
31 Ibid, 102
32 *The Most Frequent Objections to Socialism Answered* (Regina: Saskatchewan CCF, n.d.), 3
33 For examples of this, see Lewis and Scott (1943) and Coldwell (1945).

34 It was also well known in western Canadian labour circles, especially in Winnipeg. See McCormack (1977), 15 and 78.

35 Keir Hardie, *All about the I.L.P.* (London: Independent Labour Party, 1920), 11

36 Ibid, 15

37 *The Alberta Non-Partisan*, 19 July 1918, 13

38 Carlyle King, *What Is Democratic Socialism?* (Regina: Saskatchewan C.C.F., Victory and Reconstruction Series, no. 3, 1943), 10-13

39 See, for example, LSR (1938), 137 to 141.

40 See, for example, Lewis and Scott (1943), 16, 31, 53, and 90.

41 *Manifesto*, 7-8, 'Objectives,' nos. 1-4

42 Ibid, 7

43 Walter D. Young, *Anatomy of a Party: The National CCF, 1932-1961* (Toronto: University of Toronto Press, 1969), chapter 3

44 See Duff Spafford, 'The Origins of the Farmers' Union of Canada,' *Saskatchewan History*, vol. 18, no. 3 (1965) 1-9, and Spafford (1968).

45 See Spafford, 'Origins,' and *The Western Producer*, letter to the editor re. SFPA, 9 July 1925.

46 *Manifesto of the Farmers' Educational League* (1927), 4

47 United Farmers of Canada (Saskatchewan Section), 3rd Annual Convention, *Minutes and Reports*, 43-5

48 Ibid, 45

49 UFC (SS) 4th Annual Convention, *Minutes and Reports*, 16

50 UFC (SS), '1932 Economic Policy and Convention Resolutions,' 2 and 7

51 See M.J. Coldwell, 'Evils of a Party System,' *The Western Producer*, 23 May 1929.

52 See Woodsworth, 'The Non-Partisan Movement,' *Alberta Non-Partisan*, 12 September 1918, 11.

53 *The Western Producer*, 19 August 1926; J.S. Woodsworth, 'Political Democracy,' *University of Toronto Quarterly*, vol. 4, no. 3 (1935), 300-1. The latter article was reprinted in several CCF and farmer newspapers shortly after it appeared in the *Quarterly*; see Kenneth McNaught, *A Prophet in Politics: A Biography of J.S. Woodsworth* (Toronto: University of Toronto Press, 1959), 15, note 45.

54 *The Western Producer*, 19 August 1926

55 *C.C.F. Research Review*, August 1933, 5

56 Young (1969) 28, 48ff

57 See Myron Johnson, 'The Failure of the CCF in Alberta,' in Carl Caldorola, ed., *Society and Politics in Alberta* (Toronto: Methuen, 1979), and Finkel (1985).

58 *The C.C.F. (Farmer, Labour, Socialist): An Outline of Its Origins, Organization and Objectives* (Toronto: Co-operative Commonwealth Federation, 1932), 8

59 This approach was common in Alberta and Saskatchewan CCF attacks on Social Credit. See G.H. Williams's Radio Addresses, 9 December 1936, and 28 May 1938 (Archives of Saskatchewan, Saskatoon), and William Irvine's editorials in *The People's Weekly*, 1937 and 1938.

60 LSR (1938), 27-8

61 Lewis and Scott (1943), 89-90, 118-19

62 The same feeling was behind the creation of the various Labour parties on the prairies, and continued when these organizations found a home in the CCF. See McCormack (1977), 79-80, 170.

63 David E. Smith, *Prairie Liberalism: The Liberal Party in Saskatchewan, 1905-1971* (Toronto: University of Toronto Press, 1975), 212

64 S.M. Lipset, *Agrarian Socialism: The Co-operative Commonwealth Federation in Saskatchewan* (Berkeley: University of California Press, 1950), 61

65 A comparison of UFA, Alberta's Canadian Labour Party, UFC(SS), and Saskatchewan ILP programs and declarations in 1931-2 shows how close the groups were in their analyses and objectives.

66 See, for example, Smith (1975), 215: 'From the time of its founding convention, the Farmer-Labor movement showed an appreciation ... of organization matched only by the Liberals themselves.'

67 In support of this, see Young (1969), 142.

68 See ibid, chapter 6.

69 'The Socialist and the Non-Partisan Movement,' *The Alberta Non-Partisan*, 29 March 1918, 7

70 *Alberta Non-Partisan*, 5 June 1919, 9

71 *Manifesto of the No-Party League of Western Canada* (1913), 11 and 13. See also Spafford, ' "Independent" Politics.'

72 See UFC(SS), *Economic Policy and Convention Resolutions* (1932), 2-3

73 See Young (1969), 153, 169, 183-5; Frederick C. Engelmann, 'Membership Participation in Policy-Making in the C.C.F.,' *Canadian Journal of Economics and Political Science*, vol. 22, no. 2 (May 1956), 162, 164-6, 171-2.

74 See Johnson (1979).

75 See *The People's Weekly*, 20 February 1937.

76 Lipset (1950), 297

77 Ibid, chapters 9 and 10

78 *The C.C.F. (Farmer, Labour, Socialist): An Outline of Its Origins* (1932), 8

79 *CCF Land Policy* (Regina: Co-operative Commonwealth Federation, Saskatchewan Section, 1938), 2
80 See, for example, Young (1969).
81 Ibid, chapter 6
82 Ibid, 141
83 *Manifesto,* 8
84 UFC(SS), *Economic Policy and Convention Resolutions* (1932), 2
85 Woodsworth, 'President's Address,' reprinted in *C.C.F. Research Review,* August 1933, 2
86 'Manifesto,' in Michael Cross, ed., *Decline and Fall of a Good Idea: CCF–NDP Manifestos, 1932-1969* (Toronto: New Hogtown Press, 1974), 20
87 See ibid, 18.
88 See Allen Mills, 'The Later Thought of J.S. Woodsworth,' *Journal of Canadian Studies,* vol. 17, no. 3 (1982), 80-1, and Woodsworth, 'Political Democracy' (1935), 304-6, 310-12.
89 See *Hansard,* 21 April 1922, 1061; 2 June 1924, 2709-11; 11 May 1934, 3106-7.
90 Cross (1974), 21
91 *The Present Crisis and the Progressives in Parliament* (Regina: Saskatchewan Grain Growers' Association, 1922), in Archives of Saskatchewan, Saskatoon.
92 For details, see David Laycock, 'The Political Ideas of William Irvine: A Study in the Development of Western Canadian Political Thought,' MA Thesis, Department of Political Economy, University of Toronto, 1977, chapters 3 and 4.
93 Cited in ibid, 90.
94 See 'The Structure of Society: A Spider's Web, with the Dollar Dominating Our Whole Civilization,' *The UFA,* 2 January 1929; 'Political Democracy,' 310-11; and *Labour's Case in Parliament* (A summary and compilation of speeches in the Canadian House of Commons 1921-8) (Ottawa: Canadian Brotherhood of Railway Employees, 1929), 31.
95 Williams (1939), 8
96 Lewis and Scott (1943), 82-3
97 See his contribution to the 1932 *Speeches on the Co-operative Commonwealth,* 32.
98 See Lewis and Scott (1943), 45, 78, and 184-5.
99 'Farmers and Workers,' *The Western Producer,* 27 September 1928, 10
100 William Irvine, *Political Servants of Capitalism: Answering Lawson and Mackenzie King* (Ottawa: Labour Publishing Co., 1933), 22-3
101 *Manifesto,* 8

102 Regarding Alberta, see Mardiros (1979), 112; for Saskatchewan, see Dominion Labor Party, *Reconstruction Program for Canada* (Regina: Dominion Labor Party, 1919), 2-4, in Archives of Saskatchewan (Saskatoon); for Manitoba, see Mills (1981) and Wiseman (1984).

103 *The Nutcracker*, 26 May 1917, 13

104 *The Alberta Non-Partisan*, 15 June 1919, 9

105 Ibid, 11

106 'The Socialist and the Non-Partisan Movement,' *Alberta Non-Partisan*, 29 March 1918, 7

107 'The Future of Socialism,' *The Nutcracker*, 13 April 1917, 9-10

108 Laycock (1977), chapter 4

109 Cross (1974), 20

110 1934 UFA Annual Convention, *Reports and Proceedings*, 2

111 See *Economic Policy* (Saskatoon: Saskatchewan Farmer-Labor Group, 1932), 2-4.

112 'George H. Williams – Farmer-Labor Group Candidate for the Constituency of Wadena' (Wadena Farmer-Labor Group [CCF] Constituency Committee, 1934).

113 'ILP-CCF Candidates for Winnipeg' (Winnipeg ILP-CCF Election Committee, 1936), 2

114 For an account of the activities of the league in western Canada, see Michiel Horn, 'The L.S.R. in Western Canada,' in R. Francis and H. Ganzevoort, eds., *The Dirty Thirties in Western Canada* (Vancouver: Tantalus Research, 1980), 65-76.

115 See League for Social Reconstruction, *Social Planning for Canada* (Toronto: Thomas Nelson, 1935; reprint, University of Toronto Press, 197), 231.

116 Ibid, 237

117 See Lipset (1950), 131 and 151.

118 Ibid, 131; and Peter Sinclair, 'The Saskatchewan CCF: Ascent to Power and Decline of Socialism,' *Canadian Historical Review*, vol. 54, no. 4 (December 1973), 419-33.

119 For details, see George Cadbury, 'Planning in Saskatchewan,' and Meyer Brownstone, 'The Douglas-Lloyd Governments: Innovation and Bureaucratic Response,' in L. LaPierre et al., *Essays on the Left: Essays in Honour of T.C. Douglas* (Toronto: McClelland and Stewart, 1970); A.L. Johnson, 'Biography of a Government: Policy Formation in Saskatchewan, 1944-1961' (1963); Evelyn Eager, *Saskatchewan Government* (Saskatoon: Western Producer Prairie Books, 1980); L.H. Thomas, ed., *The Making of a Socialist: Recollections of T.C. Douglas* (Edmonton: University of Alberta Press, 1982), and 'The CCF Victory in Saskatchewan' (paper presented to

1979 Canadian Historical Association meetings); and Richards and Pratt (1979).

120 Cross (1974), 18

121 *The UFA*, 1 February 1933, 4

122 See *The UFA*, 17 August 1934, 9

123 Laycock (1977), chapters 4 and 5

124 See J.H. Robson, *An Economic Remedy* (Saskatoon: Farmers' Union of Canada [Saskatchewan Section], 1924).

125 Turner had been introduced to Douglas's Social Credit writings in 1919. For typical editorials and articles advocating Social Credit reforms, see *The Western Producer*, 31 December 1924; 19 February 1925; 19 April 1925 ('The Cause of World Unrest' – C.H. Douglas); 23 April 1925 (front-page article covering British Independent Labour Party convention call for socialization of banking); 10 September to 22 October 1925 (series on 'Social Credit and Economic Democracy' taken from the British Labour press); 4 December 1925 (editorial); and 4 July 1929 (reprint of W. Irvine's address, 'Parliament and Credit Reform').

126 See, for example, *The UFA*, 2 May 1932; 1 February 1933; 2 April 1934; 27 July 1934; 17 August 1934 (UFA policy on 'socialization of finance'); 4 and 11 October 1935.

127 This was illustrated clearly in editor W.N. Smith's tribute to A.R. Orage, a prominent propagandist for, first, Guild Socialism, then, Social Credit in Britain: 'He did believe in the Douglas Formula and believed he ought to propagate it, but he was a socialist as well and never thought that Douglasism could be applied except by Socialists,' *The UFA*, 23 November 1934, 4.

128 See, for example, Woodsworth, 'The Structure of Society' (1929).

129 George Williams, as early as 1925, made clear his concern that monetary and credit reform be placed within a larger context of socialist economic transformation. In a letter to the editor of *The Western Producer* (9 July 1925, 10), Williams plugs the newly established Saskatchewan Farmers' Political Association, and closes by asking 'What do you say, Western Producer? Do you believe you can get monetary reform without overthrowing capitalist governments?'

130 Canovan (1981). Goodwyn (1976) pays special attention to this for the American case.

131 See Michael Bleaney, *Underconsumption Theory* (New York: International Publishers, 1976); John Finlay, *Social Credit: The English Origins* (Montreal: McGill-Queen's University Press, 1972); 1926 ILP Program, *For a Living Wage*.

132 See Mills (1982), 78.
133 For an overview of this, see T. Regehr, 'Bankers and Farmers in Western Canada, 1900-1939,' in John Foster, ed., *The Developing West* (Edmonton: University of Alberta Press, 1983).
134 See Williams (1939), 26; *Handbook for Speakers* (Farmer-Labor Group, 1933), 5-9.
135 See Lipset (1950); Macpherson (1953); Young (1969 and 1978); Hoffman (1974); Whitaker (1977); Bennett and Krueger (1968); Richards and Pratt (1979).
136 N. Priestly, 'The Co-operative Commonwealth Federation and Agriculture,' reprinted in *The UFA*, 1 April 1933, 22-4
137 *The UFA*, 1 March 1934, 5
138 Ibid
139 Ibid
140 Ibid, 1 August 1933, 6
141 Cross (1974), 21
142 See Smith (1975) and Lipset (1950).
143 George Hoffman, 'The Saskatchewan Farmer-Labor Party, 1932-34: How Radical Was It at Its Origins?' *Saskatchewan History*, vol. 28, no. 2 (Spring 1975), 52-64; Sinclair (1973).
144 Support for state farming with some 'Soviet' characteristics was not unknown in the British Labour Party during the 1930s. But its advocates were seldom in the mainstream, and never government ministers, when making these proposals. Sir Stafford Cripps addressed an Ottawa audience in 1934 on 'The Economic Planning of Agriculture,' and endorsed some Soviet methods for agricultural development. But Cripps was in his most uncompromising phase after Labour's 1931 election defeat, and was not articulating a position sanctioned by his troubled party. Cripps was attacking the large and unproductive land-holdings of the British aristocracy, not rejecting all forms of private ownership in agricultural production.
145 *Saskatchewan Farmer-Labor Group, Economic Policy* (1932), 3-4
146 1933 Convention of the Farmer-Labor Group, *Minutes*, 13-14
147 *Saskatchewan CCF Agricultural Policy* (Regina: Saskatchewan CCF Research Bureau, 1933), 4-5
148 See the 1933 Farmer-Labor Group pamphlet, *Is Your Home Safe?*
149 *The Most Frequent Objections to Socialism Answered* (Regina: CCF, 1938), 3
150 See Cadbury (1970); Lipset (1950); L.H. Thomas (1979 and 1981); Ivan Avacomovic, *Socialism in Canada: A Study of the CCF-NDP in Federal and*

Provincial Politics (Toronto: McClelland and Stewart, 1978), Coldwell (1945), chapter 10, and Ian MacPherson, 'The CCF and the Co-operative Movement in the Douglas Years: An Uneasy Alliance,' in Brennan, ed. (1984).

151 See Norman Penner, *The Canadian Left: A Critical Analysis* (Scarborough: Prentice-Hall, 1977), 161-3 and 244.

152 On the FUL, see I. Avacumovic, 'The Communist Party of Canada and the Prairie Farmer: The Interwar Years,' in D.J. Bercuson, ed., *Western Perspectives I* (Toronto: Holt, Rinehart and Winston, 1974), 78-87.

153 *Farmers' Unity League Manifesto* (Saskatoon: Farmers' Unity League, 1930), 3 and 6

154 For excellent documentation of one aspect of the FUL's activities in Alberta, see A.B. Makuch, 'In the Populist Tradition: Organizing the Ukrainian Farmer in Alberta, 1909-1935,' MA Thesis, University of Alberta, 1983.

155 Cross (1974), 20

156 *House of Commons Debates*, 1 February 1933

157 Ibid, 2 February 1933

158 LSR (1935), 229-30

159 Ibid, 226

160 Ibid, 237

161 *The Way of Reason* (Calgary: Educational Committee of the Calgary CCF Clubs, 1938), 15

162 Ibid, 40

163 Ibid, 22-3

164 Ibid, 43

165 Ibid, 41

166 *Handbook*, 10

167 King (1943), 8

168 See, for example, LSR (1938), 48, 51-5, and 62.

169 See Lewis and Scott (1943), chapter 3, and chapter 10, 145, 161, and 171.

170 Ibid, 150-4

171 *CCF Study Course, Group 1, Lesson 4, 'Regina Manifesto'* (n.d.), 3

172 CCF Subject Files, 1931-52, #270: Technocracy 1938, 27986-7, Archives of Saskatchewan, Saskatoon

173 Williams (1939), 53

174 The *Review*, published from 1933 to 1936 in Regina, was an organ of Saskatchewan CCF's left-wing intellectual element. Editor Jack King was clearly a Marxist, and many writers for the review accepted a good deal of Marxist analysis without rejecting the CCF in favour of the Communist Party.

175 *C.C.F. Research Review*, Regina, vol. 3, no. 2 (June 1936), 15
176 Ibid, 16
177 'Political Democracy,' 310
178 LSR (1938), 61
179 Lewis and Scott (1943), 177-80, 184-5
180 Coldwell (1945), 80-2
181 Lewis and Scott (1943), 151
182 *Handbook*, 9-10
183 LSR (1935), 37
184 The most influential American 'left-technocrats' were Edward Bellamy, Thorstein Veblen, and the prolific popular journalist Stuart Chase. British 'technocratic socialism' was dominated by the Fabians, particularly Sidney and Beatrice Webb and G.B. Shaw. All of these writers were well known in prairie social democratic circles.
185 In *A War on Poverty* (3), Partridge referred to them as 'the snugly salaried and high fee-ed champions of capitalism, that from the pulpit and the professional chair, in the press, on the public platform, and the floor of Parliament, assail our ears and confuse our minds.'
186 See, for example, 'What Is Profit?' *The Western Producer,* 24 May 1928, 3; UFC (SS), Annual Convention, *Minutes and Reports*, presidential addresses, 1930, 1931, 1934.
187 Irvine (1933), 89
188 This is well articulated in a 1942 Saskatchewan CCF pamphlet, *Socialism and Co-operatives*.
189 Lipset (1950), 149
190 *Saskatchewan Farmer-Labor Economic Policy*, 2
191 *The Most Frequent Objections to Socialism Answered*, 3
192 *The Way of Reason*, 18
193 'Co-operative Institutions,' *C.C.F. Research Review*, July 1934, 3
194 *Socialism and Co-operatives* (Regina: CCF, 1942), 3
195 *House of Commons Debates*, 22 March 1943
196 See Lipset (1950) and Sinclair (1973).
197 This bias came through in intra-party communications as well as public propaganda. A nice example of this is in a 1941 letter from the Tisdale CCF constituency executive to members: 'Today in Saskatchewan, progress is being made in the Field of Co-operation. CCF supporters are everywhere doing their utmost to forward Co-operation and this is correct as Co-operatives are a step towards the Co-operative Commonwealth. If our Democratic Governments could regard themselves as the Board of Directors

of a Co-operative and then put true co-operative principles into effect great benefit would result to all.'

198 Norman Priestly, for example, admitted that certain co-operative enterprises, including producers' pools, could and did function relatively successfully 'under capitalism,' which showed that 'producer co-operation is not the highest form of socio-economic organization' ('Co-operative Institutions,' 5).

199 'Presidential Address,' 5

200 1932 UFC (SS) Annual Convention, *Minutes and Proceedings*, 35-6

201 Williams (1939), 16

202 *The Ethical Implications of the CCF* (1934), 1, in W.N. Smith Papers, Glenbow Museum Archives, Calgary

203 Ibid, 7

204 Ibid, 9

205 Ibid, 20-1

206 William Irvine, *Co-operation or Catastrophe* (1934), *The Forces of Reconstruction* (1934), and *Can a Christian Vote for Capitalism?* (1935), all published by Labour Publishing Company, Ottawa

207 Irvine (1935), 3

208 *The Most Frequent Objections to Socialism*, 3

209 Alberta CCF Clubs, Educational Committee (1938), 17-18

210 King (1943), 26

211 Ibid, 28

212 *Speeches on the Co-operative Commonwealth*, 20

213 Ibid, 41

214 Irvine (1934), 27-8

215 See William Irvine, *Scarcity or Abundance: The People Must Choose* (Winnipeg: Contemporary Publishers, 1944).

216 See, for example, Williams (1939), 25 and 30.

217 See, for example, Coldwell (1945), 119.

218 See, for example, Radio Address, 12 June 1944, in Archives of Saskatchewan, Saskatoon, file B7, VI, 65780.

219 *The CCF Goal* (Regina: Saskatchewan CCF Central Office, 1938), 1 and 3

220 Douglas, 'Radio Address,' 65780

221 Partridge (1926), 2

Chapter 5

1 Well-known examples are Charles DeGaulle, Huey Long, Adolf Hitler, and Juan Perón.

2   Their use in municipal government elections on questions of single issues, often particular expenditures leading to mill-rate increases is more common in current popular discourse. However, this practice is not directly comparable to the plebiscitarian concept used here, since the former measures do not provide elected officials with *carte blanche* powers to pursue ill-defined objectives with a variety of public policy instruments, by themselves or through officials delegated this authority by elected politicians.

3   C.B. Macpherson, *Democracy in Alberta* (Toronto: University of Toronto Press, 1953), 247

4   See Mary Hallett, 'The Social Credit Party and the New Democracy Movement: 1939-1940,' *Canadian Historical Review*, vol. 47, no. 4 (December 1966), 301-25.

5   For the clearest account of this, see Macpherson (1953), chapters 4 and 5. See also John Finlay, *Social Credit: The English Origins* (Montreal: McGill-Queen's University Press, 1972).

6   W. Mann, *Sect, Cult and Church in Alberta* (Toronto: University of Toronto Press, 1955), and D.R. Elliott, 'Antithetical Elements in William Aberhart's Theology and Political Ideology,' *Canadian Historical Review*, vol. 59, no. 1 (1978), 38-58

7   Lewis H. Thomas, *William Aberhart and Social Credit in Alberta* (Toronto: Copp-Clark, 1977), 160

8   W. Aberhart, *Social Credit Manual* (Calgary: Western Printing, 1935), 11

9   Ibid, 13-14

10 Richard Hofstader, *The Age of Reform: From Bryan to F.D.R.* (New York: Random House, 1955), is still the most influential interpretation of American populism. Hofstader links what he sees as the anti-industrial, racist, xenophobic and conspiracy theory tendencies of American populism (from 1880 to 1914) to the quasi-populist right-wing politics of Joseph McCarthy at the outset of the Cold War.

11 See *Report of the Royal Commission on Dominion-Provincial Relations*, Book I (Ottawa: King's Printer, 1940), 170. For details on this, and an interesting Social Credit commentary, see Government of Alberta, *The Case for Alberta* (Edmonton: 1938): Part I, chapter 6, section II: 'The Problem of Private Debt in Alberta.'

12 Government of Alberta, Bureau of Information and News, *And This Is Democracy* (Edmonton, 1937), 3

13 Macpherson (1953), 152

14 See, for example, John Irving, *The Social Credit Movement in Alberta* (Toronto: University of Toronto Press, 1959), 338.

15   W. Aberhart and E. Manning, transcript of CFCN Calgary radio address, 3, W.N. Smith Papers, Glenbow Museum Archives, Calgary

16   J.L. Mallory, *Social Credit and the Federal Power in Canada* (Toronto: University of Toronto Press, 1954), 60. Even Mackenzie King had developed a sense of this antagonism, and was for several years quite cautious in moving against Aberhart's early legislation to cancel interest owed on mortgages. As a correspondent of one of King's confidants remarked in September 1936: 'The possibility of Social Credit arising in other Western Provinces ... is something that every Canadian must consider very carefully. The people of the West are in an angry mood, and they are particularly offended at the Banking and other financial interests. Notwithstanding all the concessions, and all the fairness that has been displayed by individual organizations, there is a deep-rooted feeling that the financial interests have been unduly harsh and, in fact, are in large part responsible for the depression itself. In other words, the people in large numbers are determined to give the financial institutions a trimming' (H. Blair Neatby, *William Lyon Mackenzie King, Vol. 3: 1932-39: The Prism of Unity* [Toronto: University of Toronto Press, 1976], 196).

17   See, for example, 'Are You Taking a Stand against Capitalistic Injustice?' *Alberta Social Credit Chronicle*, 13 December 1935, 4. See also Irving (1959), 237, 240, 284, 291.

18   *Premier Aberhart on Agricultural Reform* (Edmonton: Bureau of Information, 1940), 5-6

19   William Aberhart, *Post-War Reconstruction: Second Series of Broadcasts* (Edmonton: Bureau of Information, 1943), 29

20   Ibid, 30

21   See Macpherson (1953) for the classic account of this.

22   See, for example, *Alberta Social Credit Chronicle*, 27 July 1934, 4, and 9 August 1935, 1: 'The reason Alberta will vote for Social Credit at the next Provincial election is that they have decided they will no longer be hoodwinked by the old political parties who have proven themselves to be just servants of the capitalist.' (The *Chronicle*, hereafter *ASSC*)

23   For a general account of this, see Harold Schultz, 'A Second Term: 1940,' *Alberta Historical Review*, vol. 10 (1962), 17-26; John Irving, 'The Evolution of the Social Credit Movement,' *Canadian Journal of Economics and Political Science*, vol. 14, no. 3 (1948), 321-41; Thomas (1977); and David Elliott and Iris Miller, *Bible Bill: A Biography of William Aberhart* (Edmonton: Reidmore Books, 1987).

24   W. Aberhart, 'Will the People Know How to Vote?' *ASSC*, 7 December 1934, 1

25 Macpherson (1953), 155-6
26 'Political Parties Fear Social Credit Principles Unreasonable Attack' [sic], by Apex, ASSC, 5 October 1934, 1
27 'Give Purchasing Power to the Consumer,' ASSC, 19 October 1934, 1
28 ASSC, 14 September 1934, 5
29 See, for example, W. Aberhart Broadcast on CFCN radio, 14 May 1935, transcript in W.N. Smith papers, Glenbow Museum Archives, Calgary; G.F. Powell, A Sovereign People Demands Results (Edmonton: Democracy House, 1937); Government of Alberta, Bureau of Information and News (1937); and Thomas (1977), chapter 6.
30 Macpherson (1953), 155-6
31 'The Solution of Our Economic Problems,' ASSC, 21 September 1934, 2
32 ASSC, editorial, 27 July 1934, 4
33 For a good sampling of the latter, see Irving (1959).
34 Aberhart to Rt Hon. Wm Lyon Mackenzie King, 26 August, 1937; copy in J.W. Dafoe Papers, University of Manitoba, Winnipeg; reprinted in Michiel Horn, ed., The Dirty Thirties: Canadians in the Great Depression (Toronto: Copp Clark, 1972), 659-64.
35 Ibid
36 The Case for Alberta (1938), 49 and 51
37 Post-War Reconstruction: Second Series of Broadcasts (1943), 33
38 Ibid, 39-41
39 Ibid, 45-6
40 Ibid, 57-8
41 See, for example, Prepare Now: A Suggested Programme of Post-War Reconstruction Embodying the Principles Essential to British Democracy (Edmonton: Bureau of Information, 1943).
42 For a general account of the pathetic later developments of Douglas's doctrine, see Macpherson (1953), chapter 7, part 2.
43 Alan Brinkley, Voices of Protest: Huey Long, Father Coughlin, and the Great Depression (New York: Random House, 1981), 54-60
44 Irving (1959), 50ff
45 Irving's suggestion that these were primarily members of 'fringe' Protestant sects has been recently disputed by David Elliott. He claims that while fundamentalist Protestants were 'overrepresented' in the early movement (relative to their percentage of the whole population), the average Social Credit supporter was a member of the United or Anglican Church (Elliott [1978], 54-5).
46 Irving (1959), 86, 208-9, 244-5
47 Ibid, 183-96

48 Jean Burnet, *Next Year Country: A Study of Rural Social Organization in Alberta* (Toronto: University of Toronto Press, 1951), 45, 88, and 147

49 Linda and Paul Grayson, 'The Social Base of Interwar Political Protest in Urban Alberta,' *Canadian Journal of Political Science*, vol. 7, no. 2 (June 1974), 310

50 Ibid, 308-11. See also Alvin Finkel, 'Social Credit and the Unemployed,' *Alberta History*, vol. 31, no. 1 (1983), 24-32.

51 Larry Hannant, 'The Calgary Working Class and the Social Credit Movement in Alberta, 1932-35,' *Labour/LeTravail*, vol. 16 (Fall 1985), 97-116; Alvin Finkel, 'Populism and the Proletariat: Social Credit and the Alberta Working Class,' *Studies in Political Economy*, vol. 13, no. 2 (1984), 109-35

52 See Brinkley (1981).

53 Macpherson (1953), Irving (1959), Mallory (1954), Richards and Pratt (1979), Young (1969 and 1978), and Maurice Pinard, *The Rise of a Third Party: A Study in Crisis Politics* (Montreal: McGill-Queen's University Press, 1975) are the major works attempting macro-level explanations.

54 Macpherson (1953), 142

55 *ASSC*, 2, 9 and 16 August 1935

56 See, for example, Irving (1959), 302 and 307.

57 The following instances were typical: Aberhart's 1939 attack on the leader of the Conservative Party as a tool of the financiers, in the Alberta legislature, reprinted in 'Lets Look at the Record' (1939); the famous 'bankers' toadies' case which sent the two English Social Credit Secretariat 'experts' to jail for libel in 1937 (Mallory [1954], 81-3); attacks on Mackenzie King and federal Liberals as tools of financiers, 1937; 1940 Social Credit campaign literature denouncing the opposition as puppets of financiers; 1943 broadcasts by Aberhart cited in note 19 above; and, variously, annual reports of Social Credit Board, 1939-47.

58 Macpherson (1953), 203. See also Irving (1959), 296 and *passim*.

59 'The Big Problem of Introduction,' *ASSC*, 30 November 1934, 1

60 Irving (1959), chapter 10

61 Macpherson (1953), 203-10

62 This phrase was used often; for one example, see *ASSC*, 30 November 1934, 1.

63 Macpherson (1953), 99

64 *Manual*, 62

65 *Human Law Must Bow to Divine Law: Historic Speech Given in the Legislature of the Province of Alberta, Aug. 6, 1937, by Hon. Lucien Maynard* (Edmonton: United Democrats, 1937)

66 Government of Alberta, Bureau of Information and News (1937), 2

67 See, for example, Mallory (1954), Irving (1959), Thomas (1977), Conway (1984), and Regehr (1983).

68 Government of Alberta, Bureau of Information and News (1937), 2

69 H. Schultz, 'Aberhart, the Organization Man,' *Alberta Historical Review,* vol. 7. no. 3 (1959), 19-26, and 'Portrait of a Premier,' *Canadian Historical Review,* vol. 45, no. 3 (1964), 185-211, and Irving (1959) stress these factors most. See also Peter Sinclair, 'Populism in Alberta and Saskatchewan: A Comparative Analysis of the Co-operative Commonwealth Federation and Social Credit,' PhD dissertation, University of Edinburgh, 1972, chapter 8, and Elliott and Miller (1987).

70 Schultz (1964), 185

71 Thomas (1977), 62

72 Owen Anderson, 'Party Politics in Alberta, 1905-1975,' in Carl Caldorola, ed., *Society and Politics in Alberta* (Toronto: Methuen, 1979), 40

73 Irving (1959), 343

74 Ibid, 330

75 In 1930, the UFA took 39.4 per cent of the popular vote, compared to the Liberal's 24.6 per cent; in 1935, with an increase in the total popular vote from 67.1 per cent to 82.6 per cent of eligible voters, Social Credit took 54.2 per cent of the popular vote, compared to 23.1 per cent for the Liberals and 11.1 per cent for the UFA The Social Credit vote in 1935 was over twice that of the UFA in 1930 (163,700 to 74,187), although it is worth noting that the eligible voting population had increased from 293,758 to 378,249 (Loren Simerl, 'A Survey of Canadian Provincial Election Results, 1905-81' [1981], 686-9).

76 Joseph Boudreau, *Alberta, Aberhart and Social Credit* (Toronto: Holt, Rinehart and Winston, 1975), 101

77 See Irving (1959) and Elliott and Miller (1987).

78 Elmore Philpott, March 1940, quoted in Schultz (1964), 203

79 Brinkley (1981), 193

80 *ASSC*, 12 April 1935, 4

81 Irving (1959), 264, 289, and 339

82 This is covered well in Irving (1959) and Elliott (1978).

83 *ASSC*, 12 April, 1935, 1

84 Quoted in Macpherson (1953), 158

85 *ASSC*, 12 April 1935, 4

86 Ibid, 4

87 Harold Schultz, 'A Second Term,' *Alberta Historical Review*, vol. 10 (Winter 1962), 21-2

88 Ibid, 25, and Hallett (1966)

89 See Kenneth Andrews, 'Progressive Counterparts of the CCF: Social Credit and the Conservative Party of Saskatchewan, 1935-1938,' *Journal of Canadian Studies*, vol. 17, no. 3 (1982), 61-4.

90 Given its limited substantive mandate, the latter was not a 'purely' plebiscitarian manoeuvre; however, its origins in a radio appeal loaded with unsubtle instruction to the followers, and its purpose as a way of building and legitimizing the entry of the league into politics, gave it a clearly plebiscitarian stamp.

91 Schultz (1959), 23

92 Irving (1959), 124

93 See draft in *ASSC*, 29 March 1935, and final version in *ASSC*, 12 April 1935.

94 Thomas (1977), 70

95 Macpherson (1953), 154

96 Ibid, 169-79; Mallory (1954), 72-4 and *passim*; Boudreau (1975), 60-77

97 *Think It Over* (Edmonton: United Democrats, 1937), 2

98 Macpherson (1953), 172 and *passim*; Schultz (1959), 22-3; Irving (1959), 120, 273-4, 328, and *passim*

99 *ASSC*, 16 November 1934, 3

100 The Battle Cry of Freedom,' *ASSC*, 16 August 1935, 1

101 *Democracy Denied* (Edmonton: Bureau of Information and News, Alberta Legislature, 1939), 2-3

102 Anderson (1979), 40

103 See Elliott and Miller (1987), whose account includes several revealing cartoons from Alberta's daily press. The authors tend to accept this portrait of Aberhart, calling him a 'left-wing fascist' (320).

104 Hanna F. Pitkin, *The Concept of Representation* (1967), 142-3

105 Macpherson (1953), 126, 152, and 157

106 W. Aberhart, 'Lecture Re. Social Credit,' 23 May 1935, 8 and 10. W.N. Smith Papers, Glenbow Museum Archives, Calgary

107 W. Aberhart, Broadcast over CFCN (Calgary), 14 May 1935, 1. W.N. Smith Papers, Glenbow Museum Archives

108 Ibid. For a facsimile copy of the 'Alberta Citizens' Registration Covenant' which the Social Credit government distributed to register citizens for receipt of promised dividends, see Elliott and Miller (1987), 242. The covenant promised a wide range of benefits from the government, including 'a just rate of wages with reasonable hours.'

109 Macpherson (1953), 158

110 'Premier Says Constitution Talks to be Held,' *The Albertan*, 18 August 1937; also cited in Macpherson (1953), 195

111 Ironically, Aberhart commented here that public acceptance of these schemes led him to 'marvel how gullible the rank and file of the people can become.'
112 *Post-War Reconstruction: Second Series of Broadcasts* (1943), 59-60
113 See *ASSC*, 5 June 1935, 3 and 7, for an extract from Douglas's 'The Nature of Democracy.'
114 Macpherson (1953), 186-92
115 'A Sovereign People ...' (Edmonton: Today and Tomorrow Publishers, 1937), 5 and 6
116 Government of Alberta, Bureau of Information and News (1937), 4
117 Ibid, 1-3
118 *ASSC*, 9 August 1935, 4
119 'Suggested Social Credit Platform Discussed at Constituency Convention,' *ASSC*, 29 March 1935, 4; cited in Macpherson (1953), 153
120 See Irving (1959), 312-14
121 *ASSC*, 29 March 1935, 4
122 Government of Alberta, Bureau of Information and News (1937), 3-4
123 *Alberta's Charter of Freedom* (Edmonton: King's Printer, 1945), 2-3
124 Macpherson (1953), 163, 173-8, and 193-200
125 Joseph Schumpeter, *Capitalism, Socialism, and Democracy* (New York: Harper and Row, 1942; reprint, 1975), 284-5
126 Pitkin (1967), 11
127 Ibid, 39
128 Schumpeter (1975), 291-5
129 Pitkin (1967), 57
130 'Suggested Social Credit Platform discussed at Constituency Convention,' *ASSC*, 29 March 1935, 4
131 'Convention Is Great Success,' *ASSC*, 12 April 1935, 5
132 See Thomas (1977), 73.
133 The Legislative Assembly (Recall) Act, *Statutes of Alberta*, 1 Edward VIII, 1st Session, 8th Legislative Assembly, Chapter 82, 253-8
134 Macpherson (1953), 153. Aberhart was not above using this language. In his broadcast on the day after his election in 1935, he announced: 'We are your servants. You, yourselves, veritably constitute the government' (Thomas [1977], 84).
135 *ASSC*, 9 August 1935, 4
136 'Lecture re. Social Credit,' 23 May 1935, 10
137 Mallory (1954), 79
138 Pitkin (1967), 58
139 Ibid, chapter 2. The *Chronicle* characterized the ballot in very Hobbesian

terms – for example, as the means by which 'we delegate all of our authority' to the new leader. (*ASSC*, 6 December 1934, 4).

140 Macpherson (1953), 160, and 230-7

141 See John Stuart Mill, *Considerations on Representative Government* (London, 1861), chapters 5 and 14.

142 Macpherson (1953), 193-200, and 234-7

143 See, most notably, Macpherson (1953); Mallory (1954); Irving (1959), Morton (1950); Thomas (1977); John Conway, 'The Nature of Populism: A Clarification,' *Studies in Political Economy*, no. 13 (Spring 1984), 137-44, and 'The UFA and Social Credit Regimes in Alberta: Some Continuities' (paper presented to the annual meetings of the Canadian Political Science Association, Montreal, 1980); and Richards and Pratt (1979).

144 They were not entirely unorthodox, if one considers the range of debt adjustment schemes advanced and implemented in the prairie provinces from 1921 to 1945.

145 See his 1943 *Post-War Reconstruction* broadcasts.

146 Even in the pre-election *Social Credit Manual*, a sense of compulsion comes across, with dividends made conditional on 'loyalty to the State and the best interests of the country' (21) and punishments threatened for squandering dividends (33-5). See also 47: What to do with people 'who do not wish to join with the Social Credit idea.'

147 *Manual*, 21

148 See Mallory (1954), Boudreau (1975), and 1940 Alberta CCF literature for examples of this.

149 *ASSC*, 29 March 1935, 4

150 Norman B. James, *Autobiography of a Nobody* (Toronto: J.M. Dent, 1947), 218-19

151 *Manual*, 33

152 *Prepare Now: A Suggested Programme of Post-War Reconstruction Embodying the Features Essential to British Democracy* (Edmonton 1943), 63

153 For a good example, see the 1943 report, which makes the claim that the 'existing system' was not capitalism at all, but a 'financial dictatorship,' directed by centralizing, socialistic planners and bureaucrats (Alberta Social Credit Board, *1943 Report,* 24).

154 'Lecture Re. Social Credit,' 23 May 1935

155 *Social Credit Manual*, 5

156 *ASSC*, 11 January 1935, 112

157 *Manual*, 41; *ASSC*, 2 November 1934, 1

158 For a rambling and confusing account of these proposals by C.H. Douglas,

see his *Credit Power and Democracy* (London: Cecil Palmer, 1921), and *Social Credit* (London: Cecil Palmer, 1924).

159 A variety of authors have tried to assess them. For some interesting contemporary assessments, see: *A Cross-Examination of the Aberhart Plan of Social Credit* (Edmonton: UFA, 1935); J.F. Parkinson, 'The Economics of Aberhart,' *Canadian Forum*, vol. 15, no. 178 (November 1935), 368-70; William and Kathryn Cordell, 'Alberta and Social Credit,' *North American Review*, vol. 241, no. 1 (March 1936), 121-33; S.J. Farmer, *Social Credit or Social Ownership* (Winnipeg: The Garry Press, 1936); Fred Henderson, *The Social Credit Illusion* (Vancouver: The Commonwealth Press, 1935). For more recent assessments, see especially Macpherson (1953), Mallory (1954), Richards and Pratt (1979).

160 See for example, *ASSC*, 3 August 1934, 1, and various books, including Douglas (1921) and (1924).

161 See, for example, *Social Credit Manual*, 23-35.

162 Ibid, 19-21

163 Macpherson (1953), 233

164 Pitkin (1967), 128-30

165 *Edmonton Journal*, 27 December 1934, cited in Thomas (1977), 68-9

166 Thomas (1977), 70-3. See the *Manual*, 13-15, for related promises of equity.

167 *Premier Aberhart on Agricultural Reform* (Edmonton: Bureau of Information, 1940), 6

168 See Government of Alberta, *The Records Tell the Story* (Edmonton: King's Printer, 1939).

169 See Thomas (1977), 91, and Conway (1984), 123.

170 See Finkel (1985), Grayson and Grayson (1974).

171 See *ASSC*, 4 January 1935 and 2 August 1935.

172 Mallory (1954), 165 and 172

173 Aberhart (1943), 59

174 Ibid, 93

175 *Manual*, 7

176 Ibid, 55

177 Ibid, 62

178 *ASSC*, 19 October 1934, 6

179 *ASSC*, 26 July 1935, 4

180 *ASSC,* 2 August 1935, 4

181 The January 1934 convention of the Alberta Federation of Labour supported a resolution calling for a provincial legislative inquiry into the feasibility of Douglas Social Credit for Alberta. In a late 1934 provincial by-election,

both the Labour-CCF and Progressive-Labour (Communist) candidates endorsed Douglas Social Credit (Conway [1980], 32 and 132).

182 On the first two factors, see Finkel (1985) and Johnson (1979).

183 *Manual*, 5-7

184 *B.N.A. Act and Social Credit*, cited in Irving (1959), 94

185 See ibid, and *ASSC*, 2 November 1934, 1.

186 *ASSC*, 30 November, 1934, 1. Canovan (1981, 296) notes that populism is often characterized by distrust of constitutional arrangements and procedures, which are viewed as the tools of entrenched élites. Aberhart and Social Credit were thus in the populist mainstream here.

187 Macpherson (1953), chapter 7, sections 3 and 4; Irving (1959), 75-84, 171-2, 303; Elliott and Miller (1987), chapter 7; *ASSC*, 27 September 1935, 1 and 7

188 See *Cross-Examination of the Aberhart Plan*; *The UFA*, August 1934 to August 1935; Irving (1959), 86-93, 118, 176, 229-306; Thomas (1977), chapters 1 and 2.

189 *A.S.S.C*, 7 December 1934, 1

190 'Lecture Re. Social Credit' (Edmonton, 23 May 1935)

191 Address in Leask, Saskatchewan, 21 September, 1935, reported in *ASSC*, 27 September 1935, 8

192 Quoted in *Is Mackenzie King Sincere?* (Edmonton: United Democrats, 1937), 1

193 Neatby (1976), 267

194 See 26 August 1937 letter to W.L.M. King, in Horn (1972), 659-64

195 See, for example, ibid; L. Maynard's 'Human Law Must Bow to Divine Law' speech of 6 August, 1937, in the Alberta legislature (reprinted as pamphlet by United Democrats); and press reports on Aberhart's response in Boudreau (1975), 97-101.

196 Government of Alberta, *The Case for Alberta* (1938), Part II, 47

197 Ibid, 48

198 Ibid, 48-9

199 Ibid, 50, 52, 53, 55

200 Ibid, 49

201 Ibid, 50

202 Ibid

203 Ibid, 51

204 Ibid, 52

205 Mallory (1954), 144-6

206 Mallory, 150-2; Social Credit Board, *Annual Report, 1940* (Edmonton: King's Printer, 1941); Social Credit Board, 'Some Notes on the

Recommendations of the Royal Commission on Dominion-Provincial Relations' (Edmonton: n.p., 1940), 1-3, in Archives of Saskatchewan, Saskatoon

207 'Some Notes,' 2

208 See The Alberta Social Credit Act, in *Statutes of Alberta*, George VI, 1937, 3rd Session, 8th Legislature, 53-4.

209 Mallory (1954), 186; Macpherson (1953), 175 and 194

210 Schultz (1964), 204; Thomas (1977), 90

211 Schultz (1964), 205; Thomas (1977), 91. For a positive account of both school and municipal district reorganization see E.J. Hanson, *Local Government in Alberta* (Toronto: McClelland and Stewart, 1956), chapter 7.

212 *Let's Look at the Record* (Aberhart on 17 February 1939, re. Speech from the Throne), 15

213 See, for example, A.J. Hooke, *The Eclipse of Democracy* (1945), 60.

214 *Case*, Part II, 46

215 Ibid, 47

216 This tired metaphor was a favourite of Aberhart's. In testimony to the Alberta Legislature's Agriculture Committee in 1934, he opined: 'in the day in which we live, we have to have the progressive engineering or philosophic type mind, which examines carefully ... the principles involved and the difficulties entailed. Then it builds the bridge or digs the tunnel where none previously existed. This latter attitude of mind is essential if we wish to progress.' *The Douglas System of Social Credit: Evidence Taken by the Agricultural Committee of the Alberta Legislature, Session 1934* (Edmonton: King's Printer, 1934), 13

217 ASSC, 'The Problem of Introduction,' 30 November 1935, 5

218 Mallory (1954), 185

219 *Manual*, 21 and 41. After this, it seems to have disappeared: it was not mentioned in the Alberta Social Credit Act of 1937, which outlined the powers of the Social Credit Board and its subordinate body, the Provincial Credit Commission.

220 See Elliott and Miller (1987), 244, for an advertisement in the 1 August 1936 *Edmonton Journal* offering a five-week training program for 'Social Credit Supervisors' in 'State Credit Houses.'

221 ASSC, 9 August 1935, 4

222 Macpherson (1953), 196-8

223 ASSC, 5 October 1934, 1

224 Macpherson (1953), 163-4

225 They were empowered, for example, to 'examine Social Credit legislation and make recommendations for legislative action in respect thereof,' to search

for technical experts and 'administration methods' applicable to Alberta, and to assist in the administration of all Social Credit legislation designed to 'ensure to the People of the Province the full benefit of the increment arising from their association' (Alberta Social Credit Act, 52-3).

226 *A Sovereign People Demand Results* (Edmonton: Today and Tomorrow, n.d. [1938?]), 8 and 9

227 Macpherson (1953), 17-77

228 Ibid, 103-5

229 Friesen (1984) devotes particular attention to western enthusiasm for the opportunities of the region from 1890 to 1930.

230 'Give Purchasing Power to the Consumer,' *ASSC*, 19 October 1934, 1 and 6

231 'Scientific Arrangement for Distribution of Goods,' *ASSC*, 30 November 1934, 1

232 Aberhart (1943), 93

233 Richards and Pratt (1979), 23, note that right populism 'had few links to the co-operative movement.'

234 Aberhart (1943), 83. See also *Social Credit Manual*, 59: 'What is meant by the increment of association? *A*: The increment of association is the value of association together for self-protection or cooperative support.'

235 *The Douglas System of Social Credit*, 91

236 *Premier Aberhart on Agricultural Reform* (Edmonton: Bureau of Information, 1940), 6

237 Aberhart (1943), 38

238 Thomas (1977), 91; *The Records Tell the Story* (1940)

239 Thomas Flanagan, 'Social Credit in Alberta: A Canadian "Cargo Cult"?' *Archives de Sociologie des Religions*, vol. 34 (1972), 39-48

240 Elliott and Miller (1987) pay extensive attention to this relationship in Aberhart's career.

241 See Flanagan (1972); Elliott (1978); Elliott and Miller (1987); Irving (1959); and Mann (1955).

242 Macpherson, (1953), chapter 4, sections 2, 3, and 5

243 Finlay (1972), chapters 5, 8, 9, and 11

244 *Manual*, 7 and 13

245 Ibid, 55

246 Robert Dahl, 'Democracy in the Workplace,' *Dissent*, Winter 1984, 58

247 Government of Alberta, Bureau of Information and News (1937), 1-2

248 Ibid, 4

249 'The Bias of Prairie Politics,' *Transactions of the Royal Society of Canada*, vol. 49, series 3 (June 1955), section two, 58 and 63

Chapter 6

1 Roger Gibbins, *Prairie Politics and Society: Regionalism in Decline* (Toronto: Butterworths, 1980).

2 The 1980-2 and 1987-9 constitutional reform processes provide both a confirmation and, in the case of women's and natives' groups' 1981 lobbying efforts, a partial qualification of this.

3 See chapter 2, above, regarding their ruling against Manitoba's 1917 direct legislation statute.

4 See Gerald Friesen, *The Canadian Prairies: A History* (Toronto: University of Toronto Press, 1984), chapters 12 and 14; Martin Robin, *Radical Politics and Canadian Labour, 1880-1930* (Kingston: Industrial Relations Centre, Queen's University 1968); Norman Penner, *The Canadian Left: A Critical Analysis* (Toronto: Prentice-Hall, 1977); A. Ross McCormack, *Reformers, Rebels and Revolutionaries: The Western Canadian Radical Movement, 1899-1919* (Toronto: University of Toronto Press, 1977); and John Herd Thompson and Allen Seager, *Canada 1922-1939 Decades of Discord* (Toronto: McClelland and Stewart, 1985).

5 Cook, *The Regenerators: Social Criticism in Late Victorian English Canada* (Toronto: University of Toronto Press, 1985)

6 See Carl Berger, 'A Canadian Utopia: The Cooperative Commonwealth of Edward Partridge,' in S. Clarkson, ed., *Visions 2020* (Edmonton: Hurtig Publishers, 1970).

7 Except to support the transfer of crown lands and natural resource control to the prairie provinces.

8 See S. Lynd, *Intellectual Origins of American Radicalism* (1969), and E.P. Thompson, *The Making of the English Working Class* (1971).

9 See Reg Whitaker, 'The Liberal Corporatist Ideas of Mackenzie King,' *Labour/Le Travailleur*, vol. 2 (1977), 137-69.

10 W.L. Morton, *The Progressive Party in Canada* (Toronto: University of Toronto Press, 1950) tends in this direction, as does Paul Sharp, *The Agrarian Revolt in Western Canada: A Survey Showing American Parallels* (Minneapolis: University of Minnesota Press, 1949). Marxist caricatures of their positions can be found in Gary Teeple and R.T. Naylor, 'Appendix: The Ideological Origins of Social Democracy and Social Credit,' in G. Teeple, ed., *Capitalism and the National Question in Canada* (Toronto: University of Toronto Press, 1972), and John Conway, 'Populism in the United States, Russia, and Canada: Explaining the Roots of Canada's Third Parties,' *Canadian Journal of Political Science*, vol. 11, no. 1 (March 1978), 99-124.

11 A. Walicki, *The Controversy over Capitalism: Studies in the Social*

Philosophy of Russian Populists (Oxford: Clarendon Press, 1969); R. Hofstader, *The Age of Reform* (1955). See also their contributions to Gellner and Ionescu, eds., *Populism: Its Meaning and National Characteristics* (London: Weidenfeld and Nicholson, 1969).

12 Friesen (1984), 381. Friesen integrates this theme into his account of western Canadian politics and culture more effectively than any other contemporary historian.

13 See Friesen (1981) and Jones (1982).

14 See, for example, 'The Farmers' Platform,' Canadian Council of Agriculture, 1921, plank 8; reprinted in the appendix to this volume.

15 Macpherson (1953), chapter 8, section 2

16 See C.B. Macpherson, *Democratic Theory: Essays in Retrieval* (London: Oxford University Press, 1973), chapter 3.

17 See especially Macpherson (1953), Lipset (1950), Sanford Silverstein, 'Occupational Class and Voting Behaviour: Electoral Support for a Left Wing Protest Movement in a Period of Prosperity,' in S.M. Lipset, ed., *Agrarian Socialism* (Berkeley: University of California Press, 1968), Sinclair (1974), James McCrorie, 'Change and Paradox in Agrarian Social Movements: The Case of Saskatchewan,' in Richard J. Ossenberg, ed., *Canadian Society: Pluralism, Change and Conflict* (Scarborough: Prentice-Hall, 1971), Grayson and Grayson (1974), and Finkel (1984).

18 It is interesting to note that most liberal academic commentators on prairie populism have tended to join Marxist scholars in focusing on the economic demands of the elected prairie populists, to the detriment of the 'democratic' demands and rationale that accompany these demands in their organizations' discourses. Thus liberals, too, underestimate the extent of political and ideological differentiation in these organizations. By viewing prairie populisms primarily as modified lobby group efforts to redress an economically defined regionalism and alienation in a complicated federal polity, this liberal approach fails to challenge the class reductionism of some recent Marxist analysis.

19 See, among others, Kenneth McNaught, *A Prophet in Politics: A Biography of J.S. Woodsworth* (1959); W.K. Rolph, *Henry Wise Wood of Alberta* (1950); H.J. Schultz, 'Portrait of a Premier: William Aberhart' (1964); David Elliott, 'William Aberhart: Right or Left' (1980), Elliott, 'Antithetical Elements in William Aberhart's Theology and Political Ideology' (1978), and Elliott and Iris Miller, *Bible Bill: A Biography of William Aberhart* (1987); Anthony Mardiros, *William Irvine: The Life of a Prairie Radical* (1979); D. Laycock, 'The Political Ideas of William Irvine' (1977); A.E. Smith, *All My Life* (Toronto: Progress Books, 1949); I.J. Mills, *Stout*

Hearts Stand Tall (Vancouver: Evergreen Press, 1971); D. Shackleton, *Tommy Douglas* (Toronto: McClelland and Stewart, 1975); L.H. Thomas, ed., *The Making of a Socialist: The Recollections of T.C. Douglas* (1982); F. Steininger, 'George Williams, Agrarian Socialist' (MA thesis, University of Regina, 1975); Walter Young, 'M.J. Coldwell: The Making of a Canadian Social Democrat, '*Journal of Canadian Studies*, vol. 9, no. 3 (1974), 50-60; J.F.C. Wright, *The Louise Lucas Story* (Montreal: Harvest House, 1975); Ramsay Cook, *The Politics of John W. Dafoe and the Free Press* (1963); Allen Mills, 'Single Tax, Socialism and the Independent Labour Party of Manitoba' (1980); Foster Griezic, 'The Honorable Thomas Alexander Crerar: The Political Career of a Western Liberal Progressive in the 1920s' (1972); Lewis H. Thomas, 'Milton Campbell, Independent Progressive,' in Carl Berger and Ramsay Cook, ed., *The West and the Nation: Essays in Honour of W.L. Morton* (Toronto: McClelland and Stewart, 1976); J.W. Brennan, 'C.A. Dunning and the Challenge of the Progressives, 1921-25,' *Saskatchewan History*, vol. 22, no. 1 (1969), 1-12; Brennan, 'C.A. Dunning, 1916-1930: The Rise and Fall of a Western Agrarian Liberal,' in John Foster, ed., *The Developing West* (1983); David E. Smith, 'James G. Gardiner: Political Leadership in the Agrarian Community,' *Saskatchewan History*, vol. 40, no. 2 (Spring 1987), 42-61; Norman Ward and David Smith's forthcoming political biography of Jimmy Gardiner, *Jimmy Gardiner: Relentless Liberal* (to be published by the University of Toronto Press, 1990); and Ed Rea's forthcoming political biography of Thomas A. Crerar.

20 With the 'Free Trade election' of 1988 and the April 1989 federal budget just behind us, the politics of unaccountability seem especially prominent in Canada now.

21 Friesen (1984) devotes particular attention to the second of these blindspots.

22 John Richards, 'Populism: A Qualified Defense,' *Studies in Political Economy*, no. 5 (1981), 5-28

Index

61, 165, 167, 170, 179, 182, 184-5,
188-9, 193, 200-1, 269, 274, 276-7,
290; *see also* citizenship
Partridge, E.A.: anti-party sentiments
of, 140, 149; as 'utopian co-
operator,' 63, 277; as radical
democratic/social democratic 'hybrid,'
273; as social democratic populist,
63; Carl Berger on, 351 n6;
establishes No-Party League of
Western Canada, 328 n6; on
capitalist control of state, 162, 337
no185; on existence of material
abundance, 199; on participatory
democracy, 155, 158; on
'people/plutocracy' antinomy, 141;
on 'the people,' 144; on role of state
in promoting economic democracy,
165; supports direct legislation, 37,
158; *A War on Poverty*, 14, 277
party politics: crypto-Liberal critiques
of, 26, 34, 36-7, 39-40, 42-51, 59,
69-70, 113, 115, 273, 285; populist
alternatives to, *see* participatory
democracy; populist critiques of, 4, 6,
9, 19, 27, 69, 295-7; radical
democratic populist critiques of, 20,
69, 71-85, 88-90, 95-6, 100, 102-5,
107, 113, 115, 269-70, 273, 283-4;
Social Credit critiques of, 206-8, 211-
13, 218, 222, 262, 264, 270-1, 274-
5; social democratic populist critiques
of, 139-40, 149-54, 160, 269, 274,
276, 283-4
Patrons of Industry: as early Canadian
populists, 5, 25; as predecessor of the
UFO, 26; B. McCutcheon on, 308 n7;
promotes decentralization of state
power, 49; promotes labour-farmer
political alliance, 65; R. Cook on,

307 n6; S.D. Shortt on, 308 n11;
*Handbook Introducing Facts and
Figures in Support of the Patron
Platform and Principles*, 308 n7
people, the: as an element of prairie
populist democratic thought, 7, 268;
crypto-Liberal conceptions of 33-6,
269; radical democratic populist
conceptions of, 74-80, 269-70;
Social Credit conceptions of, 203-11,
269-70; social democratic populist
conceptions of, 139-46, 269-70
People's Party (United States): and
American co-operative movement,
28-9, 76; H.W. Wood's view of, 71,
76; platform of, 321 n135
petite bourgeoisie: and analysis of
populism, 4, 14, 16; role of in prairie
populisms, 6, 7, 100, 170, 178, 203,
210, 272, 277-8, 282, 286, 288,
291-2, 295
physiocratic beliefs: in crypto-
Liberalism, 26, 32-5, 57-8, 66, 297;
in radical democratic populism, 130,
289; in Social Credit thought, 292-3;
in social democratic populism, 175-
8, 200
Pitkin, Hanna F.: on 'accountability'
view of representation, 230, 232; on
'authorization dimension' of
representation, 223; on 'formalistic
authorization' concept of
representation, 227, 229-30; on
'substantive dimension' of
representation, 223; on 'trusteeship'
analogy of representation, 241; *The
Concept of Representation*, 324 n50
plebiscite: Social Credit application of,
203, 225, 264; use of in Saskatchewan politics, 317 n71

THE STATE AND ECONOMIC LIFE

Editors: Mel Watkins, University of Toronto; Leo Panitch, York University

This series, begun in 1978, includes original studies in the general area of Canadian political economy and economic history, with particular emphasis on the part played by the government in shaping the economy. Collections of shorter studies, as well as theoretical or internationally comparative works, may also be included.